# THE LIFE

OF

# ABRAHAM LINCOLN

VOLUME I

# THE LIFE OF
# ABRAHAM
# LINCOLN

Drawn from original sources and containing many speeches, letters and telegrams hitherto unpublished

BY

## IDA M. TARBELL

*VOLUME ONE*

NEW YORK
Lincoln Memorial Association

*To my Father*

# PREFACE

THE work here offered the public was begun in 1894 at the suggestion of Mr. S. S. McClure and Mr. J. S. Phillips, editors of "McClure's Magazine." Their desire was to add to our knowledge of Abraham Lincoln by collecting and preserving the reminiscences of such of his contemporaries as were then living. In undertaking the work it was determined to spare neither labor nor money and in this determination Mr. McClure and his associates have never wavered. Without the sympathy, confidence, suggestion and criticism which they have given the work it would have been impossible. They established in their editorial rooms what might be called a Lincoln Bureau and from there an organized search was made for reminiscences, pictures and documents. To facilitate the work all persons possessing or knowing of Lincoln material were asked through the Magazine to communicate with the editor. The response was immediate and amazing. Hundreds of persons from all parts of the country replied. In every case the clews thus obtained were investigated and if the matter was found to be new and useful was secured. The author wrote thousands of letters and travelled thousands of miles in collecting the material which came to the editor simply as a result of this request in the magazine. The work thus became one in which the whole country co-operated.

At the outset it was the intention of the editors to use the results of the research simply as a series of unpublished reminiscences, but after a few months the new material gathered, while valuable seemed to them too fragmentary to be published as it stood, and the author was asked to prepare a series of articles on Lincoln covering his life up to 1858 and embodying as far as possible the unpublished material collected. These articles, which appeared in "McClure's Magazine" for 1895 and 1896, were received favorably, and it was decided to follow them by a series on the later life of Lincoln. This latter series was concluded in September, 1899, and both series, with considerable supplementary matter, are published in the present volumes.

It is impossible in this brief preface to mention all who have aided in the work, but there are a few whose names must not be omitted, so essential has their assistance been to the enterprise.

From the beginning Mr. J. McCan Davis of Springfield, Illinois, has been of great service, particularly in examining the files of Illinois newspapers and in interviewing. It is to Mr. Davis's intelligent and patient research that we owe the report of Lincoln's first published speech, the curious letters on the Adams law case, most of the documents of Lincoln's early life in New Salem and Springfield, such as his first vote, his reports and maps of surveys, his marriage certificate and many of the letters printed in the appendix. Mr. William H. Lambert of Philadelphia has also assisted us constantly by his sympathy and suggestions, and his large and valuable Lincoln collection has been freely at our disposal. Other collections that have been generously opened are those of O. H. Oldroyd of Washington, R. T. Durrett, Louisville, Ky., C. F. Gunther, Chicago, Ill., and Louis Vanuxem, Philadelphia, Pa. The War Department of the United States Government has extended many courtesies, the War Records being freely opened and the members of the War Records Commission aiding us in every way in their power. The librarians of the War Department, of the Congressional Library, of the Boston Public Library and of the Astor Library of New York, have also been most helpful.

The chief obligation which any student of Abraham Lincoln owes is to the great work of Messrs. Nicolay and Hay. In it are collected nearly all the documents essential to a study of Lincoln's life. Their History has been freely consulted in preparing this work and whenever letters and speeches of Lincoln appearing in their collection of his writings have been quoted, their version has been followed. Other lives of Lincoln that have been found useful are those of W. H. Herndon, W. O. Stoddard, John T. Morse, Isaac Arnold, Ward H. Lamon, H. C. Whitney, and J. G. Holland.

The new material collected will, we believe, add considerably to our knowledge of Lincoln's life. Documents are presented establishing clearly that his mother was not the nameless girl that she has been so generally believed. His father, Thomas Lincoln, is shown to have been something more than a shiftless " poor white," and Lincoln's early life, if hard and crude, to have been full of honest, cheerful effort at betterment. His struggles for a livelihood and his intellectual development from the time he started out for himself until he was admitted to the bar are traced with more detail than in any other biography, and considerable new light is thrown on this period of his life. The sensational account of his running away from his own wedding, accepted generally by historians, is shown to be false. To the period of Lincoln's life from 1849, when he gave up politics, until 1858, the period of the Lincoln and Douglas Debates, the most important contribution made is the report of what is known as the " Lost Speech."

The second volume of the Life contains as an appendix

196 pages of letters, telegrams and speeches which do not appear in Lincoln's "Complete Works," published by his private secretaries Messrs. Nicolay and Hay. The great majority of these documents have never been published at all. The source from which they have been obtained is given in each case.

No attempt has been made to cover the history of Lincoln's times save as necessary in tracing the development of his mind and in illustrating his moral qualities. It is Lincoln the man, as seen by his fellows and revealed by his own acts and words, that the author has tried to picture. This has been the particular aim of the second series of articles.

I. M. T.

# CONTENTS

xi

# LIFE OF LINCOLN

## CHAPTER I

### THE ORIGIN OF THE LINCOLN FAMILY—THE LINCOLNS IN KENTUCKY—BIRTH OF ABRAHAM LINCOLN

BETWEEN the years 1635 and 1645 there came to the town of Hingham, Massachusetts, from the west of England, eight men named Lincoln. Three of these, Samuel, Daniel, and Thomas, were brothers. Their relationship, if any, to the other Lincolns who came over from the same part of England at about the same time, is not clear. Two of these men, Daniel and Thomas, died without heirs; but Samuel left a large family, including four sons. Among the descendants of Samuel Lincoln's sons were many good citizens and prominent public officers. One was a member of the Boston Tea Party, and served as a captain of artillery in the War of the Revolution. Three served on the brig *Hazard* during the Revolution. Levi Lincoln, a great-great-grandson of Samuel, born in Hingham in 1749, and graduated from Harvard, was one of the minute-men at Cambridge immediately after the battle of Lexington, a delegate to the convention in Cambridge for framing a state constitution, and in 1781 was elected to the continental congress, but declined to serve. He was a member of the house of representatives and of the senate of Massachusetts, and was appointed attorney-general of the United States by Jefferson; for a few months preceding the arrival of Madison he was secretary of state, and in 1807 he was elected lieutenant-governor of Massachusetts.

(1)

In 1811 he was appointed associate justice of the United States Supreme Court by President Madison, an office which he declined. From the close of the Revolutionary war he was considered the head of the Massachusetts bar.

His eldest son, Levi Lincoln, born in 1782, had also an honorable career. He was a Harvard graduate, became governor of the state of Massachusetts, and held other important public offices. He received the degree of LL. D. from both Williams College, and Harvard College.

Another son of Levi Lincoln, Enoch Lincoln, served in congress from 1818 to 1826. He became governor of Maine in 1827, holding the position until his death in 1829. Enoch Lincoln was a writer of more than ordinary ability.

The fourth son of Samuel Lincoln was called Mordecai. Mordecai was a rich " blacksmith," as an iron-worker was called in those days, and the proprietor of numerous iron-works, saw-mills, and grist-mills, which with a goodly amount of money he distributed at his death among his children and grandchildren. Two of his children, Mordecai and Abraham, did not remain in Massachusetts, but removed to New Jersey, and thence to Pennsylvania, where both became rich, and dying, left fine estates to their children. Their descendants in Pennsylvania have continued to this day to be well-to-do people, some of them having taken prominent positions in public affairs. Abraham Lincoln, of Berks county, who was born in 1736 and died in 1806, filled many public offices, being a member of the general assembly of Pennsylvania, of the state convention of 1787, and of the state constitutional convention in 1790.

One of the sons of this second Mordecai, John, received from his father " three hundred acres of land, lying in the Jerseys." But evidently he did not care to cultivate his inheritance, for about 1758 he removed to Virginia. " Virginia John," as this member of the family was called, had five sons one of whom, Jacob, entered the Revolutionary army and served as a lieutenant at Yorktown. The third son was named Abraham and to him his father conveyed, in 1773, a tract of 210 acres of land in what is now Rockingham county, Virginia. But though Abraham Lincoln prospered and added to these acres he was not satisfied to remain many years in Virginia. It was not strange. The farm on which he lived lay close to the track of one of the earliest of those wonderful western migrations which from time to time have taken place in this country. Soon after John Lincoln came into Virginia vague rumors began to be circulated there of a rich western land called Kentucky. These rumors rapidly developed into facts, as journeys were made into the new land by John Finley, Daniel Boone and other adventure-loving men, and settlers began to move thither from Pennsylvania, Virginia and North Carolina. There were but two roads by which Kentucky could be reached then, the national highway from Philadelphia to Pittsburg and thence by the Ohio, and the highway which ran from Philadelphia south-westward through the Virginia valley to Cumberland Gap and thence by a trail called the Wilderness Road, northwest to the Ohio at Louisville. The latter road was considered less dangerous and more practical than the former and by it the greater part of the emigrants journeyed. Now this road lay through Rockingham county. Abraham Lincoln was thus directly under the influence of a moving procession of restless seekers after new lands and unknown goods. The spell came upon him and, selling two hundred and forty acres of land in Rockingham County for five thousand pounds of the current money of Virginia—a sum worth at that time not more than one hundred and twenty-five pounds sterling—he joined a party of travelers to the Wilderness. Returning a few months later he moved his whole family, consisting of a wife and five children, into Kentucky.

Abraham Lincoln was ambitious to become a landed proprietor in the new country, and he entered a generous amount of land—four hundred acres on Long run, in Jefferson county; eight hundred acres on Green river, near the Green river lick; five hundred acres in Campbell county. He settled near the first tract, where he undertook to clear a farm. It was a dangerous task, for the Indians were still troublesome, and the settlers, for protection, were forced to live in or near forts or stations. In 1784, when John Filson published his "History of Kentucky," though there was a population of thirty thousand in the territory, there were but eighteen houses outside of the stations. Of these stations, or stockades, there were but fifty-two. According to the tradition in the Lincoln family, Abraham Lincoln lived at Hughes Station on Floyd creek in Jefferson county.

All went well with him and his family until 1788. Then, one day, while he and his three sons were at work in their clearing, an unexpected Indian shot killed the father. His death was a terrible blow to the family. The large tracts of land which he had entered were still uncleared, and his personal property was necessarily small. The difficulty of reaching the country at that date, as well as its wild condition, made it impracticable for even a wealthy pioneer to own more stock or household furniture than was absolutely essential. Abraham Lincoln was probably as well provided with personal property as most of his neighbors. The inventory of his estate, now owned by R. T. Durrett, LL. D., of Louisville, Kentucky, was returned by the appraisers on March 10, 1789. It gives a clearer idea of the condition in which he left his wife and children, than any description could do:

|  | £. | s. | d. |
|---|---|---|---|
| 1 Sorrel horse .. .......................... | 8 |  |  |
| 1 Black horse ...... ...................... | 9 | 10 |  |
| 1 Red cow and calf...................... | 4 | 10 |  |

|  | £ | s. | d. |
|---|---|---|---|
| 1 Brindle cow and calf.................... | 4 | 10 | |
| 1 Red cow and calf........................ | 5 | | |
| 1 Brindle bull yearling.................... | 1 | | |
| 1 Brindle heifer yearling.................. | 1 | | |
| Bar spear-plough and tackling.......... | 2 | 5 | |
| 3 Weeding hoes........................... | 7 | 6 | |
| Flax wheel............. ................. | | 6 | |
| Pair smoothing irons..................... | | 15 | |
| 1 Dozen pewter plates.................... | 1 | 10 | |
| 2 Pewter dishes........................... | | 17 | 6 |
| Dutch oven and cule, weighing 15 lbs... | | 15 | |
| Small iron kettle and cule, weighing 12 lbs. | | 12 | |
| Tool adds.... ........................... | | 10 | |
| Hand saw............................... | | 5 | |
| One-inch auger.......................... | | 6 | |
| Three-quarter auger..................... | | 4 | 6 |
| Half-inch auger.......................... | | 3 | |
| Drawing-knife....... ................... | | 3 | |
| Currying-knife........................... | | 10 | |
| Currier's knife and barking-iron......... | | 6 | |
| Old smooth-bar gun..................... | | 10 | |
| Rifle gun............................... | | 55 | |
| Rifle gun............................... | 3 | 10 | |
| 2 Pott trammels........................... | | 14 | |
| 1 Feather bed and furniture.............. | 5 | 10 | |
| Ditto.................................... | 8 | 5 | |
| 1 Bed and turkey feathers and furniture... | 1 | 10 | |
| Steeking-iron............................ | | 1 | 6 |
| Candle-stick..... ....................... | | 1 | 6 |
| 1 Axe................................... | | 9 | |
| | £68 | 16s | 6d |

Soon after the death of Abraham Lincoln, his widow moved from Jefferson county to Washington county. Here the eldest son, Mordecai, who inherited nearly all of the large estate, became a well-to-do and popular citizen. The deed-book of Washington county contains a number of records of lands bought and sold by him. At one time he was sheriff of his county and according to a tradition of his descendants a member of the Kentucky legislature. His name is not to be found however in the fullest collection of journals of the Kentucky legislature which exists, that of Dr. R. T. Durett of Louisville, Kentucky.  Mordecai Lincoln is remembered especially for his sporting tastes, his bitter hatred of the Indians and his ability as a story-teller.  He remained in Kentucky until late in life, when he removed to Hancock County, Illinois.

Of Josiah, the second son, we know very little more than that the records show that he owned and sold land.  He left Kentucky when a young man, to settle on the Blue river, in Harrison County, Indiana, and there he died.  The two daughters married into well-known Kentucky families; the elder, Mary, marrying Ralph Crume; the younger, Nancy, William Brumfield.

The death of Abraham Lincoln was saddest for the youngest of the children, a lad of ten years at the time, named Thomas, for it turned him adrift to become a "wandering laboring-boy" before he had learned even to read.  Thomas seems not to have inherited any of the father's estate, and from the first to have been obliged to shift for himself.  For several years he supported himself by rough farm work of all kinds, learning, in the meantime, the trade of carpenter and cabinet-maker.  According to one of his acquaintances, "Tom had the best set of tools in what was then and now Washington County," and was "a good carpenter for those days, when a cabin was built mainly with the axe, and not a nail or bolt-hinge in it; only leathers and pins to the door, and no glass."  Although a skilled craftsman for his day, he never became a thrifty or ambitious man.  "He would work energetically enough when a job was brought to him, but he would never seek a job."  But if Thomas Lincoln plied his trade spasmodically, he shared the pioneer's love for land, for when but twenty-five years old, and still without the responsibility of a family, he bought a farm in Hardin

County, Kentucky. This fact is of importance, proving as it does that Thomas Lincoln was not the altogether shiftless man he has been pictured. Certainly he must have been above the grade of the ordinary country boy, to have had the energy and ambition to learn a trade and secure a farm through his own efforts by the time he was twenty-five. He was illiterate, never doing more "in the way of writing than to bunglingly write his own name." Nevertheless, he had the reputation in the country of being good-natured and obliging, and possessing what his neighbors called "good strong horse-sense." Although he was a "very quiet sort of a man," he was known to be determined in his opinions, and quite competent to defend his rights by force if they were too flagrantly violated. He was a moral man, and, in the crude way of the pioneer, religious.

In 1806 Thomas Lincoln married. The early history of his wife, Nancy Hanks, has been until recently obscured by contradictory traditions. The compilation of the genealogy of the Hanks family in America, which has been completed by Mrs. Caroline Hanks Hitchcock, though not yet printed, has fortunately cleared up the mystery of her birth. According to the records which Mrs. Hitchcock has gathered and a brief summary of which she has published in a valuable little volume called "Nancy Hanks," the family to which Thomas Lincoln's wife belonged first came to this country in 1699 and settled in Plymouth, Massachusetts.

This early settler, Benjamin Hanks, had eleven children, one of whom, William, went to Virginia, settling near the mouth of the Rappahannock river. William Hanks had five sons, four of whom, about the middle of the eighteenth century, moved to Amelia County, Virginia, where, according to old deeds unearthed by Mrs. Hitchcock, they owned nearly a thousand acres of land. Joseph Hanks, the youngest of these sons, married Nancy Shipley. This Miss Shipley was

a daughter of Robert and Rachel Shipley of Lurenburg
County, Virginia, and a sister of Mary Shipley, who married
Abraham Lincoln of Rockingham County, and who was the
mother of Thomas Lincoln.

About 1789 Joseph Hanks and a large number of his relatives in Amelia County moved into Kentucky, where he settled near what is now Elizabethtown. He remained here
until his death in 1793. Joseph Hanks's will may still be seen
in the county records of Bardstown. He leaves to each of his
sons a horse, to each of his daughters a " heifer yearling,"
though these bequests, as well as the " whole estate " of one
hundred and fifty acres of land was to be the property of his
wife during her life, when it was to be divided equally
among all the children.

Soon after Joseph Hanks's death his wife died and the
family was scattered. The youngest of the eight children left
fatherless and motherless by the death of Joseph Hanks and
his wife was a little girl called Nancy. She was but nine
years old at the time and a home was found for her with her
aunt, Lucy Shipley, wife of Richard Berry, who had a farm
in Washington county, near Springfield. Nancy had a large
number of relatives near there, all of whom had come from
Virginia with her father. The little girl grew up into a
sweet-tempered and beautiful woman whom tradition paints
not only as the center of all the country merry-making but as
a famous spinner and housewife.

It was probably at the house of Richard Berry that
Thomas Lincoln met Nancy Hanks, for he doubtless spent
more or less time nearby with his oldest brother, Mordecai
Lincoln, who was a resident of Washington County and a
friend and neighbor of the Berry's. He may have seen her,
too, at the home of her brother, Joseph Hanks, in Elizabethtown. This Joseph Hanks was a carpenter and had inherited the old home of the family and it was with him that

MAP OF NEW SALEM, ILLINOIS.

Drawn for this biography by J. McCann Davis, aided by surviving inhabitants of New Salem. Dr. John Allen, who lived across the road from Berry & Lincoln's store, attended Ann Rutledge in her last illness. None of the buildings are in existence to-day.

Thomas Lincoln learned his trade.  At all events, the two
cousins became engaged and on June 10, 1806, their marriage bond was issued according to the law of the time.
Two days later according to the marriage returns of the Rev-
erend Jesse Head, they were married,—a fact duly attested
also by the marriage certificate made out by the officiating
minister.

The marriage took place at the home of Richard Berry,
near Beechland in Washington County, Kentucky.  It was
celebrated in the boisterous style of one hundred years ago,
and was followed by an infare, given by the bride's guardian.
To this celebration came all the neighbors, and, according
to an entertaining Kentucky centenarian, Dr. Christopher
Columbus Graham, even those who happened in the neighborhood were made welcome.  He tells how he heard of the
wedding while " out hunting for roots," and went " just to
get a good supper.  I saw Nancy Hanks Lincoln at her wedding," continues Mr. Graham, " a fresh looking girl, I should
say over twenty.  I was at the infare, too, given by John H.
Parrott, her guardian—and only girls with money had
guardians appointed by the court.  We had bearmeat; . . .
venison; wild turkey and ducks; eggs, wild and tame, so
common that you could buy them at two bits a bushel; maple
sugar, swung on a string, to bite off for coffee or whiskey;
syrup in big gourds; peach-and-honey; a sheep that the two
families barbecued whole over coals of wood burned in a
pit, and covered with green boughs to keep the juice in; and
a race for the whiskey bottle."

After his marriage Thomas Lincoln settled in Elizabethtown.  His home was a log cabin, but at that date few people in the state had anything else.  Kentucky had been in the
union only fourteen years.  When admitted, the few brick
structures within its boundaries were easily counted, and
there were only log school-houses and churches.  Fourteen

Know all men by these presents that we Thomas Lincoln and
Richard Berry are held and firmly bound unto his
Excellency the Governor of Kentucky for the debt and full sum of
fifty pounds current money to the payment of which well and
truly to be made to the said Governor and his successors
we bind our selves our heirs &c. jointly and severally firmly
by these presents sealed with our seals and dated this 10th
day of June. 1806 The condition of the above
obligation is such that whereas there is a marriage shortly
intended between the above bound Thomas Lincoln and
Nancy Hanks
now if there be no lawful cause to obstruct the said
Marriage then this obligation to be Void or else to Remain
in full force & Virtue in Law

Witness
Jno. H. Parrott

Thomas Lincoln (Seal)
Richard Berry (Seal)
Bondsman.

Washington Co.

I do hereby certify that the following
is a true list of Marriages Solemnized by me the Sub
Scriber from the Sixth June the 28th of April 1806 untill
the date hereof

Sun 26th 1806 Joined together in the Holy estate of
Matrimony agreeable to the rules of the M.E.C.

Morris Berry & Peggy Simms
Nov 27th 1806 David Mize & Hanah Xtu
March 5th 1807 Charles Ridge & Anna Davis
March 24th 1807 John Head & Sally Clark
March 27th Benjamin Clark & Polly Head
Jany 14th Edward Pyle & Rosanah McMahon
Dec 22nd 1806 Silas Chamberlyn & Betsey West
Sun 17th 1806 John Spranger & Elizabeth Inyram
Jan 12th 1806 Thomas Lincoln & Nancy Hanks
September 23rd 1806 John Cambron & Hanah White
October 2nd 1806 Anthony Lypey & Kizziah Pettt
October 23rd 1806 Aaron Harding & Hanah Pottot
April 5th 1807 Daniel Rayne & Chrishena Pene
July 26th 1806 Benjamin Clark & Polly Clark
May 1806 Hugh Haskins & Betsey Dyer
September 25th 1806 John Graham & Cathrine Jones
Given under my hand this 22nd day of April
1807
John Head D.M.E.C.

RETURN OF MARRIAGE OF THOMAS LINCOLN AND NANCY HANKS.

From a tracing of the original, made by Henry Whitney Cleveland. This certificate was discovered about
1885 by W. F. Booker, Esq., Clerk of Washington County, Kentucky.

years had brought great improvements, but the majority of the population still lived in log cabins, so that the home of Thomas Lincoln was as good as most of his neighbors. Little is known of his position in Elizabethtown, though we have proof that he had credit in the community, for the descendants of two of the early store-keepers still remember seeing on their grandfathers' account books sundry items charged to T. Lincoln. Tools and groceries were the chief purchases he made, though on one of the ledgers a pair of " silk suspenders," worth one dollar and fifty cents, was entered. He not only enjoyed a certain credit with the people of Elizabethtown; he was sufficiently respected by the public authorities to be appointed in 1816 a road surveyor, or, as the office

FACSIMILE OF THE APPOINTMENT OF THOMAS LINCOLN AS ROAD SURVEYOR.

is known in some localities, supervisor. It was not, to be sure, a position of great importance, but it proved that he was considered fit to oversee a body of men at a task of considerable value to the community. Indeed, all of the documents mentioning Thomas Lincoln which have been discovered show him to have had a much better position in Hardin county than he has been credited with.

It was at Elizabethtown that the first child of the Lincolns, a daughter, was born. Soon after this event Thomas Lincoln decided to combine farming with his trade, and moved to the farm he had bought in 1803 on the Big South fork of Nolin creek, in Hardin County, now La Rue County, three miles from Hodgensville, and about fourteen miles from Elizabethtown. Here he was living when, on February 12, 1809, his second child, a boy, was born. The little newcomer was called Abraham, after his grandfather—a name which had persisted through many preceding generations in both the Lincoln and Hanks families.

The home into which the child came was the ordinary one of the poorer western pioneer—a one-roomed cabin with a huge outside chimney, a single window, and a rude door. The description of its squalor and wretchedness, which are so familiar, have been overdrawn. Dr. Graham, than whom there is no better authority on the life of that day, and who knew Thomas Lincoln well, declares energetically that "It is all stuff about Tom Lincoln keeping his wife in an open shed in a winter. The Lincolns had a cow and calf, milk and butter, a good feather bed—for I have slept on it. They had home-woven 'kiverlids,' big and little pots, a loom and wheel. Tom Lincoln was a man and took care of his wife."

The Lincoln home was undoubtedly rude, and in many ways uncomfortable, but it sheltered a happy family, and its poverty affected the new child but little. He grew to be robust and active and soon learned how endless are the delights and interests the country offers to a child. He had several companions. There was his sister Nancy, or Sarah —both names are given her—two years his senior; there was a cousin of his mother's, ten years older, Dennis Friend (commonly called Dennis Hanks), an active and ingenious leader in sports and mischief; and there were the neighbors' boys. One of the latter, Austin Gollaher, lived to be over ninety years of age and to his death related with pride how he played with young Lincoln in the shavings of his father's carpenter shop, hunted coons and ran the woods with him, and once even saved his life.

"Yes," Mr. Gollaher was accustomed to say, "the story that I once saved Abraham Lincoln's life is true. He and I had been going to school together for a year or more, and had become greatly attached to each other. Then school disbanded on account of there being so few scholars, and we did not see each other much for a long while. One Sunday my mother visited the Lincolns, and I was taken along. Abe and I played around all day. Finally, we concluded to cross the creek to hunt for some partridges young Lincoln had seen the day before. The creek was swollen by a recent rain, and, in crossing on the narrow footlog, Abe fell in. Neither of us could swim. I got a long pole and held it out to Abe, who grabbed it. Then I pulled him ashore. He was almost dead, and I was badly scared. I rolled and pounded him in good earnest. Then I got him by the arms and shook him, the water meanwhile pouring out of his mouth. By this means I succeeded in bringing him to, and he was soon all right.

"Then a new difficulty confronted us. If our mothers discovered our wet clothes they would whip us. This we dreaded from experience, and determined to avoid. It was June, the sun was very warm, and we soon dried our clothing by spreading it on the rocks about us. We promised never to tell the story, and I never did until after Lincoln's tragic end."

When the little boy was about four years old the first real excitement of his life occurred. His father moved from the farm on Nolin creek to another some fifteen miles northeast on Knob creek, and here the child began to go to school. At that day the schools in the west were usually accidental, depending upon the coming of some poor and ambitious young man who was willing to teach a few terms while he looked for an opening to something better. The terms were irregular, their length being decided by the time the settlers felt able to board the master and pay his small salary. The chief qualifications for a school-master seem to have been enough strength to keep the "big boys" in order, though one high authority affirms that pluck went "for a heap sight more'n sinnoo with boys."

Many of the itinerant masters were Catholics, strolling Irishmen from the colony in Tennessee, or French priests from Kaskaskia. Lincoln's first teacher, Zachariah Riney, was a Catholic. Of his second teacher, Caleb Hazel, we know even less than of Riney. Mr. Gollaher says that Abraham Lincoln, in those days when he was his schoolmate, was "an unusually bright boy at school, and made splendid progress in his studies. Indeed, he learned faster than any of his schoolmates. Though so young, he studied very hard. He would get spicewood bushes, hack them up on a log, and burn them two or three together, for the purpose of giving light by which he might pursue his studies."

Probably the boy's mother had something to do with the spice-wood illuminations. Tradition has it that Mrs. Lincoln took great pains to teach her children what she knew, and that at her knee they heard all the Bible lore, fairy tales, and country legends that she had been able to gather in her poor life.

Besides the "A B C schools," as Lincoln called them, the only other medium of education in the country districts of Kentucky in those days was "preaching." Itinerants like the school-masters, the preachers, of whatever denomination, were generally uncouth and illiterate; the code of morals they taught was mainly a healthy one, and they, no doubt, did much to keep the consciences of the pioneers awake. It is difficult to believe that they ever did much for the moral training of young Lincoln, though he certainly got his first notion of public speaking from them; and for years in his boyhood one of his chief delights was to gather his playmates about him, and preach and thump until he had his auditors frightened or in tears.

As soon as the child was strong enough to follow his father in the fields, he was put to work at simple tasks;—bringing tools, carrying water, picking berries, dropping seeds. He learned to know his father's farm from line to line and years after, when President of the United States, he recalled in a conversation at the White House, in the presence of Dr. J. J. Wright of Emporia, Kansas, the arrangement of the fields and an incident of his own childish experience as a farmer's son. " Mr. President," one of the visitors had asked, " how would you like when the war is over to visit your old home in Kentucky? " " I would like it very much," Mr. Lincoln replied. " I remember that old home very well. Our farm was composed of three fields. It lay in the valley surrounded by high hills and deep gorges. Sometimes when there came a big rain in the hills the water would come down through the gorges and spread all over the farm. The last thing that I remember of doing there was one Saturday afternoon; the other boys planted the corn in what we called the big field; it contained seven acres—and I dropped the pumpkin seed. I dropped two seeds every other hill and every other row. The next Sunday morning there came a big rain in the hills, it did not rain a drop in the valley, but the water coming down through the gorges washed ground, corn, pumpkin seeds and all clear off the field."

## CHAPTER II

In 1816 a great event happened to the little boy. His father emigrated from Knob creek to Indiana. " This removal was partly on account of slavery, but chiefly on account of the difficulty in land titles in Kentucky," says his son. It was due, as well, no doubt, to the fascination which an unknown country has always for the adventurous, and to that restless pioneer spirit which drives even men of sober judgment continually towards the frontier, in search of a place where the conflict with nature is less severe—some spot farther on, to which a friend or a neighbor has preceded, and from which he sends back glowing reports. It may be that Thomas Lincoln was tempted into Indiana by the reports of his brother Joseph, who had settled on the Big Blue river in that State. At all events, in the fall of 1816 he started with wife and children and household stores to journey by horseback and by wagon from Knob creek to a farm selected on a previous trip he had made. This farm, located near Little Pigeon creek, about fifteen miles north of the Ohio river, and a mile and a half east of Gentryville, Spencer County, was in a forest so dense that the road for the travellers had to be hewed out as they went.

To a boy of seven years, free from all responsibility, and too vigorous to feel its hardships, such a journey must have been a long delight and wonder. Life suddenly ceased its routine, and every day brought forth new scenes and adventures. Little Abraham saw forests greater than he had ever

18

dreamed of, peopled by strange birds and beasts, and he crossed a river so wide that it must have seemed to him like the sea. To Thomas and Nancy Lincoln the journey was probably a hard and sad one; but to the children beside them it was a wonderful journey into the unknown.

On arriving at the new farm an axe was put into the boy's hands, and he was set to work to aid in clearing a field for corn, and to help build the " half-face camp " which for a year was the home of the Lincolns. There were few more primitive homes in the wilderness of Indiana in 1816 than this of young Lincoln, and there were few families, even in that day, who were forced to practice more make-shifts to get a living. The cabin which took the place of the " half-face camp " had but one room, with a loft above. For a long time there was no window, door, or floor; not even the traditional deer-skin hung before the exit; there was no oiled paper over the opening for light; there was no puncheon covering on the ground.

The furniture was of their own manufacture. The table and chairs were of the rudest sort—rough slabs of wood in which holes were bored and legs fitted in. Their bedstead, or, rather bed-frame, was made of poles held up by two outer posts, and the ends made firm by inserting the poles in auger-holes that had been bored in a log which was a part of the wall of the cabin; skins were its chief covering. Little Abraham's bed was even more primitive. He slept on a heap of dry leaves in the corner of the loft, to which he mounted by means of pegs driven into the wall.

Their food, if coarse, was usually abundant; the chief difficulty in supplying the larder was to secure any variety. Of game there was plenty—deer, bear, pheasants, wild turkeys, ducks, birds of all kinds. There were fish in the streams, and wild fruits of many kinds in the woods in the summer, and these were dried for winter use; but the difficulty of raising and milling corn and wheat was very great. Indeed, in many places in the west the first flour cake was an historical event. Corn-dodger was the every-day bread of the Lincoln household, the wheat cake being a dainty reserved for Sunday mornings.

Potatoes were the only vegetable raised in any quantity, and there were times in the Lincoln family when they were the only food on the table; a fact proved to posterity by the oft-quoted remark of Abraham to his father after the latter had asked a blessing over a dish of roasted potatoes—" that they were mighty poor blessings." Not only were they all the Lincolns had for dinner sometimes; one of their neighbors tells of calling there when raw potatoes, pared and washed, were passed around instead of apples or other fruit. They even served as a kind of pioneer chauffrette—being baked and given to the children to carry in their hands as they started to school or on distant errands in winter time.

The food was prepared in the rudest way, for the supply of both groceries and cooking utensils was limited. The former were frequently wanting entirely, and as for the latter, the most important item was the Dutch oven. An indispensable article in the primitive kitchen outfit was the " gritter." It was made by flattening out an old piece of tin punching it full of holes, and nailing it on a board. Upon this all sorts of things were grated, even ears of corn, in which slow way, enough meal was sometimes secured for bread. Old tin was used for many other contrivances besides the " gritter," and every scrap was carefully saved. Most of the dishes were of pewter; the spoons, iron; the knives and forks horn-handled.

The Lincolns of course made their own soap and candles, and if they had cotton or wool to wear they had literally to grow it. It is probable that young Abraham Lincoln wore little cotton or linsey-woolsey. His trousers were of roughly tanned deer-skin, his foot-covering a home-made moccasin.

his cap a coon-skin; it was only the material for his blouse or shirt that was woven at home. If this costume had some obvious disadvantages, it was not to be despised. So good an authority as Governor Reynolds says of one of its articles— the linsey-woolsey shirt—" It was an excellent garment. I have never felt so happy and healthy since I put it off."

These "pretty pinching times," as Abraham Lincoln once described the early days in Indiana, lasted until 1819. The year before Nancy Lincoln had died, and for many months no more forlorn place could be conceived than this pioneer home bereft of its guiding spirit; but finally Thomas Lincoln went back to Kentucky and returned with a new wife—Sally Bush Johnston, a widow with three children, John, Sarah, and Matilda. The new mother came well provided with household furniture, bringing many things unfamiliar to little Abraham—"one fine bureau, one table, one set of chairs, one large clothes-chest, cooking utensils, knives, forks, bedding, and other articles." She was a woman of energy, thrift, and gentleness, and at once made the cabin home-like and taught the children habits of cleanliness and comfort.

Abraham was ten years old when his new mother came from Kentucky, and he was already an important member of the family. He was remarkably strong for his years, and the work he could do in a day was a decided advantage to Thomas Lincoln. The axe which had been put into his hand to help in making the first clearing, he had never been allowed to drop; indeed, as he says himself, " from that till within his twenty-third year he was almost constantly handling that most useful instrument." Besides, he drove the team, cut the elm and linn brush with which the stock was often fed, learned to handle the old shovel-plough, to wield the sickle, to thresh the wheat with a flail, to fan and clean it with a sheet, to go to mill and turn the hard-earned grist into flour. In short, he learned all the trades the settler's

boy must know, and so well that when his father did not
need him he could hire him to the neighbors.  Thomas
Lincoln also taught him the rudiments of carpentry and
cabinet-making, and kept him busy much of the time as his
assistant in his trade.  There are houses still standing, in
and near Gentryville, on which it is said he worked.

As he grew older he became one of the strongest and most
popular " hands " in the vicinity, and much of his time was
spent as a " hired boy " on some neighbor's farm.   For
twenty-five cents a day—paid to his father—he was hostler,
ploughman, wood-chopper, and carpenter, besides helping
the women with the " chores."   For them he was ready to
carry water, make the fire, even tend the baby.   No wonder
that a laborer who never refused to do anything asked of
him, who could " strike with a maul heavier blows " and
" sink an axe deeper into the wood " than anybody else in
the community, and who at the same time was general help
for the women, never lacked a job in Gentryville.

Of all the tasks his rude life brought him, none seems to
have suited him better than going to the mill.  It was, perhaps, as much the leisure enforced by this trip as anything
else that attracted him.  The machinery was primitive, and
each man waited his turn, which sometimes was long in coming.   A story is told by one of the pioneers of Illinois of going many miles with a grist, and waiting so long for his turn,
that when it came, he and his horse had eaten all the corn
and he had none to grind.  This waiting with other men
and boys on like errands gave an opportunity for talk,
story-telling, and games, which were Lincoln's delight.

If Abraham Lincoln's life was rough and hard it was
not without amusements.  At home the rude household was
overflowing with life.  There were Abraham and his sister,
a stepbrother and two stepsisters, and a cousin of Nancy

Thomas Lincoln married to ~~~~
Johnston December 2"d 1819 —
Sarah Lincoln, daughter of Thos.
Lincoln was married ~~~~
Aug. ~~~~ 18~~

Abraham Lincoln son of Tho[s]
Lincoln was married to Mary
Todd Nov. 4th 1842 —
John D. Johnston was married to
second wife, Nancy Jane William[s]
March 5 1851

John D. Johnston son
of John D. and Nancy
Jane Johnston was
borne April the 11. 1854

1856
1616
46

1856
16
40

Nancy Lincoln wife of Tho[s] Lincoln died October 5th 1818
Sarah daughter of Tho[s] Lincoln
wife of Aaron Grigsby died
~~uary 20th 1828 —

Thomas Lincoln died January ~~
aged 73 years 11 days —

Hanks Lincoln, Dennis (Friend) Hanks, whom misfortune had made an inmate of the Lincoln home—quite enough to plan sports and mischief and keep time from growing dull. Thomas Lincoln and Dennis Hanks were both famous story-tellers, and the Lincolns spent many a cozy evening about their cabin fire, repeating the stories they knew.

Of course the boys hunted. Not that Abraham ever became a true sportsman; indeed, he seems to have lacked the genuine sporting instinct. In a curious autobiography, written entirely in the third person, which Lincoln prepared at the request of a friend in 1860, he says of his exploits as a hunter: "A few days before the completion of his eighth year, in the absence of his father, a flock of wild turkeys approached the new log cabin; and Abraham with a rifle gun, standing inside, shot through a crack and killed one of them. He has never since pulled the trigger on any larger game." This exploit is confirmed by Dennis Hanks, who says: "No doubt about A. Lincoln's killing the turkey. He done it with his father's rifle, made by William Lutes of Bullitt county, Kentucky. I have killed a hundred deer with her myself; turkeys too numerous to mention."

But there were many other country sports which he enjoyed to the full. He went swimming in the evenings; fished with the other boys in Pigeon creek, wrestled, jumped, and ran races at the noon rests. He was present at every country horse-race and fox-chase. The sports he preferred were those which brought men together; the spelling-school, the husking-bee; the "raising;" and of all these he was the life by his wit, his stories, his good nature, his doggerel verses, his practical jokes, and by a rough kind of politeness—for even in Indiana in those times there was a notion of politeness, and one of Lincoln's school-masters had given "lessons in manners." Lincoln seems to have profited in a degree by them; for Mrs. Crawford, at whose home he worked for

some time, declares that he always "lifted his hat and bowed"
when he made his appearance.

There was, of course, a rough gallantry among the young
people; and Lincoln's old comrades and friends in Indiana
have left many tales of how he "went to see the girls," of how
he brought in the biggest back-log and made the brightest
fire; of how the young people, sitting around it, watching the way the sparks flew, told their fortunes. He helped
pare apples, shell corn and crack nuts. He took the girls to
meeting and to spelling-school, though he was not often allowed to take part in the spelling-match, for the one who
"chose first" always chose "Abe Lincoln," and that was
equivalent to winning, as the others knew that "he would
stand up the longest."

The nearest approach to sentiment at this time, of which
we know, is recorded in a story Lincoln once told to an acquaintance in Springfield. It was a rainy day, and he was sitting with his feet on the window-sill, his eyes on the street,
watching the rain. Suddenly he looked up and said:

"Did you ever write out a story in your mind? I did when
I was a little codger. One day a wagon with a lady and two
girls and a man broke down near us, and while they were
fixing up, they cooked in our kitchen. The woman had books
and read us stories, and they were the first I had ever heard.
I took a great fancy to one of the girls; and when they were
gone I thought of her a great deal, and one day when I was
sitting out in the sun by the house I wrote out a story in my
mind. I thought I took my father's horse and followed the
wagon, and finally I found it, and they were surprised to see
me. I talked with the girl and persuaded her to elope with
me; and that night I put her on my horse, and we started off
across the prairie. After several hours we came to a camp;
and when we rode up we found it was the one we had left a
few hours before, and we went in. The next night we tried
again, and the same thing happened—the horse came back to
the same place; and then we concluded that we ought not to

elope. I stayed until I had persuaded her father to give her to me. I always meant to write that story out and publish it, and I began once; but I concluded that it was not much of a story. But I think that was the beginning of love with me."

His life had its tragedies as well as its touch of romance—tragedies so real and profound that they gave dignity to all the crudeness and poverty which surrounded him, and quickened and intensified the melancholy temperament which he inherited from his mother. Away back in 1816, when Thomas Lincoln had started to find a farm in Indiana, bidding his wife be ready to go into the wilderness on his return, Nancy Lincoln had taken her boy and girl to a tiny grave, that of her youngest child; and the three had there said good-by to a little one whom the children had scarcely known, but for whom the mother's grief was so keen that the boy never forgot the scene.

Two years later he saw his father make a green pine box and put his dead mother into it, and he saw her buried not far from their cabin, almost without prayer. Young as he was, it was his efforts, it is said, which brought a parson from Kentucky, three months later, to preach the sermon and conduct the service which seemed to the child a necessary honor to the dead. As sad as the death of his mother was that of his only sister, Sarah. Married to Aaron Grigsby in 1826, she had died a year and a half later in child-birth, a death which to her brother must have seemed a horror and a mystery.

Apart from these family sorrows there was all the crime and misery of the community—all of which came to his ears and awakened his nature. He even saw in those days one of his companions go suddenly mad. The young man never recovered his reason but sank into idiocy. All night he would croon plaintive songs, and Lincoln himself tells how, fascinated by this mysterious malady, he used to rise before day light to cross the fields to listen to this funeral dirge of the reason. In spite of the poverty and rudeness of his life the depths of his nature were unclouded. He could feel intensely, and his imagination was quick to respond to the touch of mystery

# CHAPTER III

ABRAHAM LINCOLN'S EARLY OPPORTUNITIES—THE BOOKS
HE READ—TRIPS TO NEW ORLEANS—IMPRESSION HE
MADE ON HIS FRIENDS

WITH all his hard living and hard work, Lincoln was getting, in this period, a desultory kind of education. Not that he received much schooling. He went to school " by littles," he says; "in all it did not amount to more than a year." And, if we accept his own description of the teachers, it was, perhaps, just as well that it was only " by littles." No qualification was required of a teacher beyond " readin', writin,' and cipherin' to the rule of three." If a straggler supposed to know Latin happened to sojourn in the neighborhood, he was looked upon as a "wizard." But more or less of a school-room is a matter of small importance if a boy has learned to read, and to think of what he reads. And that, this boy had learned. His stock of books was small, but he knew them thoroughly, and they were good books to know; the Bible, "Æsop's Fables," "Robinson Crusoe," Bunyan's "Pilgrim Progress," a "History of the United States," Weems's "Life of Washington," and the "Statutes of Indiana."* These are the chief

*The first authorized sketch of Lincoln's life was written by the late John L. Scripps of the Chicago " Tribune," who went to Springfield at Mr. Lincoln's request, and by him was furnished the data for a campaign biography. In a letter written to Mr. Herndon after the death of Lincoln, which Herndon turned over to me, Scripps relates that in writing his book he stated that Lincoln as a youth read Plutarch's " Lives." This he did simply because, as a rule, every boy in the West in the early days did read Plutarch. When the advance sheets of the book reached Mr. Lincoln, he sent for the author and said, gravely: " That paragraph wherein you state that I read Plutarch's ' Lives ' was not true when you wrote it, for up to that moment in my life I had never seen that early contribution to human history; but I want your book, even if it is

ones we know about. Some of these books he borrowed from
the neighbors; a practice which resulted in at least one casu-
alty, for Weems's "Life of Washington" he allowed to get
wet, and to make good the loss he had to pull fodder three
days. No matter. The book became his then, and he could
read it as he would. Fortunately he took this curious work in
profound seriousness, which a wide-awake boy would hardly
be expected to do to-day. Washington became an exalted
figure in his imagination; and he always contended later,
when the question of the real character of the first President
was brought up, that it was wiser to regard him as a god-
like being, heroic in nature and deeds, as Weems does, than
to contend that he was only a man who, if wise and good,
still made mistakes and was guilty of follies, like other men.

Besides these books he borrowed many others. He once
told a friend that he "read through every book he had ever
heard of in that country, for a circuit of fifty miles." From
everything he read he made long extracts, with his turkey-
buzzard pen and brier-root ink. When he had no paper he
would write on a board, and thus preserve his selections until he secured a copybook. The wooden fire-shovel was his
usual slate, and on its back he ciphered with a charred stick
shaving it off when it had become too grimy for use. The
logs and boards in his vicinity he covered with his figures
and quotations. By night he read and worked as long as
there was light, and he kept a book in the crack of the logs in
his loft, to have it at hand at peep of day. When acting as
ferryman on the Ohio, in his nineteenth year, anxious, no
doubt, to get through the books of the house where he
boarded, before he left the place, he read every night until
midnight.

---

nothing more than a campaign sketch, to be faithful to the facts; and
in order that the statement might be literally true, I secured the book a
few weeks ago, and have sent for you to tell you that I have just read
it through."—Jesse W. Weik.

An army of a 1000 men having plundered a
city took so much money that when it was
shared among them each man (had) 2£. I demand
how much money was taken in all

$$1000.0$$
$$23$$
$$\overline{\phantom{00}}$$
$$30000$$
$$20000$$
$$20000.0\,0000$$
$$27.0000$$

Abraham Lincoln His Book

FRAGMENT FROM A LEAF IN LINCOLN'S EXERCISE-BOOK.

Every lull in his daily labor he used for reading, rarely
going to his work without a book. When ploughing or culti-
vating the rough fields of Spencer county, he found frequently a half hour for reading, for at the end of every long
row the horse was allowed to rest, and Lincoln had his book
out and was perched on stump or fence, almost as soon as the
plough had come to a standstill. One of the few people still
left in Gentryville who remembers Lincoln, Captain John
Lamar, tells to this day of riding to mill with his father, and
seeing, as they drove along, a boy sitting on the top rail of an
old-fashioned stake-and-rider worm fence, reading so intently that he did not notice their approach. His father turning to him, said: "John, look at that boy yonder, and mark
my words, he will make a smart man out of himself. I may
not see it, but you'll see if my words don't come true." "That
boy was Abraham Lincoln," adds Mr. Lamar impressively.

In his habits of reading and study the boy had little encouragement from his father, but his stepmother did all she
could for him. Indeed, between the two there soon grew up a
relation of touching gentleness and confidence. In one of the
interviews a biographer of Mr. Lincoln sought with her before her death, Mrs. Lincoln said:

"I induced my husband to permit Abe to read and study at
home, as well as at school. At first he was not easily recon-
ciled to it, but finally he too seemed willing to encourage him
to a certain extent. Abe was a dutiful son to me always, and
we took particular care when he was reading not to disturb
him—would let him read on and on till he quit of his own
accord." This consideration of his stepmother won the boy's
confidence, and he rarely copied anything that he did not take
it to her to read, asking her opinion of it; and often, when
she did not understand it, explaining the meaning in his plain
and simple language.

Among the books which fell into young Lincoln's hand

when he was about eighteen years old was a copy of the "Revised Statutes of Indiana."* We know from Dennis Hanks and from Mr. Turnham of Gentryville, to whom the book belonged, and from other associates of Lincoln at the time, that he read the book intently and discussed its contents intelligently. It was a remarkable volume for a thoughtful lad whose mind had already been fired by the history of Washington. It opened with that wonderful document, the Declaration of Independence, following the Declaration of Independence was the Constitution of the United States, the Act of Virginia passed in 1783 by which the "Territory North Westward of the river Ohio" was conveyed to the United States, and the ordinance of 1787 for governing this territory, containing that clause on which Lincoln in the future based many an argument on the slavery question. This article, No. 6 of the Ordinance, reads: "There shall be neither slavery nor involuntary servitude in the said territory, otherwise than in the punishment of crimes, whereof the party shall have been duly convicted: provided always, that any person escaping into the same, from whom labor or service is lawfully claimed in any one of the original States, such fugitive may be lawfully reclaimed, and conveyed to the person claiming his or her labor or service, as aforesaid."

---

*The book was owned by Mr. David Turnham of Gentryville, and was given by him in 1865 to Mr. Herndon, who placed it in the Lincoln Memorial collection of Chicago. In December, 1894, this collection was sold in Philadelphia, and the "Statutes of Indiana" was bought by Mr. William Hoffman Winters, Librarian of the New York Law Institute, where it now may be seen. The book is worn, the title page is gone, and a few leaves from the end are missing. The title page of a duplicate volume reads: "The Revised Laws of Indiana, adopted and enacted by the General Assembly at their eighth session. To which are prefixed the Declaration of Independence, the Constitution of the United States, the Constitution of the State of Indiana, and sundry other documents connected with the Political History of the Territory and State of Indiana. Arranged and published by authority of the General Assembly. Corydon: Printed by Carpenter and Douglass, 1824."

(3)

Following this was the Constitution and the Revised Laws of Indiana, three hundred and seventy-five pages, of five hundred words each, of statutes. When Lincoln finished this book, as he had, probably, before he was eighteen, we have reason to believe that he understood the principles on which the nation was founded, how the State of Indiana came into being, and how it was governed. His understanding of the subject was clear and practical, and he applied it in his reading, thinking, and discussion. After he had read the Statutes of Indiana, Lincoln had free access to the library of an admirer, Judge John Pitcher of Rockport, Indiana, where he examined many books.

Although so far away from the center of the world's activity, he was learning something of current history. One man in Gentryville, Mr. Jones, the storekeeper, took a Louisville paper, and here Lincoln went regularly to read and discuss its contents. All the men and boys of the neighborhood gathered there, and everything which the paper printed was subjected to their keen, shrewd common sense. It was not long before young Lincoln became the favorite member of the group, the one listened to most respectfully. Politics were warmly discussed by these Gentryville citizens, and it may be that sitting on the counter of Jones's grocery, Lincoln even argued on slavery. It certainly was one of the live questions in Indiana at that date.

For several years after the organization of the Territory, and in spite of the Ordinance of 1787, a system of thinly disguised slavery had existed; and it took a sharp struggle to bring the State in without some form of the institution. So uncertain was the result that, when decided, the word passed from mouth to mouth all over Hoosierdom, "She has come in free, she has come in free!" Even in 1820, four years after the admission to Statehood, the census showed one hundred and ninety slaves, nearly all of them in the southwest corner, where the Lincolns lived, and it was not, in reality, until 1821 that the State Supreme Court put an end to the question. In Illinois in 1822-1824 there was carried on one of the most violent contests between the friends and opponents of slavery which occurred before the repeal of the Missouri Compromise. The effort to secure slave labor was nearly successful. In the campaign, pamphlets pro and con literally inundated the State; the pulpits took it up; and "almost every stump in every county had its bellowing, indignant orator." So violent a commotion so near at hand could hardly have failed to reach Gentryville.

There had been other anti-slavery agitation going on within hearing for several years. In 1804 a number of Baptist ministers of Kentucky started a crusade against the institution, which resulted in a hot contest in the denomination, and the organization of the "Baptist Licking-Locust Association Friends of Humanity." The Rev. Jesse Head, the minister who married Thomas Lincoln and Nancy Hanks, talked freely and boldly against slavery; and one of their old friends, Christopher Columbus Graham, the man who was present at their wedding, says: "Tom and Nancy Lincoln and Sally Bush were just steeped full of Jesse Head's notions about the wrong of slavery and the rights of man as explained by Thomas Jefferson and Thomas Paine." In 1806 Charles Osborne began to preach "immediate emancipation" in Tennessee. Ten years later he started a paper in Ohio, devoted to the same idea, and in 1819 he transferred his crusade to Indiana. In 1821 Benjamin Lundy started, in Tennessee, the famous "Genius," devoted to the same doctrine; and in 1822, at Shelbyville, only about one hundred miles from Gentryville, was started a paper similar in its views, the "Abolition Intelligencer."

At that time there were in Kentucky five or six abolition societies, and in Illinois was an organization called the

"Friends of Humanity." Probably young Lincoln heard but
vaguely of these movements; but of some of them he must
have heard, and he must have connected them with the
"Speech of Mr. Pitt on the Slave Trade;" with Merry's
elegy, "The Slaves," and with the discussion given in his
"Kentucky Preceptor," "Which has the Most to Complain
of, the Indian or the Negro?" all of which tradition declares
he was fond of repeating. It is not impossible that, as Frederick Douglas first realized his own condition in reading a
school-speaker, the "Columbian Orator," so Abraham Lincoln first felt the wrong of slavery in reading his "Kentucky" or "American Preceptor."

Lincoln was not only winning in these days in the Jones
grocery store a reputation as a talker and a story-teller; he
was becoming known as a kind of backwoods orator. He
could repeat with effect all the poems and speeches in his various school readers, he could imitate to perfection the wandering preachers who came to Gentryville, and he could make a
political speech so stirring that he drew a crowd about him
every time he mounted a stump. The applause he won was
sweet; and frequently he indulged his gifts when he ought
to have been working—so thought his employers and
Thomas, his father. It was trying, no doubt, to the hard-
pushed farmers, to see the men who ought to have been cutting grass or chopping wood throw down their scythes or
axes and group around a boy, whenever he mounted a stump
to develop a pet theory or repeat with variations yesterday's
sermon. In his fondness for speech-making young Lincoln
attended all the trials of the neighborhood, and frequently
walked fifteen miles to Boonville to attend court.

He wrote as well as spoke, and some of his productions
were printed, through the influence of his admiring neighbors. Thus a local Baptist preacher was so struck with one
of Abraham's essays on temperance that he sent it to Ohio,

where it is said to have appeared in a newspaper. Another article on "National Politics," so pleased a lawyer of the vicinity that he declared the "world couldn't beat it."

In considering the different opportunities for development which the boy had at this time it should not be forgotten that he spent many months at one time or another on the Ohio and Mississippi rivers. In fact, all that Abraham Lincoln saw of men and the world outside of Gentryville and its neighborhood, until after he was twenty-one years of age he saw on these rivers. For many years the Ohio and the Mississippi were the Appian Way, the one route to the world for the western settlers. To preserve it they had been willing in early times to go to war with Spain or with France, to secede from the Union, even to join Spain or France against the United States if either country would insure their right to the highway. In the long years in which the ownership of the great river was unsettled, every man of them had come to feel with Benjamin Franklin, "a neighbor might as well ask me to sell my street door." In fact, this water-way was their "street door," and all that many of them ever saw of the world passed here. Up and down the rivers was a continual movement. Odd craft of every kind possible on a river went by: "arks" and "sleds," with tidy cabins where families lived, and where one could see the washing stretched, the children playing, the mother on pleasant days rocking and sewing; keel-boats, which dodged in and out and turned inquisitive noses up all the creeks and bayous; great fleets from the Alleghanies, made up of a score or more of timber rafts, and manned by forty or fifty rough boatmen; "Orleans boats," loaded with flour, hogs, produce of all kinds; pirogues, made from great trees; "broad-horns;" curious nondescripts worked by a wheel; and, after 1812, steamboats.

All this traffic was leisurely. Men had time to tie up and

tell the news and show their wares.   Even the steamboats
loitered as it pleased them.   They knew no schedule.   They
stopped anywhere to let passengers off.   They tied up
wherever it was convenient, to wait for fresh wood to be cut
and loaded, or for repairs to be made.   Waiting for repairs,
seems, in fact, to have absorbed a great deal of the time of
these early steamers.   They were continually running onto
"sawyers," or "planters," or "wooden islands," and they
blew up with a regularity which was monotonous.   Even
as late as 1842, when Charles Dickens made the trip down
the Mississippi, he was often gravely recommended to keep
as far aft as possible, "because the steamboats generally blew
up forward."

With this varied river life Abraham Lincoln first came
into contact as a ferryman and boatman, when in 1826 he
spent several months as a ferryman at the mouth of Anderson creek, where it joins the Ohio.   This experience suggested new possibilities to him.   It was a custom among the
farmers of Ohio, Indiana and Illinois at this date to collect a
quantity of produce, and float down to New Orleans on a
raft, to sell it.   Young Lincoln saw this, and wanted to try
his fortune as a produce merchant.   An incident of his pro-
jected trip he related once to Mr. Seward:

"Seward," he said, "did you ever hear how I earned my
first dollar?"

"No," said Mr. Seward.

"Well," replied he, "I was about eighteen years of age,
and belonged, as you know, to what they call down south the
'scrubs;' people who do not own land and slaves are nobody there; but we had succeeded in raising, chiefly by my
labor, sufficient produce, as I thought, to justify me in taking
it down the river to sell. After much persuasion I had got
the consent of my mother to go, and had constructed a flatboat large enough to take the few barrels of things we had
gathered to New Orleans.   A steamer was going down the

river. We have, you know, no wharves on the western streams, and the custom was, if passengers were at any of the landings they were to go out in a boat, the steamer stopping, and taking them on board. I was contemplating my new boat, and wondering whether I could make it stronger or improve it in any part, when two men with trunks came down to the shore in carriages, and looking at the different boats, singled out mine, and asked, 'Who owns this?' I answered modestly, 'I do.' 'Will you,' said one of them, 'take us and our trunks out to the steamer?' 'Certainly,' said I. I was very glad to have the chance of earning something, and supposed that each of them would give me a couple of bits. The trunks were put in my boat, the passengers seated themselves on them, and I sculled them out to the steamer. They got on board, and I lifted the trunks and put them on the deck. The steamer was about to put on steam again, when I called out, 'You have forgotten to pay me.' Each of them took from his pocket a silver half-dollar and threw it on the bottom of my boat. I could scarcely believe my eyes as I picked up the money. You may think it was a very little thing, and in these days it seems to me like a trifle, but it was a most important incident in my life. I could scarcely credit that I, the poor boy, had earned a dollar in less than a day; that by honest work I had earned a dollar. I was a more hopeful and thoughtful boy from that time."

Soon after this, while he was working for Mr. Gentry, the leading citizen of Gentryville, his employer decided to send a load of produce to New Orleans, and chose young Lincoln to go as "bow-hand," "to work the front oars." For this trip he received eight dollars a month and his passage back. Who can believe that he could see and be part of this river life without learning much of the ways and thoughts of the world beyond him? Every time a steamboat or a raft tied up near Anderson creek and he with his companions boarded it and saw its mysteries and talked with its crew, every time he rowed out with passengers to a passing steamer, who can doubt that he came back with new ideas and fresh energy? The trips to New Orleans were, to a thoughtful boy, an education of no mean value. It was the most cosmopolitan and brilliant city of the United States at that date, and there young Lincoln saw life at its intensest.

Such was Abraham Lincoln's life in Indiana; such were the avenues open to him for study and for seeing the world. In spite of the crudeness of it all; in spite of the fact that he had no wise direction, that he was brought up by a father with no settled purpose, and that he lived in a pioneer community, where a young man's life at best is but a series of makeshifts, Lincoln soon developed a determination to make something out of himself, and a desire to know, which led him to neglect no opportunity to learn.

The only unbroken outside influence which directed and stimulated him in these ambitions was that coming first from his mother, then from his stepmother. These two women, both of them of unusual earnestness and sweetness of spirit, were one or the other of them at his side throughout his youth and young manhood. The ideal they held before him was the simple ideal of the early American, that if a boy is upright and industrious he may aspire to any place within the gift of the country. The boy's instinct told him they were right. Everything he read confirmed their teachings, and he cultivated, in every way open to him, his passion to know and to be something. His zeal in study, his ambition to excel made their impression on his acquaintances. Even then they pointed him out as a boy who would "make something" of himself. In 1865, thirty-five years after he left Gentryville, Wm. H. Herndon, for many years a law partner of Lincoln, anxious to save all that was known of Lincoln in Indiana, went among his old associates, and with a sincerity and thoroughness worthy of grateful respect, interviewed them. At that time there were still living numbers of the people with whom Lincoln had been brought up. They all remembered something of him. It is curious to note that all of these people tell of his doing something different from what other boys did, something sufficiently superior to have made a keen impression upon them. In almost every case each person had his own special reason for admiring Lincoln. A facility in making rhymes and writing essays was the admiration of many, who considered it the more remarkable because "essays and poetry were not taught in school," and "Abe took it up on his own account."

Many others were struck by the clever application he made of this gift for expression. At one period he was employed as a "hand" by a farmer who treated him unfairly. Lincoln took a revenge unheard of in Gentryville. He wrote doggerel rhymes about his employer's nose—a long and crooked feature about which the owner was very sensitive. The wit he showed in taking revenge for a social slight by a satire on the Grigsbys, who had failed to invite him to a wedding, made a lasting impression in Gentryville. That he should write so well as to be able to humiliate his enemies more deeply than if he had resorted to the method of taking revenge current in the country, and thrashed them, seemed to his friends a mark of surprising superiority.

His schoolmates all remembered his spelling. He stood at the head of his class invariably and at the spelling-matches in which the young people of the neighborhood passed many an evening the one who first began "choosing sides" always chose "Abe Lincoln." So often did he spell the school down that finally, tradition says, he was no longer allowed to take part in the matches.

Very many of his old neighbors recalled his reading habits and how well stored his mind was with information. His explanations of natural phenomena were so unfamiliar to his companions that he sometimes was jeered at for them.

though as a rule his listeners were sympathetic, taking a certain pride in the fact that one of their number knew as much as Lincoln did. "He was better read than the world knows or is likely to know exactly," said one old acquaintance. "He often and often commented or talked to me about what he had read—seemed to read it out of the book as he went along—did so with others. He was the learned boy among us unlearned folks. He took great pains to explain; could do it so simply. He was diffident, then, too."

One man was impressed by the character of the sentences Lincoln had given him for a copybook. "It was considered at

FACSIMILE OF LINES FROM LINCOLN'S COPY BOOK.

that time," said he, "that Abe was the best penman in the neighborhood. One day, while he was on a visit at my mother's, I asked him to write some copies for me. He very willingly consented. He wrote several of them, but one of them I have never forgotten, although a boy at that time. It was this:

"'Good boys who to their books apply
Will all be great men by and by.'"

His wonderful memory was recalled by many. To save that which he found to his liking in the books he borrowed Lincoln committed much to memory. He knew many long poems, and most of the selections in the "Kentucky Preceptor." By the time he was twenty-one, in fact, his mind was well stored with verse and prose.

All of his comrades remembered his stories and his clearness in argument. " When he appeared in company," says Nat Grigsby, "the boys would gather and cluster around him to hear him talk. Mr. Lincoln was figurative in his speech, talks, and conversation. He argued much from analogy, and explained things hard for us to understand by stories, maxims, tales, and figures. He would almost always point his lesson or idea by some story that was plain and near us, that we might instantly see the force and bearing of what he said." This ability to explain clearly and to illustrate by simple figures of speech must be counted as the great mental acquirement of Lincoln's boyhood. It was a power which he gained by hard labor. Years later he related his experience to an acquaintance who had been surprised by the lucidity and simplicity of his speeches and who had asked where he was educated.

"I never went to school more than six months in my life," he said, "but I can say this: that among my earliest recollections I remember how, when a mere child, I used to get irritated when anybody talked to me in a way I could not understand. I do not think I ever got angry at anything else in my life; but that always disturbed my temper, and has ever since. I can remember going to my little bedroom, after hearing the neighbors talk of an evening with my father, and spending no small part of the night walking up and down and trying to make out what was the exact meaning of some of their, to me, dark sayings.

"I could not sleep, although I tried to, when I got on such a hunt for an idea until I had caught it; and when I thought I had got it, I was not satisfied until I had repeated it over and over; until I had put it in language plain enough, as I thought, for any boy I knew to comprehend. This was a kind of passion with me, and it has stuck by me; for I am never easy now, when I am handling a thought, till I have bounded it north and bounded it south, and bounded it east and bounded it west."

Mr. Herndon in his interviewing in Indiana found that everywhere Lincoln was remembered as kind and helpful. The man or woman in trouble never failed to receive all the aid he could give him. Even a worthless drunkard of the village called him friend, as well he might, Lincoln having gathered him up one night from the roadside where he lay freezing and carried him on his back a long distance to a shelter and a fire. The thoughtless cruelty to animals so common among country children revolted the boy. He wrote essays on "cruelty to animals," harangued his playmates, protested whenever he saw any wanton abuse of a dumb creature. This gentleness made a lasting impression on his mates, coupled as it was with the physical strength and courage to enforce his doctrines. Stories of his good heart and helpful life might be multiplied but they are summed up in what his stepmother said of the boy:

"Abe was a good boy, and I can say what scarcely one woman—a mother—can say in a thousand: Abe never gave me a cross word or look, and never refused, in fact or appearance, to do anything I requested him. I never gave him a cross word in all my life. . . . His mind and mine—what little I had—seemed to run together. He was here after he was elected president. He was a dutiful son to me always. I think he loved me truly. I had a son, John, who was raised with Abe. Both were good boys; but I must say, both now being dead, that Abe was the best boy I ever saw, or expect to see."

# CHAPTER IV

### THE LINCOLNS LEAVE INDIANA—THE JOURNEY TO ILLINOIS —ABRAHAM LINCOLN STARTS OUT FOR HIMSELF

IN THE spring of 1830 when Abraham Lincoln was twenty-one years old, his father, Thomas Lincoln, decided to leave Indiana. The reason Dennis Hanks gives for this removal was a disease called the "milk-sick." Abraham Lincoln's mother, Nancy Hanks Lincoln, and several of their relatives who had followed them from Kentucky had died of it. The cattle had been carried off by it. Neither brute nor human life seemed to be safe. As Dennis Hanks says: "This was reason enough (ain't it) for leaving?" Any one who has traveled through the portions of Spencer County in which the Lincolns settled will respect Thomas Lincoln for his energy in moving. When covered with timber, as the land was when he chose his farm, it no doubt promised well; but fourteen years of hard labor showed him that the soil was niggardly and the future of the country unpromising. To-day, sixty-five years since the Lincolns left Spencer County, the country remains as it was then, dull, commonplace, unfruitful. The towns show no signs of energy or prosperity. There are no leading streets or buildings; no man's house is better than his neighbor's, and every man's house is ordinary. For a long distance on each side of Gentryville as one passes by rail, no superior farm is to be seen, no prosperous farm or manufactory. It is a dead monotonous country, where no possibilities of quick wealth have been discovered, and which only centuries of tilling and fertilizing can make prosperous.

The place chosen for their new home was the Sangamon country in central Illinois. It was at that day a country of great renown in the West, the name meaning "The land where there is plenty to eat." One of the family—John Hanks, a cousin of Abraham's mother—was already there, and the inviting reports he had sent to Indiana were no doubt what led the Lincolns to decide on Illinois as their future home. Gentryville saw young Lincoln depart with genuine regret, and his friends gave him a score of rude proofs that he would not be forgotten. After he was gone, one of these friends planted a cedar tree in his memory. It still marks the site of the Lincoln home—the first monument erected to the memory of a man to whom the world will never cease to raise monuments.

The spot on the hill overlooking Buckthorne valley, where the Lincolns said good-by to their old home and to the home of Sarah Lincoln Grigsby, to the grave of the mother and wife, to all their neighbors and friends, is still pointed out. Buckthorne valley held many recollections dear to them all, but to no one of the company was the place dearer than to Abraham. It is certain that he felt the parting keenly, and that he never forgot his years in the Hoosier State. One of the most touching experiences he relates in all his published letters is his emotion at visiting his old Indiana home fourteen years after he had left it. So strongly was he moved by the scenes of his first conscious sorrows, efforts, joys, ambitions, that he put into verse the feelings they awakened.

While he never attempted to conceal the poverty and hardship of these days, and would speak humorously of the "pretty pinching times" he experienced, he never regarded his life at this time as mean or pitiable. Frequently he talked to his friends in later days of his boyhood, and always with apparent pleasure. "Mr. Lincoln told this story (of his youth)," says Leonard Swett, "as the story of a happy childhood. There was nothing sad or pinched, and nothing of want, and no allusion to want in any part of it. His own description of his youth was that of a happy, joyous boyhood. It was told with mirth and glee, and illustrated by pointed anecdotes, often interrupted by his jocund laugh."

And he was right. There was nothing ignoble or mean in this Indiana pioneer life. It was rude, but only with the rudeness which the ambitious are willing to endure in order to push on to a better condition than they otherwise could know. These people did not accept their hardships apathetically. They did not regard them as permanent. They were only the temporary deprivations necessary in order to accomplish what they had come into the country to do. For this reason they endured hopefully all that was hard. It is worth notice, too, that there was nothing belittling in their life; there was no pauperism, no shirking. Each family provided for its own simple wants, and had the conscious dignity which comes from being equal to a situation. If their lives lacked culture and refinement, they were rich in independence and self-reliance.

The company which emigrated to Illinois included the family of Thomas Lincoln and those of Dennis Hanks and Levi Hall, married to Lincoln's stepsisters—thirteen persons in all. They sold land, cattle and grain, and much of their household goods, and were ready in March of 1830 for their journey. All the possessions which the three families had to take with them were packed into big wagons— to which oxen were attached, and the caravan was ready. The weather was still cold, the streams were swollen, and the roads were muddy; but the party started out bravely. Inured to hardships, alive to all the new sights on their route, every day brought them amusement and adventures, and especially to young Lincoln the journey must have been of keen interest.

He drove one of the teams, he tells us, and, according to a story current in Gentryville, he succeeded in doing a fair peddler's business on the route. Captain William Jones, in whose father's store Lincoln had spent so many hours in discussion and in story-telling, and for whom he had worked the last winter he was in Indiana, says that before leaving the State Abraham invested all his money, some thirty-odd dollars, in notions. Though all the country through which they expected to pass was but sparsely settled, he believed he could dispose of them. "A set of knives and forks was the largest item entered on the bill," says Captain Jones; "the other items were needles, pins, thread, buttons, and other little domestic necessities. When the Lincolns reached their new home near Decatur, Illinois, Abraham wrote back to my father, stating that he had doubled his money on his purchases by selling them along the road. Unfortunately we did not keep that letter, not thinking how highly we would have prized it in years afterwards."

The pioneers were a fortnight on their journey. All we know of the route they took is from a few chance remarks of Lincoln's to his friends to the effect that they passed through Vincennes, where he saw a printing-press for the first time, and through Palestine, where he saw a juggler performing sleight-of-hand tricks. They reached Macon County, their new home, from the south. Mr. H. C. Whitney says that once in Decatur, when he and Lincoln were passing the courthouse together, "Lincoln walked out a few feet in front, and, after shifting his position two or three times, said, as he looked up at the building, partly to himself and partly to me: 'Here is the exact spot where I stood by our wagon when we moved from Indiana, twenty-six years ago; this isn't six feet from the exact spot.' . . . He then told me he had frequently thereafter tried to locate the route by which they had come, and that he had decided that it was near the main line of the Illinois Central railroad."

The party settled some ten miles west of Decatur, in Macon County.   Here John Hanks had the logs already cut for their new home, and Lincoln, Dennis Hanks, and Hall soon had a cabin erected.   Mr. Lincoln says in his short autobiography of 1860:  "Here they built a log cabin, into which they removed, and made sufficient of rails to fence ten acres of ground, fenced and broke the ground, and raised a crop of sown corn upon it the same year.  These are, or are supposed to be, the rails about which so much is being said just now, though these are far from being the first or only rails ever made by Abraham."   If they were far from being his "first and only rails," they certainly were the most famous ones he or anybody else ever split.

This was the last work Lincoln did for his father, for in the summer of that year (1830) he exercised the right of majority and started out to shift for himself.  When he left his home, he went empty-handed.  He was already some months over twenty-one years of age, but he had nothing in the world, not even a suit of respectable clothes; and one of the first pieces of work he did was "to split four hundred rails for every yard of brown jeans dyed with white-walnut bark that would be necessary to make him a pair of trousers."   He had no trade, no profession, no spot of land, no patron, no influence.   Two things recommended him to his neighbors— he was strong, and he was a good fellow.

His strength made him a valuable laborer. Not that he was fond of hard labor.  One of his Indiana employers says: "Abe was no hand to pitch into work like killing snakes;" but when he did work, it was with an ease and effectiveness which compensated his employer for the time he spent in practical jokes and extemporaneous speeches.  He could lift as much as three ordinary men, and "My, how he would chop," says

(4)

Dennis Hanks. "His axe would flash and bite into a sugar-tree or sycamore and down it would come. If you heard him fellin' trees in a clearin', you would say there was three men at work by the way the trees fell."

Standing six feet four, he could out-lift, out-work and out-wrestle any man he came in contact with. Friends and employers were proud of his prowess, and boasted of it, never failing to pit him against any hero whose strength they heard vaunted. He himself was proud of it, and throughout his life was fond of comparing himself with tall and strong men. When the committee called on him in Springfield in 1860, to notify him of his nomination as President, Governor Morgan, of New York, was of the number, a man of great height and brawn. "Pray, Governor, how tall may you be?" was Mr. Lincoln's first question. There is a story told of a poor man seeking a favor from him once at the White House. He was overpowered by the idea that he was in the presence of the President, and, his errand done, was edging shyly away, when Mr. Lincoln stopped him, insisting that he *measure* with him. The man was the taller, as Mr. Lincoln had thought; and he went away evidently as much abashed that he dared be taller than the President of the United States as that he had dared to venture into his presence.

Governor Hoyt tells an excellent story illustrating this interest of Lincoln's in manly strength, and his involuntary comparison of himself with whomsoever showed it. It was in 1859, after Lincoln had delivered a speech at the Wisconsin State Agricultural Fair in Milwaukee. Governor Hoyt had asked him to make the rounds of the exhibits, and they went into a tent to see a "strong man" perform. He went through the ordinary exercises with huge iron balls, tossing them in the air, and catching them and rolling them on his arms and back; and Mr. Lincoln, who evidently had never before seen such a combination of agility and strength, watched him with

intense interest, ejaculating under his breath now and then:
"By George! By George!" When the performance was over,
Governor Hoyt, seeing Mr. Lincoln's interest, asked him to
go up and be introduced to the athlete. He did so; and, as he
stood looking down musingly on the man, who was very
short, and evidently wondering that one so much smaller
than he could be so much stronger, he suddenly broke out
with one of his quaint speeches. "Why," he said, "why, I
could lick salt off the top of your hat."

His strength won him popularity, but his good-nature, his
wit, his skill in debate, his stories, were still more efficient in
gaining him good-will. People liked to have him around, and
voted him a good fellow to work with. Yet such were the
conditions of his life at this time that, in spite of his popularity, nothing was open to him but hard manual labor. To
take the first job which he happened upon—rail-splitting,
ploughing, lumbering, boating, store-keeping—and make the
most of it, thankful if thereby he earned his bed and board
and yearly suit of jeans, was apparently all there was before
Abraham Lincoln in 1830, when he started out for himself.

Through the summer and fall of 1830 and the early winter
of 1831, Mr. Lincoln worked in the vicinity of his father's
new home, usually as a farm-hand and rail-splitter. Most of
his work was done in company with John Hanks. Before the
end of the winter he secured employment of which he has
given an account himself, though in the third person:

"During that winter, Abraham, together with his stepmother's son, John D. Johnston, and John Hanks, yet resid-
ing in Macon County, hired themselves to Denton Offutt to
take a flatboat from Beardstown, Illinois, to New Orleans,
and for that purpose were to join him—Offutt—at Springfield, Illinois, as soon as the snow should go off. When it did
go off, which was about the first of March, 1831, the country
was so flooded as to make traveling by land impracticable; to
obviate which difficulty they purchased a large canoe and

came down the Sangamon river in it. This is the time and manner of Abraham's first entrance into Sangamon County. They found Offutt at Springfield, but learned from him that he had failed in getting a boat at Beardstown. This led to their hiring themselves to him for twelve dollars per month each, and getting the timber out of the trees, and building a boat at old Sangamon town, on the Sangamon river, seven miles northwest of Springfield, which boat they took to New Orleans, substantially on the old contract."

Sangamon town, where Lincoln built the flatboat, has, since his day, completely disappeared from the earth; but then it was one of the flourishing settlements on the river of that name. Lincoln's advent in the town did not go unnoticed. In a small community, cut off from the world, as old Sangamon was, every new-comer is scrutinized and discussed before he is regarded with confidence. Lincoln did not escape this scrutiny. His appearance was so striking in fact that he attracted everybody's attention. "He was a tall, gaunt young man," says Mr. John Roll, of Springfield, then a resident of Sangamon, "dressed in a suit of blue homespun jeans, consisting of a round-about jacket, waistcoat, and breeches which came to within about four inches of his feet. The latter were encased in rawhide boots, into the tops of which, most of the time, his pantaloons were stuffed. He wore a soft felt hat which had at one time been black, but now, as its owner dryly remarked, 'was sun-burned until it was a combine of colors.'"

It took some four weeks to build the raft, and in that period Lincoln succeeded in captivating the entire village by his story-telling. It was the custom in Sangamon for the "men-folks" to gather at noon and in the evening, when resting, in a convenient lane near the mill. They had rolled out a long peeled log, on which they lounged while they whittled and talked. Lincoln had not been long in Sangamon before he joined this circle. At once he became a favorite by his jokes and good-humor. As soon as he appeared at the assembly ground the men would start him to story-telling. So irresistibly droll were his "yarns" that, says Mr. Roll, "whenever he'd end up in his unexpected way the boys on the log would whoop and roll off." The result of the rolling off was to polish the log like a mirror. The men, recognizing Lincoln's part in this polishing, christened their seat "Abe's log." Long after Lincoln had disappeared from Sangamon, "Abe's log" remained, and until it had rotted away people pointed it out, and repeated the droll stories of the stranger.

When the flatboat was finished Lincoln and his friends prepared to leave Sangamon. Before he started, however, he was the hero of an adventure so thrilling that he won new laurels in the community. Mr. Roll, who was a witness of the whole exciting scene, tells the story:

"It was the spring following the winter of the deep snow.* Walter Carman, John Seamon and myself, and at times others of the Carman boys had helped Abe in building the boat, and when we had finished we went to work to make a dugout, or canoe, to be used as a small boat with the flat. We found a suitable log about an eighth of a mile up the river, and with our axes went to work under Lincoln's direction. The river was very high, fairly 'booming.' After the dugout was ready to launch we took it to the edge of the water, and made ready to 'let her go,' when Walter Carman and John Seamon jumped in as the boat struck the water, each one anxious to be the first to get a ride. As they shot out from the shore they found they were unable to make any headway against the strong current. Carman had the paddle, and Seamon was in the stern of the boat. Lincoln shouted to them to 'head up stream,' and 'work back to shore,' but they found themselves powerless against the stream. At last they began to pull for the wreck of an old flatboat, the first ever built on

---

*1830—1831. "The winter of the deep snow" is the date which is the starting point in all calculations of time for the early settlers of Illinois, and the circumstance from which the old settlers of Sangamon County receive the name by which they are generally known, "Snow-birds.'

the Sangamon, which had sunk and gone to pieces, leaving
one of the stanchions sticking above the water. Just as they
reached it Seamon made a grab, and caught hold of the
stanchion, when the canoe capsized, leaving Seamon clinging
to the old timber, and throwing Carman into the stream. It
carried him down with the speed of a mill-race. Lincoln
raised his voice above the roar of the flood, and yelled to Carman to swim for an old tree which stood almost in the channel, which the action of the high water had changed.

" Carman, being a good swimmer, succeeded in catching
a branch, and pulled himself up out of the water, which was
very cold, and had almost chilled him to death; and there he
sat shivering and chattering in the tree. Lincoln, seeing Carman safe, called out to Seamon to let go the stanchion and
swim for the tree. With some hesitation he obeyed, and
struck out, while Lincoln cheered and directed him from the
bank. As Seamon neared the tree he made one grab for a
branch, and, missing it, went under the water. Another desperate lunge was successful, and he climbed up beside Carman. Things were pretty exciting now, for there were two
men in the tree, and the boat was gone.

"It was a cold, raw April day, and there was great danger
of the men becoming benumbed, and falling back into the
water. Lincoln called out to them to keep their spirits up and
he would save them. The village had been alarmed by this
time, and many people had come down to the bank. Lincoln
procured a rope, and tied it to a log. He called all hands to
come and help roll the log into the water, and after this had
been done, he, with the assistance of several others, towed it
some distance up the stream. A daring young fellow by the
name of 'Jim' Dorrell then took his seat on the end of the log,
and it was pushed out into the current, with the expectation
that it would be carried down stream against the tree where
Seamon and Carman were.

"The log was well directed, and went straight to the tree;
but Jim, in his impatience to help his friends, fell a victim
to his good intentions. Making a frantic grab at a branch,
he raised himself off the log, which was swept from under
him by the raging water, and he soon joined the other two
victims upon their forlorn perch. The excitement on shore

increased, and almost the whole population of the village gathered on the river bank. Lincoln had the log pulled up the stream, and, securing another piece of rope, called to the men in the tree to catch it if they could when he should reach the tree. He then straddled the log himself, and gave the word to push out into the stream. When he dashed into the tree, he threw the rope over the stump of a broken limb, and let it play until it broke the speed of the log, and gradually drew it back to the tree, holding it there until the three now nearly frozen men had climbed down and seated themselves astride. He then gave orders to the people on the shore to hold fast to the end of the rope which was tied to the log, and, leaving his rope in the tree he turned the log adrift. The force of the current, acting against the taut rope, swung the log around against the bank, and all 'on board' were saved. The excited people, who had watched the dangerous experiment with alternate hope and fear, now broke into cheers for Abe Lincoln and praises for his brave act. This adventure made quite a hero of him along the Sangamon, and the people never tired telling of the exploit."

The flatboat built and loaded, the party started for New Orleans about the middle of April. They had gone but a few miles when they met with another adventure. At the village of New Salem there was a mill-dam. On it the boat stuck, and here for nearly twenty-four hours it hung, the bow in the air and the stern in the water, the cargo slowly setting backwards—shipwreck almost certain. The village of New Salem turned out in a body to see what the strangers would do in their predicament. They shouted, suggested, and advised for a time, but finally discovered that one big fellow in the crew was ignoring them and working out a plan of relief. Having unloaded the cargo into a neighboring boat, Lincoln had succeeded in tilting his craft. Then, by boring a hole in the end extending over the dam, the water was let out. This done, the boat was easily shoved over and reloaded. The ingenuity which he had exercised in saving his boat made a deep impression on the crowd on the bank, and it was talked over for many a day. The proprietor of boat and cargo was even more enthusiastic than the spectators, and vowed he would build a steamboat for the Sangamon and make Lincoln the captain. Lincoln himself was interested in what he had done, and nearly twenty years later he embodied his reflections on this adventure in a curious invention for getting boats over shoals.

The raft over the New Salem dam, the party went on to New Orleans, reaching there in May, 1831, and remaining a month. It must have been a month of intense intellectual activity for Lincoln. Since his first visit, made with young Gentry, New Orleans had entered upon her "flush times." Commerce was increasing at a rate which dazzled speculators and drew them from all over the United States. From 1830 to 1840 no other American city increased in such a ratio; exports and imports, which in 1831 amounted to $26,000,000, in 1835 had more than doubled. The Creole population had held the sway so far in the city; but now it came into competition, and often into conflict, with a pushing, ambitious, and frequently unscrupulous native American party. To these two predominating elements were added Germans, French, Spanish, negroes, and Indians. Cosmopolitan in its make-up, the city was even more cosmopolitan in its life. Everything was to be seen in New Orleans in those days, from the idle luxury of the wealthy Creole to the organization of filibustering juntas. The pirates still plied their trade in the Gulf, and the Mississippi river brought down hundreds of river boatmen—one of the wildest, wickedest set of men that ever existed in any city.

Lincoln and his companions ran their boat up beside thousands of others. It was the custom to tie such craft along the river front where St. Mary's Market now stands, and one could walk a mile, it is said, over the tops of these boats

without going ashore.  No doubt Lincoln went too, to live in
the boatmen's rendezvous, called the "swamp," a wild, rough
quarter, where roulette, whiskey, and the flint-lock pistol
ruled.  All of the picturesque life, the violent contrasts of the
city, he would see as he wandered about; and he would carry
away the sharp impressions which are produced when mind
and heart are alert, sincere, and healthy.

In this month spent in New Orleans, Lincoln must have
seen much of slavery.  At that time the city was full of slaves,
and the number was constantly increasing; indeed, one-third
of the New Orleans increase in population between 1830 and
1840 was in negroes.  One of the saddest features of the institution was to be seen there in its aggravated form—the
slave market.  The better class of slave-holders of the South,
who looked on the institution as patriarchal, and who
guarded their slaves with conscientious care, knew little,
it should be said, of this terrible traffic.  Their transfer of
slaves was humane, but in the open markets of the city it was
attended by shocking cruelty and degradation.  Lincoln witnessed in New Orleans for the first time the revolting sight of
men and women sold like animals.  Mr. Herndon says that he
often heard Mr. Lincoln refer to this experience:

"In New Orleans for the first time," he writes, "Lincoln
beheld the true horrors of human slavery.  He saw 'negroes
in chains—whipped and scourged.'  Against this inhumanity
his sense of right and justice rebelled, and his mind and conscience were awakened to a realization of what he had often
heard and read.  No doubt, as one of his companions has said,
'slavery ran the iron into him then and there.'  One morning
in their rambles over the city the trio passed a slave auction.
A vigorous and comely mulatto girl was being sold.  She underwent a thorough examination at the hands of the bidders;
they pinched her flesh, and made her trot up and down the
room like a horse, to show how she moved, and in order, as
the auctioneer said, that 'bidders might satisfy themselves

whether the article they were offering to buy was sound or
not.' The whole thing was so revolting that Lincoln moved
away from the scene with a deep feeling of 'unconquerable
hate.' Bidding his companions follow him, he said: 'Boys,
let's get away from this. If ever I get a chance to hit that
thing' (meaning slavery), 'I'll hit it hard.' "

Mr. Herndon gives John Hanks as his authority for this
statement, but, according to Mr. Lincoln's autobiography,
Hanks did not go on to New Orleans, but, having a family,
and finding that he was likely to be detained from home
longer than he had expected, he turned back at St. Louis.
Though the story as told above probably grew to its present
proportions by much telling, there is reason to believe that
Lincoln was deeply impressed on this trip by something he
saw in a New Orleans slave market, and that he often referred to it.

# CHAPTER V

LINCOLN SECURES A POSITION—HE STUDIES GRAMMAR—
FIRST APPEARANCE IN POLITICS

THE month in New Orleans passed swiftly, and in June, 1831, Lincoln and his companions took passage up the river. He did not return, however, in the usual condition of the river boatman "out of a job." According to his own way of putting it, "during this boat-enterprise acquaintance with Offutt, who was previously an entire stranger, he conceived a liking for Abraham, and believing he could turn him to account he contracted with him to act as a clerk for him on his return from New Orleans, in charge of a store and mill at New Salem." The store and mill were, however, so far only in Offutt's imagination, and Lincoln had to drift about until his employer was ready for him. He made a short visit to his father and mother, now in Coles County, near Charleston (fever and ague had driven the Lincolns from their first home in Macon County), and then, in July, 1831, he went to New Salem, where, as he says, he "stopped indefinitely, and for the first time, as it were, by himself."

The village of New Salem, the scene of Lincoln's mercantile career, was one of the many little towns which, in the pioneer days, sprang up along the Sangamon river, a stream then looked upon as navigable and as destined to be counted among the highways of commerce. Twenty miles northwest of Springfield, strung along the left bank of the Sangamon, parted by hollows and ravines, is a row of high hills. On one of these—a long, narrow ridge, beginning with a sharp and sloping point near the river, running south, and parallel with the stream a little way, and then, reaching its highest point, making a sudden turn to the west, and gradually widening until lost in the prairie—stood this frontier village. The crooked river for a short distance comes from the east, and, seemingly surprised at meeting the bluff, abruptly changes its course, and flows to the north. Across the river the bottom stretches out half a mile back to the highlands. New Salem, founded in 1829 by James Rutledge and John Cameron, and a dozen years later a deserted village, is rescued only from oblivion by the fact that Lincoln was once one of its inhabitants. The town never contained more than fifteen houses, all of them built of logs, but it had an energetic population of perhaps one hundred persons, among whom were a blacksmith, a tinner, a hatter, a schoolmaster and a preacher. New Salem boasted a grist-mill, a saw-mill, two stores and a tavern, but its day of hope was short. In 1837 it began to decline and by 1840, Petersburg, two miles down the river, had absorbed its business and population. Salem Hill is now only a green cow pasture.

Lincoln's first sight of the town had been in April, 1831, when he and his crew had been detained in getting their flatboat over the Rutledge and Cameron mill-dam. When he walked into New Salem, three months later, he was not altogether a stranger, for the people remembered him as the ingenious flat-boatman who had freed his boat from water by resorting to the miraculous expedient of boring a hole in the bottom.

Offutt's goods had not arrived when Mr. Lincoln reached New Salem; and he "loafed" about, so those who remember his arrival say, good-naturedly taking a hand in whatever he could find to do, and in his droll way making friends of everybody. By chance, a bit of work fell to him almost at once, which introduced him generally and gave him an opportunity to make a name in the neighborhood.  It was election day.  In those days elections in Illinois were conducted by the *viva voce* method.  The people did try voting by ballot, but the experiment was unpopular.  It required too much form and in 1829 the former method of voting was restored.  The judges and clerks sat at a table with the poll-book before them.  The voter walked up, and announced the candidate of his choice, and it was recorded in his presence.  There was no ticket peddling, and ballot-box stuffing was impossible.  The village school-master, Mentor Graham by name, was clerk at this particular election, but his assistant was ill.  Looking about for some one to help him, Mr. Graham saw a tall stranger loitering around the polling-place, and called to him: " Can you write? "  " Yes," said the stranger, " I can make a few rabbit tracks."  Mr. Graham evidently was satisfied with the answer, for he promptly initiated him; and he filled his place not only to the satisfaction of his employer, but also to the delectation of the loiterers about the polls, for whenever things dragged he immediately began " to spin out a stock of Indian yarns."  So droll were they that men who listened to Lincoln that day repeated them long after to their friends.  He had made a hit in New Salem, to start with, and here, as in Sangamon town, it was by means of his story-telling.

A few days later he accepted an offer to pilot down the Sangamon and Illinois rivers, as far as Beardstown, a flat-boat bearing the family and goods of a pioneer bound for Texas.  At Beardstown he found Offutt's goods, waiting to be taken to New Salem.  As he footed his way home he found two men with a wagon and ox-team going for the goods.  Offutt had expected Lincoln to wait at Beardstown until the ox-team arrived, and the teamsters, not having any credentials, asked Lincoln to give them an order for the goods.

This, sitting down by the roadside, he wrote out; one of the men used to relate that it contained a misspelled word, which he corrected.

When the oxen and their drivers returned with the goods, the store was opened in a little log house on the brink of the hill, almost over the river. The precise date of the opening of Denton Offutt's store is not known. We only know that on July 8, 1831, the County Commissioners' Court of Sangamon County granted Offutt a license to retail merchandise at New Salem, for which he paid five dollars, a fee which supposed him to have one thousand dollars' worth of goods in stock.

The frontier store filled a unique place. Usually it was a "general store," and on its shelves were found most of the articles needed in a community of pioneers. But supplying goods and groceries was not its only function; it was the pioneer's intellectual and social center. It was the common meeting-place of the farmers, the happy refuge of the village loungers. No subject was unknown there. The habitués of the place were equally at home in discussing politics, religion, or sports. Stories were told, jokes were cracked, and the news contained in the latest newspaper finding its way into the wilderness was repeated again and again. Lincoln could hardly have chosen surroundings more favorable to the highest development of the art of story-telling, and he had not been there long before his reputation for drollery was established.

But he gained popularity and respect in other ways. There was near the village a settlement called Clary's Grove, the most conspicuous part of whose population was an organization known as the "Clary's Grove Boys." They exercised a veritable terror over the neighborhood, and yet they were not a bad set of fellows. Mr. Herndon, who knew personally many of the "boys," says:

"They were friendly and good-natured; they could trench a pond, dig a bog, build a house; they could pray and fight, make a village or create a state. They would do almost anything for sport or fun, love or necessity. Though rude and rough, though life's forces ran over the edge of the bowl, foaming and sparkling in pure deviltry for deviltry's sake, yet place before them a poor man who needed their aid, a lame or sick man, a defenceless woman, a widow, or an orphaned child, they melted into sympathy and charity at once. They gave all they had, and willingly toiled or played cards for more. Though there never was under the sun a more generous parcel of rowdies, a stranger's introduction was likely to be the most unpleasant part of his acquaintance with them."

Denton Offutt, Lincoln's employer, was just the man to love to boast before such a crowd. He seemed to feel that Lincoln's physical prowess shed glory on himself, and he declared the country over that his clerk could lift more, throw farther, run faster, jump higher, and wrestle better than any man in Sangamon county. The Clary's Grove Boys, of course, felt in honor bound to prove this false, and they appointed their best man, one Jack Armstrong, to "throw Abe." Jack Armstrong was, according to the testimony of all who remember him, a "powerful twister," "square built and strong as an ox," "the best-made man that ever lived;" and everybody knew that a contest between him and Lincoln would be close. Lincoln did not like to "tussle and scuffle," he objected to "woolling and pulling;" but Offutt had gone so far that it became necessary to yield. The match was held on the ground near the grocery. Clary's Grove and New Salem turned out generally to witness the bout, and betting on the result ran high, the community as a whole staking their jack-knives, tobacco plugs, and "treats" on Armstrong. The two men had scarcely taken hold of each other before it was evident that the Clary's Grove champion had met a match.

The two men wrestled long and hard, but both kept their feet. Neither could throw the other, and Armstrong, convinced of this, tried a "foul." Lincoln no sooner realized the game of his antagonist than, furious with indignation, he caught him by the throat, and holding him out at arm's length, he "shook him like a child." Armstrong's friends rushed to his aid, and for a moment it looked as if Lincoln would be routed by sheer force of numbers; but he held his own so bravely that the "boys," in spite of their sympathies, were filled with admiration. What bid fair to be a general fight ended in a general hand-shake, even Jack Armstrong declaring that Lincoln was the "best fellow who ever broke into the camp." From that day, at the cock-fights and horse-races, which were their common sports, he became the chosen umpire; and when the entertainment broke up in a row—a not uncommon occurrence—he acted the peacemaker without suffering the peacemaker's usual fate. Such was his reputation with the "Clary's Grove Boys," after three months in New Salem, that when the fall muster came off he was elected captain.

Lincoln showed soon that if he was unwilling to indulge in "woolling and pulling" for amusement, he did not object to it in the interests of decency and order. In such a community as New Salem there are always braggarts who can only be made endurable by fear. To them Lincoln soon became an authority more to be respected than sheriff or constable. If they transgressed in his presence he thrashed them promptly with an imperturbable air, half indolent, but wholly resolute which was more baffling and impressive than even his iron grip and well-directed blows. A man came into the store one day and began swearing. Now, profanity in the presence of women, Lincoln never would allow. He asked the man to stop; but he persisted, loudly boasting that nobody should prevent his saying what he wanted to. The women gone, the man began to abuse Lincoln so hotly that the latter said: "Well, if you must be whipped, I suppose I might as well whip you as any other man;" and going outdoors with the fellow, he threw him on the ground, and rubbed smart-weed into his eyes until he bellowed for mercy. New Salem's sense of chivalry was touched, and Denton Offutt's clerk became more of a hero than ever.

His honesty excited no less admiration. Two incidents seem to have particularly impressed the community. Having discovered on one occasion that he had taken six and one-quarter cents too much from a customer, he walked three miles that evening, after his store was closed, to return the money. Again, he weighed out a half-pound of tea, as he supposed. It was night, and this was the last thing he did before closing up. On entering in the morning he discovered a four-ounce weight in the scales. He saw his mistake, and closing up shop, hurried off to deliver the remainder of the tea. This unusual regard for the rights of others soon won him the title of "Honest Abe."

As soon as the store was fairly under way, Lincoln began to look about for books. Since leaving Indiana in March, 1830, he had had in his drifting life, little leisure or opportunity for study, though a great deal for observation of men and of life. His experience had made him realize more and more clearly that power over men depends upon knowledge. He had found that he was himself superior to many of those who were called the "great" men of the country. Soon after entering Macon county, in March, 1830, when he was only twenty-one years old, he had found he could make a better speech than at least one man who was before the public. A candidate had come along where he and John Hanks were at work, and, as John Hanks tells the story, the man made a speech. "It was a bad one, and I said Abe could beat it. I turned down a box, and Abe made his speech. The other man was a candidate, Abe wasn't. Abe beat him

(5)

to death, his subject being the navigation of the Sangamon
river. The man, after Abe's speech was through, took him
aside and asked him where he had learned so much, and how
he could do so well. Abe replied, stating his manner and
method of reading, what he had read. The man encouraged
him to persevere."

He studied men carefully, comparing himself with them.
Could he do what they did? He seems never up to this time
to have met one who was incomprehensible to him. "I have
talked with great men," he told his fellow-clerk and friend
Greene, "and I do not see how they differ from others."
Then he found, too, that people listened to him, that they
quoted his opinions, and that his friends were already saying that he was able to fill any position. Offutt even declared the country over that "Abe" knew more than any
man in the United States, and that some day he would be
President.

When he began to realize that he himself possessed the
qualities which made men great in Illinois, that success depended upon knowledge and that already his friends credited him with possessing more than most members of
the community, his ambition was encouraged and his desire
to learn increased. Why should he not try for a public position? He began to talk to his friends of his ambition and to
devise plans for self-improvement. In order to keep in practice in speaking he walked seven or eight miles to debating
clubs. "Practicing polemics," was what he called the exercise. He seems now for the first time to have begun to study
subjects. Grammar was what he chose. He sought Mentor
Graham, the schoolmaster, and asked his advice. "If you are
going before the public," Mr. Graham told him, "you ought
to do it." But where could he get a grammar? There was but
one, said Mr. Graham, in the neighborhood, and that was six
miles away. Without waiting for further information, the

young man rose from the breakfast-table, walked immediately to the place and borrowed this rare copy of Kirkham's Grammar. From that time on for weeks he gave every moment of his leisure to mastering the contents of the book. Frequently he asked his friend Greene to "hold the book" while he recited, and, when puzzled by a point, he would consult Mr. Graham.

Lincoln's eagerness to learn was such that the whole neighborhood became interested. The Greenes lent him books, the schoolmaster kept him in mind and helped him as he could, and the village cooper let him come into his shop and keep up a fire of shavings sufficiently bright to read by at night. It was not long before the grammar was mastered. "Well," Lincoln said to his fellow-clerk, Greene, "if that's what they call a science, I think I'll go at another."

Before the winter was ended he had become the most popular man in New Salem. Although he was but twenty-two years of age, in February, 1832, had never been at school an entire year in his life, had never made a speech except in debating clubs and by the roadside, had read only the books he could pick up, and known only the men who made up the poor, out-of-the-way towns in which he had lived, "encouraged by his great popularity among his immediate neighbors," as he says himself, he decided to announce himself, in March, 1832, as a candidate for the General Assembly of the State.

The only preliminary expected of a candidate for the legislature of Illinois at that date was an announcement stating his "sentiments with regard to local affairs." The circular in which Lincoln complied with this custom was a document of about two thousand words, in which he plunged at once into the subject he believed most interesting to his constituents—"the public utility of internal improvements."

At that time the State of Illinois—as, indeed, the whole

United States—was convinced that the future of the country
depended on the opening of canals and railroads, and the
clearing out of the rivers. In the Sangamon country the
population felt that a quick way of getting to Beardstown on
the Illinois river, to which point the steamer came from the
Mississippi, was, as Lincoln puts it in his circular, "indis-
pensably necessary." Of course a railroad was the dream of
the settlers; but when it was considered seriously there was
always, as Lincoln says, "a heart-appalling shock accom-
panying the amount of its cost, which forces us to shrink
from our pleasing anticipations. The probable cost of this
contemplated railroad is estimated at two hundred and
ninety thousand dollars; the bare statement of which, in my
opinion, is sufficient to justify the belief that the improvement of the Sangamon river is an object much better suited
to our infant resources.

"Respecting this view, I think I may say, without the fear
of being contradicted, that its navigation may be rendered
completely practicable as high as the mouth of the South
Fork, or probably higher, to vessels of from twenty-five to
thirty tons burden, for at least one-half of all common years,
and to vessels of much greater burden a part of the time.
From my peculiar circumstances, it is probable that for the
last twelve months I have given as particular attention to the
stage of the water in this river as any other person in the
country. In the month of March, 1831, in company with
others, I commenced the building of a flatboat on the Sangamon, and finished and took her out in the course of the
spring. Since that time I have been concerned in the mill at
New Salem. These circumstances are sufficient evidence that
I have not been very inattentive to the stages of the water.
The time at which we crossed the mill-dam being in the last
days of April, the water was lower than it had been since the
breaking of winter in February, or than it was for several
weeks after. The principal difficulties we encountered in de-
scending the river were from the drifted timber, which obstructions all know are not difficult to be removed. Knowing

almost precisely the height of water at that time, I believe I am safe in saying that it has as often been higher as lower since.

"From this view of the subject it appears that my calculations with regard to the navigation of the Sangamon cannot but be founded in reason; but, whatever may be its natural advantages, certain it is that it never can be practically useful to any great extent without being greatly improved by art. The drifted timber, as I have before mentioned, is the most formidable barrier to this object. Of all parts of this river, none will require so much labor in proportion to make it navigable as the last thirty or thirty-five miles; and going with the meanderings of the channel, when we are this distance above its mouth we are only between twelve and eighteen miles above Beardstown in something near a straight direction; and this route is upon such low ground as to retain water in many places during the season, and in all parts such as to draw two-thirds or three-fourths of the river water at all high stages.

"This route is on prairie land the whole distance, so that it appears to me, by removing the turf a sufficient width, and damming up the old channel, the whole river in a short time would wash its way through, thereby curtailing the distance and increasing the velocity of the current very considerably, while there would be no timber on the banks to obstruct its navigation in future; and being nearly straight, the timber which might float in at the head would be apt to go clear through. There are also many places above this where the river, in its zigzag course, forms such complete peninsulas as to be easier to cut at the necks than to remove the obstructions from the bends, which, if done, would also lessen the distance.

"What the cost of this work would be, I am unable to say. It is probable, however, that it would not be greater than is common to streams of the same length. Finally, I believe the improvement of the Sangamon river to be vastly important and highly desirable to the people of the county; and, if elected, any measure in the legislature having this for its object, which may appear judicious, will meet my approbation and receive my support."

Lincoln could not have adopted a measure more popular. At that moment the whole population of Sangamon was in a state of wild expectation. Some six weeks before Lincoln's circular appeared, a citizen of Springfield had advertised that as soon as the ice went off the river he would bring up a steamer, the "Talisman," from Cincinnati, and prove the Sangamon navigable. The announcement had aroused the entire country, speeches were made. and subscriptions taken. The merchants announced goods direct per steamship "Talisman," the country over, and every village from Beardstown to Springfield was laid off in town lots. When the circular appeared the excitement was at its height.

Lincoln's comments in his circular on two other subjects, on which all candidates of the day expressed themselves, are amusing in their simplicity. The practice of loaning money at exorbitant rates was then a great evil in the West. Lincoln proposed that the limits of usury be fixed, and he closed his paragraph on the subject with these words, which sound strange enough from a man who in later life showed so profound a reverence for law:

"In cases of extreme necessity, there could always be means found to cheat the law; while in all other cases it would have its intended effect. I would favor the passage of a law on this subject which might not be very easily evaded. Let it be such that the labor and difficulty of evading it could only be justified in cases of greatest necessity."

A general revision of the laws of the State was the second topic which he felt required a word. "Considering the great probability," he said, "that the framers of those laws were wiser than myself, I should prefer not meddling with them, unless they were first attacked by others; in which case I should feel it both a privilege and a duty to take that stand which, in my view, might tend most to the advancement of justice."

Of course he said a word for education.

"Upon the subject of education, not presuming to dictate any plan or system respecting it, I can only say that I view it as the most important subject which we as a people can be engaged in. That every man may receive at least a moderate education, and thereby be enabled to read the histories of his own and other countries, by which he may duly appreciate the value of our free institutions, appears to be an object of vital importance, even on this account alone, to say nothing of the advantages and satisfaction to be derived from all being able to read the Scriptures, and other works both of a religious and moral nature, for themselves.

"For my part, I desire to see the time when education— and by its means, morality, sobriety, enterprise, and industry —shall become much more general than at present, and should be gratified to have it in my power to contribute something to the advancement of any measure which might have a tendency to accelerate that happy period."

The audacity of a young man in his position presenting himself as a candidate for the legislature is fully equaled by the humility of the closing paragraphs of his announcement:

"But, fellow-citizens, I shall conclude. Considering the great degree of modesty which should always attend youth, it is probable I have already been more presuming than becomes me. However, upon the subjects of which I have treated, I have spoken as I have thought. I may be wrong in regard to any or all of them; but, holding it a sound maxim that it is better only sometimes to be right than at all times to be wrong, so soon as I discover my opinions to be erroneous, I shall be ready to renounce them.

"Every man is said to have his peculiar ambition. Whether it be true or not, I can say, for one, that I have no other so great as that of being truly esteemed of my fellow-men, by rendering myself worthy of their esteem. How far I shall succeed in gratifying this ambition is yet to be developed. I am young, and unknown to many of you. I was born, and have ever remained, in the most humble walks of life. I have no wealthy or popular relations or friends to recommend me. My case is thrown exclusively upon the independent voters of the county; and, if elected, they will have conferred a favor upon me for which I shall be unremitting in my labors to compensate. But, if the good people in their wisdom shall see fit to keep me in the background, I have been too familiar with disappointments to be very much chagrined."

Very soon after Lincoln had distributed his hand-bills, enthusiasm on the subject of the opening of the Sangamon rose to a fever. The "Talisman" actually came up the river; scores of men went to Beardstown to meet her, among them Lincoln, of course, and to him was given the honor of piloting her—an honor which made him remembered by many a man who saw him that day for the first time. The trip was made with all the wild demonstrations which always attended the first steamboat. On either bank a long procession of men and boys on foot or horse accompanied the boat. Cannons and volleys of musketry were fired from every settlement passed. At every stop speeches were made, congratulations offered, toasts drunk, flowers presented. It was one long hurrah from Beardstown to Springfield, and foremost in the jubilation was Lincoln, the pilot. The "Talisman" went to the point on the river nearest to Springfield, and there tied up for a week. When she went back Lincoln again had the conspicuous position of pilot. The notoriety this gave him was probably quite as valuable politically, as the forty dollars he received for his service was financially.

While the country had been dreaming of wealth through the opening of the Sangamon, and Lincoln had been doing his best to prove that the dream would be realized, the store in which he clerked was "petering out"—to use his expression. The owner, Denton Offutt, had proved more ambitious than wise, and Lincoln saw that an early closing by the sheriff was probable. But before the store was fairly closed, and while the "Talisman" was yet exciting the country, an event occurred which interrupted all of Lincoln's plans.

# CHAPTER VI

### THE BLACK HAWK WAR—LINCOLN CHOSEN CAPTAIN OF A COMPANY—REENLISTS AS AN INDEPENDENT RANGER—END OF THE WAR

ONE morning in April a messenger from the governor of the State rode into New Salem, scattering circulars. The circular was addressed to the militia of the northwest section of the State, and announced that the British band of Sacs and other hostile Indians, headed by Black Hawk, had invaded the Rock River country, to the great terror of the frontier inhabitants; and it called upon the citizens who were willing to aid in repelling them, to rendezvous at Beardstown within a week.

The name of Black Hawk was familiar to the people of Illinois. He was an old enemy of the settlers, and had been a tried friend of the British. The land his people had once owned in the northwest of the present State of Illinois had been sold in 1804 to the government of the United States, but with the provision that the Indians could hunt and raise corn there until it was surveyed and sold to settlers. Long before the land was surveyed, however, squatters had invaded the country, and tried to force the Indians west of the Mississippi. Particularly envious were these whites of the lands at the mouth of the Rock river, where the ancient village and burial place of the Sacs stood, and where they came each year to raise corn. Black Hawk had resisted their encroachments, and many violent acts had been committed on both sides.

Finally, however, the squatters, in spite of the fact that the line of settlement was still fifty miles away, succeeded in evading the real meaning of the treaty and in securing a survey of the desired land at the mouth of the river. Black Hawk, exasperated and broken-hearted at seeing his village violated, persuaded himself that the village had never been sold—indeed, that land could not be sold.

"My reason teaches me," he wrote, "that land cannot be sold. The Great Spirit gave it to his children to live upon, and cultivate, as far as is necessary, for their subsistence; and so long as they occupy and cultivate it they have the right to the soil, but if they voluntarily leave it, then any other people have a right to settle upon it. Nothing can be sold but such things as can be carried away."

Supported by this theory, conscious that in some way he did not understand he had been wronged, and urged on by White Cloud, the prophet, who ruled a Winnebago village on the Rock river, Black Hawk crossed the Mississippi in 1831, determined to evict the settlers. A military demonstration drove him back, and he was persuaded to sign a treaty never to return east of the Mississippi. "I touched the goose-quill to the treaty and was determined to live in peace," he wrote afterwards; but hardly had he "touched the goose-quill" before his heart smote him. Longing for his home, resentment at the whites, obstinacy, brooding over the bad counsels of White Cloud and his disciple, Neapope—an agitating Indian who had recently been east to visit the British and their Indian allies, and who assured Black Hawk that the Winnebagoes, Ottawas, Chippewas, and Pottawottomies would join him in a struggle for his land, and that the British would send him guns, ammunition, provisions, and clothing early in the spring—all persuaded the Hawk that he would be successful if he made an effort to drive out the whites. In spite of the advice of many of his friends and of the Indian agent in the country, he crossed the river on April 6, 1832, and with some five hundred braves, his squaws and children, marched to the Prophet's town, thirty-five miles up the Rock river.

As soon as they heard of Black Hawk's invasion, the settlers of the northwestern part of the State fled in a panic to the forts; and from there rained petitions for protection on Governor Reynolds. General Atkinson, who was at Fort Armstrong, wrote to the governor for reinforcements; and, accordingly on the 16th of April Governor Reynolds sent out "influential messengers" with a sonorous summons. It was one of these messengers riding into New Salem who put an end to Lincoln's canvassing for the legislature, freed him from Offutt's expiring grocery, and led him to enlist.

There was no time to waste. The volunteers were ordered to be at Beardstown, nearly forty miles from New Salem, on April 22d. Horses, rifles, saddles, blankets were to be secured, a company formed. It was work of which the settlers were not ignorant. Under the laws of the State every able-bodied male inhabitant between eighteen and forty-five was obliged to drill twice a year or pay a fine of one dollar. "As a dollar was hard to raise," says one of the old settlers, "everybody drilled."

Preparations were quickly made, and by April 22d the men were at Beardstown. The day before, at Richland, Sangamon County, Lincoln was elected captain of the company from Sangamon.

According to his friend Greene it was something beside ambition which led him to seek the captaincy. One of the "odd jobs" which Lincoln had taken since coming into Illinois was working in a saw-mill for a man named Kirkpatrick. In hiring Lincoln, Kirkpatrick had promised to buy him a cant-hook with which to move heavy logs. Lincoln had proposed, if Kirkpatrick would give him the two dollars which the cant-hook would cost, to move the logs with a common handspike.  This the proprietor had agreed to, but when pay-day came he refused to keep his word.  When the Sangamon company of volunteers was formed Kirkpatrick aspired to the captaincy, and Lincoln knowing it, said to Greene: "Bill, I believe I can make Kirkpatrick pay me that two dollars he owes me on the cant-hook.  I'll run against him for captain." And he became a candidate.  The vote was taken in a field, by directing the men at the command "march" to assemble around the one they wanted for captain.  When the order was given, three-fourths of the men gathered around Lincoln.  In Lincoln's third-person autobiography he says he was elected "to his own surprise;" and adds, "He says he has not since had any success in life which gave him so much satisfaction."

The company was a motley crowd of men.  Each had secured for his outfit what he could get, and no two were equipped alike.  Buckskin breeches prevailed, and there was a sprinkling of coon-skin caps.  Each man had a blanket of the coarsest texture.  Flint-lock rifles were the usual arm, though here and there a man had a Cramer.  Over the shoulder of each was slung a powder-horn. The men had, as a rule, as little regard for discipline as for appearances, and when the new captain gave an order were as likely to jeer at it as to obey it. To drive the Indians out was their mission, and any order which did not bear directly on that point was little respected.  Lincoln himself was not familiar with military tactics, and made many blunders of which he used to tell afterwards with relish.  One of these was an early experience in giving orders.  He was marching with a front of over twenty men across a field, when he desired to pass through a gateway into the next inclosure.

"I could not for the life of me," said he, "remember the proper word of command for getting my company *endwise,* so that it could get through the gate; so, as we came near I shouted: 'This company is dismissed for two minutes, when it will fall in again on the other side of the gate!'

Nor was it only his ignorance of the manual which caused him trouble. He was so unfamiliar with camp discipline that he once had his sword taken from him for shooting within limits. Another disgrace he suffered was on account of his disorderly company. The men, unknown to him, stole a quantity of liquor one night, and the next morning were too drunk to fall in when the order was given to march. For their lawlessness Lincoln wore a wooden sword two days.

But none of these small difficulties injured his standing with the company. They soon grew so proud of his quick wit and great strength that they obeyed him because they admired him. No amount of military tactics could have secured from the volunteers the cheerful following he won by his personal qualities.

The men soon learned, too, that he meant what he said, and would permit no dishonorable performances. A helpless Indian took refuge in the camp one day; and the men, who were inspired by that wanton mixture of selfishness, unreason, and cruelty which seems to seize a frontiersman as soon as he scents a red man—were determined to kill the refugee. He had a safe conduct from General Cass; but the men, having come out to kill Indians and not having succeeded, threatened to take revenge on the helpless savage. Lincoln boldly took the man's part, and though he risked his life in doing it, he cowed the company and saved the Indian.

It was on the 27th of April that the force of sixteen hundred men organized at Beardstown started out. The day was cold, the roads heavy, the streams turbulent. The army marched first to Yellow Banks on the Mississippi, then to Dixon on the Rock river, which they reached on May 12. At Dixon they camped, and near here occurred the first bloodshed of the war.

A body of about three hundred and forty rangers, under Major Stillman, but not of the regular army, asked to go ahead as scouts, to look for a body of Indians under Black Hawk, rumored to be about twelve miles away. The permission was given, and on the night of the 14th of May, Stillman and his men went into camp. Black Hawk heard of their presence. By this time the poor old chief had discovered that the promises of aid from the Indian tribes and the British were false, and dismayed, he had resolved to recross the Mississippi. When he heard the whites were near he sent three braves with a white flag to ask for a parley and permission to descend the river. Behind them he sent five men to watch proceedings. Stillman's rangers were in camp when the bearers of the flag of truce appeared. The men were many of them half drunk, and when they saw the Indian truce-bearers, they rushed out in a wild mob, and ran them into camp. Then catching sight of the five spies, they started after them, killing two. The three who reached Black Hawk reported that the truce-bearers had been killed as well as their two companions. Furious at this violation of faith, Black Hawk "raised a yell," and sallied forth with forty braves to meet Stillman's band, who by this time were out in search of the Indians. Black Hawk, too maddened to think of the difference of numbers, attacked the whites. To his surprise the enemy turned, and fled in a wild riot. Nor did they stop at the camp, which from its position was almost impregnable; they fled in complete panic, *sauve qui peut*, through their camp, across prairie and rivers and swamps, to Dixon, twelve miles away. The first arrival reported that two thousand savages had swept down on Stillman's camp and slaughtered all but himself. Before the next night all but eleven of the band had arrived.

Stillman's Defeat, as this disgraceful affair is called, put all notion of peace out of Black Hawk's mind, and he started out in earnest on the warpath. Governor Reynolds, excited by the reports of the first arrivals from the Stillman stampede, made out that night, "by candle light," a call for more volunteers, and by the morning of the 15th had messengers out and his army in pursuit of Black Hawk. But it was like pursuing a shadow. The Indians purposely confused their trail. Sometimes it was a broad path, then it suddenly radiated to all points. The whites broke their bands, and pursued the savages here and there, never overtaking them, though now and then coming suddenly on some terrible evidences of their presence—a frontier home deserted and burned, slaughtered cattle, scalps suspended where the army could not fail to see them.

This fruitless warfare exasperated the volunteers; they threatened to leave, and their officers had great difficulty in making them obey orders. On reaching a point in the Rock river, beyond which lay the Indian country, a company under Colonel Zachary Taylor refused to cross, and held a public indignation meeting, urging that they had volunteered to defend the State, and had the right, as independent American citizens, to refuse to go out of its borders. Taylor heard them to the end, and then spoke: "I feel that all gentlemen here are my equals; in reality, I am persuaded that many of them will, in a few years, be my superiors, and perhaps, in the capacity of members of Congress, arbiters of the fortunes and reputation of humble servants of the republic, like myself. I expect then to obey them as interpreters of the will of the people; and the best proof that I will obey them is now to observe the orders of those whom the people have already put in the place of authority to which many gentlemen around me justly aspire. In plain English, gentlemen and fellow-citizens, the word has been passed on

to me from Washington to follow Black Hawk and to take
you with me as soldiers. I mean to do both. There are
the flatboats drawn up on the shore, and here are Uncle
Sam's men drawn up behind you on the prairie." The volunteers knew true grit when they met it. They dissolved their
meeting and crossed the river without Uncle Sam's men
being called into action.

The march in pursuit of the Indians led the army to
Ottawa, where the volunteers became so dissatisfied that on
May 27 and 28 Governor Reynolds mustered them out.
But a force in the field was essential until a new levy was
raised; and a few of the men were patriotic enough to offer
their services, among them Lincoln, who on May 29 was
mustered in at the mouth of the Fox river by a man in whom,
thirty years later, he was to have a keen interest—General
Robert Anderson, commander at Fort Sumter in 1861. Lincoln became a private in Captain Elijah Iles's company of
Independent Rangers, not brigaded—a company made up,
says Captain Iles in his "Footsteps and Wanderings," of
"generals, colonels, captains, and distinguished men from
the disbanded army." General Anderson says that at this
muster Lincoln's arms were valued at forty dollars, his horse
and equipment at one hundred and twenty dollars. The Independent Rangers were a favored body, used to carry messages and to spy on the enemy. They had no camp duties,
and "drew rations as often as they pleased." So that as a
private Lincoln was really better off than as a captain.*

The achievements and tribulations of this body of rangers

---

*William Cullen Bryant, who was in Illinois in 1832 at the time of
the Black Hawk War, used to tell of meeting in his travels in the State a
company of Illinois volunteers, commanded by a "raw youth" of "quaint
and pleasant" speech, and of learning afterwards that this captain was
Abraham Lincoln. As Lincoln's captaincy ended on May 27th, and Mr.
Bryant did not reach Illinois until June 12th, and as he never came
nearer than fifty miles to the Rapids of the Illinois, where the body of
rangers to which Lincoln belonged was encamped it is evident that the

to which he belonged are told with interesting detail by its commanding officer, Captain Iles, in his "Footsteps and Wanderings."

While the other companies were ordered to scout the country, he writes, mine was held by General Atkinson in camp as a reserve.  One company was ordered to go to Rock River (now Dixon) and report to Colonel Taylor (afterwards President) who had been left there with a few United States soldiers to guard the army supplies.  The place was also made a point of rendezvous.  Just as the company got to Dixon, a man came in, and reported that he and six others were on the road to Galena, and, in passing through a point of timber about twenty miles north of Dixon, they were fired on and six killed, he being the only one to make his escape. . . . Colonel Taylor ordered the company to proceed to the place, bury the dead, go on to Galena, and get all the information they could about the Indians. But the company took fright, and came back to the Illinois river, helter-skelter.

General Atkinson then called on me, and wanted to know how I felt about taking the trip; that he was exceedingly anxious to open communication with Galena, and to find out, if possible, the whereabouts of the Indians before the new troops arrived.  I answered the general that myself and men were getting rusty, and were anxious to have something to do, and that nothing would please us better than to be ordered out on an expedition; that I would find out how many of my men had good horses and were otherwise well equipped, and what time we wanted to prepare for the trip.  I called on him again at sunset, and reported that I had about fifty men well equipped and eager, and that we wanted one day to make preparations.  He said go ahead, and he would prepare our orders.

The next day was a busy one, running bullets and getting our flint-locks in order—we had no percussion locks then.  General Henry, one of my privates, who had been promoted to the position of major of one of the companies,

"raw youth" could not have been Lincoln, much as one would like to believe that it was.

(6)

volunteered to go with us. I considered him a host, as he had served as lieutenant in the War of 1812, under General Scott, and was in the battle of Lundy's Lane, and several other battles. He was a good drill officer, and could aid me much. . . . After General Atkinson handed me my orders, and my men were mounted and ready for the trip, I felt proud of them, and was confident of our success, although numbering only forty-eight. Several good men failed to go, as they had gone down to the foot of the Illinois rapids, to aid in bringing up the boats of army supplies. We wanted to be as little encumbered as possible, and took nothing that could be dispensed with, other than blankets, tin cups, coffee-pots, canteens, a wallet of bread, and some fat side meat, which we ate raw or broiled.

When we arrived at Rock River, we found Colonel Taylor on the opposite side, in a little fort built of prairie sod. He sent an officer in a canoe to bring me over. I said to the officer that I would come over as soon as I got my men in camp. I knew of a good spring half a mile above, and I determined to camp at it. After the men were in camp I called on General Henry, and he accompanied me. On meeting Colonel Taylor (he looked like a man born to command) he seemed a little piqued that I did not come over and camp with him. I told him we felt just as safe as if quartered in his one-horse fort; besides, I knew what his orders would be, and wanted to try the mettle of my men before starting on the perilous trip I knew he would order. He said the trip was perilous, and that since the murder of the six men all communications with Galena had been cut off, and it might be besieged; that he wanted me to proceed to Galena, and that he would have my orders for me in the morning, and asked what outfit I wanted. I answered "Nothing but coffee, side meat and bread."

In the morning my orders were to collect and bury the remains of the six men murdered, proceed to Galena, make a careful search for the signs of Indians, and find out whether they were aiming to escape by crossing the river below Galena, and get all information at Galena of their possible whereabouts before the new troops were ready to follow them.

John Dixon, who kept a house of entertainment here, and had sent his family to Galena for safety, joined us, and hauled our wallets of corn and grub in his wagon, which was a great help. Lieutenant Harris, U. S. A., also joined us. I now had fifty men to go with me on the march. I detailed two to march on the right, two on the left, and two in advance, to act as look-outs to prevent a surprise. They were to keep in full view of us, and to remain out until we camped for the night. Just at sundown of the first day, while we were at lunch, our advance scouts came in under whip and reported Indians. We bounced to our feet, and, having a full view of the road for a long distance, could see a large body coming toward us. All eyes were turned to John Dixon, who, as the last one dropped out of sight coming over a ridge, pronounced them Indians. I stationed my men in a ravine crossing the road, where anyone approaching could not see us until within thirty yards; the horses I had driven back out of sight in a valley. I asked General Henry to take command. He said, "No; stand at your post," and walked along the line, talking to the men in a low, calm voice. Lieutenant Harris, U. S. A., seemed much agitated; he ran up and down the line, and exclaimed, "Captain, we will catch hell!" He had horse-pistols, belt-pistols, and a double-barreled gun. He would pick the flints, reprime, and lay the horse-pistols at his feet. When he got all ready he passed along the line slowly, and seeing the nerves of the men all quiet—after General Henry's talk to them—said, "Captain, we are safe; we can whip five hundred Indians." Instead of Indians, they proved to be the command of General Dodge, from Galena, of one hundred and fifty men, *en route,* to find out what had become of General Atkinson's army, as, since the murder of the six men, communication had been stopped for more than ten days. My look-out at the top of the hill did not notify us, and we were not undeceived until they got within thirty steps of us. My men then raised a yell and ran to finish their lunch. . . .

When we got within fifteen miles of Galena, on Apple Creek, we found a stockade filled with women and children and a few men, all terribly frightened. The Indians had shot at and chased two men that afternoon, who made their escape to the stockade. They insisted on our quartering in the fort, but instead we camped one hundred yards outside, and slept—what little sleep we did get—with our guns on our arms. General Henry did not sleep, but drilled my men all night; so the moment they were called they would bounce to their feet and stand in two lines, the front ready to fire, and fall back to reload, while the others stepped forward to take their places. They were called up a number of times, and we got but little sleep. We arrived at Galena the next day, and found the citizens prepared to defend the place. They were glad to see us, as it had been so long since they had heard from General Atkinson and his army. The few Indians prowling about Galena and murdering were simply there as a ruse.

On our return from Galena, near the forks of the Apple River and Gratiot roads, we could see General Dodge on the Gratiot road, on his return from Rock River. His six scouts had discovered my two men that I had allowed to drop in the rear—two men who had been in Stillman's defeat, and, having weak horses, were allowed to fall behind. Having weak horses they had fallen in the rear about two miles, and each took the other to be Indians, and such an exciting race I never saw, until they got sight of my company; then they came to a sudden halt, and after looking at us a few moments, wheeled their horses and gave up the chase. My two men did not know but that they were Indians until they came up with us and shouted "Indians!" They had thrown away their wallets and guns, and used their ramrods as whips.

The few houses on the road that usually accommodated the travel were all standing, but vacant, as we went. On our return we found them burned by the Indians. On my return to the Illinois River I reported to General Atkinson, saying that, from all we could learn, the Indians were aiming to escape by going north, with the intention of crossing the Mississippi river above Galena. The new troops had just arrived and were being mustered into service. My company had only been organized for twenty days, and as the time had now expired, the men were mustered out. All but myself again volunteered for the third time.

Battle Ground
of Bad Axe

Atkinson's Line of March

*Bad Axe R.*

*Kickapoo R.*

Wisconsin R.

MICHIGAN TERRITORY

(WISCONSIN)

L. Koshkonong    Whitewater
*(here disbanded)*

LAKE

MICHIGAN

43                                                              43

Fort

Galena

*Fort*
STEPHENSON    BOONE
DAVIESS    Freeport    Rockford

Stillman's Defeat

42                                              CHICAGO    42

OGLE

Dixon    DE
KALB

WHITESIDE    LEE

Rock Island    Joliet
(Fort Armstrong)
Yellow Banks    ROCK    BUREAU

Black Hawk's    Ottawa
Village    Rapids of
the Illinois River

MERCER    HENRY    LASALLE

41    KNOX    MARSHALL    41
Galesburg
WARREN    Metamora

PEORIA
Peoria
FULTON    Pekin
MC    Tremont
DONOUGH    TAZEWELL    Bloomington

Havana    Lincoln    Clinton    Urbana    Danville

SCHUYLER    LOGAN    Monticello
40    CASS    MENARD    Mt.Pulaski    Tuscola    40
Beardstown    Petersburg    New Salem
Quincy    Sangamontown    Jamestown
SPRINGFIELD    Decatur    Paris
Jacksonville    SANGAMON    Sullivan    Tuscola
Taylorville    Charlestown

39                        Vandalia                        39

Missouri R.
Alton

ST.LOUIS    Vincennes

Belleville

Data does not exist for
determining    positively
the route Lincoln followed
in the Black Hawk War.
Only the general direction of
the marches of his company
are indicated here.    In going
from Ottawa to Galena and back
Captain Iles may have very well
marched his company through
Dixon's Ferry.    In returning from
Whitewater to New Salem, Lincoln
may have followed the river to Dixon
There were undoubtedly several side
marches such as that on June 25, from
Dixon to Kellogg's Grove and back,
which are not shown in this map.

MAP OF
ILLINOIS
AND PART OF
MICHIGAN TERRITORY
SHOWING
LINCOLN'S SUPPOSED LINE OF
MARCH IN BLACK HAWK WAR.

SCALE OF MILES
0  10  20  30  40  50  60

Jonesboro

Ohio R.

Cairo

L.L.POATES, ENGR., N.Y.    Longitude    West    from    Greenwich

It was the middle of June when Captain Iles and his company returned to Dixon's Ferry from their Indian hunt and were mustered out. On June 20 Lincoln was mustered in again, by Major Anderson, as a member of an independent company under Captain Jacob M. Early. His arms were valued this time at only fifteen dollars, his horse and equipments at eighty-five dollars.

A week after re-enlistment Lincoln's company moved northward with the army. It was time they moved, for Black Hawk was overrunning the country, and scattering death wherever he went. The settlers were wild with fear, and most of the settlements were abandoned. At a sudden sound, at the merest rumor, men, women, and children fled. "I well remember these troublesome times," writes one Illinois woman. "We often left our bread dough unbaked to rush to the Indian fort near by." When Mr. John Bryant, a brother of William Cullen Bryant, visited the colony in Princeton in 1832, he found it nearly broken up on account of the war. Everywhere crops were neglected, for the able-bodied men were volunteering. William Cullen Bryant, who, in June, 1834, traveled on horseback from Petersburg to near Pekin and back, wrote home: "Every few miles on our way we fell in with bodies of Illinois militia proceeding to the American camp, or saw where they had encamped for the night. They generally stationed themselves near a stream or a spring in the edge of a wood, and turned their horses to graze on the prairie. Their way was barked or girdled, and the roads through the uninhabited country were as much beaten and as dusty as the highways on New York island. Some of the settlers complained that they made war upon the pigs and chickens. They were a hard-looking set of men, unkempt and unshaved, wearing shirts of dark calico and sometimes calico capotes."

Soon after the army moved up the Rock river, the independent spy company, of which Lincoln was a member, was sent with a brigade to the northwest, near Galena, in pursuit of the Hawk. The nearest Lincoln came to an actual engagement in the war was here. The skirmish of Kellogg's Grove took place on June 25; Lincoln's company came up soon after it was over, and helped bury the five men killed. It was probably to this experience that he referred when he told a friend once of coming on a camp of white scouts one morning just as the sun was rising. The Indians had surprised the camp, and had killed and scalped every man.

"I remember just how those men looked," said Lincoln, "as we rode up the little hill where their camp was. The red light of the morning sun was streaming upon them as they lay heads towards us on the ground. And every man had a round red spot on the top of his head about as big as a dollar, where the redskins had taken his scalp. It was frightful, but it was grotesque; and the red sunlight seemed to paint everything all over." Lincoln paused, as if recalling the vivid picture, and added, somewhat irrelevantly, "I remember that one man had buckskin breeches on."

Early's company, on returning from their expedition, joined the main army on its northward march. By the end of the month the troops crossed into Michigan Territory—as Wisconsin was then called—and July was passed floundering in swamps and stumbling through forests, in pursuit of the now nearly exhausted Black Hawk. No doubt Early's company saw the hardest service on the march for to it was allotted the scouting. The farther the army advanced the more difficult was the situation. Finally the provisions gave out and July 10, three weeks before the last battle of the war, that of Bad Axe, in which the whites finally massacred most of the Indian band, Lincoln's company was disbanded at Whitewater, Wisconsin, and he and his friends started for home. The volunteers in returning suffered much from hunger. More than one of them had nothing to eat on the journey except meal and water baked in rolls of bark laid by the fire. Lincoln not only went hungry on this return; he had to tramp most of the way. The night before his company started from Whitewater he and one of his messmates had their horses stolen; and, excepting when their more fortunate companions gave them a lift, they walked as far as Peoria, Illinois, where they bought a canoe, and paddled down the Illinois river to Havana. Here they sold the canoe, and walked across the country to New Salem.

# CHAPTER VII

LINCOLN RUNS FOR STATE ASSEMBLY AND IS DEFEATED—
STOREKEEPER—STUDENT—POSTMASTER—SURVEYOR

On returning to New Salem Lincoln at once plunged into "electioneering." He ran as "an avowed Clay man," and the country was stiffly Democratic. However, in those days political contests were almost purely personal. If the candidate was liked he was voted for irrespective of principle. "The Democrats of New Salem worked for Lincoln out of their personal regard for him," said Stephen T. Logan, a young lawyer of Springfield, who made Lincoln's acquaintance in the campaign. "He was as stiff as a man could be in his Whig doctrines. They did this for him simply because he was popular—because he was Lincoln."

It was the custom for the candidates to appear at every gathering which brought the people out, and, if they had a chance, to make speeches. Then, as now, the farmers gathered at the county-seat or at the largest town within their reach on Saturday afternoons, to dispose of produce, buy supplies, see their neighbors, and get the news. During "election times" candidates were always present, and a regular feature of the day was listening to their speeches. They never missed public sales, it being expected that after the "vandoo" the candidates would take the auctioneer's place.

Lincoln let none of these chances to be heard slip. Accompanied by his friends, generally including a few Clary's Grove Boys, he always was present. The first speech he made was after a sale at Pappsville. What he said there is not remembered; but an illustration of the kind of man he was, interpolated into his discourse, made a lasting impression. A fight broke out in his audience while he was on the stand, and observing that one of his friends was being worsted, he bounded into the group of contestants, seized the fellow who had his supporter down, threw him, according to tradition, "ten or twelve feet" mounted the platform, and finished the speech. Sangamon County could appreciate such a performance; and the crowd at Pappsville that day never forgot Lincoln.

His visits to Springfield were of great importance to him. Springfield was not at that time a very attractive place. Bryant, visiting it in June, 1832, said that the houses were not as good as at Jacksonville, "a considerable proportion of them being log cabins, and the whole town having an appearance of dirt and discomfort." Nevertheless it was the largest town in the county, and among its inhabitants were many young men of breeding, education, and energy. One of these men Lincoln had become well acquainted with in the Black Hawk War *—Major John T. Stuart, at that time a lawyer, and, like Lincoln, a candidate for the General Assembly. He met others at this time who were to be associated with him

*There were many prominent Americans in the Black Hawk War, with some of whom Lincoln became acquainted. Among the best known were General Robert Anderson; Colonel Zachary Taylor; General Scott, afterwards candidate for President, and Lieutenant-General; Henry Dodge, Governor of the Territory of Wisconsin, and United States Senator; Hon. William D. Ewing and Hon. Sidney Breese, both United States Senators from Illinois; William S. Hamilton, a son of Alexander Hamilton; Colonel Nathan Boone, son of Daniel Boone; Lieutenant Albert Sidney Johnston, afterwards a Confederate General; also Jefferson Davis, President of the Southern Confederacy. Davis was at this time a lieutenant stationed at Fort Crawford. According to the muster rolls of his company he was absent on furlough from March 26 to August 18, 1832, but, according to Davis's own statement, corroborated by many of the early settlers of Illinois who served in the Black Hawk War, Davis returned to duty as soon as he found there was to be a war. When Black Hawk was finally captured in August, after the battle of Bad Axe, he was sent down the river to Jefferson Barracks, under the charge of Lieutenant Jefferson Davis. Black Hawk, in his "Life," speaks of Davis as a "good and brave young chief, with whose conduct I was much pleased."

more or less closely in the future in both law and politics, among them Judge Logan and William Butler. With these men the manners which had won him the day at Pappsville were of little value; what impressed them was his "very sensible speech," and his decided individuality and originality.

The election came off on August 6th. Lincoln was defeated. "This was the only time Abraham was ever defeated on a direct vote of the people," says his autobiographical notes. He had a consolation in his defeat, however, for in spite of the pronounced Democratic sentiments of his precinct, he received, according to the official poll-book in the county clerk's office at Springfield, two hundred and twenty-seven votes out of three hundred cast.

This defeat did not take him out of politics. Six weeks later he filled his first civil office, that of clerk of the September election. The report in his hand still exists, his first official document. In the following years few elections were held in New Salem at which Lincoln did not act as clerk.

The election over, Lincoln began to look for work. One of his friends, an admirer of his physical strength, advised him to become a blacksmith, but it was a trade which afforded little leisure for study, and for meeting and talking with men; and he had already resolved, it is evident, that books and men were essential to him. The only employment in New Salem which offered both employment and the opportunities he sought, was clerking in a store. Now the stores in New Salem were in more need of customers than of clerks, business having been greatly overdone. In the fall of 1832 four stores offered wares to the one hundred inhabitants of New Salem. The most pretentious was that of Hill and McNeill, which carried a large line of dry goods. The three others, owned respectively by the Herndon brothers, Reuben Radford, and James Rutledge, were groceries. Failing to secure employment at any of these establish-

ments, Lincoln resolved to *buy* a store.   He was not long in
finding an opportunity to purchase.   James Herndon had
already sold out his half interest in Herndon Brothers' store
to William F. Berry;   and Rowan Herndon, not getting
along well with Berry, was only too glad to find a purchaser
of his half in the person of "Abe" Lincoln.   Berry was as
poor as Lincoln; but that was not a serious obstacle, for
their notes were accepted for the Herndon stock of goods.
They had barely hung out their sign when something happened which threw another store into their hands.   Reuben
Radford had made himself obnoxious to the Clary's Grove
Boys, and one night they broke in his doors and windows,
and overturned his counters and sugar barrels.   It was too
much for Radford, and he sold out next day to William G.
Greene, for a four-hundred-dollar note signed by Greene.
At the latter's request, Lincoln made an inventory of the
stock, and offered him six hundred and fifty dollars for it—
a proposition which was cheerfully accepted.   Berry and
Lincoln, being unable to pay cash, assumed the four-hundred-dollar note payable to Radford, and gave Greene their
joint note for two hundred and fifty dollars.   The little
grocery owned by James Rutledge was the next to suc-
cumb.   Berry and Lincoln bought it at a bargain, their
joint note taking the place of cash.   The three stocks were
consolidated.   Their aggregate cost must have been not
less than fifteen hundred dollars.   Berry and Lincoln had
secured a monopoly of the grocery business in New Salem.
Within a few weeks two penniless men had become the pro-
prietors of three stores, and had stopped buying only because there were no more to purchase.

But the partnership, it was soon evident, was unfortunate.
Berry, though the son of a Presbyterian minister, was
according to tradition "a very wicked young man," drinking,
gambling, and taking an active part in all the disturbances

of the neighborhood.    In spite of the bad habits of his partner, Lincoln left the management of the business largely to
him.    It was his love of books which was responsible for
this poor business management.    He had soon discovered
that store-keeping in New Salem, after all duties were done,
left a large amount of leisure on a man's hands.    It was his
chance to read, and he scoured the town for books.    On
pleasant days he spent hour after hour stretched under a
tree, which stood just outside the door of the store, reading
the works he had picked up.    If it rained he simply made
himself comfortable on the counter within.    It was in this
period that Lincoln discovered Shakespeare and Burns.    In
New Salem there was one of those curious individuals, sometimes found in frontier settlements, half poet, half loafer, in-
capable of earning a living in any steady employment, yet
familiar with good literature and capable of enjoying it—
Jack Kelso.    He repeated passages from Shakespeare and
Burns incessantly, over the odd jobs he undertook, or as he
idled by the streams—for he was a famous fisherman—and
Lincoln soon became one of his constant companions.    The
tastes he formed in company with Kelso he retained through
life.

It was not only Burns and Shakespeare that interfered
with the grocery keeping; Lincoln had begun seriously to
read law.    His first acquaintance with the subject, we have
already seen, had been made when, a mere lad, a copy of the
"Revised Statutes of Indiana" had fallen into his hands.

But from the time he left Indiana in 1830 he had no legal
reading until one day soon after the grocery was started,
there happened one of those trivial incidents which so
often turn the current of a life.    It is best told in Mr. Lincoln's own words.*    "One day a man who was migrating to

*This incident was told by Lincoln to Mr. A. J. Conant, the artist,
who in 1860 painted his portrait in Springfield.  Mr. Conant, in order

the West drove up in front of my store with a wagon which contained his family and household plunder. He asked me if I would buy an old barrel for which he had no room in his wagon, and which he said contained nothing of special value. I did not want it, but to oblige him I bought it, and paid him, I think, half a dollar for it. Without further examination I put it away in the store, and forgot all about it. Some time after, in overhauling things, I came upon the barrel, and emptying it upon the floor to see what it contained, I found at the bottom of the rubbish a complete edition of Blackstone's Commentaries. I began to read those famous works, and I had plenty of time; for during the long summer days, when the farmers were busy with their crops, my customers were few and far between. The more I read"—this he said with unusual emphasis—"the more intensely interested I became. Never in my whole life was my mind so thoroughly absorbed. I read until I devoured them."

But all this was fatal to business, and by spring it was evident that something must be done to stimulate the grocery sales. Liquor selling was the expedient adopted, for, on the 6th of March, 1833, the County Commissioners' Court of Sangamon County granted the firm of Berry and Lincoln a license to keep a tavern at New Salem. It is probable that the license was procured not to enable the firm to keep a tavern but to retail the liquors which they had in stock. Each of the three groceries which Berry and Lincoln acquired had the usual supply of liquors and it was only natural that they should seek a way to dispose of the surplus quickly and profitably—an end which could be best accomplished by selling it over the counter by the glass. To do this lawfully

to catch Mr. Lincoln's pleasant expression, had engaged him in conversation, and had questioned him about his early life; and it was in the course of their conversation that this incident came out. It is to be found in a delightful and suggestive article entitled, "My Acquaintance with Abraham Lincoln," contributed by Mr. Conant to the "Liber Scriptorum."

required a tavern license; and it is a warrantable conclusion that such was the chief aim of Berry and Lincoln in procuring a franchise of this character. We are fortified in this conclusion by the coincidence that three other grocers of New Salem were among those who took out tavern licenses.

In a community in which liquor drinking was practically universal, at a time when whiskey was as legitimate an article of merchandise as coffee or calico, when no family was without a jug, when the minister of the gospel could take his "dram" without any breach of propriety, it is not surprising that a reputable young man should have been found selling whiskey. Liquor was sold at all groceries, but it could not be lawfully sold in a smaller quantity than one quart. The law, however, was not always rigidly observed, and it was the custom of storekeepers to treat their patrons.

The license issued to Berry and Lincoln read as follows:

Ordered that William F. Berry, in the name of Berry and Lincoln, have a license to keep a tavern in New Salem to continue 12 months from this date, and that they pay one dollar in addition to the six dollars heretofore paid as per Treasurer's receipt, and that they be allowed the following rates (viz.):

| | | |
|---|---|---|
| French Brandy per ½ pt | ............................ | 25 |
| Peach " " " | ............................ | $18\frac{3}{4}$ |
| Apple " " " | ............................ | 12 |
| Holland Gin " " | ............................ | $18\frac{3}{4}$ |
| Domestic " " | ............................ | $12\frac{1}{2}$ |
| Wine " " | ............................ | 25 |
| Rum " " | ............................ | $18\frac{3}{4}$ |
| Whiskey " " | ............................ | $12\frac{1}{2}$ |
| Breakfast, dinner or supper | ............................ | 25 |
| Lodging per night | ............................ | $12\frac{1}{2}$ |
| Horse per night | ............................ | 25 |
| Single feed | ............................ | $12\frac{1}{2}$ |
| Breakfast, dinner or supper for Stage Passengers | ..... | $37\frac{1}{2}$ |

who gave bond as required by law.

At the granting of a tavern license, the applicants therefor were required by law to file a bond. The bond given in the case of Berry and Lincoln was as follows:

Know all men by these presents, we, William F. Berry, Abraham Lincoln and John Bowling Green, are held and firmly bound unto the County Commissioners of Sangamon county in the full sum of three hundred dollars to which payment well and truly to be made we bind ourselves, our heirs, executors and administrators firmly by these presents, sealed with our seal and dated this 6th day of March A. D. 1833. Now the condition of this obligation is such that Whereas the said Berry & Lincoln has obtained a license from the County Commissioners' Court to keep a tavern in the town of New Salem to continue one year. Now if the said Berry & Lincoln shall be of good behavior and observe all the laws of this State relative to tavern keepers—then this obligation to be void or otherwise remain in full force.

ABRAHAM LINCOLN [Seal]
WM. F. BERRY [Seal]
BOWLING GREEN [Seal]

This bond appears to have been written by the clerk of the Commissioners' Court; and Lincoln's name was signed by some other than himself, very likely by his partner Berry.

Business was not so brisk in Berry and Lincoln's grocery, even after the license was granted, that the junior partner did not welcome an appointment as postmaster which he received in May, 1833. The appointment of a Whig by a Democratic administration seems to have been made without comment. "The office was too insignificant to make his politics an objection," say his autobiographical notes. The duties of the new office were not arduous, for letters were few, and their comings far between. At that date the mails were carried by four-horse post-coaches from city to city, and on horseback from central points into the country towns. The rates of postage were high. A single-sheet letter carried thirty miles or under cost six cents; thirty to eighty miles, ten cents; eighty to one hundred and fifty miles, twelve and one-half cents; one hundred and fifty to four hundred miles, eighteen and one-half cents; over four hundred miles,

Mr Spears

At your request I send you a receipt for the postage on your paper. I am some what surprised at your request. I will however comply with it. The law requires News paper postage to be paid in advance and now that I have waited a full year you choose to wound my feelings by insinuating that unless you get a receipt I will probably make you pay it again—

Respectfully
A Lincoln

Received of George Spears in full for postage on the Sangamo Journal up to the first of July 1834

A Lincoln P M

FACSIMILE OF A LETTER WRITTEN BY POSTMASTER LINCOLN
Reproduced by permission from "Menard-Salem-Lincoln Souvenir Album."
Petersburg, 1893.

twenty-five cents. A copy of one of the popular magazines sent from New York to New Salem would have cost fully twenty-five cents. The mail was irregular in coming as well as light in its contents. Though supposed to arrive twice a week, it sometimes happened that a fortnight or more passed without any mail.   Under these conditions the New Salem post-office was not a serious care.

A large number of the patrons of the office lived in the country—many of them miles away—and generally Lincoln delivered their letters at their doors.   These letters he would carefully place in the crown of his hat, and distribute them from house to house.   Thus it was in a measure true that he kept the New Salem post-office in his hat.   The habit of carrying papers in his hat clung to Lincoln; for, many years later, when he was a practising lawyer in Springfield, he apologized for failing to answer a letter promptly, by explaining: "When I received your letter I put it in my old hat, and buying a new one the next day, the old one was set aside, and so the letter was lost sight of for a time."

But whether the mail was delivered by the postmaster himself, or was received at the store it was the habit "to stop and visit awhile." He who received a letter read it and repeated the contents; if he had a newspaper, usually the postmaster could tell him in advance what it contained, for one of the perquisites of the early post-office was the privilege of reading all printed matter before delivering it.   Every day, then, Lincoln's acquaintance in New Salem, through his position as postmaster, became more intimate.

As the summer of 1833 went on, the condition of the store became more and more unsatisfactory.   As the position of postmaster brought in only a small revenue, Lincoln was forced to take any odd work he could get.   He helped in other stores in the town, split rails, and looked after the mill; but all this yielded only a scant and uncertain support, and when in the fall he had an opportunity to learn surveying, he accepted it eagerly.

The condition of affairs in Illinois in the early thirties made a demand for the service of surveyors.   The immigration had been phenomenal.   There were thousands of farms to be surveyed and thousands of corners to be located. Speculators bought up large tracts and mapped out cities on paper. It was years before the first railroad was built in Illinois, and, as all inland traveling was on horseback or in the stage-coach, each year hundreds of miles of wagon roads were opened through woods and swamps and prairies. As the county of Sangamon was large, and eagerly sought by immigrants, the county surveyor in 1833, one John Calhoun, needed deputies; but in a country so new it was no easy matter to find men with the requisite capacity.

With Lincoln, Calhoun had little, if any, personal acquaintance, for they lived twenty miles apart. Lincoln, however, had made himself known by his meteoric race for the legislature in 1832, and Calhoun had heard of him as an honest, intelligent, and trustworthy young man. One day he sent word to Lincoln by Pollard Simmons, who lived in the New Salem neighborhood, that he had decided to appoint him a deputy surveyor if he would accept the position.

Going into the woods, Simmons found Lincoln engaged in his old occupation of making rails. The two sat down together on a log, and Simmons told Lincoln what Calhoun had said. Now Calhoun was a "Jackson man;" he was for Clay. What did he know about surveying, and why should a Democratic official offer him a position of any kind? He immediately went to Springfield, and had a talk with Calhoun. He would not accept the appointment, he said, unless he had the assurance that it involved no political obligation, and that he might continue to express his political opinions as freely and frequently as he chose. This assurance was given. The only difficulty then in the way was the fact that he knew absolutely nothing of surveying. But Calhoun, of course, understood this, and agreed that he should have time to learn.

With the promptness of action with which he always undertook anything he had to do, Lincoln procured Flint and Gibson's treatise on surveying, and sought Mentor Graham for help. At a sacrifice of some time, the schoolmaster aided him to a partial mastery of the intricate subject. Lincoln worked literally day and night, sitting up night after night until the crowing of the cock warned him of the approaching dawn. So hard did he study that his friends were greatly concerned at his haggard face. But in six weeks he had mastered all the books within reach relating to the subject—a task which, under ordinary circumstances, would hardly have been achieved in as many months. Reporting to Calhoun for duty (greatly to the amazement of that gentleman), he was at once assigned to the territory in the northwest part of the county, and the first work he did of which there is any authentic record was in January, 1834. In that month he surveyed a piece of land for Russell Godby, dating the certificate January 14, 1834, and signing it "J. Calhoun, S. S. C., by A. Lincoln."

Lincoln was frequently employed in laying out public roads, being selected for that purpose by the County Commissioners' Court. So far as can be learned from the official records, the first road he surveyed was "from Musick's Ferry on Salt creek, via New Salem, to the county line in the direction of Jacksonville." For this he was allowed fifteen dollars for five days' service, and two dollars and fifty cents for a plat of the new road. The next road he surveyed, according to the records, was that leading from Athens to Sangamon town. This was reported to the County Commissioners' Court November 4, 1834. But road surveying was only a small portion of his work. He was more frequently employed by private individuals.

According to tradition, when he first took up the business he was too poor to buy a chain, and, instead, used a long, straight grape-vine. Probably this is a myth, though surveyors who had experience in the early days say it may be true. The chains commonly used at that time were made of iron. Constant use wore away and weakened the links, and it was no unusual thing for a chain to lengthen six inches after a year's use. "And a good grape-vine," to use the words of a veteran surveyor, "would give quite as satisfactory results as one of those old-fashioned chains."

Lincoln's surveys had the extraordinary merit of being correct. Much of the government work had been rather indifferently done, or the government corners had been imperfectly preserved, and there were frequent disputes between adjacent land-owners about boundary lines. Frequently Lincoln was called upon in such cases to find the corner in controversy. His verdict was invariably the end of the dispute, so general was the confidence in his honesty and skill. Some of these old corners located by him are still in existence. The people of Petersburg proudly remember that they live in a town which was laid out by Lincoln. This he did in 1836, and it was the work of several weeks.

Lincoln's pay as a surveyor was three dollars a day, more than he had ever before earned. Compared with the compensation for like services nowadays it seems small enough; but at that time it was really princely. The Governor of the State received a salary of only one thousand dollars a year, the Secretary of State six hundred dollars, and good board and lodging could be obtained for one dollar a week. But even three dollars a day did not enable him to meet all his financial obligations. The heavy debts of the store hung over him. He was obliged to help his father's family. The long distances he had to travel in his new employment had made it necessary to buy a horse, and for it he had gone into debt.

"My father," says Thomas Watkins, of Petersburg, who remembers the circumstances well, "sold Lincoln the horse, and my recollection is that Lincoln agreed to pay him fifty

To the county commissioners court for the county of Sangamon —

We the undersigned being appointed to view and relocate a part of the road between Sangamowtown and the town of Athens respectfully report that we have performed the duty of said appointment according to law — and that we have made the said relocation on good ground — and believe the same to be necessary and proper —

Athens Nov. 4. 1854 —

James Strawhedge
Levi Cantrall —
A. Lincoln —

Herewith is the map — The court may allow me the following charges if they think proper —

1 day's labour as surveyor — $3.00
Making map — 50
$3.50.

A. Lincoln

FACSIMILE OF A REPORT OF A ROAD SURVEY BY LINCOLN.

Southern boundary line of Section 24 in Town 17 Range 6

Due North
1-00-00

N 49° W
44-79

Due North
9-00-00

Scale of 2 inches to the mile

Beasley branch

3° Intersection with the old road

Athens

FACSIMILE OF A MAP MADE BY LINCOLN OF ROAD IN MENARD COUNTY, ILL dollars for it. Lincoln was a little slow in making the payments, and after he had paid all but ten dollars, my father, who was a high-strung man, became impatient, and sued him for the balance. Lincoln, of course, did not deny the debt, but raised the money and paid it. I do not often tell this," Mr. Watkins adds, "because I have always thought there never was such a man as Lincoln, and I have always been sorry father sued him."

Between his duties as deputy surveyor and postmaster, Lincoln had little leisure for the store, and its management passed into the hands of Berry. The stock of groceries was on the wane. The numerous obligations of the firm were maturing, with no money to meet them. Both members of the firm, in the face of such obstacles, lost courage; and when, early in 1834, Alexander and William Trent asked if the store was for sale, an affirmative answer was eagerly given. A price was agreed upon, and the sale was made. Now, neither Alexander Trent nor his brother had any money; but as Berry and Lincoln had bought without money, it seemed only fair that they should be willing to sell on the same terms. Accordingly the notes of the Trent brothers were accepted for the purchase price, and the store was turned over to the new owners. But about the time their notes fell due the Trent brothers disappeared. The few groceries in the store were seized by creditors, and the doors were closed, never to be opened again. Misfortunes now crowded upon Lincoln. His late partner, Berry, soon reached the end of his wild career, and one morning a farmer from the Rock Creek neighborhood drove into New Salem with the news that he was dead.

The appalling debt which had accumulated was thrown upon Lincoln's shoulders. It was then too common a fashion among men who became deluged in debt to "clear out," in the expressive language of the pioneer, as the Trents had done; but this was not Lincoln's way. He quietly settled down among the men he owed, and promised to pay them. For fifteen years he carried this burden—a load which he cheerfully and manfully bore, but one so heavy that he habitually spoke of it as the "national debt." Talking once of it to a friend, Lincoln said: "That debt was the greatest obstacle I have ever met in life; I had no way of speculating, and could not earn money except by labor, and to earn by labor eleven hundred dollars, besides my living, seemed the work of a lifetime. There was, however, but one way. I went to the creditors, and told them that if they would let me alone, I would give them all I could earn over my living, as fast as I could earn it." As late as 1848, so we are informed by Mr. Herndon, Mr. Lincoln, then a member of Congress, sent home money saved from his salary, to be applied on these obligations. All the notes, with interest at the high rates then prevailing, were at last paid.

With a single exception Lincoln's creditors seemed to be lenient. One of the notes given by him came into the hands of a Mr. Van Bergen, who, when it fell due, brought suit. The amount of the judgment was more than Lincoln could pay, and his personal effects were levied upon. These consisted of his horse, saddle and bridle, and surveying instruments. James Short, a well-to-do farmer living on Sand Ridge, a few miles north of New Salem, heard of the trouble which had befallen his young friend. Without advising Lincoln of his plans, he attended the sale, bought in the horse and surveying instruments for one hundred and twenty dollars, and turned them over to their former owner.

Lincoln never forgot a benefactor. He not only repaid the money with interest, but nearly thirty years later remembered the kindness in a most substantial way. After Lincoln left New Salem financial reverses came to James Short, and he removed to the far West to seek his fortune anew. Early in Lincoln's presidential term he heard that "Uncle Jimmy" was living in California. One day Mr. Short received a letter from Washington, D. C. Tearing it open, he read the gratifying announcement that he had been commissioned an Indian agent.

The kindness of Mr. Short was not exceptional in Lincoln's New Salem career. When the store had "winked out," as he put it, and the post-office had been left without headquarters, one of his neighbors, Samuel Hill, invited the homeless postmaster into his store. There was hardly a man or woman in the community who would not have been glad to have done as much. It was a simple recognition on their part of Lincoln's friendliness to them. He was what they called "obliging"—a man who instinctively did the thing which he saw would help another, no matter how trivial or homely it was. In the home of Rowan Herndon, where he had boarded when he first came to the town, he had made himself loved by his care of the children. "He nearly always had one of them around with him," says Mr. Herndon. In the Rutledge tavern, where he afterwards lived, the landlord told with appreciation how, when his house was full, Lincoln gave up his bed, went to the store, and slept on the counter, his pillow a web of calico. If a traveler "stuck in the mud" in New Salem's one street, Lincoln was always the first to help pull out the wheel. The widows praised him because he "chopped their wood;" the overworked, because he was always ready to give them a lift. It was the spontaneous, unobtrusive helpfulness of the man's nature which endeared him to everybody and which inspired a general desire to do all possible in return. There are many tales told of homely service rendered him, even by the hard-working farmers' wives around New Salem. There was not one of them who did not gladly "put on a plate" for Abe Lincoln when he appeared, or would not darn or mend for him when she knew he needed it. Hannah Armstrong, the wife of the hero of Clary's Grove, made him one of her family. "Abe would come out to our house," she said, "drink milk, eat mush, cornbread and butter, bring the children candy, and rock the cradle while I got him something to eat. . . . Has stayed at our house two or three weeks at a time." Lincoln's pay for his first piece of surveying came in the shape of two buckskins, and it was Hannah who "foxed" them on his trousers.

His relations were equally friendly in the better homes of the community; even at the minister's, the Rev. John Cameron's, he was perfectly at home, and Mrs. Cameron was by him affectionately called "Aunt Polly." It was not only his kindly service which made Lincoln loved; it was his sympathetic comprehension of the lives and joys and sorrows and interests of the people. Whether it was Jack Armstrong and his wrestling, Hannah and her babies, Kelso and his fishing and poetry, the school-master and his books—with one and all he was at home. He possessed in an extraordinary degree the power of entering into the interests of others, a power found only in reflective, unselfish natures endowed with a humorous sense of human foibles, coupled with great tenderness of heart. Men and women amused Lincoln, but so long as they were sincere he loved them and sympathized with them. He was human in the best sense of that fine word.

# CHAPTER VIII

ELECTIONEERING IN ILLINOIS IN 1834—LINCOLN READS LAW
—FIRST TERM AS ASSEMBLYMAN—LINCOLN'S FIRST GREAT
SORROW

Now that the store was closed and his surveying increased,
Lincoln had an excellent opportunity to extend his acquaintance by traveling about the country. Everywhere he won
friends. The surveyor naturally was respected for his calling's sake, but the new deputy surveyor was admired for his
friendly ways, his willingness to lend a hand indoors as well
as out, his learning, his ambition, his independence.
Throughout the county he began to be regarded as a "right
smart young man." Some of his associates appear even to
have comprehended his peculiarly great character and dimly
to have foreseen a splendid future. "Often," says Daniel
Green Burner, at one time clerk in Berry and Lincoln's grocery, "I have heard my brother-in-law, Dr. Duncan, say he
would not be surprised if some day Abe Lincoln got to be
governor of Illinois. Lincoln," Mr. Burner adds, "was
thought to know a little more than anybody else among the
young people. He was a good debater, and liked it. He read
much, and seemed never to forget anything."

Lincoln was fully conscious of his popularity, and it
seemed to him in 1834 that he could safely venture to try
again for the legislature. Accordingly he announced himself
as a candidate, spending much of the summer of 1834 in electioneering. It was a repetition of what he had done in 1832,
though on the larger scale made possible by wider acquaintance. In company with the other candidates he rode up and

down the county, making speeches in the public squares, in shady groves, now and then in a log school-house. In his speeches he soon distinguished himself by the amazing candor with which he dealt with all questions, and by his curious blending of audacity and humility. Wherever he saw a crowd of men he joined them, and he never failed to adapt himself to their point of view in asking for votes. If the degree of physical strength was their test for a candidate, he was ready to lift a weight, or wrestle with the countryside champion; if the amount of grain a man could cut would recommend him, he seized the cradle and showed the swath he could cut. The campaign was well conducted, for in August he was elected one of the four assemblymen from Sangamon.

The best thing which Lincoln did in the canvass of 1834 was not winning votes; it was coming to a determination to read law, not for pleasure, but as a business. In his autobiographical notes he says: "During the canvass, in a private conversation, Major John T. Stuart (one of his fellow-candidates) encouraged Abraham to study law. After the election he borrowed books of Stuart, took them home with him and went at it in good earnest. He never studied with anybody." He seems to have thrown himself into the work with almost impatient ardor. As he tramped back and forth from Springfield, twenty miles away, to get his law books, he read sometimes forty pages or more on the way. Often he was seen wandering at random across the fields, repeating aloud the points in his last reading. The subject seemed never to be out of his mind. It was the great absorbing interest of his life. The rule he gave twenty years later to a young man who wanted to know how to become a lawyer, was the one he practiced:

"Get books and read and study them carefully. Begin with Blackstone's 'Commentaries,' and after reading carefully through, say twice, take Chitty's 'Pleadings,' Greenleaf's 'Evidence,' and Story's 'Equity,' in succession. Work, work, work is the main thing."

Having secured a book of legal forms, he was soon able to write deeds, contracts, and all sorts of legal instruments; and he was frequently called upon by his neighbors to perform services of this kind. "In 1834," says Daniel Green Burner, "my father, Isaac Burner, sold out to Henry Onstott, and he wanted a deed written. I knew how handy Lincoln was that way and suggested that we get him. We found him sitting on a stump. 'All right,' said he, when informed what we wanted. 'If you will bring me a pen and ink and a piece of paper I will write it here.' I brought him these articles, and, picking up a shingle and putting it on his knee for a desk, he wrote out the deed."

As there was no practising lawyer nearer than Springfield, Lincoln was often employed to act the part of advocate before the village squire, at that time Bowling Green. He realized that this experience was valuable, and never, so far as known, demanded or accepted a fee for his services in these petty cases.

Justice was sometimes administered in a summary way in Squire Green's court. Precedents and the venerable rules of law had little weight. The "Squire" took judicial notice of a great many facts, often going so far as to fill, simultaneously, the two functions of witness and court. But his decisions were generally just.

James McGrady Rutledge tells a story in which several of Lincoln's old friends figure and which illustrates the legal practices of New Salem. "Jack Kelso," says Mr. Rutledge, "owned, or claimed to own, a white hog. It was also claimed by John Ferguson. The hog had wandered around Bowling Green's place, until he felt somewhat acquainted with it. Ferguson sued Kelso, and the case was tried before 'Squire'

Green. The plaintiff produced two witnesses who testified positively that the hog belonged to him. Kelso had nothing to offer, save his own unsupported claim.

" 'Are there any more witnesses?' inquired the court.
"He was informed that there were no more.
" 'Well,' said 'Squire' Green, 'the two witnesses we have heard have sworn to a —— lie. I know this shoat, and I know it belongs to Jack Kelso. I therefore decide this case in his favor.' "

An extract from the record of the County Commissioners' Court illustrates the nature of the cases that came before the justice of the peace in Lincoln's day. It also shows the price put upon the privilege of working on Sunday, in 1832:

"JANUARY 29, 1832.—Alexander Gibson found guilty of Sabbath-breaking and fined 12½ cents. Fine paid into court.
    "(Signed)       EDWARD ROBINSON, J. P."

The session of the Ninth Assembly began December 1, 1834, and Lincoln went to the capital, then Vandalia, seventy-five miles southeast of New Salem, on the Kaskaskia river, in time for the opening. Vandalia was a town which had been called into existence in 1820 especially to give the State government an abiding place. Its very name had been chosen, it is said, because it "sounded well" for a State capital. As the tradition goes, while the commissioners were debating what they should call the town they were making, a wag suggested that it be named Vandalia, in honor of the Vandals, a tribe of Indians which, he said, had once lived on the borders of the Kaskaskia; this, he argued, would conserve a local tradition while giving a euphonious title. The commissioners, pleased with so good a suggestion, adopted the name. When Lincoln first went to Vandalia it was a town of about eight hundred inhabitants; its noteworthy features, according to Peck's "Gazetteer" of Illinois for 1834, being a brick court-house, a two-story brick edifice "used by State officers," "a neat framed house of worship for the Presbyterian Society, with a cupola and bell," "a framed meeting-house for the Methodist Society," three taverns, several stores, five lawyers, four physicians, a land office, and two newspapers. It was a much larger town than Lincoln had ever lived in before, though he was familiar with Springfield, then twice as large as Vandalia, and he had seen the cities of the Mississippi.

The Assembly which he entered was composed of eighty-one members—twenty-six senators and fifty-five representatives. As a rule, these men were of Kentucky, Tennessee, or Virginia origin, with here and there a Frenchman. There were but few eastern men, for there was still a strong prejudice in the State against Yankees. The close bargains and superior airs of the emigrants from New England contrasted so unpleasantly with the open-handed hospitality and the easy ways of the Southerners and French, that a pioneer's prospects were blasted at the start if he acted like a Yankee. A history of Illinois in 1837, published evidently to "boom" the State, cautioned the emigrant that if he began his life in Illinois by "affecting superior intelligence and virtue, and catechizing the people for their habits of plainness and simplicity and their apparent want of those things which he imagines indispensable to comfort," he must expect to be forever marked as "a Yankee," and to have his prospects correspondingly defeated. A "hard-shell" Baptist preacher of about this date showed the feeling of the people when he said, in preaching of the richness of the grace of the Lord: "It tuks in the isles of the sea and the uttermust part of the yeth. It embraces the Esquimaux and the Hottentots, and some, my dear brethering, go so far as to suppose that it tuks in the poor benighted Yankees, but *I don't go that fur.*"

When it came to an election of legislators, many of the people "didn't go that fur" either.

There was a preponderance of jean suits like Lincoln's in the Assembly, and there were occasional coonskin caps and buckskin trousers. Nevertheless, more than one member showed a studied garb and a courtly manner. Some of the best blood of the South went into the making of Illinois, and it showed itself from the first in the Assembly. The surroundings of the legislators were quite as simple as the attire of the plainest of them. The court-house, in good old Colonial style, with square pillars and belfry, was finished with wooden desks and benches. The State furnished her law-makers few perquisites beyond their three dollars a day. A cork inkstand, a certain number of quills, and a limited amount of stationery were all the extras an Illinois legislator in 1834 got from his position. Scarcely more could be expected from a State whose revenues from December 1, 1834, to December 1, 1836, were only about one hundred and twenty-five thousand dollars, with expenditures during the same period amounting to less than one hundred and sixty-five thousand dollars.

Lincoln thought little of these things, no doubt. To him the absorbing interest was the men he met. To get acquainted with them, measure them, compare himself with them, and discover wherein they were his superiors and what he could do to make good his deficiency—this was his chief occupation. The men he met were good subjects for such study. Among them were William L. D. Ewing, Jesse K. Dubois, Stephen T. Logan, Theodore Ford, and Governor Duncan—men destined to play large parts in the history of the State. One whom he met that winter in Vandalia was destined to play a great part in the history of the nation—the Democratic candidate for the office of State attorney for the first judicial district of Illinois; a man four years younger

(8)

than Lincoln—he was only twenty-one at the time; a new-comer, too, in the State, having arrived about a year before, under no very promising auspices either, for he had only thirty-seven cents in his pockets, and no position in view; but a man of mettle, it was easy to see, for already he had risen so high in the district where he had settled, that he dared con-test the office of State attorney with John J. Hardin, one of the most successful lawyers of the State. This young man was Stephen A. Douglas. He had come to Vandalia from Morgan county to conduct his campaign, and Lincoln met him first in the halls of the old court-house, where he and his friends carried on with success their contest against Hardin.

The ninth Assembly gathered in a more hopeful and am-bitious mood than any of its predecessors. Illinois was feel-ing well. The State was free from debt. The Black Hawk war had stimulated the people greatly, for it had brought a large amount of money into circulation. In fact, the greater portion of the eight to ten million dollars the war had cost, had been circulated among the Illinois volunteers. Immigra-tion, too, was increasing at a bewildering rate. In 1835 the census showed a population of 269,974. Between 1830 and 1835 two-fifths of this number had come in. In the northeast Chicago had begun to rise. "Even for a western town," its growth had been unusually rapid, declared Peck's "Gazet-teer," of 1834; the harbor building there, the proposed Michi-gan and Illinois canal, the rise in town lots—all promised to the State a great metropolis. To meet the rising tide of prosperity, the legislators of 1834 felt that they must devise some worthy scheme, so they chartered a new State bank, with a capital of one million five hundred thousand dollars, and revived a bank which had broken twelve years before, granting it a charter of three hundred thousand dollars. There was no surplus money in the State to supply the capital; there were no trained bankers to guide the concern; there was no clear notion of how it was all to be done; but a banking capital of one million eight hundred thousand dollars would be a good thing in the State, they were sure; and if the East could be made to believe in Illinois as much as her legislators believed in her, the stocks would go; and so the banks were chartered.

But even more important to the State than banks was a highway. For thirteen years plans for the Illinois and Michigan canal had been constantly before the Assembly.  Surveys had been ordered, estimates reported, the advantages extolled, but nothing had been done.  Now, however, the Assembly, flushed by the first thrill of the coming boom, decided to authorize a loan of a half-million on the credit of the State.  Lincoln favored both these measures.  He did not, however, do anything especially noteworthy for either of the bills, nor was the record he made in other directions at all remarkable.  He was placed on the committee of public accounts and expenditures, and attended meetings with fidelity.  His first act as a member was to give notice that he would ask leave to introduce a bill limiting the jurisdiction of justices of the peace—a measure which he succeeded in carrying through.  He followed this by a motion to change the rules, so that it should not be in order to offer amendments to any bill after the third reading, which was not agreed to; though the same rule, in effect, was adopted some years later, and is to this day in force in both branches of the Illinois Assembly.  He next made a motion to take from the table a report which had been submitted by his committee, which met a like fate.  His first resolution, relating to a State revenue to be derived from the sales of the public lands, was denied a reference, and laid upon the table.  Neither as a speaker nor an organizer did he make any especial impression on the body.

In the spring of 1835 the young representative from San-gamon returned to New Salem to take up his duties as post-master and deputy surveyor, and to resume his law studies. He exchanged his rather exalted position for the humbler one with a light heart. New Salem held all that was dear-est in the world to him at that moment, and he went back to the poor little town with a hope, which he had once sup-posed honor forbade his acknowledging even to himself, glowing warmly in his heart. He loved a young girl of that town, and now for the first time, though he had known her since he first came to New Salem, was he free to tell his love.

One of the most prominent families of the settlement in 1831, when Lincoln first appeared there, was that of James Rutledge. The head of the house was one of the founders of New Salem, and at that time the keeper of the village tavern. He was a high-minded man, of a warm and gener-ous nature, and had the universal respect of the community. He was a South Carolinian by birth, but had lived many years in Kentucky before coming to Illinois. Rutledge came of a distinguished family: one of his ancestors signed the Declaration of Independence; another was chief justice of the Supreme Court of the United States by appointment of Washington, and another was a conspicuous leader in the American Congress.

The third of the nine children in the Rutledge household was a daughter, Ann Mayes, born in Kentucky, January 7, 1813. When Lincoln first met her she was nineteen years old, and as fresh as a flower. Many of those who knew her at that time have left tributes to her beauty and gentleness, and even to-day there are those living who talk of her with moistened eyes and softened tones. "She was a beautiful girl," says her cousin, James McGrady Rutledge, "and as bright as she was beautiful. She was well educated for that early day, a good conversationalist, and always gentle and cheerful. A girl whose company people liked." So fair a maid was not, of course, without suitors. The most determined of those who sought her hand was one John McNeill, a young man who had arrived in New Salem from New York soon after the founding of the town. Nothing was known of his antecedents, and no questions were asked. He was understood to be merely one of the thousands who had come west in search of fortune. That he was intelligent, industrious, and frugal, with a good head for business, was at once apparent; for in four years from his first appearance in the settlement, besides earning a half-interest in a general store, McNeill had acquired a large farm a few miles north of New Salem. His neighbors believed him to be worth about twelve thousand dollars.

John McNeill was an unmarried man—at least so he represented himself to be—and very soon after becoming a resident of New Salem he formed the acquaintance of Ann Rutledge, then a girl of seventeen. It was a case of love at first sight, and the two soon became engaged, in spite of the rivalry of Samuel Hill, McNeill's partner. But Ann was as yet only a young girl; and it was thought very sensible in her and considerate in her lover that both acquiesced in the wishes of Ann's parents that, for some time at least, the marriage be postponed.

Such was the situation when Lincoln appeared in New Salem. He naturally soon became acquainted with the girl. She was a pupil in Mentor Graham's school, where he frequently visited, and rumor says that he first met her there. However that may be, it is certain that in the latter part of 1832 he went to board at the Rutledge tavern and there was thrown daily into her company.

During the next year, 1833, John McNeill, in spite of his fair prospects, became restless and discontented. He wanted to see his people. he said. and before the end of the year he decided to go East for a visit. To secure perfect freedom from his business while gone, he sold out his interest in his store. To Ann he said that he hoped to bring back his father and mother, and to place them on his farm. "This duty done," was his farewell word, "you and I will be married." In the spring of 1834 McNeill started East. The journey overland by foot and horse was in those days a trying one, and on the way McNeill fell ill with chills and fever. It was late in the summer before he reached his home, and wrote back to Ann, explaining his silence. The long wait had been a severe strain on the girl, and Lincoln had watched her anxiety with softened heart. It was to him, the New Salem postmaster, that she came to inquire for letters. It was to him she entrusted those she sent. In a way the postmaster must have become the girl's confidant; and his tender heart must have been deeply touched. After the long silence was broken, and McNeill's first letter of explanation came, the cause of anxiety seemed removed; but, strangely enough, other letters followed only at long intervals, and finally they ceased altogether. Then it was that the young girl told her friends a secret which McNeill had confided to her before leaving New Salem.

He had told her what she had never even suspected before, that John McNeill was not his real name, but that it was John McNamar. Shortly before he came to New Salem, he explained, his father had suffered a disastrous failure in business. He was the oldest son; and in the hope of retrieving the lost fortune, he resolved to go West, expecting to return in a few years and share his riches with the rest of the family. Anticipating parental opposition, he ran away from home; and, being sure that he could never accumulate anything with so numerous a family to support, he endeavored to lose himself by a change of name. All this Ann had believed and not repeated; but now, worn out by waiting, she took the story to her friends.

With few exceptions they pronounced the story a fabrication and McNamar an impostor. His excuse seemed flimsy. Why had he worn this mask? At best, they declared, he was a mere adventurer; and was it not more probable that he was a fugitive from justice—a thief, a swindler, or a murderer? And who knew how many wives he might have? With all New Salem declaring John McNamar false, Ann Rutledge could hardly be blamed for imagining that he was dead or had forgotten her.

It was not until McNeill, or McNamar, had been gone many months, and gossip had become offensive, that Lincoln ventured to show his love for Ann, and then it was a long time before the girl would listen to his suit. Convinced at last, however, that her former lover had deserted her, she yielded to Lincoln's wishes and promised, in the spring of 1835, soon after Lincoln's return from Vandalia, to become his wife. But Lincoln had nothing on which to support a family—indeed, he found it no trifling task to support himself. As for Ann, she was anxious to go to school another year. It was decided that in the autumn she should go with her brother to Jacksonville and spend the winter there in an academy. Lincoln was to devote himself to his law studies; and the next spring, when she returned from school and he had been admitted to the bar, they were to be married.

A happy spring and summer followed. New Salem took a cordial interest in the two lovers and presaged a happy life for them, and all would undoubtedly have gone well if the young girl could have dismissed the haunting memory of her old lover. The possibility that she had wronged him, that he might reappear, that he loved her still, though she now loved another, that perhaps she had done wrong—a torturing conflict of memory, love, conscience, doubt, and mor-

bidness lay like a shadow across her happiness, and wore
upon her until she fell ill.    Gradually her condition became
hopeless; and Lincoln, who had been shut from her, was sent
for.    The lovers passed an hour alone in an anguished parting, and soon after, on August 25, 1835, Ann died.

The death of Ann Rutledge plunged Lincoln into the deepest gloom.    That abiding melancholy, that painful sense of
the incompleteness of life which had been his mother's dowry
asserted itself.    It filled and darkened his mind and his
imagination tortured him with its black pictures.    One
stormy night Lincoln was sitting beside William Greene, his
head bowed on his hand, while tears trickled through his
fingers; his friend begged him to control his sorrow, to try
to forget.    "I cannot," moaned Lincoln; "the thought of
the snow and rain on her grave fills me with indescribable
grief."

He was seen walking alone by the river and through the
woods, muttering strange things to himself.    He seemed
to his friends to be in the shadow of madness.    They kept
a close watch over him; and at last Bowling Green, one of
the most devoted friends Lincoln then had, took him home
to his little log cabin, half a mile north of New Salem, under
the brow of a big bluff.    Here, under the loving care of
Green, and his good wife Nancy, Lincoln remained until he
was once more master of himself.

But though he had regained self-control, his grief was
deep and bitter.    Ann Rutledge was buried in Concord cem-
etery, a country burying-ground seven miles northwest of
New Salem.    To this lonely spot Lincoln frequently journeyed to weep over her grave.    "My heart is buried there,"
he said to one of his friends.

When McNamar returned (for McNamar's story was
true, and two months after Ann Rutledge died he drove into
New Salem with his widowed mother and his brothers and

sisters in the "prairie schooner" beside him) and learned of
Ann's death, he "saw Lincoln at the post-office," as he afterward said, and "he seemed desolate and sorely distressed."
On himself apparently, her death produced no deep impression. Within a year he married another woman; and his
conduct toward Ann Rutledge is to this day a mystery.

In later life, when Lincoln's sorrow had become a
memory, he told a friend who questioned him: "I really and
truly loved the girl and think often of her now." There was
a pause, and then the President added:

"And I have loved the name of Rutledge to this day."

When the death of Ann Rutledge came upon Lincoln, for
a time threatening to destroy his ambition and blast his life,
he was in a most encouraging position. Master of a profession in which he had an abundance of work and earned fair
fees, hopeful of being admitted in a few months to the bar,
a member of the State Assembly with every reason to believe
that, if he desired it, his constituency would return him—few
men are as far advanced at twenty-six as was Abraham Lincoln.

Intellectually he was far better equipped than he believed
himself to be, better than he has ordinarily been credited with
being. True, he had had no conventional college training,
but he had by his own efforts attained the chief result of all
preparatory study, the ability to take hold of a subject and
assimilate it. The fact that in six weeks he had acquired
enough of the science of surveying to enable him to serve as
deputy surveyor shows how well-trained his mind was. The
power to grasp a large subject quickly and fully is never an
accident. The nights Lincoln spent in Gentryville lying on
the floor in front of the fire figuring on the fire-shovel, the
hours he passed in poring over the Statutes of Indiana, the
days he wrestled with Kirkham's Grammar, alone made the
mastery of Flint and Gibson possible. His struggle with

Flint and Gibson made easier the volumes he borrowed from Major Stuart's law library.

Lincoln had a mental trait which explains his rapid growth in mastering subjects—seeing clearly was essential to him. He was unable to put a question aside until he understood it. It pursued him, irritated him until solved. Even in his Gentryville days his comrades noted that he was constantly searching for reasons and that he "explained so clearly." This characteristic became stronger with years. He was unwilling to pronounce himself on any subject until he understood it, and he could not let it alone until he had reached a conclusion which satisfied him.

This seeing clearly became a splendid force in Lincoln; for when he once had reached a conclusion he had the honesty of soul to suit his actions to it. No consideration could induce him to abandon the line of conduct which his reason told him was logical. Joined to these strong mental and moral qualities was that power of immediate action which so often explains why one man succeeds in life while another of equal intelligence and uprightness fails. As soon as Lincoln saw a thing to do he did it. He wants to know; here is a book—it may be a biography, a volume of dry statutes, a collection of verse; no matter, he reads and ponders it until he has absorbed all it has for him. He is eager to see the world; a man offers him a position as a " hand " on a Mississippi flatboat; he takes it without a moment's hesitation over the toil and exposure it demands. John Calhoun is willing to make him a deputy surveyor; he knows nothing of the science; in six weeks he has learned enough to begin his labors. Sangamon county must have representatives, why not he? and his circular goes out. Ambition alone will not explain this power of instantaneous action. It comes largely from that active imagination which, when a new relation or position opens, seizes on all its possibilities and from them creates a situation so real that one enters with confidence upon what seems to the unimaginative the rashest undertaking. Lincoln saw the possibilities in things and immediately appreciated them.

But the position he filled in Sangamon county in 1835 was not all due to these qualities; much was due to his personal charm. By all accounts he was big, awkward, ill-clad, shy— yet his sterling honor, his unselfish nature, his heart of the true gentleman, inspired respect and confidence. Men might laugh at his first appearance, but they were not long in recognizing the real superiority of his nature.

Such was Abraham Lincoln at twenty-six, when the tragic death of Ann Rutledge made all that he had attained, all that he had planned, seem fruitless and empty. He was too sincere and just, too brave a man, to allow a great sorrow permanently to interfere with his activities. He rallied his forces, and returned to his law, his surveying, his politics. He brought to his work a new power, that insight and patience which only a great sorrow can give.

# CHAPTER IX

THE Ninth General Assembly of Illinois held its opening
session in the winter of 1834-35. It was Lincoln's first experience as a legislator and it was rather a tame one, but in
December, 1835, the members were called to an extra session which proved to be in every way more exciting and more
eventful than its predecessors. The chief reason for its being called was in itself calculated to exhilarate the hopeful
young law-givers. A census had been taken since their last
session and so large an increase in population had been reported that it was considered necessary to summon the assembly to re-apportion the legislative districts. When the reapportionment was made it was found that the General Assembly was increased by fifty members, the number of senators being raised from twenty-six to forty, of representatives from fifty-five to ninety-one. A growth of fifty members in four years excited the imagination of the State. The
dignity and importance of Illinois suddenly assumed new importance. It was imagined that the story of New York's
growth in wealth and influence was to be repeated in this
new country and every ambitious man in the assembly determined to lead in the rise of the State.

The work on internal improvements begun in the
previous session took a new form. The governor, in calling
the members together, had said: "While I would urge the
most liberal support of all such measures as tending with perfect certainty to increase the wealth and prosperity of the

State, I would at the same time most respectfully suggest the propriety of intrusting the construction of all such works where it can be done consistently with the general interest, to individual enterprise." The legislators acquiesced and in this session began to grant a series of private charters for internal improvements which had they been carried out, would have given the State means of communication in 1840 almost if not quite equal to those of to-day. The map on page 135 shows the incorporations of railroad and canal companies made in the extra session of the Ninth Assembly, 1835-36, and in the regular session of the Tenth, 1836-37; sixteen of the railroads were chartered in the former session.

Lincoln and his colleagues did not devote their attention entirely to chartering railroads. Ten schools were chartered in this same session, some of which exist to-day. In the next session twelve academies and eighteen colleges received charters.

The absorbing topic of the winter, however, and the one in which Lincoln was chiefly concerned was the threatened naturalization of the convention system in Illinois. Up to this time candidates for office in the United States had generally nominated themselves as we have seen Lincoln doing. The only formality they imposed upon themselves was to consult a little unauthorized caucus of personal friends. Unless they were exceptionally cautious persons the disapproval of this caucus did not stand in their way at all. So long as party lines were indistinct and the personal qualities of a candidate were considered rather than his platform this method of nomination was possible, but with party organization it began to change. In the case of presidential candidates the convention with its delegates and platform had just appeared, the first full-fledged one being held but three years before, in 1832. Along with the presidential convention came the "machine," an organization of all those who belonged to a party, intended to secure unity of effort. By means of primaries and conventions one candidate was put forward by a party instead of a dozen being allowed to offer themselves. The strength which the convention gave the Democratic party, which first adopted and developed it, was enormous. The Whigs opposed the new institution; they declared it "was intended to abridge the liberties of the people by depriving individuals, on their own mere motion, of the privilege of becoming candidates and depriving each man of the right to vote for a candidate of his own selection and choice."

The efficacy of the new method was so apparent, however, that, let the Whigs preach as they would, it was rapidly adopted. In 1835 the whole machinery was well developed in New England and New York and had appeared in the West. In the north of Illinois the Democrats had begun to organize under the leadership of two men of eastern origin and training, Ebenezer Peck of Chicago, and Stephen A. Douglas of Jacksonville, and this session of the Illinois legislature the convention system became a subject of discussion.

The Whigs, Lincoln among them, violently opposed the new scheme. It was a Yankee contrivance they said, favored only by New Englanders like Douglas, or worse still by monarchists like Peck. They recalled with pious indignation that Peck was a Canadian, brought up under an aristocratic form of government, that he had even deserted the liberal party of this government to go over to the ultramonarchists. They declared it a remarkable fact that no man born and raised west of the mountains or south of the Potomac had yet returned to vindicate "the wholesale system of convention." In spite of Whig warnings, however, the convention system was approved by a vote of twenty-six to twenty-five.

The Ninth Assembly expired at the close of this extra ses-

sion and in June Lincoln announced himself as a candidate
for the Tenth Assembly.  A few days later the "Sangamon
Journal" published his simple platform:

"New Salem, June 13, 1836.

"To the Editor of the 'Journal':

"In your paper of last Saturday I see a communication,
over the signature of 'Many Voters,' in which the candidates
who are announced in the 'Journal' are called upon to 'show
their hands.'  Agreed.  Here's mine.

"I go for all sharing the privileges of the government who
assist in bearing its burdens.  Consequently, I go for ad-
mitting all whites to the right of suffrage who pay taxes or
bear arms (by no means excluding females).

"If elected, I shall consider the whole people of Sangamon
my constituents, as well those that oppose as those that support me.

"While acting as their representative, I shall be governed
by their will on all subjects upon which I have the means of
knowing what their will is; and upon all others I shall do
what my own judgment teaches me will best advance their
interests.  Whether elected or not, I go for distributing the
proceeds of the sales of the public lands to the several States,
to enable our State, in common with others, to dig canals and
construct railroads without borrowing money and paying
the interest on it.

"If alive on the first Monday in November, I shall vote
for Hugh L. White for President.

"Very respectfully,

"A. LINCOLN."

The campaign which Lincoln began with this letter was in
every way more exciting for him than those of 1832 and
1834.  In the reapportionment of the legislative districts
which had taken place the winter before Sangamon County's
delegation had been enlarged to seven representatives and
two senators.  This gave large new opportunities to political
ambition, and doubled the enthusiasm of political meetings.

But the increase of the representation was not all that made the campaign exciting. Party lines had never before been so clearly drawn in Sangamon county, nor personal abuse quite so frank. One of Lincoln's first acts was to answer a personal attack. During his absence from New Salem a rival candidate passed through the place and stated publicly that he was in possession of facts which, if known to the public, would entirely destroy Lincoln's prospects at the coming election; but he declared that he thought so much of Lincoln that he would not tell what he knew. Lincoln met this mysterious insinuation with shrewd candor. "No one has needed favors more than I," he wrote his rival, "and generally few have been less unwilling to accept them; but in this case favor to me would be injustice to the public, and therefore I must beg your pardon for declining it. That I once had the confidence of the people of Sangamon County is sufficiently evident; and if I have done anything, either by design or misadventure, which if known would subject me to a forfeiture of that confidence, he that knows of that thing and conceals it is a traitor to his country's interest.

"I find myself wholly unable to form any conjecture of what fact or facts, real or supposed, you spoke; but my opinion of your veracity will not permit me for a moment to doubt that you at least believed what you said. I am flattered with the personal regard you manifested for me; but I do hope that on mature reflection you will view the public interest as a paramount consideration and therefore let the worst come."

Usually during the campaign Lincoln was obliged to meet personal attacks, not by letter, but on the platform. Joshua Speed, who later became the most intimate friend that Lincoln probably ever had, tells of one occasion when he was obliged to meet such an attack on the very spur of the moment. A great mass-meeting was in progress at Springfield, and Lincoln had made a speech which had produced a deep impression.

" I was then fresh from Kentucky," says Mr. Speed, " and had heard many of her great orators. It seemed to me then, as it seems to me now, that I never heard a more effective speaker. He carried the crowd with him, and swayed them as he pleased. So deep an impression did he make that George Forquer, a man of much celebrity as a sarcastic speaker and with a great reputation throughout the State as an orator, rose and asked the people to hear *him*. He began his speech by saying that this young man would have to be taken down, and he was sorry that the task devolved upon him. He made what was called one of his 'slasher-gaff' speeches, dealing much in ridicule and sarcasm. Lincoln stood near him, with his arms folded, never interrupting him. When Forquer was done, Lincoln walked to the stand, and replied so fully and completely that his friends bore him from the court-house on their shoulders.

"So deep an impression did this first speech make upon me that I remember its conclusion now, after a lapse of thirty-eight years.

" 'The gentleman commenced his speech,' he said, 'by saying that this young man would have to be taken down, and he was sorry the task devolved upon him. I am not so young in years as I am in the tricks and trade of a politician; but live long or die young, I would rather die now than, like the gentleman, change my politics and simultaneous with the change receive an office worth three thousand dollars a year, and then have to erect a lightning-rod over my house to protect a guilty conscience from an offended God.'

"To understand the point of this it must be explained that Forquer had been a Whig, but had changed his politics, and had been appointed Register of the Land Office; and over his house was the only lightning-rod in the town or county. Lincoln had seen the lightning-rod for the first time on the day before."

This speech has never been forgotten in Springfield, and on my visits there I have repeatedly had the site of the house on which this particular lightning-rod was placed pointed out, and one or another of the many versions which the story has taken, related to me.

It was the practice at that date in Illinois for two rival candidates to travel over the district together. The custom led to much good-natured raillery between them; and in such contests Lincoln was rarely, if ever, worsted. He could even turn the generosity of a rival to account by his whimsical treatment. On one occasion, says Mr. Weir, a former resident of Sangamon county, he had driven out from Springfield in company with a political opponent to engage in joint debate. The carriage, it seems, belonged to his opponent. In addressing the gathering of farmers that met them, Lincoln was lavish in praise of the generosity of his friend. "I am too poor to own a carriage," he said, "but my friend has generously invited me to ride with him. I want you to vote for me if you will; but if not then vote for my opponent, for he is a fine man." His extravagant and persistent praise of his opponent appealed to the sense of humor in his rural audience, to whom his inability to own a carriage was by no means a disqualification.

The election came off in August, and resulted in the choice of a delegation from Sangamon County famous in the annals of Illinois. The nine successful candidates were Abraham Lincoln, John Dawson, Daniel Stone, Ninian W. Edwards, William F. Elkins, R. L. Wilson, Andrew McCormick, Job Fletcher, and Arthur Herndon. Each one of these men was over six feet in height, their combined stature being, it is said, fifty-five feet. "The Long Nine" was the name Sangamon County gave them.

As soon as the election was over Lincoln occupied himself in settling another matter, of much greater moment. He went to Springfield to seek admission to the bar. The "roll of attorneys and counsellors at law," on file in the office of the

# Map of Albany.

Third     Street

Public
Square

Second     Street

First     Street

Meridian     Street

Explanation

Head of Map Due North
Width of Street 66 feet
Do Alley 16 do
Front of Lots 66 do
Depth do 124 do
Stone at the S.W.
corner of the Public
square.

Blocks Nos. 1, 2, 3
4, 5. and the Public
Square are situated
on the West half
of the N.E. quarter
of Section 6. and
are the property of
John Wright. Blocks
6 and 7 are situated
on the West half of
the N.E. quarter of
Section 7 and
are the property of
John Donovan. Both tracts are of Township 19 North of
Range 3 West.

I hereby certify that the above is a correct
Map of the town of Albany, as surveyed by me

June 16th 1856

A. Lincoln
for T. M. Neale S.S.C.

FACSIMILE OF A MAP OF ALBANY, ILL., MADE BY LINCOLN.

clerk of the Supreme Court of Springfield, Illinois, shows that his license was dated September 9, 1836, and that the date of the enrollment of his name upon the official list was March 1, 1837. The first case in which he was concerned, as far as we know, was that of Hawthorne against Woolridge. He made his first appearance in court in October, 1836.

Although he had given much time during this year to politics and the law, he had by no means abandoned surveying. Indeed he never had more calls. The grandiose scheme of internal improvements initiated the winter before had stimulated speculation and Lincoln frequently was obliged to be away for three and four weeks at a time, laying out new towns or locating new roads.

Every such trip added to his political capital. Such was his reputation throughout the country that when he got a job, says the Hon. J. M. Ruggles, a friend and political supporter, there was a picnic and jolly time in the neighborhood. Men and boys gathered from far and near, ready to carry chain, drive stakes, and blaze trees, if they could only hear Lincoln's odd stories and jokes. The fun was interspersed with foot races and wrestling matches. To this day the old settlers in many a place of central Illinois repeat the incidents of Lincoln's sojourns in their neighborhood while surveying their town.

In December Lincoln put away his surveying instruments to go to Vandalia for the opening session of the Tenth Assembly. Larger by fifty members than its predecessor, this body was as much superior in intellect as in numbers. It included among its members a future President of the United States, a future candidate for the same high office, six future United States Senators, eight future members of the National House of Representatives, a future Secretary of the Interior, and three future Judges of the State Supreme Court. Here sat side by side Abraham Lincoln and Stephen A.

Douglas; Edward Dickinson Baker, who represented at different times the States of Illinois and Oregon in the national councils; O. H. Browning, a prospective senator and future cabinet officer, and William L. D. Ewing, who had just served in the senate; John Logan, father of the late General John A. Logan; Robert M. Cullom, father of Senator Shelby M. Cullom; John A. McClernand, afterwards member of congress for many years, and a distinguished general in the late civil war; and many others of national repute.

The members came to Vandalia full of hope and exultation. In their judgment it needed only a few months of legislation to put their State by the side of New York; and from the opening of the session they were overflowing with excitement and schemes. In the general ebullition of spirits which characterized the assembly, Lincoln had little share. Only a week after the opening of the session he wrote to a friend, Mary Owens, at New Salem, that he had been ill, though he believed himself to be about well then; and he added: "But that, with other things I cannot account for, have conspired, and have gotten my spirits so low that I feel I would rather be any place in the world than here. I really cannot endure the thought of staying here ten weeks."

Though depressed, he was far from being inactive. The Sangamon delegation, in fact, had its hands full, and to no one of the nine had more been entrusted than to Lincoln. In common with almost every delegation, they had been instructed by their constituents to adopt a scheme of internal improvements complete enough to give every budding town in Illinois easy communication with the world. This for the State in general; for Sangamon County in particular, they had been directed to secure the capital. The change in the State's centre of population made it advisable to move the seat of government northward from Vandalia, and Springfield was anxious to secure it. To Lincoln was entrusted the work of putting through the bill to remove the capital. In the same letter quoted from above he tells Miss Owens: "Our chance to take the seat of government to Springfield is better than I expected." Regarding the internal improvements scheme he feels less confident: "Some of the legislature are for it, and some against; which has the majority, I cannot tell."

It was not long, however, before all uncertainty about internal improvements was over. The people were determined to have them, and the assembly responded to their demands by passing an act which provided, at State expense, for railroads, canals, or river improvements in almost every county in Illinois. No finer bit of imaginative work was ever done, in fact, by a legislative body, than the map of internal improvements laid out by the Tenth Assembly.

With splendid disdain of town settlements and resources they ran the railroads into the counties they thought ought to be opened up, and if there was no terminus they laid out one. They improved the rivers and they dug canals, they built bridges and drained the swamps, they planned to make the waste places blossom and to people the forests with men. This project was to benefit every hamlet of the State, said its defenders, and to compensate the counties which were not to have railroads or canals they voted them a sum of money for roads and bridges.

There was no time to estimate exactly the cost of these fine plans. Nor did they feel any need of estimates; that was a mere matter of detail. They would vote a fund, and when that was exhausted they would vote more; and so they appropriated sum after sum: one hundred thousand dollars to improve the Rock river; one million eight hundred thousand dollars to build a road from Quincy to Danville; four million dollars to complete the Illinois and Michigan Canal; two hundred and fifty thousand for the Western Mail Route

MAP OF
**ILLINOIS**
ILLUSTRATING
*"An Act to establish and maintain a
General System of Internal Improvements,
In force 27th Feb. 1837"*

SCALE OF MILES

0  10  20  30  40  50  60

GOV. FARQUHAR, DEL.

BRADLEY & POATES, ENGR'S, N.Y.

—in all, some twelve million dollars. To carry out the elaborate scheme, they provided a commission, one of the first
duties of which was to sell the bonds of the State to raise the
money for the enterprise. The majority of the assembly
seem not to have entertained for a moment an idea that there
would be any difficulty in selling at a premium the bonds of
Illinois. "On the contrary," says General Linder, in his
"Reminiscences," "the enthusiastic friends of the measure
maintained that, instead of there being any difficulty in obtaining a loan of the fifteen or twenty millions authorized to
be borrowed, our bonds would go like hot cakes, and be
sought for by the Rothschilds, and Baring Brothers, and
others of that stamp; and that the premiums which we would
obtain upon them would range from fifty to one hundred per
cent., and that the premium itself would be sufficient to construct most of the important works, leaving the principal sum
to go into our treasury, and leave the people free from taxation for years to come."

The scheme was carried without difficulty and the work
of raising money and of grading road-beds began almost
simultaneously. All of this seems insane enough to-day,
knowing as we do that it ended in panic and bankruptcy, in
deserted road-beds and unpaid bills, but at that time the
measure seemed to the legislature only the enterprise which
the prospects of the country demanded. Illinois was not alone
in confidence and recklessness. Her folly was that of the
whole country. Never had there been a period of rasher
speculation and inflation. The entire debt of the country had
been paid, and a great income was pouring in on the federal
government. The completion of certain great works like the
Erie Canal had stimulated trade, and greatly increased the
value of lands. Every variety of industry was succeeding.
Capital was pouring in from Europe which seemed dazzled
at the thought of a nation free from debt with a revenue so

great that she was forced to distribute it quarterly to her States as the United States began to do in January, 1837. An exaggerated confidence in regard to the future of the country possessed both foreign and domestic capitalist. Credit was practically unlimited, "Debt was the road to wealth" and men could realize millions on the wildest schemes. Little wonder that Lincoln and his associates, ignorant of the history of finance and governed as they were by popular opinion, fell into the delusion of the day and sought to found a State on credit.

Although Lincoln favored and aided in every way the plan for internal improvements, his real work was in securing the removal of the capital to Springfield. The task was by no means an easy one to direct, for outside of the "Long Nine" there was, of course, nobody particularly interested in Springfield, and there were delegations from a dozen other counties hot to secure the capital for their own constituencies. It took patient and clever manipulation to put the bill through. Certain votes Lincoln, no doubt, gained for his cause by force of his personal qualities. Thus Jesse K. Dubois says that he and his colleagues voted for the bill because they liked Lincoln and wanted to oblige him; but probably the majority he won by skillful log-rolling. The very few letters written by him at this time which have been preserved show this; for instance a letter to John Bennett in which he says:

" Mr. Edwards tells me you wish to know whether the act to which your town incorporation provision was attached passed into a law. It did. You can organize under the general incorporation law as soon as you choose.

"I also tacked a provision on to a fellow's bill, to authorize the relocation of the road from Salem down to your town, but I am not certain whether or not the bill passed. Neither do I suppose I can ascertain before the law will be published —if it is a law."

There is nothing in his correspondence, however, to show that he ever sacrificed his principles in these trades. Everything we know of his transactions are indeed to the contrary. General T. H. Henderson, of Illinois, says in his reminiscences of Lincoln:

" Before I had ever seen Abraham Lincoln I heard my father, who served with him in the legislature of 1838-39 and of 1840-41, relate an incident in Mr. Lincoln's life which illustrates his character for integrity and his firmness in maintaining what he regarded as right in his public acts, in a marked manner.

" I do not remember whether this incident occurred during the session of the legislature in 1836-37 or 1838-39. But I think it was in that of 1836-37, when it was said that there was a great deal of log-rolling going on among the members. But, however that may be, according to the story related by my father, an effort was made to unite the friends of capital removal with the friends of some measure which Mr. Lincoln, for some reason, did not approve. What that measure was to which he objected, I am not now able to recall. But those who desired the removal of the capital to Springfield were very anxious to effect the proposed combination, and a meeting was held to see if it could be accomplished. The meeting continued in session nearly all night, when it adjourned without accomplishing anything, Mr. Lincoln refusing to yield his objections and to support the obnoxious measure.

Another meeting was called, and at this second meeting a number of citizens, not members of the legislature, from the central and northern parts of the State, among them my father, were present by invitation. The meeting was long protracted, and earnest in its deliberations. Every argument that could be thought of was used to induce Mr. Lincoln to yield his objections and unite with his friends, and thus secure the removal of the capital to his own city; but without effect. Finally, after midnight, when everybody seemed exhausted with the discussion, and when the candles were burning low in the room, Mr. Lincoln rose amid the silence and solemnity which prevailed, and, my father said, made one of the most eloquent and powerful speeches to which he had ever listened. He concluded his remarks by saying: 'You may burn my body to ashes, and scatter them to the winds of heaven; you may drag my soul down to the regions of darkness and despair to be tormented forever; but you will never get me to support a measure which I believe to be wrong, although by doing so I may accomplish that which I believe to be right.' And the meeting adjourned."

As was to be expected, the Democrats charged that the Whigs of Sangamon had won their victory by "bargain and corruption." These charges became so serious that, in an extra session called in the summer of 1837, a few months after the bill passed, Lincoln had a bitter fight over them with General L. D. Ewing, who wanted to keep the capital at Vandalia. "The arrogance of Springfield," said General Ewing, "its presumption in claiming the seat of government, is not to be endured; the law has been passed by chicanery and trickery; the Springfield delegation has sold out to the internal improvement men, and has promised its support to every measure that would gain a vote to the law removing the seat of government."

Lincoln answered in a speech of such severity and keenness that the House believed he was "digging his own grave," for Ewing was a high-spirited man who would not hesitate to answer by a challenge. It was, in fact, only the interference of their friends which prevented a duel at this time between Ewing and Lincoln. This speech, to many of Lincoln's colleagues, was a revelation of his ability and character. "This was the first time," said General Linder, "that I began to conceive a very high opinion of the talents and personal courage of Abraham Lincoln."

A few months later the "Long Nine" were again attacked, Lincoln specially being abused. The assailant this time was a prominent Democrat, Mr. J. B. Thomas. When he had ended, Lincoln replied in a speech which was long known in local political circles as the "skinning of Thomas."

No one doubted after this that Lincoln could defend himself. He became doubly respected as an opponent, for his reputation for good-humored raillery had already been established in his campaigns. In a speech made in January he gave another evidence of his skill in the use of ridicule. A resolution had been offered by Mr. Linder to institute an inquiry into the management of the affairs of the State bank. Lincoln's remarks on the resolution form his first reported speech. He began his remarks by good-humored but nettling chaffing of his opponent.

"Mr. Chairman," he said. "Lest I should fall into the too common error of being mistaken in regard to which side I design to be upon, I shall make it my first care to remove all doubt on that point, by declaring that I am opposed to the resolution under consideration, *in toto*. Before I proceed to the body of the subject, I will further remark, that it is not without a considerable degree of apprehension that I venture to cross the track of the gentleman from Coles (Mr. Linder). Indeed, I do not believe I could muster a sufficiency of courage to come in contact with that gentleman, were it not for the fact that he, some days since, most graciously condescended to assure us that he would never be found wasting ammunition on *small game*. On the same fortunate occasion he further gave us to understand that he regarded *himself* as being decidedly the *superior* of our common friend from Randolph (Mr. Shields); and feeling, as I really do, that I, to say the most of myself, am nothing more than the peer of our friend from Randolph, I shall regard the gentleman from Coles as decidedly my superior also; and consequently, in the course of what I shall have to say, whenever I shall have occasion to allude to that gentleman I shall endeavor to adopt that kind of court language which I understand to be due to decided superiority. In one faculty, at least, there can be no dispute of the gentleman's superiority over me, and most other men; and that is, the faculty of entangling a subject so that neither himself, or any other man, can find head or tail to it."

Taking up the resolution on the bank, he declared its meaning:

"Some gentlemen have their stock in their hands, while others, who have more money than they know what to do with, want it; and this, and this alone, is the question, to settle which we are called on to squander thousands of the people's money. What interest, let me ask, have the people in the settlement of this question? What difference is it to them whether the stock is owned by Judge Smith or Sam Wiggins? If any gentleman be entitled to stock in the bank, which he is kept out of possession of by others, let him assert his right in the Supreme Court, and let him or his antagonist, whichever may be found in the wrong, pay the costs of suit. It is an old maxim, and a very sound one, that he that dances should always pay the fiddler. Now, sir, in the present case, if any gentlemen whose money is a burden to them, choose to lead off a dance, I am decidedly opposed to the people's money being used to pay the fiddler. No one can doubt that the examination proposed by this resolution must cost the State some ten or twelve thousand dollars; and all this to settle a question in which the people have no interest, and about which they care nothing. These capitalists generally act harmoniously and in concert to fleece the people; and now that they have got into a quarrel with themselves, we are called upon to appropriate the people's money to settle the quarrel."

The resolution had declared that the bank practised various methods which were "to the great injury of the people." Lincoln took the occasion to announce his ideas of the people and the politicians.

"If the bank really be a grievance, why is it that no one of the real people is found to ask redress of it? The truth is, no such oppression exists. If it did, our people would groan with memorials and petitions, and we would not be permitted

to rest day or night till we had put it down.  The people
know their rights, and they are never slow to assert and
maintain them when they are invaded.  Let them call for an
investigation, and I shall ever stand ready to respond to the
call.  But they have made no such call.  I make the assertion
boldly, and without fear of contradiction, that no man who
does not hold an office, or does not aspire to one, has ever
found any fault of the bank.  It has doubled the prices of the
products of their farms, and filled their pockets with a sound
circulating medium; and they are all well pleased with its
operations.  No, sir, it is the politician who is the first to
sound the alarm (which, by the way, is a false one).  It is
he who, by these unholy means, is endeavoring to blow up a
storm that he may ride upon and direct.  It is he, and he
alone, that here proposes to spend thousands of the people's
public treasure, for no other advantage to them than to make
valueless in their pockets the reward of their industry.  Mr.
Chairman, this work is exclusively the work of politicians—
a set of men who have interests aside from the interests of
the people, and who, to say the most of them, are, taken as a
mass, at least one step removed from honest men.  I say this
with the greater freedom, because, being a politician myself,
none can regard it as personal."

The speech was published in full in the "Sangamon Journal" for Jan. 28, 1837, and the editor commented:

" Mr. Lincoln's remarks on Mr. Linder's bank resolution
in the paper are quite to the point.  Our friend carries the
true Kentucky rifle, and when he fires he seldom fails of
sending the shot home."

One other act of his in this session cannot be ignored.  It
is a sinister note in the hopeful chorus of the Tenth Assembly.  For months there had come from the southern States
violent protests against the growth of abolition agitation in
the North.  Garrison's paper, the " infernal Liberator," as it
was called in the pro-slavery part of the country, had been
gradually extending its circulation and its influence; and it
already had imitators even on the banks of the Mississippi.

The American Anti-slavery Society was now over three years old.  A deep, unconquerable conviction of the iniquity of slavery was spreading through the North.  The South felt it and protested, and the statesmen of the North joined them in their protest.  Slavery could not be crushed, said the conservatives.  It was sanctioned by the Constitution.  The South must be supported in its claims, and agitation stopped. But the agitation went on, and riots, violence, and hatred pursued the agitators.  In Illinois, in this very year, 1837, we have a printing-office raided and an anti-slavery editor, Elijah Lovejoy, killed by the citizens of Alton, who were determined that it should not be said among them that slavery was an iniquity.

To silence the storm, mass-meetings of citizens, the United States Congress, the State legislatures, took up the question and again and again  voted  resolutions assuring the South that the Abolitionists were not supported; that the country recognized their right to their " peculiar institution," and that in no case should they be interfered with.  At Springfield, this same year (1837) the citizens convened and passed a resolution declaring that "the efforts of Abolitionists in this community are neither necessary nor useful."  When the riot occured in Alton, the Springfield papers uttered no word of condemnation, giving the affair only a laconic mention.

The Illinois Assembly joined in the general disapproval, and on March 3d passed the following resolutions:

" Resolved by the General Assembly of the State of Illinois:

" That we highly disapprove of the formation of Abolition societies, and of the doctrines promulgated by them.

" That the right of property in slaves is sacred to the slave-holding States by the Federal Constitution, and that they cannot be deprived of that right without their consent.

" That the General Government cannot abolish slavery in

the District of Columbia against the consent of the citizens of said District, without a manifest breach of good faith.

" That the governor be requested to transmit to the States of Virginia, Alabama, Mississippi, New York and Connecticut a copy of the foregoing report and resolutions "

Lincoln refused to vote for these resolutions. In his judgment no expression on the slavery question should go unaccompanied by the statement that it was an evil, and he had the boldness to protest immediately against the action of the House. He found only one man in the assembly willing to join him in his protest. These two names are joined to the document they presented:

" Resolutions upon the subject of domestic slavery having passed both branches of the General Assembly at its present session, the undersigned hereby protest against the passage of the same.

" They believe that the institution of slavery is founded on both injustice and bad policy, but that the promulgation of abolition doctrines tends rather to increase than abate its evils.

" They believe that the Congress of the United States has no power under the Constitution to interfere with the institution of slavery in the different States.

" They believe that the Congress of the United States has the power under the Constitution, to abolish slavery in the District of Columbia, but that the power ought not to be exercised, unless at the request of the people of the District.

" The difference between these opinions and those contained in the resolutions is their reason for entering this protest.                                    " DAN STONE,
                                       " A. LINCOLN,
          " Representatives from the County of Sangamon."

The Tenth Assembly gave Lincoln an opportunity to show his ability as a political manœuvrer, his power as a speaker, and his courage in opposing what seemed to him wrong.

There had never been a session of the assembly when the members had the chance to make so wide an impression. The character of the legislation on foot had called to Vandalia numbers of persons of influence from almost every part of the State. They were invariably there to secure something for their town or county, and naturally made a point of learning all they could of the members and of getting as well acquainted with them as circumstances allowed. Game suppers seem to have been the means usually employed by visitors for bringing people together, and Lincoln became a favorite guest not only because he was necessary to the success of almost any measure, but because he was so jovial a companion. It was then that he laid the foundation of his extensive acquaintance throughout the State which in after years stood him in excellent stead.

The lobbyists were not the only ones in Vandalia who gave suppers, however. Not a bill was passed nor an election decided that a banquet did not follow. Mr. John Bryant, the brother of William Cullen, was in Vandalia that winter in the interest of his county, and he attended one of these banquets, given by the successful candidate for the United States Senate. Lincoln was present, of course, and so were all the prominent politicians of the State.

"After the company had gotten pretty noisy and mellow from their imbibitions of Yellow Seal and 'corn juice,'" says Mr. Bryant, "Mr. Douglas and General Shields, to the consternation of the host and intense merriment of the guests, climbed up on the table, at one end, encircled each other's waists, and to the tune of a rollicking song, pirouetted down the whole length of the table, shouting, singing, and kicking dishes, glasses, and everything right and left, helter skelter. For this night of entertainment to his constituents, the successful candidate was presented with a bill, in the morning, for supper, wines, liquors, and damages, which amounted to six hundred dollars."

(10)

But boisterous suppers were not by any means the only feature of Lincoln's social life that winter in Vandalia. There was another and quieter side in which he showed his rare companionableness and endeared himself to many people. In the midst of the log-rolling and jubilations of the session he would often slip away to some acquaintance's room and spend hours in talk and stories. Mr. John Bryant tells of his coming frequently to his room at the hotel, and sitting "with his knees up to his chin, telling his inimitable stories and his triumphs in the House in circumventing the Democrats."

Major Newton Walker, of Lewiston, who was in Vandalia at the time, says: "I used to play the fiddle a great deal and have played for Lincoln a number of times. He used to come over to where I was boarding and ask me to play, and I would take the fiddle with me when I went over to visit him, and when he grew weary of telling stories he would ask me to give him a tune, which I never refused to do."

# CHAPTER X

As soon as the assembly closed, Lincoln returned to New
Salem; but not to stay. He had determined to go to Springfield. Major John Stuart, the friend who had advised him
to study law and who had lent him books and with whom he
had been associated closely in politics, had offered to take
him as a partner. It was a good opening, for Stuart was one
of the leading lawyers and politicians of the State, and his influence would place Lincoln at once in command of more or
less business. From every point of view the change seems to
have been wise; yet Lincoln made it with foreboding.

To practise law he must abandon his business as surveyor,
which was bringing him a fair income; he must for a time,
at least, go without a certain income. If he failed, what
then? The uncertainty weighed on him heavily, the more so
because he was burdened by the debts left from his store and
because he was constantly called upon to aid his father's family. Thomas Lincoln had remained in Coles County, but he
had not, in these six years in which his son had risen so rapidly, been able to get anything more than a poor livelihood
from his farm. The sense of responsibility Lincoln had
towards his father's family made it the more difficult for him
to undertake a new profession. His decision was made, however, and as soon as the session of the Tenth Assembly was
over he started for Springfield. His first appearance there is
as pathetic as amusing.

"He had ridden into town," says Joshua Speed, "on a
borrowed horse, with no earthly property save a pair of sad-

dle-bags containing a few clothes. I was a merchant at Springfield, and kept a large country store, embracing dry-goods, groceries, hardware, books, medicines, bed-clothes, mattresses—in fact, everything that the country needed. Lincoln came into the store with his saddle-bags on his arm. He said he wanted to buy the furniture for a single bed. The mattress, blankets, sheets, coverlid, and pillow, according to the figures made by me, would cost seventeen dollars. He said that perhaps was cheap enough; but small as the price was, he was unable to pay it. But if I would credit him till Christmas, and his experiment as a lawyer was a success, he would pay then; saying in the saddest tone, 'If I fail in this I do not know that I can ever pay you.' As I looked up at him I thought then, and I think now, that I never saw a sadder face.

"I said to him: 'You seem to be so much pained at contracting so small a debt, I think I can suggest a plan by which you can avoid the debt, and at the same time attain your end. I have a large room with a double bed upstairs, which you are very welcome to share with me.'

" 'Where is your room?' said he.

" 'Upstairs,' said I, pointing to a pair of winding stairs which led from the store to my room.

"He took his saddle-bags on his arm, went upstairs, set them on the floor, and came down with the most changed expression of countenance. Beaming with pleasure, he exclaimed:

" 'Well, Speed, I am moved.' "

Another friend, William Butler, with whom Lincoln had become intimate at Vandalia, took him to board; life at Springfield thus began under as favorable auspices as he could hope for.

After Chicago, Springfield was at that day the most promising city in Illinois. It had some fifteen hundred inhabitants, and the removal of the capital was certain to bring many more. Already, in fact, the town felt the effect. "The owner of real estate sees his property rapidly enhancing in value," declared the "Sangamon Journal;" "the merchant anticipates a large accession to our population and a corresponding additional sale for his goods; the mechanic already has more contracts offered him for building and improvements than he can execute; the farmer anticipates the growth of a large and important town, a market for the varied products of his farm;—indeed, every class of our citizens look to the future with confidence, that, we trust, will not be disappointed."

The effect was apparent too, in society. "We used to eat all together," said an old man who in the early thirties came to Springfield as a hostler; "but about this time some one came along and told the people they oughtn't to do so, and then the hired folks ate in the kitchen." This differentiation was apparent to Lincoln and a little discouraging. He was thinking at the time of this removal of marrying, but he soon saw that it was quite out of the question for him to support a wife in Springfield.

"I am afraid you would not be satisfied," he wrote the young woman, "there is a great deal of flourishing about in carriages here, which it would be your doom to see without sharing it. You would have to be poor, without the means of hiding your poverty. Do you believe you could bear that patiently?"

Lincoln's idea of marrying Mary Owens, of whom he asked this question, was the result of a Quixotic sense of honor which had curiously blinded him to the girl's real feeling for him. The affair had begun in the fall of 1836, when a woman of his acquaintance who was going to Kentucky on a visit, proposed laughingly to bring back a sister of hers on condition that Lincoln marry her.

"I of course accepted the proposal," Lincoln wrote afterwards in a letter to Mrs. O. H. Browning, "for you know I could not have done otherwise had I really been averse to it; but privately, between you and me, I was most confoundedly well pleased with the project. I had seen the said sister some three years before, thought her intelligent and agreeable, and saw no good objection to plodding life through hand in hand with her. Time passed on, the lady took her journey and in due time returned, sister in company, sure enough. This astonished me a little, for it appeared to me that her coming so readily showed that she was a trifle too willing, but on reflection it occurred to me that she might have been prevailed on by her married sister to come, without anything concerning me ever having been mentioned to her, and so I concluded that if no other objection presented itself, I would consent to waive this."

Another objection did present itself as soon as he saw the lady. He was anything but pleased with her appearance.

"But what could I do?" he continues in his letter to Mrs. Browning. "I had told her sister that I would take her for better or for worse, and I made a point of honor and conscience in all things to stick to my word, especially if others had been induced to act on it, which in this case I had no doubt they had, for I was now fairly convinced that no other man on earth would have her, and hence the conclusion that they were bent on holding me to my bargain. 'Well, thought I, 'I have said it, and, be the consequences what they may, it shall not be my fault if I fail to do it.' At once I determined to consider her my wife, and this done, all my powers of discovery were put to work in search of perfections in her which might be fairly set off against her defects. I tried to imagine her handsome, which, but for her unfortunate corpulency, was actually true. Exclusive of this, no woman that I have ever seen has a finer face. I also tried to convince myself that the mind was much more to be valued than the person, and in this she was not inferior, as I could discover, to any with whom I had been acquainted.

"Shortly after this, without attempting to come to any positive understanding with her, I set out for Vandalia, when and where you first saw me. During my stay there I had letters from her which did not change my opinion of either her intellect or intention, but, on the contrary, confirmed it in both.

"All this while, although I was fixed 'firm as the surge-repelling rock' in my resolution, I found I was continually repenting the rashness which had led me to make it. Through life I have been in no bondage, either real or imaginary, from the thraldom of which I so much desired to be free. After my return home I saw nothing to change my opinion of her in any particular. She was the same, and so was I. I now spent my time in planning how I might get along in life after my contemplated change of circumstances should have taken place, and how I might procrastinate the evil day for a time, which I really dreaded as much, perhaps more, than an Irishman does the halter."

Lincoln was in this state of mind when he went to Springfield and discovered how unfit his resources were to support a wife there. Although he put the question of poverty so plainly he assured Miss Owens that if she married him he would do all in his power to make her happy.

"Whatever woman may cast her lot with mine," he wrote her, "should any ever do so, it is my intention to do all in my power to make her happy and contented; and there is nothing I can imagine that would make me more unhappy than to fail in the effort. I know I should be much happier with you than the way I am, provided I saw no signs of discontent in you. What you have said to me may have been in the way of jest, or I may have misunderstood it. If so, then let it be forgotten; if otherwise, I much wish you would think seriously before you decide. What I have said I will most positively abide by, provided you wish it. My opinion is that you had better not do it. You have not been accustomed to hardship, and it may be more serious than you now imagine. I know you are capable of thinking correctly on any subject, and if you deliberate maturely upon this before you decide, then I am willing to abide your decision."

This decidedly dispassionate view of their relation seems not to have brought any decision from Miss Owens; for three months later Mr. Lincoln wrote her an equally judicial letter, telling her that he could not think of her "with entire indifference," that he in all cases wanted to do right and "most particularly so in all cases with women," and summing up his position as follows:

"I now say that you can now drop the subject, dismiss your thoughts (if you ever had any) from me forever, and leave this letter unanswered, without calling forth one accusing murmur from me. And I will even go further, and say that if it will add anything to your comfort or peace of mind to do so, it is my sincere wish that you should. Do not understand by this that I wish to cut your acquaintance. I mean no such thing.
"What I do wish is that our further acquaintance shall depend upon yourself. If such further acquaintance would contribute nothing to your happiness, I am sure it would not to mine. If you feel yourself in any degree bound to me, I am now willing to release you, provided you wish it; while, on the other hand, I am willing and even anxious to bind you faster, if I can be convinced that it will, in any considerable degree, add to your happiness. This, indeed, is the whole question with me. Nothing would make me more miserable than to believe you miserable—nothing more happy than to know you were so."

Miss Owens had enough discernment to recognize the disinterestedness of this love-making, and she refused Mr. Lincoln's offer. She found him "deficient in those little links which make up the chain of a woman's happiness," she said. When finally refused Lincoln wrote the letter to Mrs. Browning from which the above citations have been taken. He concluded it with an account of the effect on himself of Miss Owens' refusal:

" I was mortified, it seemed to me, in a hundred different ways. My vanity was deeply wounded by the reflection that

I had so long been too stupid to discover her intentions, and at the same time never doubting that I understood them perfectly; and also that she, whom I had taught myself to believe nobody else would have, had actually rejected me with all my fancied greatness. And, to cap the whole, I then for the first time began to suspect that I was really a little in love with her. But let it all go! I'll try and outlive it. Others have been made fools of by the girls, but this can never with truth be said of me. I most emphatically, in this instance, made a fool of myself. I have now come to the conclusion never again to think of marrying, and for this reason—I can never be satisfied with any one who would be blockhead enough to have me."

The skill, the courage, and the good-will Lincoln had shown in his management of the bill for the removal of the capital gave him at once a position in Springfield. The entire "Long Nine," indeed, were regarded by the county as its benefactors, and throughout the summer there were barbecues and fireworks, dinners and speeches in their honor. "The service rendered Old Sangamon by the present delegation" was a continually recurring toast at every gathering. At one "sumptuous dinner" the internal improvement scheme in all its phases was toasted again and again by the banqueters. " 'The Long Nine' of Old Sangamon—well done, good and faithful servants," drew forth long applause. Among those who offered volunteer toasts at this dinner were "A. Lincoln, Esq.," and "S. A. Douglas, Esq."

At a dinner at Athens, given to the delegation, eight formal toasts and twenty-five volunteers are quoted in the report of the affair in the "Sangamon Journal." Among them were the following:

A. Lincoln. He has fulfilled the expectations of his friends and disappointed the hopes of his enemies.

A. Lincoln. One of nature's noblemen.

By A. Lincoln. Sangamon County will ever be true to her

Mason, Vank &c &c         To Stuart Lincoln         Dr
1837 April.   To attendance at trial of right
              of J. A. Carr's property before Justical   $5.00

Lucinda Mason      To Stuart Lincoln           Dr
1837 Oct    To staying of Judgment of Drew.    $5.00

Wiley & Wood       To Stuart Lincoln           Dr.
1837-8   To defence of Chancery suit of E.J.   $50.00
                                               15.00
         Robert by cost to Stuart —          $35.00

**FACSIMILE OF PAGE FROM STUART & LINCOLN'S FEE BOOK**
From the original owned by Jesse W. Weik.

best interests, and never more so than in reciprocating the good feelings of the citizens of Athens and neighborhood.

Lincoln had not been long in Springfield before he was able to support himself from his law practice, a result due, no doubt, very largely to his personal qualities and to his reputation as a shrewd politician. Not that he made money. The fee-book of Lincoln and Stuart shows that the returns were modest enough, and that sometimes they even "traded out" their account. Nevertheless it was a satisfaction to earn a livelihood so soon. Of his peculiar methods as a lawyer at this date we know very little. Most of his cases are utterly uninteresting. The very first year he was in Springfield, however, he had one case which created a sensation, and which is an admirable example of the way he could combine business and politics as well as of his merciless persistency in pursuing a man whom he believed unjust.

It seems that among the offices to be filled at the August election of 1837 was that of probate justice of the peace. One of the candidates was General James Adams, a man who had come on from the East in the early twenties, and who had at first claimed to be a lawyer. He had been an aspirant for various offices, among them that of governor of the State, but with little success. A few days before the August election of 1837 an anonymous hand-bill was scattered about the streets. It was an attack on General Adams, charging him with having acquired the title to a ten-acre lot of ground near the town by the deliberate forgery of the name of Joseph Anderson, of Fulton County, Illinois, to an assignment of a judgment. Anderson had died, and his widow, going to Springfield to dispose of the land, had been surprised to find that it was claimed by General Adams. She had employed Stuart and Lincoln to look into the matter. The hand-bill, which went into all of the details at great length, concluded as follows: "I have only made these statements because I am known by many to be one of the individuals against whom the charge of forging the assignment and slipping it into the general's papers has been made; and because our silence might be construed into a confession of the truth. I shall not subscribe my name; but hereby authorize the editor of the 'Journal' to give it up to any one who may call for it."

After the election, at which General Adams was successful, the hand-bill was reproduced in the "Sangamon Journal," with a card signed by the editor, in which he said: "To save any further remarks on this subject, I now state that A. Lincoln, Esq., is the author of the hand-bill in question." The same issue of the paper contained a lengthy communication from General Adams, denying the charge of fraud.

The controversy was continued for several weeks in the newspapers, General Adams often filling six columns of a single issue of the "Springfield Republican."

He charged that the assault upon him was the result of a conspiracy between "a knot of lawyers, doctors, and others," who wished to ruin his reputation. Lincoln's answers to Adams are most emphatic. In one case, quoting several of his assertions, he pronounced them "all as false as hell, as all this community must know." Adams's replies were always voluminous. "Such is the turn which things have lately taken," wrote Lincoln, "that when General Adams writes a book I am expected to write a commentary on it." Replying to Adams's denunciation of the lawyers, he said: "He attempted to impose himself upon the community as a lawyer, and he actually carried the attempt so far as to induce a man who was under the charge of murder to entrust the defence of his life to his hands, and finally took his money and got him hanged. Is this the man that is to raise a breeze in his favor by abusing lawyers? . . . If he is not a lawyer, he *is* a liar; for he proclaimed himself a lawyer, and got a man hanged by depending on him." Lincoln concluded:

"Farewell, General. I will see you again at court, if not be-fore—when and where we will settle the question whether you or the widow shall have the land." The widow did get the land, but this was not the worst thing that happened to Adams. The climax was reached when the "Sangamon Jour-nal" published a long editorial (written by Lincoln, no doubt) on the controversy, and followed it with a copy of an indictment found against Adams in Oswego County, New York, in 1818. The offence charged in this indictment was the forgery of a deed by Adams—"a person of evil name and fame and of a wicked disposition."

Lincoln's victory in this controversy undoubtedly did much to impress the community, not necessarily that he was a good lawyer, but rather that he was a clever strategist and a fearless enemy. It was not, in fact, as a lawyer that he was prominent in the first years after he came to Springfield. It was as a politician. The place he had taken among the lead-ers of the Whig party in the winter of 1836 and 1837 he easily kept. The qualities which he had shown from the out-start of his public life were only strengthened as he gained experience and self-confidence. He was the terror of the pre-tentious and insincere, and had a way of exposing their shams by clever tricks which were unanswerable arguments. Thus, it was considered necessary, at that day, by a candi-date to prove to the farmers that he was poor and, like them-selves, horny-handed. Those politicians who wore good clothes and dined sumptuously were careful to conceal their regard for the elegancies of life from their constituents. One of the Democrats who in this period took particu-lar pains to decry the Whigs for their wealth and aristocratic principles was Colonel Dick Taylor, gen-erally known in Illinois as "ruffled-shirt Taylor." He was a vain and handsome man, who habitually ar-rayed himself as gorgeously as the fashion allowed.

One day when he and Lincoln had met in debate at a country-side gathering, Colonel Dick became particularly bitter in his condemnation of Whig elegance. Lincoln listened for a time, and then, slipping near the speaker, suddenly caught his coat, which was buttoned up close, and tore it open. A mass of ruffled shirt, a gorgeous velvet vest, and a great gold chain from which dangled numerous rings and seals, were uncovered to the crowd. Lincoln needed to make no further reply that day to the charge of being a "rag baron."

Lincoln loved fair play as he hated shams; and throughout these early years in Springfield boldly insisted that friend and enemy have the chance due them. A dramatic case of this kind occurred at a political meeting held one evening in the Springfield court-room, which at that date was temporarily in a hall under Stuart and Lincoln's law office. Directly over the platform was a trap-door. Lincoln frequently would lie by this opening during a meeting, listening to the speeches. One evening one of his friends, E. D. Baker, in speaking angered the crowd, and an attempt was made to "pull him down." Before the assailants could reach the platform, however, a pair of long legs dangled from the trap-door, and in an instant Lincoln dropped down beside Baker, crying out, "Hold on, gentlemen, this is a land of free speech." His appearance was so unexpected, and his attitude so determined, that the crowd soon was quiet, and Baker went on with his speech.

Lincoln did not take a prominent place in his party because the Whigs lacked material. He had powerful rivals. Edward Dickinson Baker, Colonel John J. Hardin, John T. Stuart, Ninian W. Edwards, Jesse K. Dubois, O. H. Browning, were but a few of the brilliant men who were throwing all their ability and ambition into the contest for political honors in the State. Nor were the Whigs a whit superior to the Democrats. William L. D. Ewing, Ebenezer Peck, William Thomas, James Shields, John Calhoun, were in every respect as able as the best men of the Whig party. Indeed, one of the prominent Democrats with whom Lincoln came often in contact, was popularly regarded as the most brilliant and promising politician of the State— Stephen A. Douglas. His record had been phenomenal. He had amazed both parties, in 1834, by securing the appointment by the legislature to the office of State Attorney for the first judicial circuit, over John J. Hardin. In 1836 he had been elected to the legislature, and although he was at that time but twenty-three years of age, he had shown himself one of the most vigorous, capable, and intelligent members. Indeed, Douglas's work in the Tenth Assembly gave him about the same position in the Democratic party of the State at large that Lincoln's work in the same body gave him in the Whig party of his own district. In 1837 he had had no difficulty in being appointed register of the land office, a position which compelled him to make his home in Springfield. It was only a few months after Lincoln rode into town, all his earthly possessions in a pair of saddle-bags, that Douglas appeared. Handsome, polished, and always with an air of prosperity, the advent of the young Democratic official was in striking contrast to that of the sad-eyed, ill-clad, poverty-stricken young lawyer from New Salem.

From the first, Lincoln and Douglas were thrown constantly together in the social life of the town, and often pitted against each other in what were the real forums of the State at that day—the space around the huge "Franklin" stove of some obliging store-keeper, the steps of somebody's law office, a pile of lumber, or a long timber, lying in the public square, where the new State-house was going up.

In the fall of 1837 Douglas was nominated for Congress on the Democratic ticket. His Whig opponent was Lincoln's law partner, John T. Stuart. The campaign which the two conducted was one of the most remarkable in the history of the State. For five months of the spring and summer of 1838 they rode together from town to town all over the northern part of Illinois (Illinois at that time was divided into but three congressional districts; the third, in which Sangamon county was included, being made up of the twenty-two northernmost counties), speaking six days out of seven. When the election came off in August, 1838, out of thirty-six thousand votes cast, Stuart received a majority of only fourteen; but even that majority the Democrats always contended was won unfairly.

The campaign was watched with intense interest by the young politicians of Springfield; no one of them felt a deeper interest in it than Lincoln, who was himself a candidate for the State legislature, and who was spending a great deal of his time in electioneering.

As the campaign of 1840 approached Lincoln was more and more frequently pitted against Douglas. He had by this time no doubt learned something of the power of the "Little Giant," as Douglas was already called. Certainly no man in public life between 1837 and 1860 had a greater hold on his followers. The reasons for this grasp are not hard to find. Douglas was by nature buoyant, enthusiastic, impetuous. He had that sunny boyishness which is so irresistible to young and old. With it he had great natural eloquence. When his deep, rich voice rolled out fervid periods in support of the sub-treasury and the convention system, or in opposition to internal improvements by the federal government, the people applauded out of sheer joy at the pleasure of hearing him. He was one of the few men in Illinois whom the epithet of "Yankee" never hurt. He might be a Yankee, but when he sat down on the knee of some surly lawyer, and confidentially told him his plans; or, at a political meeting, took off his coat, and rolled up his sleeves, and "pitched into" his opponent, the sons of Illinois forgot his origin in love for the man.

Lincoln undoubtedly understood the charm of Douglas, and realized his power. But he already had an insight into one of his political characteristics that few people recognized at that day. In writing to Stuart in 1839, while the latter was attending Congress, Lincoln said: "Douglas has not been here since you left. A report is in circulation here now that he has abandoned the idea of going to Washington, though the report does not come in a very authentic form, so far as I can learn. Though, by the way, speaking of authenticity, you know that if we had heard Douglas say that he had abandoned the contest, it would not be very authentic."

At that time the local issues, which had formerly engaged Illinois candidates almost entirely, were lost sight of in national questions. In Springfield, where the leaders of both parties were living, many hot debates were held in private. Out of these grew, in December, 1839, a series of public discussions, extending over eight evenings, and in which several of the first orators of the State took part. Lincoln was the last man on the list. The people were nearly worn out before his turn came, and his audience was small. He began his speech with some melancholy, self-deprecatory reflections, complaining that the small audience cast a damp upon his spirits which he was sure he would be unable to overcome during the evening. He did better than he expected, overcoming the damp on his spirits so effectually that he made what was regarded as the best speech of the series. By a general request, it was printed for distribution. The speech is peculiarly interesting from the fact that while there is a little of the perfervid eloquence of 1840 in it, as well as a good deal of the rather boisterous humor of the time, a part of it is devoted to a careful examination of the statements of

(11)

his opponents, and a refutation of them by means of public documents.

As a good Democrat was expected to do, Douglas had explained with plausibility why the Van Buren administration had in 1838 spent $40,000,000. Lincoln takes up his statements one by one, and proves, as he says, that "the majority of them are wholly untrue." Douglas had attributed a part of the expenditures to the purchase of public lands from the Indians.

"Now it happens," said Lincoln, "that no such purchase was made during that year. It is true that some money was paid that year in pursuance of Indian treaties; but no more, or rather not as much as had been paid on the same account in each of several preceding years. . . . . Again, Mr. Douglas says that the removal of the Indians to the country west of the Mississippi created much of the expenditure of 1838. I have examined the public documents in relation to this matter, and find that less was paid for the removal of Indians in that than in some former years. The whole sum expended on that account in that year did not much exceed one quarter of a million. For this small sum, although we do not think the administration entitled to credit, because large sums have been expended in the same way in former years, we consent it may take one and make the most of it.

"Next, Mr. Douglas says that five millions of the expenditures of 1838 consisted of the payment of the French indemnity money to its individual claimants. I have carefully examined the public documents, and thereby find this statement to be wholly untrue. Of the forty millions of dollars expended in 1838, I am enabled to say positively that not one dollar consisted of payments on the French indemnities. So much for that excuse.

"Next comes the Post-office. He says that five millions were expended during that year to sustain that department. By a like examination of public documents, I find this also wholly untrue. Of the so often mentioned forty millions, not one dollar went to the Post-office. . . .

"I return to another of Mr. Douglas's excuses for the expenditures of 1838, at the same time announcing the pleasing intelligence that this is the last one. He says that ten millions of that year's expenditure was a contingent appropriation, to prosecute an anticipated war with Great Britain on the Maine boundary question. Few words will settle this. First, that the ten millions appropriated was not made till 1839, and consequently could not have been expended in 1838; second, although it was appropriated, it has never been expended at all. Those who heard Mr. Douglas recollect that he indulged himself in a contemptuous expression of pity for me. 'Now he's got me,' thought I. But when he went on to say that five millions of the expenditure of 1838 were payments of the French indemnities, which I knew to be untrue; that five millions had been for the Post-office, which I knew to be untrue; that ten millions had been for the Maine boundary war, which I not only knew to be untrue, but supremely ridiculous also; and when I saw that he was stupid enough to hope that I would permit such groundless and audacious assertions to go unexposed,—I readily consented that, on the score both of veracity and sagacity, the audience should judge whether he or I were the more deserving of the world's contempt."

These citations show that Lincoln had already learned to handle public documents, and to depend for at least a part of his success with an audience upon a careful statement of facts. The methods used in at least a portion of this speech are exactly those which made the irresistible strength of his speeches in 1858, 1859, and 1860.

But there was little of as good work done in the campaign of 1840, by Lincoln or anybody else, as is found in this speech. It was a campaign of fun and noise, and nowhere more so than in Illinois. Lincoln was one of the five Whig Presidential electors, and he flung himself into the campaign with confidence. "The nomination of Harrison takes first rate," he wrote to his partner Stuart, then in Washington. "You know I am never sanguine, but I believe we will carry the State. The chance of doing so appears to me twenty-five per cent. better than it did for you to beat Douglas." The Whigs, in spite of their dislike of the convention system, organized as they never had before, and even sent out a "confidential" circular of which Lincoln was the author.

This circular provided for a remarkably complete organization of the State, as the following extracts will show:

After due deliberation, the following is the plan of organization, and the duties required of each county committee:

(1) To divide their county into small districts, and to appoint in each a subcommittee, whose duty it shall be to make a perfect list of all the voters in their respective districts, and to ascertain with certainty for whom they will vote. If they meet with men who are doubtful as to the man they will support, such voters should be designated in separate lines, with the name of the man they will probably support.

(2) It will be the duty of said subcommittee to keep a constant watch on the doubtful voters, and from time to time have them talked to by those in whom they have the most confidence, and also to place in their hands such documents as will enlighten and influence them.

. . . . . . . .

(5) On the first of each month hereafter we shall expect to hear from you. After the first report of your subcommittees, unless there should be found a great many doubtful voters, you can tell pretty accurately the manner in which your county will vote. In each of your letters to us, you will state the number of certain votes both for and against us, as well as the number of doubtful votes, with your opinion of the manner in which they will be cast.

(6) When we have heard from all the counties, we shall be able to tell with similar accuracy the political complexion of the State. This information will be forwarded to you as soon as received.

Every weapon Lincoln thought of possible use in the contest he secured. "Be sure to send me as many copies of the

'Life of Harrison' as you can spare from other uses," he wrote Stuart. "Be very sure to procure and send me the 'Senate Journal' of New York, of September, 1814. I have a newspaper article which says that that document proves that Van Buren voted against raising troops in the last war. And, in general, send me everything you think will be a good 'war-club.'"

Every sign of success he quoted to Stuart; the number of subscribers to the "Old Soldier," a campaign newspaper which the Whig committee had informed the Whigs of the State that they *must take;* the names of Van Buren men who were weakening, and to whom he wanted Stuart to send documents; the name of every theretofore doubtful person who had declared himself for Harrison. "Japh Bell has come out for Harrison," he put in a postscript to one letter; "ain't that a caution?"

The monster political meetings held throughout the State did much to widen Lincoln's reputation, particularly one held in June in Springfield. Twenty thousand people attended this meeting, delegations coming from every direction. It took fourteen teams to haul the delegation from Chicago, and they were three weeks on their journey. Each party carried some huge symbolic piece—the log cabin being the favorite. One of the cabins taken to Springfield was drawn by thirty yokes of oxen. In a hickory tree which was planted beside this cabin, coons were seen playing, and a barrel of hard cider stood by the door, continually on tap. Instead of a log cabin, the Chicago delegation dragged across country a government yawl rigged up as a two-masted ship, with a band of music and a six-pounder cannon on board.

There are many reminiscences of this great celebration, and Lincoln's part in it, still afloat in Illinois. General T. J. Henderson writes, in his entertaining reminiscences of Lincoln:

"The first time I remember to have seen Abraham Lincoln was during the memorable campaign of 1840, when I was a boy fifteen years of age. It was at an immense Whig mass-meeting held at Springfield, Illinois, in the month of June of that year. The Whigs attended this meeting from all parts of the State in large numbers, and it was estimated that from forty to fifty thousand people were present. They came in carriages and wagons, on horseback and on foot. They came with log cabins drawn on wheels by oxen, and with coons, coon-skins, and hard cider. They came with music and banners; and thousands of them came from long distances. It was the first political meeting I had ever attended, and it made a very strong impression upon my youthful mind.

"My father, William H. Henderson, then a resident of Stark county, Illinois, was an ardent Whig; and having served under General William Henry Harrison, the then Whig candidate for President, in the war of 1812-1815, he felt a deep interest in his election. And although he lived about a hundred miles from Springfield, he went with a delegation from Stark county to this political meeting, and took me along with him. I remember that at this great meeting of the supporters of Harrison and Tyler there were a number of able and distinguished speakers of the Whig party of the State of Illinois present. Among them were Colonel E. D. Baker, who was killed at Ball's Bluff, on the Potomac, in the late war, and who was one of the most eloquent speakers in the State; Colonel John J. Hardin, who was killed at the battle of Buena Vista, in the Mexican war; Fletcher Webster, a son of Daniel Webster, who was killed in the late war; S. Leslie Smith, a brilliant orator of Chicago; Rev. John Hogan, Ben Bond, and Abraham Lincoln. I heard all of these men speak on that occasion. And while I was too young to be a judge of their speeches, yet I thought them all to be great men, and none of them greater than Abraham Lincoln."

The late Judge Scott of Illinois says of Lincoln's speech at that gathering, in an unpublished paper "Lincoln on the Stump and at the Bar":

"Mr. Lincoln stood in a wagon, from which he addressed

the mass of people that surrounded it. The meeting was one
of unusual interest because of him who was to make the principal address. It was at the time of his greatest physical
strength. He was tall, and perhaps a little more slender than
in later life, and more homely than after he became stouter in
person. He was then only thirty-one years of age, and yet
he was regarded as one of the ablest of the Whig speakers in
that campaign. There was that in him that attracted and
held public attention. Even then he was the subject of popular regard because of his candid and simple mode of discussing and illustrating political questions. At times he was intensely logical, and was always most convincing in his arguments. The questions involved in that canvass had relation
to the tariff, internal public improvements by the federal government, the distribution of the proceeds of the sales of public lands among the several States, and other questions that
divided the political parties of that day. They were not such
questions as enlisted and engaged his best thoughts; they did
not take hold of his great nature, and had no tendency to develop it. At times he discussed the questions of the time in a
logical way, but much time was devoted to telling stories to
illustrate some phase of his argument, though more often the
telling of these stories was resorted to for the purpose of
rendering his opponents ridiculous. That was a style of
speaking much appreciated at that early day. In that kind of
oratory he excelled most of his contemporaries—indeed, he
had no equal in the State. One story he told on that occasion was full of salient points, and well illustrated the argument he was making. It was not an impure story, yet it was
not one it would be seemly to publish; but rendered, as it
was, in his inimitable way, it contained nothing that was offensive to a refined taste. The same story might have been
told by another in such a way that it would probably have
been regarded as transcending the proprieties of popular address. One characterizing feature of all the stories told by
Mr. Lincoln, on the stump and elsewhere, was that although
the subject matter of some of them might not have been entirely unobjectionable, yet the manner of telling them was so
peculiarly his own that they gave no offence even to refined
and cultured people. On the contrary, they were much en-

joyed. The story he told on this occasion was much liked by the vast assembly that surrounded the temporary platform from which he spoke, and was received with loud bursts of laughter and applause. It served to place the opposing party and its speakers in a most ludicrous position in respect to the question being considered, and gave him a most favorable hearing for the arguments he later made in support of the measures he was sustaining."

Although so active as a Whig politician Lincoln was not prominent at this period as a legislator. Few bills originated with him. Among these few one of interest is the Illinois law requiring the examination of school teachers as to their qualifications, and providing for the granting of official certificates of authority to teach. In the pioneer days, any person whom circumstances forced into the business was permitted to teach. On December 2, 1840, Lincoln offered the following resolution in the Illinois House of Representatives:

"Resolved, That the committee on education be instructed to inquire into the expediency of providing by law for the examination as to the qualification of persons offering themselves as school teachers, that no teacher shall receive any part of the public school fund who shall not have successfully passed such examination, and that they report by bill or otherwise."

A motion to table this resolution was defeated. Within the ensuing three months the legislature passed "an act making provision for organizing and maintaining common schools"—the act which was the foundation of the common school system of Illinois. Section 81 of this act, providing for the qualification of teachers embodied Lincoln's idea. This section made it the duty of the school trustees in every township "to examine any person proposing to teach school in their vicinity in relation to the qualifications of such person as a teacher." or they might appoint a board of commis-

sioners to conduct the examination; and a certificate of qualification was to be issued by a majority of the trustees or commissioners. Since then, of course, all the States have passed
laws providing for the examination of teachers. In Illinois,
no material change has been made in Lincoln's plan (for this
section of the law was very likely drawn by Lincoln), except that the power of examination has been transferred
from the trustees or commissioners to the county superintendent of schools an office then unknown.

---

**S. T. LOGAN & E. D. BAKER,**
ATTORNEYS AND COUNSELLORS AT LAW.
WILL practice, in conjunction, in the Cir-
Courts of this Judicial District, and n the Circuit
Courts of the Counties of Pike, Schuyler and Peoria.
Springfield, march, 1837.                                8}-t

**J. T. STUART AND A. LINCOLN.**
ATTORNEYS and Counsellors at Law, will practice,
conjointly, in the Courts of this Judicial Circuit.—
Office No. 4 Hoffman's Row, up stairs.
Springfield, april 12, 1837.                              4

THE partnership heretofore existing between the un-
dersigned, has been dissolved by mutual consent.—
The business will be found in the hands of John T. Stuart.
                                 JOHN T. STUART,
April 12, 1837.   84      HENRY E. DUMMER.

STUART AND LINCOLN'S PROFESSIONAL CARD.

# CHAPTER XI

BUSY as Lincoln was with law and politics the first three
years after he reached Springfield, he did not by any means
fail to identify himself with the interests of the town and of
its people. In all the intellectual life of the place he took his
part. In the fall of 1837 with a few of the leading young
men he formed a young men's lyceum. One of the very
few of his early speeches which has been preserved was delivered before this body, its subject being the Perpetuation
of our Political Institutions. At the request of the members of the Lyceum this address was published in the "Sangamon Journal" for February 3, 1838.

The most pleasing feature of his early life in the town was
the way in which he attracted all classes of people to him. He
naturally, from his political importance and from his relation
to Mr. Stuart, was admitted to the best society. But Lincoln
was not received there from tolerance of his position only.
The few members left of that interesting circle of Springfield
in the thirties are emphatic in their statements that he was
recognized as a valuable social factor. If indifferent to forms
and little accustomed to conventional usages, he had a native
dignity and self-respect which stamped him at once as a superior man. He had a good will, an easy adaptability to people, which made him take a hand in everything that went on.
His name appears in every list of banqueters and merry-
makers reported in the Springfield papers. He even served
as committeeman for cotillion parties. "We liked Lincoln

though he was not gay," said one charming and cultivated old lady to me in Springfield. "He rarely danced, he was never very attentive to ladies, but he was always a welcome guest everywhere, and the centre of a circle of animated

COTILLION PARTY.

E PLURIBUS UNUM.

*The pleasure of your Company is respectfully solicited at a Cotillion Party, to be given at the "American House," on to=morrow evening at 7 o'clock, P. M.*

December 16th, 1839

| | |
|---|---|
| N. H. RIDGELY, | J. F. SPEED, |
| J. A. M'CLERNAND, | J. SHIELDS, |
| R. ALLEN, | E. D. TAYLOR, |
| N. H. WASH, | E. H. MERRYMAN, |
| F. W. TODD, | N. E. WHITESIDE, |
| B. A. DOUGLASS, | M. EASTHAM, |
| W. S. PRENTICE, | J. R. DILLER, |
| N. W. EDWARDS, | A. LINCOLN, |

*Managers.*

**FACSIMILE OF INVITATION TO A SPRINGFIELD COTILLION PARTY.**
From the collection of Mr. C. F. Gunther, Chicago.

talkers. Indeed, I think the only thing we girls had against Lincoln was that he always attracted all the men around him."

Lincoln's kindly interest and perfectly democratic feeling attached to him many people whom he never met save on the streets. Indeed his life in the streets of Springfield is a most touching and delightful study. He concerned himself in the progress of every building which was put up, of every new street which was opened; he passed nobody without recognition; he seemed always to have time to stop and talk. He became, in fact, part of Springfield street life, just as he did of the town's politics and society.

In 1840 Lincoln became engaged to be married to one of the favorite young women of Springfield, Miss Mary Todd, the sister-in-law of one of his political friends, a member of the "Long Nine" and a prominent citizen, Ninian W. Edwards.

Miss Todd came from a well-known family of Lexington, Kentucky; her father, Robert S. Todd, being one of the leading citizens of his State. She had come to Springfield in 1839 to live with her sister, Mrs. Edwards. She was a brilliant, witty, highly-educated girl, ambitious and spirited, with a touch of audacity which only made her more attractive, and she at once took a leading position in Springfield society. There were many young unmarried men in the town, drawn there by politics, and Mr. Edwards's handsome home was opened to them in the hospitable Southern way. After Mary Todd became an inmate of the Edwards house, the place was gayer than ever. She received much attention from Douglas, Shields, Lincoln, and several others. It was soon apparent, however, that Miss Todd preferred Lincoln. As the intimacy between them increased, Mr. and Mrs. Edwards protested. However honorable and able a man Lincoln might be, he was still a "plebeian." His family were humble and poor; he was self-educated, without address or polish, careless of forms, indifferent to society. How could Mary Todd, brought up in a cultured home, accustomed to the refinements of life, ambitious for social position, accommodate herself to so grave a nature, so dull an exterior?

Miss Todd knew her own mind, however. She loved Lincoln, and seems to have believed from the first in his future. Some time in 1840 they became engaged.

But it was not long before there came the clashing inevitable between two persons whose tastes and ambitions were so different. Miss Todd was jealous and exacting; Lincoln thoughtless and inattentive. He frequently failed to accompany her to the merry-makings which she wanted to attend and she, naturally enough, resented his neglect interpreting it as a purposed slight. Sometimes in revenge she went with Mr. Douglas or some other escort who offered. Reproaches and tears and misunderstandings followed. If the lovers made up, it was only to fall out again. At last Lincoln became convinced that they were incompatible, and resolved that he must break the engagement. But the knowledge that the girl loved him took away his courage. He felt that he must not draw back, and he became profoundly miserable.

"Whatever woman may cast her lot with mine, should any ever do so, it is my intention to do all in my power to make her happy and contented; and there is nothing I can imagine that would make me more unhappy than to fail in the effort," Lincoln had written Miss Owens three years before. How could he make this brilliant, passionate creature to whom he was betrothed happy?

A mortal dread of the result of the marriage, a harrowing doubt of his own feelings, possessed him. The experience is not so rare in the history of lovers that it should be regarded, as it often has been, as something exceptional and abnormal in Lincoln's case. A reflective nature founded in melancholy, like Lincoln's, rarely undertakes even the simpler affairs of life without misgivings. He certainly experienced dread and doubt before entering on any new relation. When it came to forming the most delicate and intimate of all human relations, he staggered under a burden of uncertainty and suffering and finally broke the engagement.

So horrible a breach of honor did this seem to him that he called the day when it occurred the "fatal first of January, 1841," and months afterward he wrote to his intimate friend Speed: "I must regain my confidence in my own ability to keep my resolves when they are made. In that ability I once prided myself as the only or chief gem of my character; that gem I lost—how and where you know too well. I have not yet regained it, and, until I do, I cannot trust myself in any matter of much importance."

The breaking of the engagement between Miss Todd and Mr. Lincoln was known at the time to all their friends. Lincoln's melancholy was evident to them all, nor did he, indeed, attempt to disguise it. He wrote and spoke freely to his intimates of the despair which possessed him, and of his sense of dishonor. The episode caused a great amount of gossip, as was to be expected. After Mr. Lincoln's assassination and Mrs. Lincoln's sad death, various accounts of the courtship and marriage were circulated. It remained, however, for one of Lincoln's law partners, Mr. W. H. Herndon, to develop and circulate the most sensational of all the versions of the rupture. According to Mr. Herndon, the engagement between the two was broken in the most violent and public way possible, by Mr. Lincoln's failing to appear at the wedding. Mr. Herndon even describes the scene in detail:

"The time fixed for the marriage was the first day of January, 1841. Careful preparations for the happy occasion were made at the Edwards mansion. The house underwent the customary renovation; the furniture was properly arranged, the rooms neatly decorated, the supper prepared, and the guests invited. The latter assembled on the evening in question, and awaited in expectant pleasure the interesting ceremony of marriage. The bride, bedecked in veil and silken gown, and nervously toying with the flowers in her hair, sat in the adjoining room. Nothing was lacking but the groom. For some strange reason he had been delayed. An hour passed, and the guests, as well as the bride, were becoming restless. But they were all doomed to disappointment. Another hour passed; messengers were sent out over town, and each returning with the same report, it became apparent that Lincoln, the principal in this little drama, had purposely failed to appear. The bride, in grief, disappeared to her room; the wedding supper was left untouched; the guests quietly and wonderingly withdrew; the lights in the Edwards mansion were blown out, and darkness settled over all for the night. What the feelings of a lady as sensitive, passionate, and proud as Miss Todd were, we can only imagine; no one can ever describe them. By daybreak, after persistent search, Lincoln's friends found him. Restless, gloomy, miserable, desperate, he seemed an object of pity. His friends, Speed among the number, fearing a tragic termination, watched him closely in their rooms day and night. 'Knives and razors, and every instrument that could be used for self-destruction, were removed from his reach.' Mrs. Edwards did not hesitate to regard him as insane, and of course her sister Mary shared in that view."

No one can read this description in connection with the rest of Mr. Herndon's text, and escape the impression that, if it is true, there must have been a vein of cowardice in Lincoln. The context shows that he was not insane enough to excuse such a public insult to a woman. To break his engagement was, all things considered, not an unusual or abnormal thing; to brood over the rupture, to blame himself, to feel that he had been dishonorable, was to be expected, after such an act, from one of his temperament. Nothing, however, but temporary insanity or constitutional cowardice could explain such conduct as here described. Mr. Herndon does not pretend to found his story on any personal knowledge of the affair. He was in Springfield at the time, a clerk in Speed's store, but did not have then, nor, indeed, did he

ever have, any social relations with the families in which
Mr. Lincoln was always a welcome guest.  His authority
for the story is a remark which he says Mrs. Ninian Edwards made to him in an interview: "Lincoln and Mary
were engaged; everything was ready and prepared for the
marriage, even to the supper.  Mr. Lincoln failed to meet his
engagement; cause, insanity."  This remark, it should be
noted, is not from a manuscript written by Mrs. Edwards,
but in a report of an interview with her, written by Mr.
Herndon.  Supposing, however, that the statement was made
exactly as Mr. Herndon reports it, it certainly does not
justify any such sensational description as Mr. Herndon
gives.

If such a thing had ever occurred, it could not have failed
to be known, of course, even to its smallest details, by all the
relatives and friends of both Miss Todd and Mr. Lincoln.
Nobody, however, ever heard of this wedding party until
Mr. Herndon gave his material to the public.

One of the closest friends of the Lincolns throughout their
lives was a cousin of Mrs. Lincoln's, Mrs. Grimsley, afterwards Mrs. Dr. Brown.  Mrs. Grimsley lived in Springfield,
on the most intimate and friendly relations with Mr. and
Mrs. Lincoln, and the first six months of their life in the
White House she spent with them.  She was a woman of unusual culture, and of the rarest sweetness and graciousness
of character.  Some months before Mrs. Brown's death, in
August, 1895, a copy of Mr. Herndon's story was sent her,
with a request that she write for publication her knowledge
of the affair.  In her reply she said:

"Did Mr. Lincoln fail to appear when the invitations were
out, the guests invited, and the supper ready for the wedding?  I will say emphatically, 'No.'

"There may have been a little shadow of foundation for
Mr. Herndon's lively imagination to play upon, in that, the
year previous to the marriage, and when Mr. Lincoln and

my cousin Mary expected soon to be married, Mr. Lincoln was taken with one of those fearful, overwhelming periods of depression, which induced his friends to persuade him to leave Springfield. This he did for a time; but I am satisfied he was loyal and true to Mary, even though at times he may have doubted whether he was responding as fully as a manly, generous nature should to such affection as he knew my cousin was ready to bestow on him. And this because it had not the overmastering depth of an early love. This everybody here knows; therefore I do not feel as if I were betray‐ ing dear friends."

Mrs. John Stuart, the wife of Lincoln's law partner at that time, is still living in Springfield, a refined, cultivated, intelligent woman, who remembers perfectly the life and events of that day. When Mr. Herndon's story first came to her attention, her indignation was intense. She protested that she never before had heard of such a thing. Mrs. Stuart was not, however, in Springfield at that particular date, but in Washington, her husband being a member of Congress. She wrote the following statement for this biography:

"I cannot deny this, as I was not in Springfield for some months before and after this occurrence was said to have taken place; but I was in close correspondence with relatives and friends during all this time, and never heard a word of it. The late Judge Broadwell told me that he had asked Mr. Ninian Edwards about it, and Mr. Edwards told him that no such thing had ever taken place.

"All I can say is that I unhesitatingly do not believe such an event ever occurred. I thought I had never heard of this till I saw it in Herndon's book. I have since been told that Lamon mentions the same thing. I read Lamon at the time he published, and felt very much disgusted, but did not remember this particular assertion. The first chapters of Lamon's book were purchased from Herndon; so Herndon is responsible for the whole.

"Mrs. Lincoln told me herself all the circumstances of her engagement to Mr. Lincoln, of his illness, and the breaking

(12)

off of her engagement, of the renewal, and her marriage. So I say I do not believe one word of this dishonorable story about Mr. Lincoln."

Another prominent member in the same circle with Mr. Lincoln and Miss Todd is Mrs. B. T. Edwards, the widow of Judge Benjamin T. Edwards, the sister-in-law of Mr. Ninian Edwards, who had married Miss Todd's sister. She came to Springfield in 1839, and was intimately acquainted with Mr. Lincoln and Miss Todd, and knew, as well as another could know, their affairs. Mrs. Edwards is still living in Springfield, a woman of the most perfect refinement and trustworthiness. In answer to the question, "Is Mr. Herndon's description true?" she writes:

"I am impatient to tell you that all that he says about this wedding—the time for which was 'fixed for the first day of January'—is a fabrication. He has drawn largely upon his imagination in describing something which never took place.

"I know the engagement between Mr. Lincoln and Miss Todd was interrupted for a time, and it was rumored among her young friends that Mr. Edwards had rather opposed it. But I am sure there had been no 'time fixed' for any wedding; that is, no preparations had ever been made until the day that Mr. Lincoln met Mr. Edwards on the street and told him that he and Mary were going to be married that evening. Upon inquiry, Mr. Lincoln said they would be married in the Episcopal church, to which Mr. Edwards replied: 'No; Mary is my ward, and she must be married at my house.'

"If I remember rightly, the wedding guests were few, not more than thirty; and it seems to me all are gone now but Mrs. Wallace, Mrs. Levering, and myself, for it was not much more than a family gathering; only two or three of Mary Todd's young friends were present. The 'entertainment' was simple, but in beautiful taste; but the bride had neither veil nor flowers in her hair, with which to 'toy nervously.' There had been no elaborate *trousseau* for the bride of the future President of the United States, nor even a handsome wedding gown; nor was it a gay wedding."

Two sisters of Mrs. Lincoln who are still living, Mrs.
Wallace of Springfield, and Mrs. Helm of Elizabethstown,
Kentucky, deny emphatically that any wedding was ever arranged between Mr. Lincoln and Miss Todd but the one
which did take place. That the engagement was broken
after a wedding had been talked of, they think possible; but
Mr. Herndon's story, they deny emphatically.

"There is not a word of truth in it!" Mrs. Wallace broke
out, impulsively, before the question about the non-appear-
ance of Mr. Lincoln had been finished. "I never was so
amazed in my life as when I read that story. Mr. Lincoln
never did such a thing. Why, Mary Lincoln never had a
silk dress in her life until she went to Washington."

As Mr. Joshua Speed was, all through this period, Mr.
Lincoln's closest friend, no thought or feeling of the one ever
being concealed from the other, Mrs. Joshua Speed, who is
still living in Louisville, Kentucky, was asked if she knew
of the story. Mrs. Speed listened in surprise to Mr. Herndon's tale. "I never heard of it before," she declared. "I
never heard of it. If it is true, I never heard of it."
While the above investigation was going on quite unex-
pectedly, a volunteer witness to the falsity of the story appeared. The Hon. H. W. Thornton of Millersburg, Illinois,
was a member of the Twelfth General Assembly, which met
in Springfield in 1840. During that winter he was boarding
near Lincoln, saw him almost every day, was a constant visitor at Mr. Edwards's house, and he knew Miss Todd well.
He wrote to the author declaring that Mr. Herndon's statement about the wedding must be false, as he was closely associated with Miss Todd and Mr. Lincoln all winter, and never
knew anything of it. Mr. Thornton went on to say that he
knew beyond a doubt that the sensational account of Lincoln's insanity was untrue, and he quoted from the House
journal to show how it was impossible that, as Lamon says,

using Herndon's notes, "Lincoln went crazy as a loon, and did not attend the legislature in 1841-1842, for this reason;" or, as Herndon says, that he had to be watched constantly. According to the record taken from the journals of the House by Mr. Thornton, and which have been verified in Springfield, Mr. Lincoln was in his seat in the House on that "fatal first of January" when he is asserted to have been groping in the shadow of madness, and he was also there on the following day. The third of January was Sunday. On Monday, the fourth, he appears not to have been present—at least he did not vote; but even this is by no means conclusive evidence that he was not there. On the fifth, and on every succeeding day until the thirteenth, he was in his seat. From the thirteenth to the eighteenth, inclusive, he is not recorded on any of the roll-calls, and probably was not present. But on the nineteenth, when "John J. Hardin announced his illness to the House," as Mr. Herndon says (which announcement seems not to have gotten into the journal), Lincoln was again in his place, and voted. On the twentieth he is not recorded; but on every subsequent day, until the close of the session on the first of March, Lincoln was in the House. Thus, during the whole of the two months of January and February, he was absent not more than seven days—as good a record of attendance, perhaps, as that made by the average member.

Mr. Thornton says further: "Mr. Lincoln boarded at William Butler's, near to Dr. Henry's, where I boarded. The missing days, from January 13th to 19th, Mr. Lincoln spent several hours each day at Dr. Henry's; a part of these days I remained with Mr. Lincoln. His most intimate friends had no fears of his injuring himself. He was very sad and melancholy, but being subject to these spells, nothing serious was apprehended. His being watched, as stated in Herndon's book, was news to me until I saw it there."

But while Lincoln went about his daily duties, even on the "fatal first of January,"—the day when he broke his word to Miss Todd, his whole being was shrouded in gloom. He did not pretend to conceal this from his friends. Writing to Mr. Stuart on January 23d, he said:

"I am now the most miserable man living. If what I feel were equally distributed to the whole human family, there would not be one cheerful face on the earth. Whether I shall ever be better, I cannot tell; I awfully forebode I shall not. To remain as I am is impossible. I must die or be better, it appears to me. The matter you speak of on my account you may attend to as you say, unless you shall hear of my condition forbidding it. I say this because I fear I shall be unable to attend to any business here, and a change of scene might help me."

In the summer he visited his friend Speed, who had sold his store in Springfield, and returned to Louisville, Kentucky. The visit did much to brighten his spirits, for, writing back in September, after his return, to his friend's sister, he was even gay.

A curious situation arose the next year (1842), which did much to restore Lincoln to a more normal view of his relation to Miss Todd. In the summer of 1841, his friend Speed had become engaged. As the time for his marriage approached, he in turn was attacked by a melancholy not unlike that from which Lincoln had suffered. He feared he did not love well enough to marry, and he confided his fear to Lincoln. Full of sympathy for the trouble of his friend, Lincoln tried in every way to persuade him that his "twinges of the soul" were all explained by nervous debility. When Speed returned to Kentucky, Lincoln wrote him several letters, in which he consoled, counselled, or laughed at him. These letters abound in suggestive passages. From what did Speed suffer? From three special causes and a general one, which Lincoln proceeds to enumerate:

"The general cause is, that you are naturally of a nervous temperament; and this I say from what I have seen of you personally, and what you have told me concerning your mother at various times, and concerning your brother William at the time his wife died. The first special cause is your exposure to bad weather on your journey, which my experience clearly proves to be very severe on defective nerves. The second is the absence of all business and conversation of friends, which might divert your mind, give it occasional rest from the intensity of thought which will sometimes wear the sweetest idea threadbare and turn it to the bitterness of death. The third is the rapid and near approach of that crisis on which all your thoughts and feelings concentrate."

Speed writes that his *fiancée* is ill, and his letter is full of gloomy forebodings of an early death. Lincoln hails these fears as an omen of happiness.

"I hope and believe that your present anxiety and distress about her health and her life must and will forever banish those horrid doubts which I know you sometimes felt as to the truth of your affection for her. If they can once and forever be removed (and I almost feel a presentiment that the Almighty has sent your present affliction expressly for that object), surely nothing can come in their stead to fill their immeasurable measure of misery. It really appears to me that you yourself ought to rejoice, and not sorrow, at this indubitable evidence of your undying affection for her. Why, Speed, if you did not love her, although you might not wish her death, you would most certainly be resigned to it. Perhaps this point is no longer a question with you, and my pertinacious dwelling upon it is a rude intrusion upon your feelings. If so, you must pardon me. You know the hell I have suffered on that point, and how tender I am upon it. . . . I am now fully convinced that you love her as ardently as you are capable of loving. Your ever being happy in her presence, and your intense anxiety about her health, if there were nothing else, would place this beyond all dispute in my mind. I incline to think it probable that your nerves will fail you occasionally for a while; but once you get them firmly guarded now, that trouble is over forever. I think, if I were you, in case my mind were not exactly right, I would avoid being idle. I would immediately engage in some business or go to making preparations for it, which would be the same thing."

Mr. Speed's marriage occurred in February, and to the letter announcing it Lincoln replied:

"I opened the letter with intense anxiety and trepidation; so much so, that, although it turned out better than I expected, I have hardly yet, at a distance of ten hours, become calm.

"I tell you, Speed, our forebodings (for which you and I are peculiar) are all the worst sort of nonsense. I fancied, from the time I received your letter of Saturday, that the one of Wednesday was never to come, and yet it *did* come, and what is more, it is perfectly clear, both from its tone and handwriting, that you were much happier, or, if you think the term preferable, less miserable, when you wrote it than when you wrote the last one before. You had so obviously improved at the very time I so much fancied you would have grown worse. You say that something indescribably horrible and alarming still haunts you. You will not say that three months from now, I will venture. When your nerves once get steady now, the whole trouble will be over forever. Nor should you become impatient at their being even very slow in becoming steady. Again you say, you much fear that that Elysium of which you have dreamed so much is never to be realized. Well, if it shall not, I dare swear it will not be the fault of her who is now your wife. I now have no doubt that it is the peculiar misfortune of both you and me to dream dreams of Elysium far exceeding all that anything earthly can realize."

His prophecy was true. In March Speed wrote him that he was "far happier than he had ever expected to be." Lincoln caught at the letter with pathetic eagerness.

"It cannot be told how it now thrills me with joy to hear you say you are 'far happier than you ever expected to be.'

That much I know is enough.   I know you too well to suppose your expectations were not, at least, sometimes extravagant, and if the reality exceeds them all, I say, Enough,
dear Lord.   I am not going beyond the truth when I tell
you that the short space it took me to read your last
letter gave me more pleasure than the total sum of all I
have enjoyed since the fatal 1st of January, 1841.   Since
then it seems to me   I should have been entirely happy, but
for the never-absent idea that there is one still unhappy
whom I have contributed to make so.   That still kills my soul.
I cannot but reproach myself for even wishing to be happy
while she is otherwise.   She accompanied a large party on
the railroad cars to Jacksonville last Monday, and on her return spoke, so that I heard of it, of having enjoyed the trip
exceedingly.   God be praised for that."

Evidently Lincoln was still unreconciled to his separation
from Miss Todd.   In the summer of 1842, only three or four
months after the above letter was written, a clever ruse on
the part of certain of their friends threw the two unexpect-
edly together; and an understanding of some kind evidently
was reached, for during the season they met secretly at the
house of one of Lincoln's friends, Mr. Simeon Francis.   It
was while these meetings were going on that a burlesque encounter occurred between Lincoln and James Shields, for
which Miss Todd was partly responsible, and which no doubt
gave just the touch of comedy necessary to relieve their
tragedy and restore them to a healthier view of their relations.

Among the Democratic officials then living in Springfield
was the auditor of the State, James Shields.   He was a hot-
headed, blustering Irishman, not without ability, and certainly courageous; a good politician, and, on the whole, a
very well-liked man.   However, the swagger and noise with
which he accompanied the execution of his duties, and his
habit of being continually on the defensive, made him the
butt of Whig ridicule.   Nothing could have given greater

satisfaction to Lincoln and his friends than having an opponent who, whenever they joked him, flew into a rage and challenged them to fight.

At the time Lincoln was visiting Miss Todd at Mr. Francis's house, the Whigs were much excited over the fact that the Democrats had issued an order forbidding the payment of State taxes in State bank-notes. The bank-notes were in fact practically worthless, for the State finances were suffering a violent reaction from the extravagant legislation of 1836 and 1837. One of the popular ways of attacking an obnoxious political doctrine in that day was writing letters from some imaginary backwoods settlement, setting forth in homely vernacular the writer's views of the question, and showing how its application affected his part of the world. These letters were really a rude form of the " Biglow Papers " or " Nasby Letters." Soon after the order was issued by the Illinois officials demanding silver instead of bank-notes in payment of taxes, Lincoln wrote a letter to a Springfield paper from the "Lost Townships," signing it "Aunt Rebecca." In it he described the plight to which the new order had brought the neighborhood, and he intimated that the only reason for issuing such an order was that the State officers might have their salaries paid in silver. Shields was ridiculed unmercifully in the letter for his vanity and his gallantry.

It happened that there were several young women in Springfield who had received rather too pronounced attention from Mr. Shields, and who were glad to see him tormented. Among them were Miss Todd and her friend Miss Julia Jayne. Lincoln's letter from the "Lost Townships" was such a success that they followed it up with one in which "Aunt Rebecca" proposed to the gallant auditor, and a few days later they published some very bad verses, signed "Cathleen," celebrating the wedding.

Springfield was highly entertained, less by the verses than by the fury of Shields. He would have satisfaction, he said, and he sent a friend, one General Whitesides, to the paper, to ask for the name of the writer of the communications. The editor, in a quandary, went to Lincoln, who, unwilling that Miss Todd and Miss Jayne should figure in the affair, ordered that his own name be given as the author of letters and poem. This was only about ten days after the first letter had appeared, on September 2d, and Lincoln left Springfield in a day or two for a long trip on the circuit. He was at Tremont when, on the morning of the seventeenth, two of his friends, E. H. Merryman and William Butler, drove up hastily. Shields and his friend Whitesides were behind, they said, the irate Irishman vowing that he would challenge Lincoln. They, knowing that Lincoln was "unpractised both as to diplomacy and weapons," had started as soon as they had learned that Shields had left Springfield, had passed him in the night, and were there to see Lincoln through.

It was not long before Shields and Whitesides arrived, and soon Lincoln received a note in which the indignant writer said: "I will take the liberty of requiring a full, positive, and absolute retraction of all offensive allusions used by you in these communications in relation to my private character and standing as a man, as an apology for the insults conveyed in them. This may prevent consequences which no one will regret more than myself."

Lincoln immediately replied that, since Shields had not stopped to inquire whether he really was the author of the articles, had not pointed out what was offensive in them, had assumed facts and hinted at consequences, he could not submit to answer the note. Shields wrote again, but Lincoln simply replied that he could receive nothing but a withdrawal of the first note or a challenge. To this he steadily held, even refusing to answer the question as to the authorship of the

letters, which Shields finally put. It was inconsistent with
his honor to negotiate for peace with Mr. Shields, he said,
unless Mr. Shields withdrew his former offensive letter.
Seconds were immediately named: Whitesides by Shields,
Merryman by Lincoln; and though they talked of peace,
Whitesides declared he could not mention it to his principal.
"He would challenge me next, and as soon cut my throat as
not."

This was on the nineteenth, and that night the party returned to Springfield. But in some way the affair had leaked
out, and fearing arrest, Lincoln and Merryman left town the
next morning. The instructions were left with Butler. If
Shields would withdraw his first note, and write another
asking if Lincoln was the author of the offensive articles,
and, if so, asking for gentlemanly satisfaction, then Lincoln
had prepared a letter explaining the whole affair. If Shields
would not do this, there was nothing to do but fight. Lincoln left the following preliminaries for the duel:

"*First*. Weapons: Cavalry broadswords of the largest
size, precisely equal in all respects, and such as now used by
the cavalry company at Jacksonville.

"*Second*. Position: A plank ten feet long, and from nine
to twelve inches broad, to be firmly fixed on edge, on the
ground, as the line between us, which neither is to pass his
foot over on forfeit of his life. Next a line drawn on the
ground on either side of said plank and parallel with it, each
at the distance of the whole length of the sword and three
feet additional from the plank; and the passing of his own
such line by either party during the fight shall be deemed a
surrender of the contest.

"*Third*. Time: On Thursday evening at five o'clock, if
you can get it so; but in no case to be at a greater distance of
time than Friday evening at five o'clock.

"*Fourth*. Place: Within three miles of Alton, on the opposite side of the river, the particular spot to be agreed on
by you."

As Mr. Shields refused to withdraw his first note, the entire party started for the rendezvous across the Mississippi. Lincoln and Merryman drove together in a dilapidated old buggy, in the bottom of which rattled a number of broadswords. It was the morning of the 22d of September when the duellists arrived in the town. There are people still living in Alton who remember their coming. "The party arrived about the middle of the morning," says Mr. Edward Levis, "and soon crossed the river to a sand-bar which at the time was, by reason of the low water, a part of the Missouri mainland. The means of conveyance was an old horse-ferry that was operated by a man named Chapman. The weapons were in the keeping of the friends of the principals, and no care was taken to conceal them; in fact, they were openly displayed. Naturally, there was a great desire among the male population to attend the duel, but the managers of the affair would not permit any but their own party to board the ferryboat. Skiffs were very scarce, and but a few could avail themselves of the opportunity in this way. I had to content myself with standing on the levee and watching proceedings at long range."

As soon as the parties reached the island the seconds began preparations for the duel, the principals meanwhile seating themselves on logs on opposite sides of the field—a half-cleared spot in the timber. One of the spectators says:

"I watched Lincoln closely while he sat on his log awaiting the signal to fight. His face was grave and serious. I could discern nothing suggestive of 'Old Abe,' as we knew him. I never knew him to go so long before without making a joke, and I began to believe he was getting frightened. But presently he reached over and picked up one of the swords, which he drew from its scabbard. Then he felt along the edge of the weapon with his thumb, like a barber feels of the edge of his razor, raised himself to his full height, stretched out his long arms and clipped off a twig from above his head with the sword. There wasn't another man of us who could have reached anywhere near that twig, and the absurdity of that long-reaching fellow fighting with cavalry sabers with Shields, who could walk under his arm, came pretty near making me howl with laughter. After Lincoln had cut off the twig he returned the sword to the scabbard with a sigh and sat down, but I detected the gleam in his eye, which was always the forerunner of one of his inimitable yarns, and fully expected him to tell a side-splitter there in the shadow of the grave—Shields's grave."

The arrangements for the affair were about completed when the duellists were joined by some unexpected friends. Lincoln and Merryman, on their way to Alton, had stopped at White Hall for dinner. Across the street from the hotel lived Mr. Elijah Lott, an acquaintance of Merryman. Mr. Lott was not long in finding out what was on foot, and as soon as the duellists had departed, he drove to Carrollton, where he knew that Colonel John J. Hardin and several other friends of Lincoln were attending court, and warned them of the trouble. Hardin and one or two others immediately started for Alton. They arrived in time to calm Shields, and to aid the seconds in adjusting matters "with honor to all concerned."

That the duellists returned in good spirits is evident from Mr. Levis's reminiscences: "It was not very long," says he, "until the boat was seen returning to Alton. As it drew near I saw what was presumably a mortally wounded man lying in the bow of the boat. His shirt appeared to be bathed in blood. I distinguished Jacob Smith, a constable, fanning the supposed victim vigorously. The people on the bank held their breath in suspense, and guesses were freely made as to which of the two men had been so terribly wounded. But suspense was soon turned to chagrin and relief when it transpired that the supposed candidate for another world was nothing more nor less than a log covered with a red shirt.

This ruse had been resorted to in order to fool the people on the levee; and it worked to perfection. Lincoln and Shields came off the boat together, chatting in a nonchalant and pleasant manner."

The Lincoln-Shields duel had so many farcical features, and Miss Todd had unwittingly been so much to blame for it, that one can easily see that it might have had considerable influence on the relations of the two young people. However that may be, something had made Mr. Lincoln feel that he could renew his engagement. Early in October, not a fortnight after the duel, he wrote Speed: "You have now been the husband of a lovely woman nearly eight months. That you are happier now than the day you married her I well know, for without you would not be living. But I have your word for it, too, and the returning elasticity of spirits which is manifested in your letters. But I want to ask a close question: Are you now in feelings as well as judgment glad that you are married as you are?

"From anybody but me this would be an impudent question, not to be tolerated; but I know that you will pardon it in me. Please answer it quickly, as I am impatient to know."

We do not know Speed's answer, nor the final struggle of the man's heart. We only know that on November 4, 1842, Lincoln was married, the wedding being almost impromptu. Mrs. Dr. Brown, Miss Todd's cousin, in the same letter quoted from above, describes the wedding:

"One morning, bright and early, my cousin came down in her excited, impetuous way, and said to my father: 'Uncle, you must go up and tell my sister that Mr. Lincoln and I are to be married this evening,' and to me: 'Get on your bonnet and go with me to get my gloves, shoes, etc., and then to Mr. Edwards's.' When we reached there we found some excitement over a wedding being sprung upon them so suddenly. However, my father, in his lovely, pacific way, 'poured oil upon the waters,' and we thought everything was 'ship-shape,' when Mrs. Edwards laughingly said: 'How fortunately you selected this evening, for the Episcopal Sewing Society is to meet here, and my supper is all ordered.'

"But that comfortable little arrangement would not hold, as Mary declared she would not make a spectacle for gossiping ladies to gaze upon and talk about; there had already

THE PEOPLE OF THE STATE OF ILLINOIS.

To any Minister of the Gospel, or other authorised Person—GREETING.

THESE are to License and permit you to join in the holy bands of Matrimony *Abraham Lincoln* and *Mary Todd* of the County of Sangamon and State of Illinois, and for so doing, this shall be your sufficient warrant.

Given under my hand and seal of office, at Springfield, in said County this 4ᵗʰ day of Novmbr 1842

*N. W. Matheny*, Clerk.

Solemnized on the same 4ᵗʰ day of Nov. 1842          *Charles Dresser*

FACSIMILE OF MARRIAGE LICENSE AND CERTIFICATE OF ABRAHAM LINCOLN.
From the original on file in the County Clerk's office of Springfield, Ill.

been too much talk about her. Then my father was despatched to tell Mr. Lincoln that the wedding would be deferred until the next evening. Clergyman, attendants and intimate friends were notified, and on Friday evening, in the midst of a small circle of friends, with the elements doing their worst in the way of rain, this singular courtship culminated in marriage. This I know to be literally true, as I was one of her bridesmaids, Miss Jayne (afterwards Mrs. Lyman Trumbull) and Miss Rodney being the others."

# CHAPTER XII

LINCOLN BECOMES A CANDIDATE FOR CONGRESS AND IS
DEFEATED—ON THE STUMP IN 1844—NOMINATED AND
ELECTED TO THE 30TH CONGRESS

For eight successive years Lincoln had been a member of
the General Assembly of Illinois. It was quite long enough,
in his judgment, and his friends seem to have wanted to give
him something better, for in 1841 they offered to support
him as a candidate for governor of the State. This, however, he refused. His ambition was to go to Washington.
In 1842 he declined renomination for the assembly and became a candidate for Congress. He did not wait to be asked,
nor did he leave his case in the hands of his friends. He
frankly announced his desire, and managed his own canvass.
There was no reason, in Lincoln's opinion, for concealing
political ambition. He recognized, at the same time, the
legitimacy of the ambition of his friends, and entertained no
suspicion or rancor if they contested places with him.

"Do you suppose that I should ever have got into notice
if I had waited to be hunted up and pushed forward by older
men?" he wrote his friend Herndon once, when the latter
was complaining that the older men did not help him on.
"The way for a young man to rise is to improve himself
every way he can, never suspecting that anybody wishes to
hinder him. Allow me to assure you that suspicion and jeal-
ousy never did help any man in any situation. There may
sometimes be ungenerous attempts to keep a young man
down; and they will succeed, too, if he allows his mind to be
diverted from its true channel to brood over the attempted

injury. Cast about, and see if this feeling has not injured every person you have ever known to fall into it."

Lincoln had something more to do, however, in 1842, than simply to announce himself in the innocent manner of early politics. The convention system introduced into Illinois in 1835 by the Democrats had been zealously opposed by all good Whigs, Lincoln included, until constant defeat taught them that to resist organization by an every-man-for-himself policy was hopeless and wasteful, and that if they would succeed they must meet organization with organization. In 1841 a Whig State convention had been called to nominate candidates for the offices of governor and lieutenant-governor; and now, in March, 1843, a Whig meeting was held again at Springfield, at which the party's platform was laid, and a committee, of which Lincoln was a member, was appointed to prepare an "Address to the People of Illinois." In this address the convention system was earnestly defended. Against this rapid adoption of the abominated system many of the Whigs protested, and Lincoln found himself supporting before his constituents the tactics he had once warmly opposed. In a letter to his friend John Bennett, of Petersburg, written in March, 1843, he said:

"I am sorry to hear that any of the Whigs of your county, or of any county, should longer be against conventions. On last Wednesday evening a meeting of all the Whigs then here from all parts of the State was held, and the question of the propriety of conventions was brought up and fully discussed, and at the end of the discussion a resolution recommending the system of conventions to all the Whigs of the State was unanimously adopted. Other resolutions were also passed, all of which will appear in the next 'Journal.' The meeting also appointed a committee to draft an address to the people of the State, which address will also appear in the next 'Journal.' In it you will find a brief argument in favor of conventions, and, although I wrote it myself, I *will* say to you

(13)

that it is conclusive upon the point, and cannot be reasonably answered.

"If there be any good Whig who is disposed still to stick out against conventions, get him, at least, to read the argument in their favor in the 'Address.' "

The "brief argument" which Lincoln thought so conclusive, "if he did write it himself," justified his good opinion. After its circulation there were few found to "stick out against conventions."

The Whigs of the various counties in the Congressional district met on April 5, as they had been instructed to do, and chose delegates. John J. Hardin of Jacksonville, Edward D. Baker and Abraham Lincoln of Springfield, were the three candidates for whom these delegates were instructed.

To Lincoln's keen disappointment, the delegation from Sangamon county was instructed for Baker. A variety of social and personal influences, besides Baker's popularity, worked against Lincoln. "It would astonish, if not amuse, the older citizens," wrote Lincoln to a friend, "to learn that I (a stranger, friendless, uneducated, penniless boy, working on a flatboat at ten dollars per month) have been put down here as the candidate of pride, wealth, and aristocratic family distinction." He was not only accused of being an aristocrat, he was called "a deist." He had fought, or been about to fight, a duel. His wife's relations were Episcopalian and Presbyterian. He and she attended a Presbyterian church. These influences alone could not be said to have defeated him, he wrote, but "they levied a tax of considerable per cent. upon my strength."

The meeting that named Baker as its choice for Congress appointed Lincoln one of the delegates to the convention. "In getting Baker the nomination," Lincoln wrote to Speed, "I shall be fixed a good deal like a fellow who is made a groomsman to a man that has cut him out, and is marrying his own dear 'gal.'" From the first, however, he stood bravely by Baker. "I feel myself bound not to hinder him in any way from getting the nomination; I should despise myself were I to attempt it," he wrote certain of his constituents who were anxious that he should attempt to secure the nomination in spite of his instructions. It was soon evident to both Lincoln and Baker that John J. Hardin was probably the strongest candidate in the district, and so it proved when the convention met in May, 1843, at Pekin.

It has frequently been charged that in this Pekin convention, Hardin, Baker, and Lincoln agreed to take in turn the three next nominations to Congress, thus establishing a species of rotation in office. This charge cannot be sustained. What occurred at the Pekin convention is here related by one of the delegates, the Hon. J. M. Ruggles of Havana, Illinois.

"When the convention assembled," writes Mr. Ruggles, "Baker was there with his friend and champion delegate, Abraham Lincoln. The ayes and noes had been taken, and there were fifteen votes apiece, and one in doubt that had not arrived. That was myself. I was known to be a warm friend of Baker, representing people who were partial to Hardin. As soon as I arrived Baker hurried to me, saying: 'How is it? It all depends on you.' On being told that notwithstanding my partiality for him, the people I represented expected me to vote for Hardin, and that I would have to do so, Baker at once replied: 'You are right—there is no other way.' The convention was organized, and I was elected secretary. Baker immediately arose, and made a most thrilling address, thoroughly arousing the sympathies of the convention, and ended by declining his candidacy. Hardin was nominated by acclamation; and then came the episode.

"Immediately after the nomination, Mr. Lincoln walked across the room to my table, and asked if I would favor a resolution recommending Baker for the next term. On being answered in the affirmative, he said: 'You prepare the resolution, I will support it, and I think we can pass it.' The resolution created a profound sensation, especially with the friends of Hardin. After an excited and angry discussion, the resolution passed by a majority of one.''

Lincoln supported Hardin energetically in the campaign which followed. In a letter to the former written on May 11th, just after the convention, he says:

"Butler informs me that he received a letter from you in which you expressed some doubt as to whether the Whigs of Sangamon will support you cordially. You may at once dismiss all fears on that subject. We have already resolved to make a particular effort to give you the very largest majority possible in our county. From this no Whig of the county dissents. We have many objects for doing it. We make it a matter of honor and pride to do it; we do it because we love the Whig cause; we do it because we like you personally; and, last, we wish to convince you that we do not bear that hatred to Morgan County that you people have seemed so long to imagine. You will see by the 'Journal' of this week that we propose, upon pain of losing a barbecue, to give you twice as great a majority in this county as you shall receive in your own. I got up the proposal.''

Lincoln was true to his promise and after Hardin was elected and in Washington he kept him informed of much that went on in the district; thus in an amusing letter written in May, 1844, while the latter was in Congress, he tells him of one disgruntled constituent who must be pacified, giving him, at the same time, a hint as to the temper of the "Locofocos."

"Knowing that you have correspondents enough, I have forborne to trouble you heretofore," he writes; "and I now only do so to get you to set a matter right which has got wrong with one of our best friends. It is old Uncle Thomas Campbell of Spring Creek (Berlin P. O.). He has received

several documents from you, and he says they are old newspapers and old documents, having no sort of interest in them.
He is, therefore, getting a strong impression that you treat
him with disrespect. This, I know, is a mistaken impression, and you must correct it. The way, I leave to yourself.
Robert W. Canfield says he would like to have a document
or two from you.

"The Locos here are in considerable trouble about Van
Buren's letter on Texas, and the Virginia electors. They are
growing sick of the tariff question, and consequently are
much confounded at Van Buren's cutting them off from the
new Texas question. Nearly half the leaders swear they
won't stand it. Of those are Ford, T. Campbell, Ewing,
Calhoun, and others. They don't exactly say they won't go
for Van Buren, but they say he will not be the candidate, and
that *they* are for Texas anyhow."

The resolution passed at the Pekin convention in 1843 was
remembered and respected by the Whigs when the time came
to nominate Hardin's successor. Baker was selected and
elected, Lincoln working for him as loyally as he had for
Hardin. In this campaign—that of 1844—Lincoln was a
presidential elector. He went into the canvass with unusual
ardor for Henry Clay was the candidate and Lincoln shared
the popular idolatry of the man. His devotion was not
merely a sentiment, however. He had been an intelligent
student of Clay's public life, and his sympathy was all with
the principles of the "gallant Harry of the West." Throughout the campaign he worked zealously, travelling all over the
State, speaking and talking. As a rule, he was accompanied
by a Democrat. The two went unannounced, simply stopping at some friendly house. On their arrival the word was
sent around, "the candidates are here," and the men of the
neighborhood gathered to hear the discussion, which was carried on in the most informal way, the candidates frequently
sitting tipped back against the side of the house, or perched
on a rail. whittling during the debates. Nor was all of this

electioneering done by argument. Many votes were still cast in Illinois out of personal liking, and the wily candidate did his best to make himself agreeable, particularly to the women of the household. The Hon. William L. D. Ewing, a Democrat who travelled with Lincoln in one campaign, used to tell a story of how he and Lincoln were eager to win the favor of one of their hostesses, whose husband was an important man in his neighborhood. Neither had made much progress until at milking-time Mr. Ewing started after the woman of the house as she went to the yard, took her pail, and insisted on milking the cow himself. He naturally felt that this was a master stroke. But receiving no reply from the hostess, to whom he had been talking loudly as he milked, he looked around, only to see her and Lincoln leaning comfortably over the bars, engaged in an animated discussion. By the time he had completed his self-imposed task, Lincoln had captivated the hostess, and all Mr. Ewing received for his pains was hearty thanks for giving her a chance to have so pleasant a talk with Mr. Lincoln.

Lincoln's speeches at this time were not confined to his own State. He made several in Indiana, being invited thither by prominent Whig politicians who had heard him speak in Illinois. The first and most important of his meetings in Indiana was at Bruceville. The Democrats, learning of the proposed Whig gathering, arranged one, for the same evening, with Lieutenant William W. Carr of Vincennes as speaker. As might have been expected from the excited state of politics at the moment, the proximity of the two mass-meetings aroused party loyalty to a fighting pitch. "Each party was determined to break up the other's speaking," writes Miss O'Flynn, in a description of the Bruceville meeting prepared from interviews with those who took part in it. "The night was made hideous with the rattle of tin pans and bells and the blare of cow-horns. In spite of all

the din and uproar of the younger element, a few grown-up
male radicals and partisan women sang and cheered loudly
for their favorites, who kept on with their flow of political
information.  Lieutenant Carr stood in his carriage, and addressed the crowd around him, while a local politician acted
as grand marshal of the night, and urged the yelling Democratic legion to surge to the schoolhouse, where Abraham
Lincoln was speaking, and run the Whigs from their headquarters.  Old men now living, who were big boys then, cannot remember any of the burning eloquence of either speaker.
As they now laughingly express it: 'We were far more interested in the noise than the success of the speakers, and we
ran backward and forward from one camp to the other.' "

Fortunately, the remaining speeches in Indiana were made
under more dignified conditions.  One was delivered at
Rockport; another "from the door of a harness shop" near
Gentryville, Lincoln's old home in Indiana; and a third at
the "Old Carter School" in the same neighborhood.  At the
delivery of the last many of Lincoln's old neighbors were
present, and they still tell of the cordial way in which he
greeted them and inquired for old friends.  After his speech
he drove home with Mr. Josiah Crawford, for whom he had
once worked as a day laborer.  His interest in every familiar
spot—a saw-pit where he had once worked—the old swimming pool, the town grocery, the mill, the blacksmith shop,
surprised and flattered everybody.  "He went round inspect-
ing everything," declares one of his hosts.  So vivid were
the memories which this visit to Gentryville aroused, so deep
were Lincoln's emotions, that he even attempted to express
them in verse.  A portion of the lines he wrote have been
preserved, the only remnants of his various early attempts
at versification.

In this campaign of 1844 Lincoln for the second time in
his political life met the slavery question.  The chief issue of

that campaign was the annexation of Texas. The Whigs, under Clay's leadership, opposed it. To annex Texas without the consent of Mexico would compromise our national reputation for fair dealing, Clay argued; it would bring on war with Mexico, destroy the existing relations between North and South and compel the North to annex Canada, and it would tend to extend rather than restrict slavery.

A large party of strong anti-slavery people in the North felt that Clay did not give enough importance to the anti-slavery argument and they nominated a third candidate, James G. Birney. This "Liberal Party" as it was called, had a fair representation in Illinois and Lincoln must have encountered them frequently, though what arguments he used against them, if any, we do not know, no extracts of his 1844 speeches being preserved.

The next year, 1845, he found the abolition sentiment stronger than ever. Prominent among the leaders of the third party in the State were two brothers, Williamson and Madison Durley of Hennepin, Illinois. They were outspoken advocates of their principles, and even operated a station of the underground railroad. Lincoln knew the Durleys, and, when visiting Hennepin to speak, solicited their support. They opposed their liberty principles. When Lincoln returned to Springfield he wrote Williamson Durley a letter which sets forth with admirable clearness his exact position on the slavery question at that period. It is the most valuable document on the question which we have up to this point in Lincoln's life.

"When I saw you at home," Lincoln began, "it was agreed that I should write to you and your brother Madison. Until I then saw you I was not aware of your being what is generally called an Abolitionist, or, as you call yourself, a Liberty man, though I well knew there were many such in your county.

"I was glad to hear that you intended to attempt to bring about, at the next election in Putnam, a union of the Whigs proper and such of the Liberty men as are Whigs in principle on all questions save only that of slavery. So far as I can perceive, by such union neither party need yield anything on *the* point in difference between them. If the Whig abolitionists of New York had voted with us last fall, Mr. Clay would now be President, Whig principles in the ascendant, and Texas not annexed; whereas, by the division, all that either had at stake in the contest was lost. And, indeed, it was extremely probable, beforehand, that such would be the result. As I always understood, the Liberty men deprecated the annexation of Texas extremely; and this being so, why they should refuse to cast their votes (so) as to prevent it, even to me seemed wonderful. What was their process of reasoning, I can only judge from what a single one of them told me. It was this: 'We are not to do *evil* that *good* may come.' This general proposition is doubtless correct; but did it apply? If by your votes you could have prevented the *extension*, etc., of slavery, would it not have been *good,* and not *evil,* so to have used your votes, even though it involved the casting of them for a slave-holder? By the *fruit* the tree is to be known. An *evil* tree cannot bring forth *good* fruit. If the fruit of electing Mr. Clay would have been to prevent the extension of slavery, could the act of electing have been evil?

"But I will not argue further. I perhaps ought to say that individually I never was much interested in the Texas question. I never could see much good to come of annexation, inasmuch as they were already a free republican people on our own model. On the other hand, I never could very clearly see how the annexation would augment the evil of slavery. It always seemed to me that slaves would be taken there in about equal numbers, with or without annexation. And if more *were* taken because of annexation, still there would be just so many the fewer left where they were taken from. It is possibly true, to some extent, that, with annexation, some slaves may be sent to Texas and continued in slavery that otherwise might have been liberated. To whatever extent this may be true, I think annexation an evil. I hold it to be a paramount duty of us in the free States, due to the Union of the States, and perhaps to liberty itself (paradox though it may seem), to let the slavery of the other States alone; while, on the other hand, I hold it to be equally clear that we should never knowingly lend ourselves, directly or indirectly, to prevent that slavery from dying a natural death—to find new places for it to live in, when it can no longer exist in the old. Of course I am not now considering what would be our duty in cases of insurrection among the slaves. To recur to the Texas question, I understand the Liberty men to have viewed annexation as a much greater evil than ever I did; and I would like to convince you, if I could, that they could have prevented it, without violation of principle, if they had chosen."

At the time that Lincoln wrote the above letter to the Durley brothers he was working for a nomination to Congress. In 1843 he had helped elect his friend Hardin. He had secured the nomination for Baker in 1844 and had worked faithfully to elect him. Now he felt that his duty to his friends was discharged and that he was free to try for himself. He undoubtedly hoped that neither of his friends would contest the nomination. Baker did not but late in 1845 it became evident that Hardin might. Lincoln was worried over the prospect. "The paper at Pekin has nominated Hardin for governor," he wrote his friend B. F. James in November, "and, commenting on this, the Alton papers indirectly nominated him for Congress. It would give Hardin a great start, and perhaps use me up, if the Whig papers of the district should nominate him for Congress. If your feelings toward me are the same as when you saw me (which I have no reason to doubt), I wish you would let nothing appear in your paper which may operate against me. You understand. Matters stand just as they did when I saw you. Baker is certainly off the track, and I fear Hardin intends to be on it."

Hardin certainly was free to run for Congress if he wanted to. He had voluntarily declined the nomination in

1844, because of the events of the Pekin convention, but he had made no promise to do so in 1846. Many of the Whigs of the district had not expected him to be a candidate, how= ever, arguing that Lincoln, because of his relation to the party, should be given his turn. "We do not entertain a doubt," wrote the editor of the "Sangamon Journal," in February, 1846, "that if we could reverse the positions of the two men, a very large portion of those who now support Mr. Lincoln most warmly would support General Hardin quite as well."

As time went on and Lincoln found in all probability that Hardin would enter the race, it made him anxious and a little melancholy. In writing to his friend Dr. Robert Boal of Lacon, Illinois, on January 7, 1846, he said:

"Since I saw you last fall, I have often thought of writing you, as it was then understood I would; but, on reflection, I have always found that I had nothing new to tell you. All has happened as I then told you I expected it would—Baker's declining, Hardin's taking the track, and so on.

"If Hardin and I stood precisely equal—that is, if *neither* of us had been to Congress, or if we *both* had—it would not only accord with what I have always done, for the sake of peace, to give way to him; and I expect I should do it. That I *can* voluntarily postpone my pretensions, when they are no more than equal to those to which they are postponed, you have yourself seen. But to yield to Hardin under present circumstances seems to me as nothing else than yielding to one who would gladly sacrifice me altogether. This I would rather not submit to. That Hardin is talented, energetic, unusually generous and magnanimous, I have, before this, affirmed to you, and do not now deny. You know that my only argument is that 'turn about is fair play.' This he, prac- tically at least, denies.

"If it would not be taxing you too much, I wish you would write me, telling the aspect of things in your county, or rather your district; and also send the names of some of your Whig neighbors to whom I might, with propriety, write,

Unless I can get some one to do this, Hardin, with his old
franking list, will have the advantage of me.  My reliance
for a fair shake (and I want nothing more) in your county
is chiefly on you, because of your position and standing, and
because I am acquainted with so few others.  Let me hear
from you soon."

Lincoln followed the vibrations of feeling in the various
counties with extreme nicety, studying every individual
whose loyalty he suspected or whose vote was not yet
pledged.  "Nathan Dresser is here," he wrote to his friend
Bennett, on January 15, 1846, "and speaks as though the
contest between Hardin and me is to be doubtful in Menard
county.  I know he is candid, and this alarms me some.  I
asked him to tell me the names of the men that were going
strong for Hardin; he said Morris was about as strong as
any.  Now tell me, is Morris going it openly?  You remember you wrote me that he would be neutral.  Nathan also
said that some man (who he could not remember) had said
lately that Menard county was again to decide the contest,
and that made the contest very doubtful.  Do you know who
that was?

"Don't fail me to write me instantly on receiving, telling
me all—particularly the names of those who are going strong
against me."

In January, General Hardin suggested that since he and
Lincoln were the only persons mentioned as candidates, there
be no convention, but the selection be left to the Whig voters
of the district.  Lincoln refused.

"It seems to me," he wrote Hardin, "that on reflection you
will see the fact of your having been in Congress has, in
various ways, so spread your name in the district as to give
you a decided advantage in such a stipulation.  I appreciate
your desire to keep down excitement; and I promise you to
'keep cool' under all circumstances. . . . I have always
been in the habit of acceding to almost any proposal that a

friend would make, and I am truly sorry that I cannot in this. I perhaps ought to mention that some friends at different places are endeavoring to secure the honor of the sitting of the convention at their towns respectively, and I fear that they would not feel much complimented if we shall make a bargain that it should sit nowhere."

After General Hardin received this refusal he withdrew from the contest, in a manly and generous letter which was warmly approved by the Whigs of the district. Both men were so much loved that a break between them would have been a disastrous thing for the party. "We are truly glad that a contest which in its nature was calculated to weaken the ties of friendship has terminated amicably," said the Sangamon " Journal."

The charge that Hardin, Baker, and Lincoln tried to ruin one another in this contest for Congress has often been denied by their associates, and never more emphatically than by Judge Gillespie, an influential politician of the State. "Hardin," Judge Gillespie says, "was one of the most unflinching and unfaltering Whigs that ever drew the breath of life. He was a mirror of chivalry, and so was Baker. Lincoln had boundless respect for, and confidence in, them both. He knew they would sacrifice themselves rather than do an act that could savor in the slightest degree of meanness or dishonor. These men, Lincoln, Hardin and Baker, were bosom friends, to my certain knowledge. . . Lincoln felt that they could be actuated by nothing but the most honorable sentiments towards him. For although they were rivals, they were all three men of the most punctilious honor, and devoted friends. I knew them intimately, and can say confidently that there never was a particle of envy on the part of one towards the other. The rivalry between them was of the most honorable and friendly character, and when Hardin and Baker were killed ( Hardin in Mexico, and Baker at Ball's Bluff) Lincoln felt that in the death of each he had lost a dear and true friend."

After Hardin's withdrawal, Lincoln went about in his characteristic way trying to soothe his and Hardin's friends. "Previous to General Hardin's withdrawal," he wrote one of his correspondents, "some of his friends and some of mine had become a little warm; and I felt . . . that for them now to meet face to face and converse together was the best way to efface any remnant of unpleasant feeling, if any such existed. I did not suppose that General Hardin's friends were in any greater need of having their feelings corrected than mine were."

In May, Lincoln was nominated. His Democratic opponent was Peter Cartwright, the famous Methodist exhorter, the most famous itinerant preacher of the pioneer era. Cartwright had moved from Kentucky to Illinois when still a young man to get into a free State, and had settled in the Sangamon valley, near Springfield. For the next forty years he travelled over the State, most of the time on horseback, preaching the gospel in his unique and rugged fashion. His district was at first so large (extending from Kaskaskia to Galena) that he was unable to traverse the whole of it in the same year. He was elected to the legislature in 1828 and again in 1832; Lincoln, in the latter year, being an opposing candidate. In 1840 when he was the Democratic nominee for Congress against Lincoln he was badly beaten. Cartwright now made an energetic canvass, his chief weapon against Lincoln being the old charges of atheism and aristocracy; but they failed of effect, and in August, Lincoln was elected.

The contest over, sudden and characteristic disillusion seized him. "Being elected to Congress, though I am grateful to our friends for having done it, has not pleased me as much as I expected," he wrote Speed.

# CHAPTER XIII

LINCOLN IN WASHINGTON IN 1847—HE OPPOSES THE MEXI-
CAN WAR—CAMPAIGNING IN NEW ENGLAND

In November, 1847, Lincoln started for Washington. The city in 1848 was little more than the outline of the Washington of 1899. The capitol was without the present wings, dome, or western terrace. The White House, the City Hall, the Treasury, the Patent Office, and the Post-Office were the only public buildings standing then which have not been rebuilt or materially changed. The streets were unpaved, and their dust in summer and mud in winter are celebrated in every record of the period. The parks and circles were still unplanted. Near the White House were a few fine old homes, and Capitol Hill was partly built over. Although there were deplorable wastes between these two points, the majority of the people lived in the southeastern part of the city, on or near Pennsylvania avenue. The winter that Lincoln was in Washington, Daniel Webster lived on Louisiana avenue, near Sixth street; Speaker Winthrop and Thomas H. Benton on C street, near Third; John Quincy Adams and James Buchanan, the latter then Secretary of State, on F street, between Thirteenth and Fourteenth. Many of the senators and congressmen were in hotels, the leading ones of which were Willard's, Coleman's, Gadsby's, Brown's, Young's, Fuller's, and the United States. Stephen A. Douglas, who was in Washington for his first term as senator, lived at Willard's. So inadequate were the hotel accommodations during the sessions that visitors to the town were frequently obliged to accept most uncomfortable makeshifts for beds. Seward, vis-

iting the city in 1847, tells of sleeping on "a cot between two
beds occupied by strangers."

The larger number of members lived in "messes," a species
of boarding-club, over which the owner of the house occupied
usually presided. The "National Intelligencer" of the day is
sprinkled with announcements of persons "prepared to accommodate a mess of members." Lincoln went to live in one
of the best known of these clubs, Mrs. Spriggs's, in "Duff
Green's Row," on Capitol Hill. This famous row has now
entirely disappeared, the ground on which it stood being occupied by the Congressional Library.

At Mrs. Spriggs's, Lincoln had as mess-mates several
congressmen: A. R. McIlvaine, James Pollock, John Strohm,
and John Blanchard, all of Pennsylvania, Patrick Tompkins
of Mississippi, Joshua R. Giddings of Ohio, and Elisha Em-
bree of Indiana. Among his neighbors in messes on Capitol
Hill were Andrew Johnson of Tennessee, Alexander H.
Stephens of Georgia, and Jefferson Davis of Mississippi.
One of the members of the mess at Mrs. Spriggs's in the winter of 1847-1848 was Dr. S. C. Busey of Washington, D. C.

" I soon learned to know and admire Lincoln," says Dr.
Busey in his " Personal Reminiscences and Recollections,"
" for his simple and unostentatious manners, kind-hearted-
ness, and amusing jokes, anecdotes, and witticisms. When
about to tell an anecdote during a meal he would lay down
his knife and fork, place his elbows upon the table, rest his
face between his hands, and begin with the words, ' That re-
minds me,' and proceed. Everybody prepared for the explosion sure to follow. I recall with vivid pleasure the scene
of merriment at the dinner after his first speech in the House
of Representatives, occasioned by the descriptions, by himself and others of the congressional mess, of the uproar in
the House during its delivery.

"Congressman Lincoln was always neatly but very plainly
dressed, very simple and approachable in manner, and unpre-

entious. He attended to his business, going promptly to the House and remaining till the session adjourned, and appeared to be familiar with the progress of legislation."

The town offered then little in the way of amusement. The Adelphi theater was opened that winter for the first time, and presented a variety of mediocre plays. At the Olympia were "lively and beautiful exhibitions of model artists." Herz and Sivori, the pianists, then touring in the United States, played several times in the season; and there was a Chinese museum. Add the exhibitions of Brown's paintings of the heroes of Palo Alto, Resaca, Monterey, and Buena Vista, and of Powers's "Greek Slave," the performances of Dr. Valentine, "Delineator of Eccentricities," a few lectures, and numerous church socials, and you have about all there was in the way of public entertainments in Washington in 1848. But of dinners, receptions, and official gala affairs there were many. Lincoln's name appears frequently in the "National Intelligencer" on committees to offer dinners to this or that great man. In the spring of 1849 he was one of the managers of the inaugural ball given to Taylor. His friend Washburn recalls an amusing incident of Lincoln at this ball. "A small number of mutual friends," says Mr. Washburn, "including Mr. Lincoln, made up a party to attend the inauguration ball together. It was by far the most brilliant inauguration ball ever given. Of course Mr. Lincoln had never seen anything of the kind before. One of the most modest and unpretending persons present, he could not have dreamed that like honors were to come to him, almost within a little more than a decade. He was greatly interested in all that was to be seen, and we did not take our departure until three or four o'clock in the morning. When we went to the cloak and hat room, Mr. Lincoln had no trouble in finding his short cloak, which little more than covered his shoulders, but, after a long search was unable to find his hat. After an hour he gave up

all idea of finding it. Taking his cloak on his arm, he walked
out into Judiciary square, deliberately adjusting it on his
shoulders, and started off bare-headed for his lodgings. It
would be hard to forget the sight of that tall and slim man,
with his short cloak thrown over his shoulders, starting for
his long walk home on Capitol Hill, at four o'clock in the
morning, without any hat on."

Another reminiscence of his homely and independent ways
comes from the librarian of the Supreme Court at that period, through Lincoln's friend, Washburn. Mr. Lincoln, the
story goes, came to the library one day for the purpose of
procuring some law books which he wanted to take to his
room for examination. Getting together all the books he
wanted, he placed them in a pile on a table. Taking a large
bandana handkerchief from his pocket, he tied them up, and
putting a stick which he had brought with him through a
knot he had made in the handkerchief, he shouldered the
package and marched off from the library to his room. In
a few days he returned the books in the same way.

Lincoln's simple, sincere friendliness and his quaint humor
soon won him a sure, if quiet, social position in Washington.
He was frequently invited to Mr. Webster's Saturday breakfasts, where his stories were highly relished for their originality and drollery. Dr. Busey recalls his popularity at one
of the leading places of amusement on Capitol Hill.

"Congressman Lincoln was very fond of bowling," he
says, "and would frequently join others of the mess, or meet
other members in a match game, at the alley of James Cas-
paris, which was near the boarding-house. He was a very
awkward bowler, but played the game with great zest and
spirit, solely for exercise and amusement, and greatly to the
enjoyment and entertainment of the other players and by-
standers by his criticisms and funny illustrations. He accepted success and defeat with like good nature and humor,
and left the alley at the conclusion of the game without a

sorrow or disappointment. When it was known that he was
in the alley, there would assemble numbers of people to witness the fun which was anticipated by those who knew of his
fund of anecdotes and jokes. When in the alley, surrounded
by a crowd of eager listeners, he indulged with great freedom in the sport of narrative, some of which were very
broad. His witticisms seemed for the most part to be impromptu, but he always told the anecdotes and jokes as if he
wished to convey the impression that he had heard them
from some one; but they appeared very many times as if they
had been made for the immediate occasion."

Another place where he became at home and was much
appreciated was in the post-office at the Capitol.

"During the Christmas holidays," says Ben. Perley Poore,
" Mr. Lincoln found his way into the small room used as the
post-office of the House, where a few jovial raconteurs used
to meet almost every morning, after the mail had been distributed into the members' boxes, to exchange such new
stories as any of them might have acquired since they had
last met. After modestly standing at the door for several
days, Mr. Lincoln was reminded of a story, and by New
Year's he was recognized as the champion story-teller of the
Capitol. His favorite seat was at the left of the open fire-
place, tilted back in his chair, with his long legs reaching over
to the chimney jamb. He never told a story twice, but appeared to have an endless *répertoire* of them always ready,
like the successive charges in a magazine gun, and always
pertinently adapted to some passing event. It was refresh-
ing to us correspondents, compelled as we were to listen to
so much that was prosy and tedious, to hear this bright specimen of western genius tell his inimitable stories, especially
his reminiscences of the Black Hawk war."

But Lincoln had gone to Washington for work, and he at
once interested himself in the Whig organization formed to
elect the officers of the House. There was only a small Whig
majority, and it took skill and energy to keep the offices in

the party. Lincoln's share in achieving this result was generally recognized. As late as 1860, twelve years after the struggle, Robert C. Winthrop of Massachusetts, who was elected speaker, said in a speech in Boston wherein he discussed Lincoln's nomination to the Presidency: "You will be sure that I remember him with interest, if I may be allowed to remind you that he helped to make me the speaker of the Thirtieth Congress, when the vote was a very close and strongly contested vote."

A week after Congress organized, Lincoln wrote to Springfield: "As you are all so anxious for me to distinguish myself, I have concluded to do so before long;" and he did it—but not exactly as his Springfield friends wished. The United States was then at war with Mexico, a war that the Whigs abhorred. Lincoln had used his influence against it; but, hostilities declared, he had publicly affirmed that every loyal man must stand by the army. Many of his friends, Hardin, Baker, and Shields, among others, were at that moment in Mexico. Lincoln had gone to Washington intending to say nothing in opposition to the war. But the administration wished to secure from the Whigs not only votes of supplies and men, but a resolution declaring that the war was just and right. Lincoln, with others of his party in Congress, refused his sanction and voted for a resolution offered by Mr. Ashburn, which declared that the war had been "unnecessarily and unconstitutionally" begun. On December 22d he made his début in the House by the famous "Spot Resolutions," a series of searching questions so clearly put, so strong historically and logically, that they drove the administration from the "spot" where the war began, and showed that it had been the aggressor in the conquest. The resolution ran:—

"*Whereas*, The President of the United States, in his message of May 11, 1846, has declared that 'the Mexican

Government not only refused to receive him (the envoy of the United States), or to listen to his propositions, but, after a long-continued series of menaces, has at last invaded our territory and shed the blood of our fellow-citizens on our own soil.'

"And again, in his message of December 8, 1846, that ' we had ample cause of war against Mexico long before the breaking out of hostilities; but even then we forbore to take redress into our own hands until Mexico herself became the aggressor, by invading our soil in hostile array, and shedding the blood of our citizens.'

" And yet again, in his message of December 7, 1847, that ' the Mexican Government refused even to hear the terms of adjustment which he (our minister of peace) was authorized to propose, and finally, under wholly unjustifiable pretexts, involved the two countries in war, by invading the territory of the State of Texas, striking the first blow, and shedding the blood of our citizens on our own soil.'

"*And whereas,*   This House is desirous to obtain a full knowledge of all the facts which go to establish whether the particular spot on which the blood of our citizens was so shed was or was not at that time our own soil: therefore,

" *Resolved,* by the House of Representatives, that the President of the United States be respectfully requested to inform this House—

" First.   Whether the spot on which the blood of our citizens was shed, as in his message declared, was or was not within the territory of Spain, at least after the treaty of 1819 until the Mexican revolution.

" Second.  Whether that spot is or is not within the territory which was wrested from Spain by the revolutionary Government of Mexico.

" Third.  Whether that spot is or is not within a settlement of people, which settlement has existed ever since long before the Texas revolution, and until its inhabitants fled before the approach of the United States army.

" Fourth. Whether that settlement is or is not isolated from any and all other settlements by the Gulf and the Rio Grande on the south and west, and by wide uninhabited regions on the north and east.

"Fifth. Whether the people of that settlement, or a majority of them, or any of them, have ever submitted themselves to the government or laws of Texas or of the United States, by consent or by compulsion, either by accepting office, or voting at elections, or paying tax, or serving on juries, or having process served upon them, or in any other way.

"Sixth. Whether the people of that settlement did or did not flee from the approach of the United States army, leaving unprotected their homes and their growing crops, *before* the blood was shed, as in the message stated; and whether the first blood, so shed, was or was not shed within the inclosure of one of the people who had thus fled from it.

"Seventh. Whether our citizens, whose blood was shed, as in his message declared, were or were not, at that time, armed officers and soldiers, sent into that settlement by the military order of the President, through the Secretary of War.

"Eighth. Whether the military force of the United States was or was not so sent into that settlement after General Taylor had more than once intimated to the War Department that, in his opinion, no such movement was necessary to the defence or protection of Texas."

In January Lincoln followed up these resolutions with a speech in support of his position. His action was much criticised in Illinois, where the sound of the drum and the intoxication of victory had completely turned attention from the moral side of the question, and Lincoln found himself obliged to defend his position with even Mr. Herndon, his law partner, who, with many others, objected to Lincoln's voting for the Ashburn resolution.

"That vote," wrote Lincoln in answer to Mr. Herndon's letter, "affirms that the war was unnecessarily and unconstitutionally commenced by the President; and I will stake my life that if you had been in my place you would have voted just as I did. Would you have voted what you felt and knew to be a lie? I know you would not. Would you have gone out of the House—skulked the vote? I expect not. If you had skulked one vote, you would have had to skulk many more before the end of the session. Richardson's resolutions, introduced before I made any move or gave any vote upon the subject, make the direct question of the justice of the war; so that no man can be silent if he would. You are compelled to speak; and your only alternative is to tell the truth or a lie. I cannot doubt which you would do.

" This vote has nothing to do in determining my votes on the questions of supplies. I have always intended, and still intend, to vote supplies; perhaps not in the precise form recommended by the President, but in a better form for all purposes, except Locofoco party purposes." * * *

This determination to keep the wrong of the Mexican war before the people even while voting supplies for it Lincoln held to steadily. In May a pamphlet was sent him in which the author claimed that "in view of all the facts" the government of the United States had committed no aggression in Mexico.

"Not in view of all the facts," Lincoln wrote him. "There are facts which you have kept out of view. It is a fact that the United States army in marching to the Rio Grande marched into a peaceful Mexican settlement, and frightened the inhabitants away from their homes and their growing crops. It is a fact that Fort Brown, opposite Matamoras, was built by that army within a Mexican cotton-field, on which at the time the army reached it a young cotton crop was growing, and which crop was wholly destroyed and the field itself greatly and permanently injured by ditches, embankments, and the like. It is a fact that when the Mexicans captured Captain Thornton and his command, they found and captured them within another Mexican field.

" Now I wish to bring these facts to your notice, and to ascertain what is the result of your reflections upon them. If you deny that they are facts, I think I can furnish proofs which shall convince you that you are mistaken. If you admit that they are facts, then I shall be obliged for a reference to any law of language, law of States, law of nations, law of morals, law of religions, any law, human or divine, in which an authority can be found for saying those facts constitute 'No aggression.'

"Possibly you consider those acts too small for notice. Would you venture to so consider them had they been committed by any nation on earth against the humblest of our people? I know you would not. Then I ask, is the precept ' Whatsoever ye would that men should do to you, do ye even so to them ' obsolete? of no force? of no application? "

The routine work assigned Lincoln in the Thirtieth Congress was on the committee on the post-office and post roads. Several reports were made by him from this committee. These reports, with a speech on internal improvements, cover his published work in the House up to July.

As the Whigs were to hold their national convention for nominating a candidate for the presidency in June, Lincoln gave considerable time during the spring to electioneering. In his judgment the Whigs could elect nobody but General Taylor and he urged his friends in Illinois to give up Henry Clay, to whom many of them still clung. "Mr. Clay's chance for an election," he wrote, "is just no chance at all."

Lincoln went to the convention, which was held in Philadelphia, and as he prophesied, "Old Rough and Ready" was nominated. He went back to Washington full of enthusiasm. "In my opinion we shall have a most overwhelming, glorious triumph," he wrote a friend. "One unmistakable sign is that all the odds and ends are with us—Barnburners, Native Americans, Tyler men, disappointed office-seekers, Locofocos, and the Lord knows what. This is important, if in nothing else, in showing which way the wind blows."

In connection with Alexander H. Stephens, of whom he had become a warm friend, Toombs, and Preston, Lincoln formed the first Congressional Taylor club, known as the "Young Indians." Campaigning had already begun on the floor of Congress, and the members were daily making speeches for the various candidates. On July 27th Lincoln made a speech for Taylor. It was a boisterous election speech, full of merciless caricaturing, and delivered with inimitable drollery. It kept the House in an uproar, and was reported the country over by the Whig press. The "Baltimore American," in giving a synopsis of it, called it the "crack speech of the day," and said of Lincoln: "He is a very able, acute, uncouth, honest, upright man, and a tremendous wag, withal. . . . Mr. Lincoln's manner was so good-natured, and his style so peculiar, that he kept the House in a continuous roar of merriment for the last half hour of his speech. He would commence a point in his speech far up one of the aisles, and keep on talking, gesticulating, and walking until he would find himself, at the end of a paragraph, down in the centre of the area in front of the clerk's desk. He would then go back and take another *head*, and *work down* again. And so on, through his capital speech."

This speech, as well as the respect Lincoln's work in the House had inspired among the leaders of the party, brought him an invitation to deliver several campaign speeches in New England at the close of Congress, and he went there early in September. There was in New England, at that date, much strong anti-slavery feeling. The Whigs claimed to be "Free Soilers" as well as the party which appropriated that name, and Lincoln, in the first speech he made, defined carefully his position on the slavery question. This was at Worcester, Massachusetts, on September 12th. The Whig State convention had met to nominate a candidate for governor, and the most eminent Whigs of Massachusetts were present. Curiously enough the meeting was presided over by ex-Governor Levi Lincoln, a descendant, like Abraham Lincoln, from the original Samuel of Hingham. There were many brilliant speeches made; but if we are to trust the reports of the day, Lincoln's was the one which by its logic, its clearness, and its humor, did most for the Whig cause. "Gentle-

men inform me," says one Boston reporter, who came too
late for the exercises, "that it was one of the best speeches
ever heard in Worcester, and that several Whigs who had
gone off on the "free soil" fizzle have come back again to the
Whig ranks."

A report of the speech was printed in the Boston "Advertiser." According to this report Lincoln spent the first part
of his hour in defending General Taylor against the charge
of having no principles and in proving him a good Whig.

"Mr. Lincoln then passed," says the Advertiser, "to the
subject of slavery in the States, saying that the people of Illinois agreed entirely with the people of Massachusetts on this
subject, except, perhaps, that they did not keep so constantly
thinking about it. All agreed that slavery was an evil, but
that we were not responsible for it, and cannot affect it in
States of this Union where we do not live. But the question
of the *extension* of slavery to new territories of this country
is a part of our responsibility and care, and is under our control. In opposition to this Mr. Lincoln believed that the self-
named 'Free Soil' party was far behind the Whigs. Both
parties opposed the extension. As he understood it, the new
party had no principle except this opposition. If their platform held any other, it was in such a general way that it
was like the pair of pantaloons the Yankee peddler offered
for sale, 'large enough for any man, small enough for any
boy.' They therefore had taken a position calculated to break
down their single important declared object. They were
working for the election of either General Cass or General
Taylor. The speaker then went on to show, clearly and elo-
quently, the danger of extension of slavery likely to result
from the election of General Cass. To unite with those who
annexed the new territory, to prevent the extension of
slavery in that territory, seemed to him to be in the highest
degree absurd and ridiculous. Suppose these gentlemen succeed in electing Mr. Van Buren, they had no specific means
to *prevent* the extension of slavery to New Mexico and California; and General Taylor, he confidently believed, would
not encourage it, and would not prohibit its restriction. But

if General Cass was elected, he felt certain that the plans of farther extension of territory would be encouraged, and those of the extension of slavery would meet no check. The ' Free Soil ' men, in claiming that name, indirectly attempt a deception, by implying that Whigs were *not* Free Soil men. In declaring that they would 'do their duty and leave the consequences to God,' they merely gave an excuse for taking a course they were not able to maintain by a fair and full argument. To make this declaration did not show what their duty was. If it did, we should have no use for judgment; we might as well be made without intellect; and when divine or human law does not clearly point out what *is* our duty, we have no means of finding out what it is but using our most intelligent judgment of the consequences. If there were divine law or human law for voting for Martin Van Buren, or if a fair examination of the consequences and first reasoning would show that voting for him would bring about the ends they pretended to wish, then he would give up the argument. But since there was no fixed law on the subject, and since the whole probable result of their action would be an assistance in electing General Cass, he must say that they were behind the Whigs in their advocacy of the freedom of the soil.

"Mr. Lincoln proceeded to rally the Buffalo convention for forbearing to say anything—after all the previous declarations of those members who were formerly Whigs—on the subject of the Mexican War because the Van Burens had been known to have supported it. He declared that of all the parties asking the confidence of the country, this new one had *less* of principle than any other.

"He wondered whether it was still the opinion of these Free Soil gentlemen, as declared in the ' whereas ' at Buffalo, that the Whig and Democratic parties were both entirely dissolved and absorbed into their own body. Had the *Vermont election* given them any light? They had calculated on making as great an impression in that State as in any part of the Union, and there their attempts had been wholly ineffectual. Their failure there was a greater success than they would find in any other part of the Union.

"At the close of this truly masterly and convincing speech," the "Advertiser" goes on, "the audience gave three

enthusiastic cheers for Illinois, and three more for the eloquent Whig member from that State."

After the speech at Worcester, Lincoln spoke at Lowell,
Dedham, Roxbury, Chelsea and Cambridge, and on September 22d, in Tremont Temple, Boston, following a splendid
oration by Governor Seward. His speech on this occasion
was not reported, though the Boston papers united in calling it "powerful and convincing." His success at Worcester
and Boston was such that invitations came from all over
New England asking him to speak.

But Lincoln won something in New England of vastly
deeper importance than a reputation for making popular campaign speeches. Here for the first time he caught a glimpse
of the utter impossibility of ever reconciling the northern
conviction that slavery was evil and unendurable, and the
southern claim that it was divine and necessary; and he began here to realize that something must be done.

The first impression of slavery which Abraham Lincoln
received was in his childhood in Kentucky. His father and
mother belonged to a small company of western abolitionists, who at the beginning of the century boldly denounced
the institution as an iniquity. So great an evil did Thomas
and Nancy Lincoln hold slavery that to escape it they were
willing to leave their Kentucky home and move to a free
State. Thus their boy's first notion of the institution was
that it was something to flee from, a thing so dreadful that it
was one's duty to go to pain and hardship to escape it.

In his new home in Indiana he heard the debate on slavery
go on. The State he had moved into was in a territory made
free forever by the ordinance of 1787, but there were still
slaves and believers in slavery within its boundaries and it
took many years to eradicate them. Close to his Indiana
home lay Illinois and here the same struggle went on
through all his boyhood. The lad was too thoughtful not

to reflect on what he heard and read of the differences of opinions on slavery. By the time the Statutes of Indiana fell into his hands—some time before he was eighteen years old—he had gathered a large amount of practical information about the question which he was able then to weigh in the light of the great principles of the Constitution, the ordinance of 1787, and the laws of Indiana, which he had begun to study with passionate earnestness.

When he left Indiana for Illinois he continued to be thrown up against slavery. In his trip in 1831 to New Orleans he saw its most terrible features. As a young legislator he saw the citizens of his town, and his fellows in the legislature ready to condemn as " dangerous agitators," those who dared call slavery an evil, saw them secretly sympathize with outlawry like the Alton riot and the murder of Elijah Lovejoy. So keenly did he feel the danger of passing resolutions against abolitionists which tacitly implied that slavery was as the South was beginning to claim, a divine institution that in 1837, he was one of the only two members of the Illinois assembly who were willing to publicly declare "that the institution of slavery is founded on both injustice and bad policy."

From time to time as he travelled on the Mississippi and Ohio he saw the workings of slavery. In 1841 coming home from a visit to Louisville, Ky., he was in the same boat with a number of negroes, the sight so impressed him that he described it to a friend:

" A gentleman had purchased twelve negroes in different parts of Kentucky, and was taking them to a farm in the South. They were chained six and six together. A small iron clevis was around the left wrist of each, and this fastened to the main chain by a shorter one, at a convenient distance from the others, so that the negroes were strung together precisely like so many fish upon a trout-line. In this condition they were being separated forever from the scenes of their childhood, their friends, their fathers and mothers, and brothers and sisters, and many of them from their wives and children, and going into perpetual slavery, where the lash of the master is proverbially more ruthless and unrelenting than any other where; and yet amid all these distressing circumstances, as we would think them, they were the most cheerful and apparently happy creatures on board. One whose offense for which he had been sold was an over-fondness for his wife, played the fiddle almost continually, and the others danced, sang, cracked jokes, and played various games with cards from day to day. How true it is that 'God tempers the wind to the shorn lamb,' or in other words, that he renders the worst of human conditions tolerable, while he permits the best to be nothing better than tolerable.''

Runaway slaves, underground railway stations, masters and men tracking negroes, the occasional capture of a man or woman to be taken back to the South, trials of fugitives—all the features common in those years particularly in the States bordering on bond territory Lincoln saw. In 1847 he was even engaged to defend a slave-owner's claim, a case he lost, the negro being allowed to go free.

It was not until 1844-45, however, that the matter became an important element in his political life. Heretofore it had been a moral question only, now, however, the annexation of Texas made it a political one. It became necessary that every politician and voter decide whether the new territory should be bond or free. The abolitionists or Liberty party grew rapidly in Illinois. Lincoln found himself obliged not only to meet Democratic arguments, but the abolition theories and convictions. When in 1847 he went to Congress it was already evident that the Mexican war would be settled by the acquisition of large new territory. What was to be done with it? The North had tried to forestall the South by bringing in a provision that whatever territory was acquired should be free forever. This Wilmot proviso as it was called from the name of the originator, went through as many forms as Proteus, though its intent was always the same. From first to last Lincoln voted for it. " I may venture to say that I voted for it at least forty times during the short time I was there," he said in after years. Although he voted so persistently he did little or no debating on the question in the House and in the hot debates from which he could not escape, he acted as a peace-maker.

At Mrs. Spriggs's mess, where he boarded in Washington, the Wilmot proviso was the topic of frequent conversation and the occasion of very many angry controversies. Dr. Busey, who was a fellow boarder, says of Lincoln's part in these discussions, that though he may have been as radical as any in the household, he was so discreet in giving expression to his convictions on the slavery question as to avoid giving offence to anybody, and was so conciliatory as to create the impression, even among the pro-slavery advocates, that he did not wish to introduce or discuss subjects that would provoke a controversy.

"When such conversation would threaten angry or even unpleasant contention he would interrupt it by interposing some anecdote, thus diverting it into a hearty and general laugh, and so completely disarrange the tenor of the discussion that the parties engaged would either separate in good humor or continue conversation free from discord. This amicable disposition made him very popular with the household."

But when in 1848 Lincoln went to New England he experienced for the first time the full meaning of the "free soil" sentiment as the new abolition sentiment was called. Massachusetts was quivering at that moment under the impassioned protests of the great abolitionists. Sumner was just deciding to abandon literature to devote his life to the cause of freedom and was speaking wherever he had the chance and often in scenes which were riots. "Ah me such an assembly," wrote Longfellow in his Journal after one of these speeches of Sumner. "It was like one of Beethoven's symphonies played in a saw-mill." Whittier was laboring at Amesbury by letters of counsel and encouragement to friends, by his pure, high-souled poems of protest and promise and by his editorials to the "National Era," which he and his friends had just started in Washington. Lowell was publishing the last of the Biglow Papers and preparing the whole for the book form. He was writing, too, some of his noblest prose. Emerson, Palfrey, Hoar, Adams, Phillips, Garrison, were all at work. Giddings had been there from Ohio.

Only a few days before Lincoln arrived a great convention of free soilers and bolting Whigs had been held in Tremont Temple and its earnestness and passion had produced a deep impression. Sensitive as Lincoln was to every shade of popular feeling and conviction the sentiment in New England stirred him as he had never been stirred before, on the question of slavery. Listening to Seward's speech in Tremont Temple, he seems to have had a sudden insight into the truth, a quick illumination; and that night, as the two men sat talking, he said gravely to the great anti-slavery advocate:

"Governor Seward, I have been thinking about what you said in your speech. I reckon you are right. We have got to deal with this slavery question, and got to give much more attention to it hereafter than we have been doing."

# CHAPTER XIV

### LINCOLN AT NIAGARA—SECURES A PATENT FOR AN INVENTION—ABANDONS POLITICS AND DECIDES TO DEVOTE HIMSELF TO THE LAW

IT was late in September when Lincoln started westward from his campaigning in New England. He stopped in Albany, N. Y., and in company with Thurlow Weed called on Fillmore then candidate for Vice-President. From Albany he went to Niagara. Mr. Herndon once asked him what made the deepest impression on him when he stood before the Falls.

"The thing that struck me most forcibly when I saw the Falls," he responded, "was, where in the world did all that water come from?" The memory of Niagara remained with him and aroused many speculations. Among various notes for lectures which Nicolay and Hay found among Mr. Lincoln's papers after his death and published in his "Complete Works," is a fragment on Niagara which shows how deeply his mind was stirred by the majesty of that mighty wonder.

"Niagara Falls! By what mysterious power is it that millions and millions are drawn from all parts of the world to gaze upon Niagara Falls? There is no mystery about the thing itself. Every effect is just as any intelligent man, knowing the causes, would anticipate without seeing it. If the water moving onward in a great river reaches a point where there is a perpendicular jog of a hundred feet in descent in the bottom of the river, it is plain the water will have a violent and continuous plunge at that point. It is also plain, the water, thus plunging, will foam and roar, and send up a mist continuously, in which last, during sunshine, there will be perpetual rainbows. The mere physical of Niagara Falls is only this. Yet this is really a very small part of that world's wonder. Its power to excite reflection and emotion is its great charm. The geologist will demonstrate that the plunge, or fall, was once at Lake Ontario, and has worn its way back to its present position; he will ascertain how fast it is wearing now, and so get a basis for determining how long it has been wearing back from Lake Ontario, and finally demonstrate by it that this world is at least fourteen thousand years old. A philosopher of a slightly different turn will say, 'Niagara Falls is only the lip of the basin out of which pours all the surplus water which rains down on two or three hundred thousand square miles of the earth's surface.' He will estimate with approximate accuracy that five hundred thousand tons of water fall with their full weight a distance of a hundred feet each minute—thus exerting a force equal to the lifting of the same weight, through the same space, in the same time. . . .

"But still there is more. It calls up the indefinite past. When Columbus first sought this continent—when Christ suffered on the cross—when Moses led Israel through the Red Sea—nay, even when Adam first came from the hand of his Maker; then, as now, Niagara was roaring here. The eyes of that species of extinct giants whose bones fill the mounds of America have gazed on Niagara, as ours do now. Contemporary with the first race of men, and older than the first man, Niagara is strong and fresh to-day as ten thousand years ago. The Mammoth and Mastodon, so long dead that fragments of their monstrous bones alone testify that they ever lived, have gazed on Niagara—in that long, long time never still for a single moment, never dried, never froze, never slept, never rested."

In his trip westward to Springfield from Niagara there occurred an incident which started Lincoln's mind on a new line of thought  one which all that fall divided it with politics. It happened that the boat by which he made part of the trip stranded in shallow water. The devices employed to float her, interested Lincoln much. He no doubt recalled the days when on the Ohio, the Mississippi, and the Sangamon he had seen his own or his neighbor's boats stuck on a sand-bar for hours, even days. Was there no way that these vexatious delays could be prevented in shallow streams? He set himself resolutely at the task of inventing a practical device for getting boats over shoals. When he reached Springfield he began to build a model representing his idea. He showed the deepest interest in the work and Mr. Herndon says he would sometimes bring the model into his office and while whittling on it would talk of its merits and the revolution it was going to work on the western rivers.

When Lincoln returned to Washington he took the model with him, and through Mr. Z. C. Robbins, a lawyer of Washington, secured a patent. "He walked into my office one morning with a model of a western steamboat under his arm," says Mr. Robbins. "After a friendly greeting he placed his model on my office-table and proceeded to explain the principles embodied therein that he believed to be his own invention, and which, if new, he desired to secure by letters-patent. During my former residence in St. Louis, I had made myself thoroughly familiar with everything appertaining to the construction and equipment of the flat-bottomed steamboats that were adapted to the shallow rivers of our western and southern States, and therefore, I was able speedily to come to the conclusion that Mr. Lincoln's proposed improvement of that class of vessels was new and patentable, and I so informed him. Thereupon he instructed me to prepare the necessary drawings and papers and prosecute an application for a patent for his invention at the United States patent office. I complied with his instructions and in due course of proceedings procured for him a patent that fully covered all the distinguishing features of his improved steamboat. The identical model that Mr. Lincoln brought to my office can now be seen in the United States patent office."

But it was only his leisure which Lincoln spent in the fall of 1848 on his invention. All through October and the first days of November he was speaking up and down the State for Taylor. His zeal was rewarded in November by the election of the Whig ticket and a few weeks later he went back to Washington for the final session of the Thirtieth Congress. He went back resolved to do something regarding slavery. He seems to have seen but two things at that moment which could constitutionally be done. The first was to allow the slave-holder no more ground than he had; to accomplish this he continued to vote for the Wilmot proviso. The second was to abolish slavery in the District of Columbia. Over ten years before, in 1837, Lincoln had declared, in the assembly of Illinois, that the Congress of the United States had the power, under the constitution, to abolish slavery in the District of Columbia, but that the power ought not to be exercised unless at the request of the people of the District. When he went to Washington in 1847 he found a condition of things which made him feel that Congress ought to exercise the power it had. There had existed for years in the city a slave market: "a sort of negro livery stable, where droves of negroes were collected, temporarily kept, and finally taken to southern markets, precisely like droves of horses," Lincoln said in describing it in later years; and this frightful place was in view from the windows of the Capitol. Morally and intellectually shocked and irritated by this spectacle, Lincoln brooded over it until now, in the second session of his term, he decided to ask that Congress exercise the power he had affirmed ten years before belonged to it, and on January 16, 1849, he drew up and presented a bill to abolish slavery in the District of Columbia, "with the consent of the voters of the District and with compensation to owners"

The bill caused a noise in the House, but came to naught, as indeed at that date any similar bill was bound to do. It showed, however, more plainly than anything Lincoln had done so far in Congress his fearlessness when his convictions were aroused.

The inauguration of Taylor on March 4, 1849, ended Lincoln's congressional career. The principle, "turn about is fair play," which he had insisted on in 1846 when working for the nomination for himself, he regarded as quite as applicable now. It was not because he did not desire to return to Congress.

" I made the declaration that I would not be a candidate again," he wrote Herndon in January, 1848, "more from a wish to deal fairly with others, to keep peace among our friends, and to keep the district from going to the enemy, than from any cause personal to myself; so that, if it should so happen that nobody else wishes to be elected, I could not refuse the people the right of sending me again. But to enter myself as a competitor of others, or to authorize any one so to enter me, is what my word and honor forbid."

And yet he was not willing to leave public life. The term in Congress had only increased his fondness for politics. It had given him a touch of that fever for public office from which so few men who have served in Congress ever entirely recover. The Whigs owed much to him, and there was a general disposition to gratify any reasonable ambition he might have. "I believe that, so far as the Whigs in Congress are concerned, I could have the General Land Office almost by common consent," he wrote Speed; "but then Sweet and Don Morrison and Browning and Cyrus Edwards all want it, and what is worse, while I think I could easily take it myself, I fear I shall have trouble to get it for any other man in Illinois."

Although he feared his efforts would be useless, he pledged his support to his friend, Cyrus Edwards. While Lincoln

was looking after Edwards's interests, a candidate appeared
who was most objectionable to the Whigs, General Justin
Butterfield.   Lincoln did all he could to defeat Butterfield
save the one thing necessary—ask the position for himself.
This he would not do until he learned that Edwards had no
chance.   Then he applied; but it was too late.   Butterfield
had secured the office while Lincoln had been holding back.
When Edwards found that Lincoln had finally applied for
the place, he accused him of treachery.   Lincoln was deeply
hurt by the suspicion.

" The better part of one's life consists of his friendships," he wrote to Judge Gillespie, " and, of them,
mine with Mr. Edwards was one of the most cherished.
I have not been false to it.   At a word I could have had
the office any time before the Department was committed
to Mr. Butterfield—at least Mr. Ewing and the President
say as much.   That word I forbore to speak, partly for other
reasons, but chiefly for Mr. Edwards's sake—losing the
office that he might gain it.   I was always for (him) ; but to
lose his *friendship*, by the effort for him, would oppress me
very much, were I not sustained by the utmost consciousness
of rectitude.   I first determined to be an applicant, unconditionally, on the 2d of June; and I did so then upon being informed by a telegraphic despatch that the question was narrowed down to Mr. B. and myself, and that the Cabinet had
postponed the appointment three weeks for my benefit.   Not
doubting that Mr. Edwards was wholly out of the question,
I, nevertheless, would not then have become an applicant had
I supposed he would thereby be brought to suspect me of
treachery to him.   Two or three days afterwards a conversation with Levi Davis convinced me Mr. Edwards was dissatisfied; but I was then too far in to get out.   His own letter, written on the 25th of April, after I had fully informed
him of all that had passed, up to within a few days of that
time, gave assurance I had that entire confidence from him
which I felt my uniform and strong friendship for him entitled me to.   Among other things it says: 'Whatever course

your judgment may dictate as proper to be pursued shall never be excepted to by me." I also had had a letter from Washington saying Chambers, of the "Republic," had brought a rumor there, that Mr. E. had declined in my favor, which rumor I judged came from Mr. E. himself, as I had not then breathed of his letter to any living creature. In saying I had never, before the 2d of June, determined to be an applicant, *unconditionally,* I mean to admit that, before then, I had said, substantially, I would take the office rather than it should be lost to the State, or given to one in the State whom the Whigs did not want; but I aver that in every instance in which I spoke of myself I intended to keep, and now believe I did keep, Mr. E. above myself. Mr. Edwards's first suspicion was that I had allowed Baker to overreach me, as his friend, in behalf of Don Morrison. I know this was a mistake; and the result has proved it. I understand his view now is, that if I had gone to open war with Baker I could have ridden him down, and had the thing all my own way. I believe no such thing. With Baker and some strong man from the Military tract and elsewhere for Morrison, and we and some strong men from the Wabash and elsewhere for Mr. E., it was not possible for either to succeed. I believed this in March, and I *know* it now. The only thing which gave either any chance was the very thing Baker and I proposed—an adjustment with themselves.

"You may wish to know how Butterfield finally beat me. I cannot tell you particulars now, but will when I see you. In the meantime let it be understood I am not greatly dissatisfied—I wish the office had been so bestowed as to encourage our friends in future contests, and I regret exceedingly Mr. Edwards's feelings towards me. These two things away, I should have no regrets—at least I think I would not."

It was not until eleven years later that Edwards forgave Lincoln. Then at Judge Gillespie's request he promised to "bury the hatchet with Lincoln" and to enter the campaign for him.

Lincoln declared that he had no regrets about the way the General Land Office went, but, if he had not, his Whig

friends in Washington had. They determined to do something for him, and in the summer of 1849 summoned him to
the capital to urge him to accept the governorship of Oregon.
The Territory would soon be a State, it was believed, and
Lincoln would then undoubtedly be chosen to represent it in
the United States Senate. Unquestionably, a splendid political prospect was thus opened. Many of Lincoln's friends advised him to accept; his wife, however, disliked the idea of
life in the far West, and on her account he refused the place.

The events of the summer of 1849 seemed to Lincoln to
end his political career. He had no time to brood over his
situation, however. The necessity of earning a livelihood
was too imperative. His financial obligations were, in fact,
considerable. The old debt for the New Salem store still
hung over him; he had a growing family; and his father and
mother, who were still living in Coles county, whither they
had moved in 1831, were dependent upon him for many of
the necessaries, as well as all the comforts, of their lives. At
intervals ever since he had left home he had helped them;
now by saving their land from the foreclosing of a mortgage,
now by paying their doctor's bills, now by adding to the
cheerfulness of their home.

He was equally kind to his other relatives, visiting them
and aiding them in various ways. Among these relatives
were two cousins, Abraham and Mordecai, the sons of his
uncle Mordecai Lincoln, who lived in Hancock County, in his
congressional district. At Quincy, also in his district, lived
with his family a brother of his mother—Joseph Hanks. Lincoln never went to Quincy without going to see his uncle Joseph and "uncle Joe's Jake," as he called one of his cousins.
"On these occasions," writes one of the latter's family, Mr.
J. M. Hanks of Florence, Colorado, "mirth and jollity
abounded, for Mr. Lincoln indulged his bent of story-telling to the utmost, until a late hour." His half-brother, John

Johnston, he aided for many years. His help did not always take the form of money. Johnston was shiftless and always in debt, and consequently restless and discontented. In 1851 he was determined to borrow money or sell his farm, and move to Missouri. He proposed to Mr. Lincoln that he lend him eighty dollars. Mr. Lincoln answered:

" What I propose is, that you shall go to work, ' tooth and nail,' for somebody who will give you money for it. . . . I now promise you, that for every dollar you will, between this and the first of May, get for your own labor, either in money or as your own indebtedness, I will then give you one other dollar. . . . In this I do not mean you shall go off to St. Louis, or the lead mines, or the gold mines in California, but I mean for you to go at it for the best wages you can get close to home in Coles county. Now, if you will do this, you will be soon out of debt, and, what is better, you will have a habit that will keep you from getting in debt again. But, if I should now clear you out of debt, next year you would be just as deep in as ever. You say you would almost give your place in Heaven for seventy or eighty dollars. Then you value your place in Heaven very cheap, for I am sure you can, with the offer I make, get the seventy or eighty dollars for four or five months' work."

A few months later Lincoln wrote Johnston in regard to his contemplated move to Missouri:

"What can you do in Missouri better than here? Is the land any richer? Can you there, any more than here, raise corn and wheat and oats without work? Will anybody there, any more than here, do your work for you? If you intend to go to work, there is no better place than right where you are; if you do not intend to go to work, you cannot get along anywhere. Squirming and crawling about from place to place can do no good. You have raised no crop this year; and what you really want is to sell the land, get the money, and spend it. Part with the land you have, and, my life upon it, you will never after own a spot big enough to bury you in. Half you will get for the land you will spend in moving to Missouri, and the other half you will eat, drink, and wear out, and no foot of land will be bought. Now, I feel it my duty to have no hand in such a piece of foolery."

All this plain advice did not prevent Johnston trying to sell a small piece of land on which Mr. Lincoln had paid the mortgage in order to secure it to his step-mother during her life. When Mr. Lincoln received this proposition he replied:

"Your proposal about selling the east forty acres of land is all that I want or could claim for *myself;* but I am not satisfied with it on *mother's* account. I want her to have her living, and I feel that it is my duty, to some extent, to see that she is not wronged. She had a right of dower (that is, the use of one-third for life) in the other two forties; but, it seems, she has already let you take that, hook and line. She now has the use of the whole of the east forty as long as she lives, and if it be sold, of course she is entitled to the interest on *all* the money it brings as long as she lives; but you propose to sell it for three hundred dollars, take one hundred away with you, and leave her two hundred at eight per cent., making her the *enormous* sum of sixteen dollars a year. Now, if you are satisfied with treating her in that way, I am not. It is true that you are to have that forty for two hundred dollars *at* mother's death; but you are not to have it *before.* I am confident that land can be made to produce for mother at least thirty dollars a year, and I cannot, to oblige any living person, consent that she shall be put on an allowance of sixteen dollars a year."

It was these obligations which made Lincoln resume at once the practice of the law. He decided to remain in Springfield, although he had an opportunity to go in with a well-established Chicago lawyer. For many reasons life in Springfield was satisfactory to him. He had bought a home there in 1844, and was deeply attached to it. There, too, he was surrounded by scores of friends who had known him since his first appearance in the town, and to many of whom he was related by marriage; and he had the good will of the community. In short, he was a part of Springfield. The very children knew him, for there was not one of them for whom he had not done some kind deed. "My first strong impression of Mr. Lincoln," says a lady of Springfield, "was made by one of his kind deeds. I was going with a little friend for my first trip alone on the railroad cars. It was an epoch of my life. I had planned for it and dreamed of it for weeks. The day I was to go came, but as the hour of the train approached, the hackman, through some neglect, failed to call for my trunk. As the minutes went on, I realized, in a panic of grief, that I should miss the train. I was standing by the gate, my hat and gloves on, sobbing as if my heart would break, when Mr. Lincoln came by.

"'Why, what's the matter?' he asked, and I poured out all my story.

"'How big's the trunk? There's still time, if it isn't too big.' And he pushed through the gate and up to the door. My mother and I took him up to my room, where my little old-fashioned trunk stood, locked and tied. 'Oh, ho,' he cried; 'wipe your eyes and come on quick.' And before I knew what he was going to do, he had shouldered the trunk, was down stairs, and striding out of the yard. Down the street he went, fast as his long legs could carry him. I trotting behind, drying my tears as I went. We reached the station in time. Mr. Lincoln put me on the train, kissed me good-bye, and told me to have a good time. It was just like him."

This sensitiveness to a child's wants made Mr. Lincoln a most indulgent father. He continually carried his boys about with him, and their pranks, even when they approached rebellion, seemed to be an endless delight to him. Like most boys, they loved to run away, and neighbors of the Lincolns tell many tales of Mr. Lincoln's captures of the culprits. One of the prettiest of all these is a story told of an escape Willie once made, when three or four years old, from the hands of his mother, who was giving him a tubbing. He scampered out of the door without the vestige of a garment on him, flew up the street, slipped under a fence into a great green field, and took across it. Mr. Lincoln was sitting on the porch, and discovered the pink and white runaway as he was cutting across the greensward. He stood up, laughing aloud, while the mother entreated him to go in pursuit; then he started in chase. Half-way across the field he caught the child, and gathering him up in his long arms, he covered his rosy form with kisses. Then mounting him on his back, the chubby legs around his neck, he rode him back to his mother and his tub.

It was a frequent custom with Lincoln, this of carrying his children on his shoulders. He rarely went down street that he did not have one of his younger boys mounted on his shoulder, while another hung to the tail of his long coat. The antics of the boys with their father, and the species of tyranny they exercised over him, are still subjects of talk in Springfield. Mr. Roland Diller, who was a neighbor of Mr. Lincoln, tells one of the best of the stories. He was called to the door one day by hearing a great noise of children crying, and there was Mr. Lincoln striding by with the boys, both of whom were wailing aloud. "Why, Mr. Lincoln, what's the matter with the boys?" he asked.

"Just what's the matter with the whole world," Lincoln replied; "I've got three walnuts and each wants two."

Another of Lincoln's Springfield acquaintances, the Rev. Mr. Alcott of Elgin, Ill., tells of seeing him coming away from church, unusually early one Sunday morning. "The sermon could not have been more than half way through," says Mr. Alcott. " 'Tad' was slung across his left arm like a pair of saddle-bags, and Mr. Lincoln was striding along with long, and deliberate steps toward his home. On one of the street corners he encountered a group of his fellow-townsmen. Mr. Lincoln anticipated the question which was about to be put by the group, and, taking his figure of speech from practices with which they were only too familiar, said: ' Gentlemen, I entered this colt, but he kicked around so I had to withdraw him.' "

There was no institution in Springfield in which Lincoln had not taken an active interest in the first years of his residence; and now that he had decided to remain in the town, he resumed all his old relations, from the daily visits to the drug-stores on the public square, which were the recognized rendezvous of Springfield politicians and lawyers, to his weekly attendance at the First Presbyterian church. That he was as regular in his attendance on the latter as on the former, all his old neighbors testify. In fact, Lincoln, all his life, went regularly to church. The serious attention which he gave the sermons he heard is shown in a well-authenticated story of a visit he made in 1837, with a company of friends, to a camp-meeting held six miles west of Springfield at the "Salem Church." The sermon on this occasion was preached by one of the most vigorous and original individuals in the pulpit of that day—the Rev. Dr. Peter Akers. In this discourse was a remarkable and prophetic passage, long remembered by those who heard it. The speaker prophesied the downfall of castes, the end of tyrannies, and the crushing out of slavery. As Lincoln and his friends returned home there was a long discussion of the sermon.

"It was the most instructive sermon, and he is the most impressive preacher, I have ever heard," Lincoln said. "It is wonderful that God has given such power to men. I firmly believe his interpretation of prophecy, so far as I understand it, and especially about the breaking down of civil and religious tyrannies; and, odd as it may seem, when he described those changes and revolutions, I was deeply impressed that I should be somehow strangely mixed up with them."

If Lincoln was not at this period a man of strictly orthodox beliefs, he certainly was, if we accept his own words, profoundly religious. In the letters which passed between Lincoln and Speed in 1841 and 1842, when the two men were doubting their own hearts and wrestling with their disillusions and forebodings, Lincoln frequently expressed the idea to Speed that the Almighty had sent their suffering for a special purpose. When Speed finally acknowledged himself happily married, Lincoln wrote to him: "I always was superstitious; I believe God made me one of the instruments of bringing your Fanny and you together, which union I have no doubt he had foreordained." Then, referring to his own troubled heart, he added: "Whatever He designs He will do for me yet. 'Stand still, and see the salvation of the Lord,' is my text just now."

Only a few months after Lincoln decided to settle permanently in Springfield his father, Thomas Lincoln, fell dangerously ill. Lincoln in writing to John Johnston, his halfbrother, said: "I sincerely hope father may recover his health, but, at all events, tell him to remember to call upon and confide in our great and good and merciful Maker, who will not turn away from him in any extremity. He notes the fall of a sparrow, and numbers the hairs of our heads, and He will not forget the dying man who puts his trust in Him."

Lincoln's return to the law was characterized by a marked change in his habits. He gave much more attention to study than he ever had before. His colleagues in Springfield and on the circuit noticed this change. After court closed in the town on the circuit, and the lawyers were gathered in the barroom or on the veranda of the tavern, telling stories and chaffing one another, Lincoln would join them, though often but for a few minutes. He would tell a story as he passed, and while they were laughing at its climax, would slip away to his room to study. Frequently this work was carried on far into the night. "Placing a candle on a chair at the head of the bed," says Mr. Herndon, "he would study for hours. I have known him to study in this position until two o'clock in the morning. Meanwhile, I and others who chanced to occupy the same room would be safely and soundly asleep." Although he worked so late, "he was in the habit of rising earlier than his brothers of the bar," says Judge Weldon. "On such occasions he was wont to sit by the fire, having uncovered the coals, and muse, ponder, and soliloquize."

But it was not only the law that occupied him. He began a serious course of general education, studying mathematics, astronomy, poetry, as regularly as a school-boy who had lessons to recite. In the winter of 1849-50 he even joined a club of a dozen gentlemen of Springfield who had begun the study of German, the meetings of the class being held in his office.

Much of Lincoln's devotion to study at this period was due to his desire to bring himself in general culture up to the men whom he had been meeting in the East. No man ever realized his own deficiencies in knowledge and experience more deeply than Abraham Lincoln, nor made a braver struggle to correct them. He often acknowledged to his friends the consciousness he had of his own limitations in the simplest matters of life. Mr. H. C. Whitney, one of his old friends, gives a pathetic example of this. Once on the circuit his friends missed him after supper. When he returned, some one asked where he had been.

" Well, I have been to a little show up at the Academy," he said.

"He sat before the fire," says Mr. Whitney, "and narrated all the sights of that most primitive of county shows, given chiefly to school children. Next night he was missing again; the show was still in town, and he stole in as before, and entertained us with a description of new sights—a magic lantern, electrical machine, etc. I told him I had seen all these sights at school. ' Yes,' said he sadly, ' I now have an advantage over you, for the first time in my life seeing these things which are, of course, common to those who had, what I did not, a chance at an education when they were young.' "

It was to make up for the "chance at an education" which he did not have in youth that Abraham Lincoln at forty years of age, after having earned the reputation of being one of the ablest politicians in Illinois, spent his leisure in study.

# CHAPTER XV

WHEN in 1849 Lincoln decided to abandon politics finally
and to devote himself to the law, he had been practising for
thirteen years. In spite of the many interruptions electioneering and office-holding had caused he was well-established. Rejoining his partner Herndon—the firm of Lincoln and Herndon had been only a name during Lincoln's
term in Washington—he took up the law with a singleness
of purpose which had never before characterized his practice.

Lincoln's headquarters were in Springfield, but his practice was itinerant. The arrangements for the administration
of justice in Illinois in the early days were suited to the conditions of the country, the State being divided into judicial
circuits including more or less territory according to the
population. To each circuit a judge was appointed, who
each spring and fall travelled from county-seat to county-
seat to hold court. With the judge travelled a certain number of the best-known lawyers of the district. Each lawyer
had, of course, a permanent office in one of the county-seats,
and often at several of the others he had partners, usually
young men of little experience, for whom he acted as counsel in special cases. This peripatetic court prevailed in Illinois
until the beginning of the fifties; but for many years after,
when the towns had grown so large that a clever lawyer
might have enough to do in his own county, a few lawyers,

Lincoln among them, who from long association felt that
the circuit was their natural habitat refused to leave it.

The circuit which Lincoln travelled was known as the
"Eighth Judicial Circuit." It included fifteen counties in
1845, though the territory has since been divided into more.
It was about one hundred and fifty miles long by as many
broad. There were no railroads in the Eighth Circuit until
about 1854, and the court travelled on horseback or in carriages. Lincoln had no horse in the early days of his practice. It was his habit then to borrow one, or to join a company of a half dozen or more in hiring a "three-seated spring
wagon." Later he owned a turn-out of his own, which
figures in nearly all the traditions of the Eighth Circuit; the
horse being described as "poky" and the buggy as "rattling."

There was much that was irritating and uncomfortable in
the circuit-riding of the Illinois court, but there was more
which was amusing to a temperament like Lincoln's. The
freedom, the long days in the open air, the unexpected if
trivial adventures, the meeting with wayfarers and settlers
—all was an entertainment to him. He found humor and
human interest on the route where his companions saw nothing but commonplaces. "He saw the ludicrous in an assemblage of fowls," says H. C. Whitney, one of his fellow-
itinerants, "in a man spading his garden, in a clothes-line full
of clothes, in a group of boys, in a lot of pigs rooting at a
mill door, in a mother duck teaching her brood to swim—in
everything and anything." The sympathetic observations
of these long rides furnished humorous settings for some of
his best stories. If frequently on these trips he fell into
sombre reveries and rode with head bent, ignoring his companions, generally he took part in all the frolicking which
went on, joining in practical jokes, singing noisily with the
rest, sometimes even playing a Jew's-harp.

When the county-seat was reached, the bench and bar

quickly settled themselves in the town tavern. It was usually
a large two-story house with big rooms and long verandas.
There was little exclusiveness possible in these hostelries.

FACSIMILE OF MAP OF CIRCUIT WHICH LINCOLN TRAVELLED IN PRACTISING LAW.

Ordinarily judge and lawyer slept two in a bed, and three
or four beds in a room. They ate at the common table with
jurors, witnesses, prisoners out on bail, travelling peddlers,

teamsters, and laborers. The only attempt at classification on the landlord's part was seating the lawyers in a group at the head of the table. Most of them accepted this distinction complacently. Lincoln, however, seemed to be indifferent to it. One day, when he had come in and seated himself at the foot with the "fourth estate," the landlord called to him, "You're in the wrong place, Mr. Lincoln; come up here."

"Have you anything better to eat up there, Joe?" he inquired quizzically; "if not, I'll stay here."

The accommodations of the taverns were often unsatisfactory—the food poorly cooked, the beds hard. Lincoln accepted everything with uncomplaining good nature, though his companions habitually growled at the hardships of the life. It was not only repugnance to criticism which might hurt others, it was the indifference of one whose thoughts were always busy with problems apart from physical comfort, who had little notion of the so-called " refinements of life," and almost no sense of luxury and ease.

The judge naturally was the leading character in these nomadic groups. He received all the special consideration the democratic spirit of the inhabitants bestowed on any one, and controlled his privacy and his time to a degree. Judge David Davis, who from 1848 presided over the Eighth Circuit as long as Mr. Lincoln travelled it, was a man of unusual force of character, of large learning, quick impulses, and strong prejudices. Lincoln was from the beginning of their association a favorite with Judge Davis. Unless he joined the circle which the judge formed in his room after supper, his honor was impatient and distraught, interrupting the conversation constantly by demanding: "Where's Lincoln?" "Why don't Lincoln come?" And when Lincoln did come, the judge would draw out story after story, quieting everybody who interrupted with an impatient, "Mr. Lincoln's talking." If anyone came to the door to see the host in the midst of one of Lincoln's stories he would send a lawyer into the hall to see what was wanted, and, as soon as the door closed, order Lincoln to "go ahead."

The appearance of the court in a town was invariably a stimulus to its social life. In all of the county-seats there were a few fine homes of which the dignity, spaciousness, and elegance still impress the traveller through Illinois. The hospitality of these houses was generous. Dinners, receptions, and suppers followed one another as soon as the court began. Lincoln was a favorite figure at all these gatherings.

His favorite field, however, was the court. The court-houses of Illinois in which he practised were not log houses, as has been frequently taken for granted. "It is not probable," says a leading member of the Illinois bar, "Mr. Lincoln ever saw a log court-house in central Illinois, where he practised law, unless he saw one at Decatur, in Macon County. In a conversation between three members of the Supreme Court of Illinois, all of whom had been born in this State and had lived in it all their lives, and who were certainly familiar with the central portions of the State, all declared they had never seen a log court-house in the State."

The court-houses in which Lincoln practised were stiff, old-fashioned wood or brick structures, usually capped by cupola or tower, and fronted by verandas with huge Doric or Ionic pillars. They were finished inside in the most uncompromising style—hard white walls, unpainted woodwork, pine floors, wooden benches. Usually they were heated by huge Franklin stoves, with yards of stove-pipe running wildly through the air, searching for an exit, and threatening momentarily to unjoint and tumble in sections. Few of the lawyers had offices in the town; and a corner of the court-room, the shade of a tree in the court-yard, a sunny side of a building, were where they met their clients and transacted business.

In the courts themselves there was a certain indifference to formality engendered by the primitive surroundings, which, however, the judges never allowed to interfere with the seriousness of the work. Lincoln habitually, when not busy, whispered stories to his neighbors, frequently to the annoyance of Judge Davis. If Lincoln persisted too long, the judge would rap on the chair and exclaim: "Come, come, Mr. Lincoln, I can't stand this! There is no use trying to carry on two courts; I must adjourn mine or you yours, and I think you will have to be the one." As soon as the group had scattered, the judge would call one of the men to him and ask: "What was that Lincoln was telling?"

"I was never fined but once for contempt of court," says one of the clerks of the court in Lincoln's day. "Davis fined me five dollars. Mr. Lincoln had just come in, and leaning over my desk had told me a story so irresistibly funny that I broke out into a loud laugh. The judge called me to order in haste, saying, 'This must be stopped. Mr. Lincoln, you are constantly disturbing this court with your stories.' Then to me, 'You may fine yourself five dollars for your disturbance.' I apologized, but told the judge that the story was worth the money. In a few minutes the judge called me to him. 'What was the story Lincoln told you?' he asked. I told him, and he laughed aloud in spite of himself. 'Remit your fine,' he ordered."

The partiality of Judge Davis for Lincoln was shared by the members of the court generally. The unaffected friendliness and helpfulness of his nature had more to do with this than his wit and cleverness. If there was a new clerk in court, a stranger unused to the ways of the place, Lincoln was the first—sometimes the only one—to shake hands with him and congratulate him on his election.

"No lawyer on the circuit was more unassuming than was

Mr. Lincoln," says one who practised with him. "He arrogated to himself no superiority over anyone—not even the most obscure member of the bar. He treated everyone with that simplicity and kindness that friendly neighbors manifest in their relations with one another. He was remarkably gentle with young lawyers becoming permanent residents at the several county-seats in the circuit where he had practised for so many years. . . . The result was, he became the much-beloved senior member of the bar. No young lawyer ever practised in the courts with Mr. Lincoln who did not in all his after life have a regard for him akin to personal affection."

"I remember with what confidence I always went to him," says Judge Lawrence Welden, who first knew Lincoln at the bar in 1854, "because I was certain he knew all about the matter and would most cheerfully help me. I can see him now, through the decaying memories of thirty years, standing in the corner of the old court-room; and as I approached him with a paper I did not understand, he said, 'Wait until I fix this plug of my "gallis" and I will pitch into that like a dog at a root.' While speaking he was busily engaged in trying to connect his suspenders with his pants by making a plug perform the function of a button."

If for any reason Lincoln was absent from court, he was missed perhaps as no other man on the Eighth Circuit would have been, and his return greeted joyously. He was not less happy himself to rejoin his friends. "Ain't you glad I've come?" he would call out, as he came up to shake hands.

The cases which fell to Lincoln on the Eighth Circuit were of the sort common to a new country. Litigation over bordering lines and deeds, over damages by wandering cattle, over broils at country festivities. Few of the cases were of large importance. When a client came to Lincoln his first effort was to arrange matters, if possible, and to avoid a suit. In a few notes for a law lecture prepared about 1850, he says:

"Discourage litigation. Persuade your neighbors to compromise whenever you can. Point out to them how the nominal winner is often a real loser—in fees, expenses, and waste of time. As a peacemaker the lawyer has a superior opportunity of being a good man. There will still be business enough.

"Never stir up litigation. A worse man can scarcely be found than one who does this. Who can be more nearly a fiend than he who habitually overhauls the register of deeds in search of defects in titles, whereon to stir up strife, and put money in his pocket? A moral tone ought to be infused into the profession which should drive such men out of it."

He carried out this in his practice. "Who was your guardian?" he asked a young man who came to him to complain that a part of the property left him had been withheld. "Enoch Kingsbury," replied the young man.

"I know Mr. Kingsbury," said Lincoln, "and he is not the man to have cheated you out of a cent, and I can't take the case, and advise you to drop the subject." And it was dropped.

"We shall not take your case," he said to a man who had shown that by a legal technicality he could win property worth six hundred dollars. "You must remember that some things legally right are not morally right. We shall not take your case, but will give you a little advice for which we will charge you nothing. You seem to be a sprightly, energetic man; we would advise you to try your hand at making six hundred dollars in some other way."

Where he saw injustice he was quick to offer his services to the wronged party. A pleasant example of this is related by Joseph Jefferson in his "Autobiography." In 1839, Jefferson, then a lad of ten years, travelled through Illinois with his father's theatrical company.  After playing at Chicago, Quincy, Peoria and Pekin, the company went in the fall to Springfield, where the sight of the legislature tempted the elder Jefferson and his partner to remain throughout the season.  But there was no theatre.  Not to be daunted they built one.  But hardly had they completed it before a religious revival broke out in the town, and the church people turned all their influence against the theatre.  So effectually did they work that a law was passed by the municipality imposing a license which was practically prohibitory.  "In the midst of our trouble," says Jefferson, "a young lawyer called on the managers.  He had heard of the injustice, and offered, if they would place the matter in his hands, to have the license taken off, declaring that he only desired to see fair play, and he would accept no fee whether he failed or succeeded.  The young lawyer began his harangue.  He handled the subject with tact, skill, and humor, tracing the history of the drama from the time when Thespis acted in a cart to the stage of to-day.  He illustrated his speech with a number of anecdotes, and kept the council in a roar of laughter.  His good humor prevailed, and the exorbitant tax was taken off."  The "young lawyer" was Lincoln.

Having accepted a case, Lincoln's first object seemed to be to reduce it to its simplest elements.  "If I can clean this case of technicalities, and get it properly swung to the jury, I'll win it," he told his partner Herndon one day.  He began by getting at what seemed to him the pivot on which it rested.  Sure of that, he cared little for anything else.  He trusted very little to books; a great deal to common sense and his ideas of right and wrong.

"In the make of his character Mr. Lincoln had many elements essential to the successful circuit lawyer," says one of his fellow-practitioners.  "He knew much of the law as written in the books, and had that knowledge ready for use at all

times. That was a valuable possession in the absence of law
books, where none were obtainable on the circuit. But he
had more than a knowledge of the law. He knew right and
justice, and knew how to make their application to the affairs of every-day life. That was an element in his character that gave him power to prevail with the jury when arguing a case before them. Few lawyers ever had the influence
with a jury that Mr. Lincoln had."

When a case was clear to him and he was satisfied of its
justice, he trusted to taking advantage of the developments
of the trial to win. For this reason he made few notes beforehand, rarely writing out his plan of argument. Those
he left are amusingly brief; for instance, the notes made for

*When you cant find it anywhere else look into this*

**FACSIMILE OF A LINCOLN MEMORANDUM.**

From the Lincoln collection in the law offices of Messrs. Vanuxem & Potter, of Philadelphia. This characteristic memorandum was found by Messrs. Herndon & Weik in looking
over the papers in Lincoln's law office. It was the label to a package of letters, pamphlets,
and newspapers which he had tied together and marked.

a suit he had brought against a pension agent who had withheld as fee half of the pension he had obtained for the aged
widow of a Revolutionary soldier. Lincoln was deeply indignant at the agent, and had resolved to win his suit. He
read up the Revolutionary war afresh, and when he came
to address the jury drew a harrowing picture of the private
soldier's sufferings and of the trials of his separation from
his wife. The notes for this argument ran as follows:

"No contract—Not professional services. Unreasonable
charge,—Money retained by Def't not given by Pl'ff.—
Revolutionary War.—Soldier's bleeding feet.—Pl'ff's husband.—Soldier leaving home for army.—*Skin def't.*—
Close."

Lincoln's reason for not taking notes, as he told it to H. W. Beckwith, when a student in the Danville office of Lincoln and Lamon, was: " Notes are a bother, taking time to make, and more to hunt them up afterwards; lawyers who do so soon get the habit of referring to them so much that it confuses and tires the jury." " He relied on his well-trained memory," says Mr. Beckwith, " that recorded and indexed every passing detail. And by his skilful questions, a joke, or pat retort as the trial progressed, he steered his jury from the bayous and eddies of side issues and kept them clear of the snags and sandbars. if any were put in the real channel of his case."

Much of his strength lay in his skill in examining witnesses. "He had a most remarkable talent for examining witnesses," says an intimate associate; "with him it was a rare gift. It was a power to compel a witness to disclose the whole truth. Even a witness at first unfriendly, under his kindly treatment would finally become friendly. and would wish to tell nothing he could honestly avoid against him, if he could state nothing for him."

He could not endure an unfair use of testimony or the misrepresentation of his own position. "In the Harrison murder case," says Mr. T. W. S. Kidd of Springfield, a crier of the court in Lincoln's day, "the prosecuting attorney stated that such a witness made a certain statement, when Mr. Lincoln rose and made such a plaintive appeal to the attorney to correct the statement, that the attorney actually made the *amende honorable,* and afterwards remarked to a brother lawyer that he could deny his own child's appeal as quickly as he could Mr. Lincoln's."

Sometimes under provocation he became violently angry. In the murder case referred to above, the judge ruled contrary to his expectations, and, as Mr. Lincoln said, contrary to the decision of the Supreme Court in a similar case. "Both

Mr. Lincoln and Judge Logan, who was with him in the case," says Mr. Kidd, "rose to their feet quick as thought. I do think he was the most unearthly looking man I had ever seen. He roared like a lion suddenly aroused from his lair, and said and did more in ten minutes than I ever heard him say or saw him do before in an hour."

He depended a great deal upon his stories in pleading, using them as illustrations which demonstrated the case more conclusively than argument could have done. Judge H. W. Beckwith of Danville, Illinois, in his "Personal Recollections of Lincoln," tells a story which is a good example of Lincoln's way of condensing the law and the facts of an issue in a story.

"A man, by vile words, first provoked and then made a bodily attack upon another. The latter in defending himself gave the other much the worst of the encounter. The aggressor, to get even, had the one who thrashed him tried in our circuit court upon a charge of an assault and battery. Mr. Lincoln defended, and told the jury that his client was in the fix of a man who, in going along the highway with a pitchfork on his shoulder, was attacked by a fierce dog that ran out at him from a farmer's door-yard. In parrying off the brute with the fork its prongs stuck into the brute and killed him.

" 'What made you kill my dog?' said the farmer.

" 'What made him try to bite me?'

" 'But why did you not go at him with the other end of the pitchfork?'

" 'Why did he not come after me with his other end?' At this Mr. Lincoln whirled about in his long arms an imaginary dog and pushed its tail end toward the jury. This was the defensive plea of *'son assault demesne'*—loosely, that 'the other fellow brought on the fight,'—quickly told, and in a way the dullest mind would grasp and retain."

Mr. T. W. S. Kidd says that he once heard a lawyer opposed to Lincoln trying to convince a jury that precedent was superior to law, and that custom made things legal in all cases. When Lincoln arose to answer him he told the jury he would argue his case in the same way. Said he: "Old 'Squire Bagly, from Menard, came into my office and said, 'Lincoln, I want your advice as a lawyer. Has a man what's been elected justice of the peace a right to issue a marriage license?' I told him he had not; when the old 'squire threw himself back in his chair very indignantly, and said: 'Lincoln, I thought you was a lawyer. Now Bob Thomas and me had a bet on this thing, and we agreed to let you decide; but if this is your opinion I don't want it, for I know a thunderin' sight better, for I have been 'squire now eight years and have done it all the time.' "

His manner of telling stories was most effective. "When he chose to do so," writes Judge Scott, " he could place the opposite party, and his counsel too, for that matter, in a most ridiculous attitude by relating in his inimitable way a pertinent story. That often gave him a great advantage with the jury. A young lawyer had brought an action in trespass to recover damages done to his client's growing crops by defendant's hogs. The right of action under the law of Illinois, as it was then, depended on the fact whether plaintiff's fence was sufficient to turn ordinary stock. There was some little conflict in the evidence on that question; but the weight of the testimony was decidedly in favor of plaintiff, and sustained beyond all doubt his cause of action. Mr. Lincoln appeared for defendant. There was no controversy as to the damage done by defendant's stock. The only thing in the case that could possibly admit of any discussion was the condition of plaintiff's fence; and as the testimony on that question seemed to be in favor of plaintiff, and as the sum involved was little in amount, Mr. Lincoln did not deem it necessary to argue the case seriously, but by way of saying something in behalf of his client he told a little story about a *fence* that was so *crooked* that when a hog went through an opening in it, invariably it came out on the same side from whence it started. His description of the confused look of the hog after several times going through the fence and still finding itself on the side from which it had started, was a humorous specimen of the best story-telling. The effect was to make plaintiff's case appear ridiculous; and while Mr. Lincoln did not attempt to apply the story to the case, the jury seemed to think it had some kind of application to the fence in controversy—otherwise he would not have told it— and shortly returned a verdict for the defendant."

Those unfamiliar with his methods frequently took his stories as an effort to wring a laugh from the jury. A lawyer, a stranger to Mr. Lincoln, once expressed to General Linder the opinion that this practice of Lincoln was a waste of time. "Don't lay that flattering unction to your soul," Linder answered; "Lincoln is like Tansey's horse, he 'breaks to win.' "

But it was not his stories, it was his clearness which was his strongest point. He meant that the jury should see that he was right. For this reason he never used a word which the dullest juryman could not understand. Rarely, if ever, did a Latin term creep into his arguments. A lawyer quoting a legal maxim one day in court, turned to Lincoln, and said: "That is so, is it not, Mr. Lincoln?"

"If that's Latin," Lincoln replied, "you had better call another witness."

His illustrations were almost always of the homeliest kind. He did not care to "go among the ancients for figures," he said.

" Much of the force of his argument," writes Judge Scott, " lay in his logical statement of the facts of a case. When he had in that way secured a clear understanding of the facts, the jury and the court would seem naturally to follow him in his conclusions as to the law of the case. His simple and natural presentation of the facts seemed to give the impression that the jury were themselves making the statement. He had the happy and unusual faculty of making the jury believe *they*—and not *he*—were trying the case. Mr. Lincoln kept himself in the background, and apparently assumed nothing more than to be an *assistant* counsel to the court or the jury, on whom the primary responsibility for the final decision of the case in fact rested."

He rarely consulted books during a trial, lest he lose the attention of the jury, and if obliged to, translated their statements into the simplest terms. In his desire to keep his case clear he rarely argued points which seemed to him unessential. "In law it is good policy never to plead what you need not, lest you oblige yourself to prove what you can not," he wrote. He would thus give away point after point with an indifferent "I reckon that's so," until the point which he considered pivotal was reached, and there he hung.

"In making a speech," says Mr. John Hill, "Mr. Lincoln was the plainest man I ever heard. He was not a speaker but a talker. He talked to jurors and to political gatherings plain, sensible, candid talk, almost as in conversation, no effort whatever in oratory. But his talking had wonderful effect. Honesty, candor, fairness, everything that was convincing, were in his manner and expressions."

This candor of which Mr. Hill speaks characterized his entire conduct of a trial. "It is well understood by the profession," says General Mason Brayman, "that lawyers do not read authorities favoring the opposing side. I once heard Mr. Lincoln, in the supreme court of Illinois, reading from a reported case some strong points in favor of his argument. Reading a little too far, and before becoming aware of it, he plunged into an authority against himself. Pausing a moment, he drew up his shoulders in a comical way, and half laughing, went on, 'There, there, may it please the court, I reckon I've scratched up a snake. But, as I'm in for it, I guess I'll read it through.' Then, in his most ingenious and matchless manner, he went on with his argument, and won his case, convincing the court that it was not much of a snake after all."

# CHAPTER XVI

LINCOLN'S IMPORTANT LAW CASES—DEFENCE OF A SLAVE
GIRL—THE MCCORMICK CASE—THE ARMSTRONG MUR-
DER CASE—THE ROCK ISLAND BRIDGE CASE

ABRAHAM LINCOLN'S place in the legal circle of Illinois
has never been clearly defined. The ordinary impression is
that, though he was a faithful and trusted lawyer, he never
rose to the first rank of his profession. This idea has come
from imperfect information concerning his legal career. An
examination of the reports of the Illinois Supreme Court
from 1840, when he tried his first case before that body, to
1861, when he gave up his profession to become President of
the United States, shows that in this period of twenty years,
broken as it was, from 1847 to 1849, by a term in Congress,
and interrupted constantly, from 1854 to 1860, by his labors
in opposition to the repeal of the Missouri Compromise, Lincoln was engaged in nearly one hundred cases before that
court, some of them of great importance. This fact shows
him to have been one of the leading lawyers of his State.
Between ninety and one hundred cases before the Supreme
Court of a State in twenty years is a record surpassed by but
few lawyers. It was exceeded by none of Lincoln's Illinois
contemporaries.

Among the cases in which he was prominent and of which
we have reports, there are several of dramatic import.
viewing them, as we can now, in connection with his
later life. One of the first in which he appeared before the
Illinois Supreme Court involved the freedom of a negro girl
called Nance. In spite of the fact that Illinois had been free

since its admission as a State, many traces of slavery still remained, particularly in the southern and central parts of the State. Among the scattered slaveholders was one Nathan Cromwell of Tazewell County, who for some years had in his service a negro girl, Nance. He claimed that Nance was bound to him by indenture, and that he had the right to sell her as any other property, a right he succeeded finally in exercising. One of his neighbors, Baily by name, bought the girl; but the purchase was conditional: Baily was to pay for his property only when he received from Cromwell title papers showing that Nance was bound to serve under the laws of the State. These papers Cromwell failed to produce before his death. Later his heirs sued Baily for the purchase price. Baily employed Lincoln to defend him. The case was tried in September, 1839, and decided against Baily. Then in July, 1841, it was tried again, before the Supreme Court of the State. Lincoln proved that Nance had lived for several years in the State, that she was over twenty-one years of age, that she had declared herself to be free, and that she had even purchased goods on her own account. The list of authorities he used in the trial to prove that Nance could not be held in bondage shows that he was already familiar with both Federal and State legislation on the slavery question up to that date. He went back to the Ordinance of 1787, to show that slavery was forbidden in the Northwest Territory; he recalled the Constitution that had made the State free in 1818; he showed that by the law of nations no person can be sold in a free State. His argument convinced the court; the judgment of the lower court was overruled, and Nance was free.

After Lincoln's return from Congress in 1849, he was engaged in some of the most important cases of the day. One of these was a contest between the Illinois Central Railroad, at that time building, and McLean County, Illinois. This road had been exempted by the legislature from all State taxation on condition that it pay perpetually into the State treasury seven per cent. of its annual gross earnings. When the line was laid in McLean County the county authorities declared that the State legislature could not excuse the railroad company from paying county taxes; accordingly the company's property was assessed and a tax levied. If this claim of the county could be sustained, it was certain to kill the railroad; and great preparations were made for the defence. The solicitor of the Illinois Central at that time was General Mason Brayman, who retained Lincoln. The case was tried at Bloomington, before the supreme court, and, largely through the efforts of Lincoln, was won for the road. According to Herndon, Lincoln charged for his services a fee of two thousand dollars. Going to Chicago he presented his bill. "Why," said the officer to whom he applied, "this is as much as a first-class lawyer would have charged."

Stung by the ungrateful speech, Lincoln withdrew the bill, left the office, and at the first opportunity submitted the matter to his friends. Five thousand dollars, they all agreed, was a moderate fee, considering what he had done for the road, and six leading lawyers of the State signed a paper in which they declared that such a charge would not be "unreasonable." Lincoln then sued the road for that amount, and won his case. "He gave me my half," says Herndon; "and as much as we deprecated the avarice of great corporations, we both thanked the Lord for letting the Illinois Central Railroad fall into our hands."

The current version of this story names General George B. McClellan as the testy official who snubbed Lincoln when he presented the bill. This could not have been. The incident occurred in 1855; that year Captain McClellan spent in the Crimea, as one of a commission of three sent abroad to study the European military service as displayed in the Crimean

**war.** It was not until January, 1857, that McClellan resigned his commission in the United States army to become the chief engineer, and afterwards vice-president, of the Illinois Central Railroad. It was when an officer of the Illinois Central, however, that McClellan first met Lincoln. "Long before the war," he says, in "McClellan's Own Story," "when vice-president of the Illinois Central Railroad, I knew Mr. Lincoln, for he was one of the counsel of the company. More than once I have been with him in out-of-the-way county-seats where some important case was being tried, and, in the lack of sleeping accommodations, have spent the night in front of a stove, listening to the unceasing flow of anecdotes from his lips. He was never at a loss, and I could never quite make up my mind how many of them he had really heard before, and how many he invented on the spur of the moment. His stories were seldom refined, but were always to the point."

It was through his legal practice that Lincoln first met still another man who was to sustain a relation of the greatest importance to him in the war. This man was Edwin M. Stanton. The meeting occurred in Cincinnati in 1855, in connection with a patent case which is famous in the legal history of the country, and in which both Lincoln and Stanton had been retained as counsel. So much that is false has been written of this meeting, that a full and exact statement of the circumstances has been obtained for this work from Mr. George Harding of Philadelphia, the only one of either judges or counsel in the case living at this writing.

"Cyrus H. McCormick owned reaping-machine patents granted in 1845 and 1847," says Mr. Harding, "upon which he sued John M. Manny and Co. of Rockford, Illinois. Mr. Manny had obtained patents also. Manny and Co. were large manufacturers of reaping-machines under Manny's patents. McCormick contended that his patents were valid and secured to him a virtual monopoly of all practical reaping machines as constructed at that date.   If McCormick had been successful in his contention, Manny would have been enjoined, his factory stopped, and a claim of four hundred thousand dollars damages demanded from his firm.   McCormick's income from that monopoly would have been vastly increased.   Hence the suit was very important to all parties and to the farming public.   The plaintiff McCormick had retained Mr. E. N. Dickerson and Reverdy Johnson.   The former was entrusted with the preparation of the plaintiff's case and the argument before the court on the mechanics of the case.   Mr. P. H. Watson, who had procured Manny's patents, was given by Manny the entire control of the defendant's case.   He employed Mr. George Harding to prepare the defence for Manny, and to argue the mechanics of the case before the court.   In those times it was deemed important in patent cases to employ associate counsel not specially familiar with mechanical questions, but of high standing in the general practice of the law, and of recognized forensic ability.   If such counsel represented the defendant he urged upon the court the importance of treating the patentee as a quasi-monopolist, whose claims should be limited to the precise mechanical contributions which he had made to the art; while, on the other hand, the plaintiff's forensic counsel was expected to dwell upon the privations and labor of the patentee, and insist on a very liberal view of his claims, and to hold that defendants who had appropriated any of his ideas should be treated as pirates.   The necessity of the forensic contribution in the argument of patent cases is not now recognized.

"McCormick had selected Mr. Reverdy Johnson for the forensic part of his case.   Mr. Watson was in doubt as to whom to select to perform this duty for the defendants.   At the suggestion of Mr. Manny, Mr. Watson wrote to Mr. Lincoln, sending to him a retainer of five hundred dollars, and requesting him to read the testimony, which was sent to him from time to time as taken, so that if Mr. Watson afterward concluded to have him argue the case he would be prepared.   Mr. Harding had urged the employment of Mr. Stanton, who was personally known to him, and who then resided at Pittsburg.

"With a view to determining finally who should argue the forensic part of Manny's case, Mr. Watson personally visited Springfield and conferred with Mr. Lincoln. On his way back from Springfield he called upon Mr. Stanton at Pittsburg, and, after a conference, retained Mr. Stanton, and informed him distinctly that he was to make the closing argument in the case. Nevertheless Mr. Lincoln was sent copies of the testimony; he studied the testimony, and was paid for so doing, the same as Mr. Stanton. Mr. Watson considered that it would be prudent for Mr. Lincoln to be prepared, in case of Mr. Stanton's inability, for any cause, to argue the case; so that, at the outset, Mr. Stanton was selected by Mr. Manny's direct representative to perform this duty.

"When all the parties and counsel met at Cincinnati, Mr. Lincoln was first definitely informed by Mr. Watson of his determination that Mr. Stanton was to close the case for defendants. Mr. Lincoln was evidently disappointed at Mr. Watson's decision. Mr. Lincoln had written out his argument in full. He was anxious to meet Mr. Reverdy Johnson in forensic contest. The case was important as to the amount in dispute, and of widespread interest to farmers. Mr. Lincoln's feelings were embittered, moreover, because the plaintiff's counsel subsequently, in open court, of their own motion, stated that they perceived that there were three counsel present for defendant, and that plaintiff had only two counsel present; but they were willing to allow all three of defendant's counsel to speak, provided Mr. Dickerson, who had charge of the mechanical part of McCormick's case, were permitted to make two arguments, besides Mr. Johnson's argument. Mr. Watson, who had charge of defendant's case, declined this offer, because the case ultimately depended upon mechanical questions; and he thought that if Mr. Dickerson were allowed to open the mechanical part of the case, and then make a subsequent argument on the mechanics, the temptation would be great to make an insufficient or misleading mechanical opening of the case at first, and, after Mr. Harding had replied thereto, to make a fuller or different mechanical presentation, which could not be replied to by Mr. Harding. It was conceded that neither Mr. Lincoln nor Mr. Stanton was prepared to handle the me-

chanics of the case either in opening or reply. In view of
these facts, Mr. Watson decided that only two arguments
would be made for Manny, and that Mr. Harding would
open the case for defendant on the mechanical part, and Mr.
Stanton would close on the general propositions of law applicable to the case. Mr. Stanton said in court that personally he had no desire to speak, but he agreed with Mr.
Watson that only two arguments should be made for defendants whether he spoke or not. Mr. Lincoln, knowing
Mr. Watson's wishes, insisted that Mr. Stanton should make
the closing argument, and that he would not himself speak.
Mr. Stanton accepted the position, and did speak, because he
knew that such was the expressed wish and direction of Mr.
Watson, who controlled the conduct of defendant's case.

"Mr. Lincoln kindly and gracefully, but regretfully, accepted the situation. He attended, and exhibited much interest in the case as it proceeded. He sent to Mr. Harding
the written argument which he had prepared, that he might
have the benefit of it before he made his opening argument;
but requested Mr. Harding not to show it to Mr. Stanton.
The chagrin of Mr. Lincoln at not speaking continued, however, and he felt that Mr. Stanton should have insisted on
his, Mr. Lincoln's, speaking also; while Mr. Stanton merely
carried out the positive direction of his client that there
should be only two arguments for defendant, and that he,
Mr. Stanton, should close the case, and Mr. Harding should
open the case. Mr. Lincoln expressed to Mr. Harding satisfaction at the manner in which the mechanical part of the
case had been presented by him, and after Mr. Lincoln had
been elected President, he showed his recollection of it by
tendering Mr. Harding, of his own motion, a high position.

"In regard to the personal treatment of Mr. Lincoln while
in attendance at Cincinnati, it is to be borne in mind that Mr.
Lincoln was known to hardly any one in Cincinnati at that
date, and that Mr. Stanton was probably not impressed with
the appearance of Mr. Lincoln. It is true there was no personal intimacy formed between them while at Cincinnati.
Mr. Lincoln was disappointed and unhappy while in Cincinnati, and undoubtedly did not receive the attention which
he should have received. Mr. Lincoln felt all this, and par-

ticularly, but unjustly, reflected upon Mr. Stanton as the main cause. When Mr. Lincoln was nominated for President, Mr. Stanton, like many others in the country, sincerely doubted whether Mr. Lincoln was equal to the tremendous responsibility which he was to be called upon to assume as President. This is to be borne in mind, in view of events subsequent to the case at Cincinnati. Mr. Stanton never called upon Mr. Lincoln after he came to Washington as President. Mr. Lincoln in alluding to Mr. Stanton (both before and after his election as President) did not attempt to conceal his unkind feeling towards him, which had its origin at Cincinnati. This feeling did not undergo a change until after he met Mr. Stanton as Secretary of War.

"The occurrences narrated show how one great man may underrate his fellow man. Mr. Stanton saw at Cincinnati in Mr. Lincoln only his gaunt, rugged features, his awkward dress and carriage, and heard only his rural jokes; but Stanton lived to perceive in those rugged lineaments only expressions of nobility and loveliness of character, and to hear from his lips only wisdom, prudence, and courage, couched in language unsurpassed in literature. But above all they show the nobility of Mr. Lincoln's character in forgetting all unkind personal feeling engendered at Cincinnati towards Mr. Stanton, and subsequently appointing him his Secretary of War.

"The above was narrated by Mr. Harding for the main purpose of correcting the popular impression that Mr. Stanton, of his own motion, rode over and displaced Mr. Lincoln in the case at Cincinnati; for the truth is that Mr. Stanton, in the course he pursued, was directed by his clients' representative, Mr. Watson, who believed that he was serving the best interests of his clients."

Lincoln was first suggested to Mr. Manny as counsel in this case by a younger member of the firm, Mr. Ralph Emerson, of Rockford, Illinois. Mr. Emerson, as a student of law, had been thrown much into company with Mr. Lincoln, and had learned to respect his judgment and ability. Indeed, it was Lincoln who was instrumental in deciding him to abandon the law. The young man had seen much in the practice of his chosen profession which seemed to him unjust, and he had begun to feel that the law was incompatible with his ideals. One evening, after a particularly trying day in court, he walked out with Lincoln. Suddenly turning to his companion, he said: "Mr. Lincoln, I want to ask you a question. Is it possible for a man to practice law and always do by others as he would be done by?" Lincoln's head dropped on his breast, and he walked in silence for a long way; then he heaved a heavy sigh. When he finally spoke, it was of a foreign matter. "I had my answer," said Mr. Emerson, "and that walk turned the course of my life."

During the trial at Cincinnati, Lincoln and Mr. Emerson were thrown much together, and Mr. Emerson's recollections are particularly interesting.

" As I was the sole intimate friend of Mr. Lincoln in the case, when it was decided that he should not take part in the argument, he invited me to his room to express his bitter disappointment; and it was with difficulty that I persuaded him to remain as counsel during the hearing. We generally spent the afternoons together. The hearing had hardly progressed two days before Mr. Lincoln expressed to me his satisfaction that he was not to take part in the argument. So many and so deep were the questions involved that he realized he had not given the subject sufficient study to have done himself justice.

"The court-room, which during the first day or two was well filled, greatly thinned out as the argument proceeded day after day. But as the crowd diminished, Mr. Lincoln's interest in the case increased. He appeared entirely to forget himself, and at times, rising from his chair, walked back and forth in the open space of the court-room, as though he were in his own office, pausing to listen intently as one point after another was clearly made out in our favor. He manifested such delight in countenance and unconscious action that its effect on the judges, one of whom at least already highly respected him, was evidently stronger than any set speech of his could possibly have been. The impression produced on the judges was evidently that Mr. Lincoln was thoroughly convinced of the justice of our side, and anxious that we should prevail, not merely on account of his interest in his clients, but because he thought our case was just and should triumph.

"The final summing up on our side was by Mr. Stanton; and though he took but about three hours in its delivery, he had devoted as many, if not more, weeks to its preparation. It was very able, and Mr. Lincoln was throughout the whole of it a rapt listener. Mr. Stanton closed his speech in a flight of impassioned eloquence. Then the court adjourned for the day, and Mr. Lincoln invited me to take a long walk with him. For block after block he walked rapidly forward, not saying a word, evidently deeply dejected.

"At last he turned suddenly to me, exclaiming, 'Emerson, I am going home.' A pause. 'I am going home to study law.'

"'Why,' I exclaimed, 'Mr. Lincoln, you stand at the head of the bar in Illinois now! What are you talking about?'

"'Ah, yes,' he said, 'I do occupy a good position there, and I think that I can get along with the way things are done there now. But these college-trained men, who have devoted their whole lives to study, are coming West, don't you see? And they study their cases as we never do. They have got as far as Cincinnati now. They will soon be in Illinois.' Another long pause; then stopping and turning toward me, his countenance suddenly assuming that look of strong determination which those who knew him best sometimes saw upon his face, he exclaimed, 'I am going home to study law! I am as good as any of them, and when they get out to Illinois I will be ready for them.'"

The fee which Lincoln received in the McCormick case, including the retainer, which was five hundred dollars—the largest retainer ever received by Lincoln—amounted to nearly two thousand dollars. Except the sum paid him by the Illinois Central Railroad it was probably the largest fee he ever received. The two sums came to him about the same

time, and undoubtedly helped to tide over the rather unfruitful period, from a financial standpoint which followed
—the period of his contest with Douglas for the Senate.
Lincoln never made money.  From 1850 to 1860 his income
averaged from two thousand to three thousand dollars a
year.  In the forties it was considerably less.  The fee-book
of Lincoln and Herndon for 1847 shows total earnings of
only fifteen hundred dollars.  The largest fee entered was
one of one hundred dollars.  There are several of fifty dollars, a number of twenty, more of ten, still more of five, and
a few of three dollars.

But Lincoln's fees were as a rule smaller than his clients
expected or his fellow lawyers approved of.  Mr. Abraham
Brokaw of Bloomington, Illinois, tells the following story
illustrating Lincoln's idea of a proper fee.  One of Mr. Brokaw's neighbors had borrowed about $500.00 from him and
given his note.  When it became due the man refused to pay.
Action was brought, and the sheriff levied on the property
of the debtor and finally collected the entire debt; but at
about that time the sheriff was in need of funds and used
the money collected.  When Brokaw demanded it from him
he was unable to pay it and was found to be insolvent.
Thereupon Brokaw employed Stephen A. Douglas to sue the
sureties on the official bond of the sheriff.  Douglas brought
the suit and soon collected the claim.  But Douglas was at
that time in the midst of a campaign for Congress and the
funds were used by him with the expectation of being able
to pay Brokaw later.  However, he neglected the matter
and went to Washington without making any settlement.
Brokaw, although a life-long and ardent Democrat and a
great admirer of Douglas, was a thrifty German and
did not propose to lose sight of his money.  After fruit-
lessly demanding the money from Douglas, Brokaw went
to David Davis, then in general practice at Blooming-

ton, told him the circumstances and asked him to undertake the collection of the money from Douglas. Davis protested that he could not do it, that Douglas was a personal
friend and a brother lawyer and Democrat and it would be
very disagreeable for him to have anything to do with the
matter. He finally said to Brokaw, "You wait until the next
term of court and Lincoln will be here. He would like nothing better than to have this claim for collection. I will introduce you to him and I have no doubt he will undertake it."
Shortly after, Brokaw was presented to Lincoln, stated his
case and engaged his services. Lincoln promptly wrote
Douglas, still at Washington, that he had the claim for collection and that he must insist upon prompt payment. Douglas, very indignant, wrote directly to Brokaw that he thought
the placing of the claim in Lincoln's hands a gross outrage,
that he and Brokaw were old friends and Democrats and
that Brokaw ought not to place any such weapon in the
hands of such an Abolitionist opponent as Lincoln and if he
could not wait until Douglas returned he should at least have
placed the claim for collection in the hands of a Democrat.
Brokaw's thrift again controlled and he sent Douglas' letter
to Lincoln. Thereupon Lincoln placed the claim in the hands
of "Long" John Wentworth, then a Democratic member of
Congress from Chicago Wentworth called upon Douglas
and insisted upon payment, which shortly after was made,
and Brokaw at last received his money. "And what do you
suppose Lincoln charged me?" Brokaw says in telling the
story. After hearing a few guesses he answers, "He charged
me exactly $3.50 for collecting nearly $600.00."

Such charges were felt by the lawyers of the Eighth Circuit, with some reason, to be purely Quixotic. They protested and argued, but Lincoln went on serenely charging
what he thought his services worth. Ward Lamon who was
one of Lincoln's numerous circuit partners says that he and

Lincoln frequently fell out on the matter of fees. On one occasion Lamon was particularly incensed. He had charged and received a good sized fee for a case which the two had tried together and won. When Lamon offered Lincoln his share he refused it. The fee was too large, he said, part of it must be refunded and he would not accept a cent until part of it had been refunded. Judge Davis heard of this transaction. He was himself a shrewd money-maker, never hesitating to take all he could legally get and he felt strong disgust at this disinterested attitude about money. Calling Lincoln to him the judge scolded roundly. "You are pauperizing this court, Mr. Lincoln, you are ruining your fellows. Unless you quit this ridiculous policy, we shall all have to go to farming." But not even the ire of the bench moved Lincoln.

If a fee was not paid, Lincoln did not believe in suing for it. Mr. Herndon says that he would consent to be swindled before he would contest a fee. The case of the Illinois Central railroad, however, was an exception to this rule. He was careless in accounts, never entering anything on the book. When a fee was paid to him, he simply divided the money into two parts, one of which he put into his pocket, and the other into an envelope which he labelled "Herndon's half." Lincoln's whole theory of the conduct of a lawyer in regard to money is summed up in the "notes" for a law lecture which he left among his papers:

" The matter of fees is important, far beyond the mere question of bread and butter involved. Properly attended to, fuller justice is done to both lawyer and client. An exorbitant fee should never be claimed. As a general rule never take your whole fee in advance, nor any more than a small retainer. When fully paid beforehand, you are more than a common mortal if you can feel the same interest in the case, as if something was still in prospect for you, as well as for your client. And when you lack interest in the case the job will very likely lack skill and diligence in the performance. Settle the amount of fee and take a note in advance. Then you will feel that you are working for something, and you are sure to do your work faithfully and well. Never sell a fee note—at least not before the consideration service is performed. It leads to negligence and dishonesty—negligence by losing interest in the case, and dishonesty in refusing to refund when you have allowed the consideration to fail."

If a client was poor, and Lincoln's sympathies were aroused, he not infrequently refused pay. There are a few well authenticated cases of his offering his services to those whom he believed he could help, stipulating when he did it that he would make no charge. The best known example of this is the Armstrong murder case.

William, or "Duff" Armstrong, as he was generally called, was the son of Lincoln's New Salem friends, Jack and Hannah Armstrong. In August, 1857, Duff and a number of his mates had joined a crowd of ruffians who had gathered on the outskirts of a camp-meeting held near Havana, in Macon county. He had drunk heavily for some days, and, finally, in a broil on the night of August 29, had beaten a comrade, one Metzker, who had provoked him to a fight. That same night Metzker was hit with an ox-yoke by another drunken reveller, Norris by name. Three days later he died. Both Armstrong and Norris were arrested. Marks of two blows were on the victim, either of which might have killed him. That Norris had dealt one was proved. Did Armstrong deal the other? He claimed he had used nothing but his fists in the broil; but both the marks on Metzker were such as must have been made by some instrument. The theory was developed that one blow was from a slung-shot used by Armstrong, and that he and Norris had acted in concert, deliberately planning to murder Metzker. Outraged by the cruelty of the deed, the whole countryside demanded the punishment of the prisoners. Just at the time that Armstrong was thrown into prison his father died, his last charge to his wife Hannah being, "Sell everything you have and clear Duff." True to her trust, Hannah engaged two lawyers of Havana, both of whom are still living, to defend her boy. Anxious lest the violence of public feeling should injure Duff's chances, the lawyers secured a change of venue to Cass county, their client remaining in prison until spring. Norris, in the meantime, was convicted, and sentenced to eight years in the penitentiary.

When the lawyers and witnesses assembled in Beardstown, May, 1858, for Armstrong's trial, it happened that Lincoln was attending court in the town. At that moment he was, after Stephen A. Douglas, the most conspicuous man in Illinois. His future course in politics was a source of interest in the East as well as the West. The coming contest with Douglas for the senatorship—for it was already probable that he would be the candidate in the convention which was only a month away—was causing him intense anxiety. Yet occupied as he was with his profession, and harassed by the critical political situation, he did not hesitate an instant when Hannah Armstrong came to him for advice. Going to her lawyers, he said he should like to assist them. They, of course, were glad of his aid, and he at once took the case in hand. His first care was the selection of a jury. Not knowing the neighborhood well, he could not discriminate closely as to individuals; but he took pains, as far as he could control the choice, to have only young men chosen, believing that they would be more favorable to the prisoner. A surviving witness in the case estimates that the average age of the jury was not over twenty-three years.

The jury empanelled, the examination of witnesses seems to have been conducted, on behalf of the defence chiefly by Lincoln. Many of the witnesses bore familiar names. Some were sons of "Clary's Grove Boys," and Lincoln had known their fathers. "The witnesses were kept out of the court-room until called to testifv," says William A. Douglas. "I happened to be the firsι witness called, and so heard the whole trial. When William Killian was called to the stand, Lincoln asked him his name.

" 'William Killian,' was the reply.

" 'Bill Killian,' Lincoln repeated in a familiar way; 'tell me, are you a son of old Jake Killian?'

" 'Yes, sir,' answered the witness.

" 'Well,' said Lincoln, somewhat aside, 'you are a smart boy if you take after your dad.' "

As the trial developed it became evident that there could have been no collusion between Armstrong and Norris, but there was strong evidence that Armstrong had used a slung-shot. The most damaging evidence was that of one Allen, who swore that he had seen Armstrong strike Metzker about ten or eleven o'clock in the evening. When asked how he could see, he answered that the moon shone brightly. Under Lincoln's questioning he repeated the statement until it was impossible that the jury should forget it. With Allen's testi-mony unimpeached, conviction seemed certain.

Lincoln's address to the jury was full of genuine pathos. It was not as a hired attorney that he was there, he said, but to discharge a debt of friendship. "Uncle Abe," says Duff Armstrong himself, "did his best talking when he told the jury what true friends my father and mother had been to him in the early days. . . . He told how he used to go out to 'Jack' Armstrong's and stay for days; how kind mother was to him; and how, many a time, he had rocked me to sleep in the old cradle."

But Lincoln was not relying on sympathy alone to win his case. In closing he reviewed the evidence, showing that all depended on Allen's testimony, and this he said he could prove to be false. Allen never saw Armstrong strike Metz-ker by the light of the moon, for at the hour when he said he saw the fight, between ten and eleven o'clock, the moon was not in the heavens. Then producing an almanac, he passed it to the judge and jury. The moon, which was on that night only in its first quarter, had set before midnight. This unexpected overthrow of the testimony by which Lincoln had taken care that the jury should be most deeply impressed, threw them into confusion. There was a complete change of feeling. Lincoln saw it; and as he finished his address, and the jury left the room, turning to the boy's mother, he said, "Aunt Hannah, your son will be free before sundown."

Lincoln had not misread his jury. Duff Armstrong was discharged as not guilty.

There has long been a story current that the dramatic introduction of the almanac, by which certainly the audience and jury were won, was a pure piece of trickery on Lincoln's part; that the almanac was not one of 1857, but of 1853, in which the figure three had been changed throughout to seven. The best reply to this charge of forgery is the very evident one that it was utterly unnecessary. The almanac for August, 1857, shows that the moon was exactly in the position where it served Lincoln's client's interests best. He did not need to forge an almanac, the one of the period being all that he could want.

Another murder case in which Lincoln defended the accused occurred in August, 1859. The victim was a student in his own law office, Greek Crafton. The murderer, Peachy Harrison, was the grandson of Lincoln's old political antagonist, Peter Cartwright. Both young men were connected with the best families of the county; the brother of one was married to the sister of the other; they had been life-long friends. In an altercation upon some political question hot words were exchanged, and Harrison, beside himself, stabbed Crafton, who three days later died from the wound. The best known lawyers of the State were engaged for the case. Senator John M. Palmer and General A. McClernand were on the side of the prosecution. Among those who represented the defendant were Lincoln, Herndon, Logan, and Senator Shelby M. Cullom. The tragic pathos of a case which involved, as this did, the deepest affections of almost an entire community, reached its climax in the appearance in court of the venerable Peter Cartwright. No face in Illinois was better known than his, no life had been spent in a more relentless war on evil. Eccentric and aggressive as he was, he was honored far and wide; and when he arose in the witness stand, his white hair crowned with this cruel sorrow, the most indifferent spectator felt that his examination would be unbearable. It fell to Lincoln to question Cartwright. With the rarest gentleness he began to put his questions.

"How long have you known the prisoner?"

Cartwright's head dropped on his breast for a moment; then straightening himself, he passed his hand across his eyes and answered in a deep, quavering voice:

"I have known him since a babe, he laughed and cried on my knee."

The examination ended by Lincoln drawing from the witness the story of how Crafton had said to him, just before his death: "I am dying; I will soon part with all I love on earth, and I want you to say to my slayer that I forgive him. I want to leave this earth with a forgiveness of all who have in any way injured me."

This examination made a profound impression on the jury. Lincoln closed his argument by picturing the scene anew, appealing to the jury to practice the same forgiving spirit that the murdered man had shown on his death-bed.

It was undoubtedly to his handling of the grandfather's evidence that Harrison's acquittal was due.

A class of legal work which Lincoln enjoyed particularly was that in which mathematical or mechanical problems were involved. He never lost interest in his youthful pot-boiling profession of surveying, and would go out himself to make sure of boundaries if a client's case required particular investigation. Indeed, he was generally recognized by his fellow lawyers as an authority in surveying, and as late as 1859 his opinion on a disputed question was sought by a convention of surveyors who had met in Springfield. One of the most interesting cases involving mechanical problems which Lincoln ever argued was that of the Rock Island Bridge. It was not, however, the calculations he used which made it striking. The case was a dramatic episode in the war long waged by the Mississippi against the plains beyond. For decades the river had been the willing burden-bearer of the West. Now, however, the railroad had come. The Rock Island road had even dared to bridge the stream to carry away the traffic which the river claimed.

In May, 1856, a steamboat struck one of the piers of the bridge, and was wrecked and burned. One pier of the bridge was also destroyed. The boat owners sued the railroad company. The suit was the beginning of the long and violent struggle for commercial supremacy between St. Louis and Chicago. In Chicago it was commonly believed that the St. Louis Chamber of Commerce had bribed the captain of the boat to run upon the pier; and it was said that later, when the bridge itself was burned, the steamers gathered near and whistled for joy. The case was felt to involve the future course of western commerce; and when it was called in September, 1857, at Chicago, people crowded there from all over the West. Norman B. Judd, afterwards so prominent in the politics of the State, was the attorney of the road, and he engaged Lincoln, among others, as counsel. Lincoln made an address to the jury which those who remember it declare to have been one of his strongest legal arguments.

" The two points relied upon by the opponents of the bridge," says Judge Blodgett of Chicago, " were:

"First. That the river was the great waterway for the commerce of the valley, and could not legally be obstructed by a bridge.

"Second. That this particular bridge was so located with reference to the channel of the river at that point as to make it a peril to all water craft navigating the river and an unnecessary obstruction to navigation.

"The first proposition had not at that time been directly passed upon by the Supreme Court of the United States, although the Wheeling Bridge case involved the question; but the court had evaded a decision upon it, by holding that the Wheeling Bridge was so low as to be an unnecessary obstruction to the use of the river by steamboats. The discussion of the first proposition on the part of the bridge company devolved mainly upon Mr. Abraham Lincoln.

"I listened with much interest to his argument on this point, and while I was not impressed by it as a specially eloquent effort (as the word eloquent is generally understood), I have always considered it as one of the ablest efforts I ever heard from Mr. Lincoln at the bar. His illustrations were apt and forcible, his statements clear and logical, and his reasons in favor of the policy (and necessarily the right) to bridge the river, and thereby encourage the settlement and building up of the vast area of fertile country to the west of it, were broad and statesmanlike.

"The pith of his argument was in his statement that *one man had as good a right to cross a river as another had to sail up or down it;* that these were equal and mutual rights which must be exercised so as not to interfere with each other, like the right to cross a street or highway and the right to pass along it. From this undeniable right to cross the river he then proceeded to discuss the means for crossing. Must it always be by canoe or ferryboat? Must the products of all the boundless fertile country lying west of the river for all time be compelled to stop on its western bank, be unloaded from the cars and loaded upon a boat, and after the transit across the river, be reloaded into cars on the other side, to continue their journey east?   In this connection he drew a vivid picture of the future of the great West lying beyond the river, and argued that the necessities of commerce demanded that the bridges across the river be a conceded right, which the steamboat interests ought not to be allowed to successfully resist, and thereby stay the progress of development and civilization in the region to the west.

" While I cannot recall a word or sentence of the argument, I well remember its effect on all who listened to it, and the decision of the court fully sustained the right to bridge so long as it did not unnecessarily obstruct navigation."

All the papers in regard to the trial are supposed to have been burned in the Chicago fire of 1871, but the speech, which was reported by Congressman Hitt of Illinois, at that time court stenographer, was published on September 24, 1857, in the Chicago " Daily Press," afterwards united with the " Tribune."

According to this report the first part of the speech was devoted to the points Judge Blodgett outlines; the second part was given to a careful explanation of the currents of the Mississippi at the point where the bridge crossed.  Lincoln succeeded in showing that had the pilot of the boat been as familiar as he ought to have been with the river, he could easily have prevented the accident.  His argument was full of nice mathematical calculations clearly put, and was marked by perfect candor.   Indeed, the honesty with which he admitted the points made by the opposite counsel caused considerable alarm to some of his associates. Mrs. Norman B. Judd (Mr. Judd was the attorney of the road) says that Mr. Joseph B. Knox, who was also engaged with Mr. Lincoln in the defence, dined at her house the day that Lincoln made his speech.   " He sat down at the dinner table in great excitement," writes Mrs. Judd, "saying, 'Lincoln has lost the case for us. The admissions he made in regard to the currents in the Mississippi at Rock Island and Moline will convince the court that a bridge at that point will always be a serious and constant detriment to navigation on the river.' 'Wait until you hear the conclusion of his speech,' replied Mr. Judd; 'you will find his admission is a strong point instead of a weak one, and on it he will found a strong argument that will satisfy you.'" And as it proved, Mr. Judd was right.

The few cases briefly outlined here show something of the range of Lincoln's legal work. They show that not only his friends like Hannah Armstrong believed in his power with a jury, but that great corporations like the Illinois Central Railroad were willing to trust their affairs in his hands; that he was not only a "jury lawyer," as has been often stated, but trusted when it came to questions of law pure and simple. If this study of his cases were continued, it would only be to accumulate evidence to prove that Lincoln was considered by his contemporaries one of the best lawyers of Illinois.

It is worth notice, too, that he made his reputation as a lawyer and tried his greatest cases *before* his debate with Douglas gave him a national reputation. It was in 1855 that the Illinois Central engaged him first as counsel; in 1855 that he went to Cincinnati on the McCormick case; in 1857 that he tried the Rock Island Bridge case. Thus his place was won purely on his legal ability unaided by political prestige. His success came, too, in middle life. Lincoln was forty years old in 1849, when he abandoned politics definitely, as he thought, for the law. He tried his greatest cases when he was from forty-five to forty-eight.

# CHAPTER XVII

## LINCOLN RE-ENTERS POLITICS

FROM 1849 to 1854 Abraham Lincoln gave almost his entire time to his profession. Politics received from him only the attention which any public spirited citizen without personal ambition should give. He kept close watch upon Federal, State and local affairs. He was active in the efforts made in Illinois in 1851 to secure a more thorough party organization. In 1852 he was on the Scott electoral ticket and did some canvassing. But this was all. He was yearly becoming more absorbed in his legal work, losing more and more of his old inclination for politics, when in May, 1854, the Repeal of the Missouri Compromise aroused him as he had never been before in all his life. The Missouri Compromise was the second in that series of noble provisions for making new territory free territory, which liberty-loving men have wrested from the United States Congress, whenever the thirst for expansion has seized this country. The first of these was the " Ordinance of 1787," prohibiting slavery in all the great Northwest Territory. The second the Missouri Compromise, passed in 1820, was the result of a struggle to keep the Louisiana Purchase free. It provided that Missouri might come in as a slave State if slavery was never allowed north of 36° 30′ north latitude. The next great expansion of the United States after the Louisiana Purchase resulted from the annexation of Texas, and of the territory acquired by the Mexican War. The North was determined that this new territory should be free. The South wanted it for slaves. The struggle between them threatened the Union for a time, but it was adjusted by the compromise of 1850, in which, according to Mr. Lincoln's summing up, " the South got their new fugitive-slave law, and the North got California (by far the best part of our acquisition from Mexico) as a free State. The South got a provision that New Mexico and Utah, when admitted as States, may come in with or without slavery, as they may then choose; and the North got the slave-trade abolished in the District of Columbia. The North got the western boundary of Texas thrown farther back eastward than the South desired; but, in turn, they gave Texas ten millions of dollars with which to pay her old debts."

For three years matters were quiet. Then Nebraska sought territorial organization. Now by the Missouri Compromise slavery was forbidden in that section of the Union, but in spite of this fact Stephen A. Douglas, then a member of the Senate of the United States, introduced a bill to give Nebraska and Kansas the desired government, to which later he added an amendment repealing the Missouri Compromise and permitting the people who should settle in the new territories to reject or establish slavery as they should see fit. It was the passage of this bill which brought Abraham Lincoln from the court room to the stump. His friend Richard Yates was running for re-election to Congress. Lincoln began to speak for him, but in accepting invitations he stipulated that it should be against the Kansas-Nebraska bill that he talk. His earnestness surprised his friends. Lincoln was coming back into politics, they said, and when Douglas, the author of the repeal, was announced to speak in Springfield in October of 1854, they called on Lincoln to meet him.

Douglas was having a serious struggle to reconcile his

Illinois constituency. All the free sentiment of the State had been bitterly aroused by his part in the repeal of the Missouri Compromise, and when he first returned to Illinois it looked as if he would not be given even a hearing. Indeed, when he first attempted to speak in Chicago, September 1, he was hooted from the platform. With every day in the State, however, he won back his friends, so great was his power over men, and he was beginning to arouse something of his old enthusiasm when he went to Springfield to speak at the annual State Fair. There was a great crowd present from all parts of the State, and Douglas spoke for three hours. When he closed it was announced that Lincoln would answer him the next day. Lincoln's friends expected him to do well in his reply, but his speech was a surprise even to those who knew him best. It was profound, finished, vigorous, eloquent. When had he mastered the history of the slavery question so completely? they asked each other. "The anti-Nebraska speech of Mr. Lincoln," said the Springfield "Journal" the next day, "was the profoundest, in our opinion that he has made in his whole life. He felt upon his soul the truths burn which he uttered, and all present felt that he was true to his own soul. His feelings once or twice swelled within, and came near stifling utterance. He quivered with emotion. The whole house was as still as death. He attacked the Nebraska bill with unusual warmth and energy; and all felt that a man of strength was its enemy, and that he intended to blast it if he could by strong and manly efforts. He was most successful, and the house approved the glorious triumph of truth by loud and continued huzzas."

The vigor and earnestness of Lincoln's speech aroused the crowd to such enthusiasm that Senator Douglas felt obliged to reply to him the next day. These speeches of October 3, 4 and 5, 1854, form really the first of the series of Lincoln-

Douglas Debates. They proved conclusively to the anti-Nebraska politicians in Illinois that Lincoln was to be their leader in the fight they had begun against the extension of slavery.

Although the speech of October 4 was not preserved, we know from Paul Selby, at that time editor of an independent paper in Jacksonville, Illinois, which had been working hard against the repeal of the Missouri Compromise, that Lincoln's speech at Springfield was practically the same as one delivered twelve days later at Peoria in reply to Douglas. Of this latter a full report was preserved.

In his reply at Peoria, Lincoln began by a brief but sufficient résumé of the efforts of the North to apply the Declaration of Independence to all new territory which it acquired, and failing in that to provide for the sake of peace a series of compromises reserving as much territory as possible to freedom. He showed that the Kansas-Nebraska bill was a direct violation of one of the greatest of these solemn compromises. This he declared was "wrong." "Wrong in its direct effect, letting slavery into Kansas and Nebraska, and wrong in its prospective principle, allowing it to spread to every other part of the wide world where men can be found inclined to take it. This declared indifference, but, as I must think, covert real zeal, for the spread of slavery, I cannot but hate. I hate it because of the monstrous injustice of slavery itself. I hate it because it deprives our republican example of its just influence in the world; enables the enemies of free institutions with plausibility to taunt us as hypocrites; causes the real friends of freedom to doubt our sincerity; and especially because it forces so many men among ourselves into an open war with the very fundamental principles of civil liberty, criticizing the Declaration of Independence, and insisting that there is no right principle of action but self-interest."

**Disavowing** all " prejudice against the Southern people," **he** generously declared :

" They are just what we would be in their situation. If slavery did not exist among them, they would not introduce it. If it did now exist among us, we should not instantly give it up. . . I surely will not blame them for not doing what I should not know how to do myself. If all earthly power were given me, I should not know what to do as to the existing institution. My first impulse would be to free all the slaves, and send them to Liberia, to their own native land. But a moment's reflection would convince me that whatever of high hope . . . . there may be in this in the long run, its sudden execution is impossible. If they were all landed there in a day, they would all perish in the next ten days, and there are not surplus shipping and surplus money enough to carry them there in many times ten days. . . . I think I would not hold one in slavery at any rate, yet the point is not clear enough for me to denounce people upon . . . . . . It does seem to me that systems of gradual emancipation might be adopted, but for their tardiness in this I will not undertake to judge our brethren of the South. . . . The law which forbids the bringing of slaves from Africa, and that which has so long forbidden the taking of them into Nebraska, can hardly be distinguished on any moral principle, and the repeal of the former could find quite as plausible excuses as that of the latter."

Taking up the arguments by which the repeal of the Missouri Compromise was justified, he answered them one by one with clearness and a great array of facts. The chief of these arguments was that the repeal was in the interest of the " sacred right of self-government " that the people of Nebraska had a right to govern themselves as they chose, voting for or against slavery as they pleased.

" The doctrine of self-government is right," Lincoln said, " absolutely and eternally right, but it has no just application as here attempted. Or perhaps I should rather say that whether it has such application depends upon whether a negro is not or is a man. If he is not a man, in that case he who is a man may as a matter of self-government do just what he pleases with him. But if the negro is a man, is it not to that extent a total destruction of self-government to say that he too shall not govern himself? When the white man governs himself, that is self-government; but when he governs himself and also governs another man, that is more than self-government—that is despotism. If the negro is a man, why then my ancient faith teaches me that 'all men are created equal,' and that there can be no moral right in connection with one man's making a slave of another.

"Judge Douglas frequently, with bitter irony and sarcasm, paraphrases our argument by saying: 'The white people of Nebraska are good enough to govern themselves, but they are not good enough to govern a few miserable negroes!'

"Well! I doubt not that the people of Nebraska are and will continue to be as good as the average of people elsewhere. I do not say the contrary. What I do say is that no man is good enough to govern another man without that other's consent. I say this is the leading principle, the sheet-anchor of American republicanism."

This Peoria speech, which is very long, is particularly interesting to students of Mr. Lincoln's speeches, because in it is found the germ of many of the arguments which he elaborated in the next six years and used with tremendous effect.

With the Peoria speech Douglas had had enough of Lincoln as an antagonist, and he made a compact with him that neither should speak again in the campaign. It was characteristic of Douglas that on his way to Chicago he should stop and deliver a speech at Princeton!

But though Lincoln had temporarily withdrawn from the stump he was by no means abandoning the struggle. The iniquity of the Kansas-Nebraska bill grew greater to him every day. He meant to fight it to the end and he wanted to go where he could fight it directly. He became a candidate for the General Assembly of Illinois from Sangamon County and was elected by a large majority in November. A little later he saw an opportunity for a larger position. Although Illinois was strongly Democratic, the revolt against the Nebraska bill had driven from the party a number of men, members of the Legislature who had signified their determination to vote only for an Anti-Nebraska Senator. This gave the Whigs a chance, and several candidates offered themselves—among them Lincoln. Resigning from the Legislature (members of the Legislature could not become candidates for the senatorship), he began his electioneering in the frank Western style of those days by requesting his friends to support him.

"I have really got it into my head to try to be United States Senator," he wrote his friend Gillespie, "and, if I could have your support, my chances would be reasonably good. But I know, and acknowledge, that you have as just claims to the place as I have; and therefore I cannot ask you to yield to me, if you are thinking of becoming a candidate yourself. If, however, you are not, then I should like to be remembered affectionately by you; and also to have you make a mark for me with the Anti-Nebraska members, down your way."

He sent a large number of similar letters to friends, and by the first of January, when the Legislature re-assembled, he felt his chances of election were good. "I have more committals than any other man," he wrote his friend Washburne. Nevertheless he failed of the election. Just how he explained to Washburne early in February:

"I began with 44 votes, Shields (Democratic) 41, and Trumbull (Anti-Nebraska) 5,—yet Trumbull was elected. In fact, 47 different members voted for me,—getting three new ones on the second ballot, and losing four old ones. How came my 47 to yield to Trumbull's 5? It was Governor Matteson's work. He has been secretly a candidate ever since (before, even) the fall election. All the members round about the canal were Anti-Nebraska, but were nevertheless nearly all Democrats and old personal friends of his. His plan was to privately impress them with the belief that he was as good Anti-Nebraska as any one else—at least could be secured to be so by instructions, which could be easily passed. . . . . . . . . . . . . . .

"The Nebraska men, of course, were not for Matteson; but when they found they could elect no avowed Nebraska man, they tardily determined to let him get whomever of our men he could, by whatever means he could, and ask him no questions. . . . . . . . . . . . . .

The Nebraska men were very confident of the election of Matteson, though denying that he was a candidate, and we very much believing also that they would elect him. But they wanted first to make a show of good faith to Shields by voting for him a few times, and our secret Matteson men also wanted to make a show of good faith by voting with us a few times. So we led off. On the seventh ballot, I think, the signal was given to the Nebraska men to turn to Matteson, which they acted on to a man, with one exception. . .

Next ballot the remaining Nebraska man and one pretended Anti went over to him, giving him 46. The next still another, giving him 47, wanting only three of an election. In the meantime our friends, with a view of detaining our expected bolters, had been turning from me to Trumbull till he had risen to 35 and I had been reduced to 15. These would never desert me except by my direction; but I became satisfied that if we could prevent Matteson's election one or two ballots more, we could not possibly do so a single ballot after my friends should begin to return to me from Trumbull. So I determined to strike at once, and accordingly advised my remaining friends to go for him, which they did and elected him on the tenth ballot.

"Such is the way the thing was done. I think you would have done the same under the circumstances. . . . . . I could have headed off every combination and been elected, had it not been for Matteson's double game—and his defeat now gives me more pleasure than my own gives me pain.

On the whole, it is perhaps as well for our general cause that Trumbull is elected. The Nebraska men confess that they hate it worse than anything that could have happened. It is a great consolation to see them worse whipped than I am."

Not only had Lincoln made the leading orator of the Nebraska cause cry enough, he had by his quick wit and his devotion to the cause secured an Anti-Nebraska Senator for the State.

Although for the time being campaigning was over, Lincoln by no means dropped the subject. The struggle between North and South over the settlement of Kansas grew every day more bitter. Violence was beginning, and it was evident that if the people of the new territory should vote to make the State free it would be impossible to enforce the decision without bloodshed. Lincoln watched the developments with a growing determination never to submit to the repeal of the Missouri Compromise. He would advocate its restoration so long as Kansas remained a territory, and if it ever sought to enter the Union as a slave State he would oppose it. He discussed the subject incessantly with his friends as he travelled the circuit; and wrestled with it day and night in solitude. A new conviction was gradually growing upon him. He had long held that slavery was wrong but that it could not be touched in the State where it was recognized by the Constitution; all that the free States could require, in his judgment, was that no new territory should be opened to slavery. He held that all compromises adjusting difficulties between the North and South on the slavery question were as sacred as the Constitution. Now he saw the most important of them all violated. Was it possible to devise a compromise which would settle forever the conflicting interests? He turned over the question continually. Judge T. Lyle Dickey of Illinois once told the Hon. William Pitt Kellogg that

when the excitement over the Kansas-Nebraska bill first
broke out, he was with Lincoln and several friends attending court. One evening several persons, including himself and Lincoln, were discussing the slavery question. Judge
Dickey contended that slavery was an institution, which the
Constitution recognized, and which could not be disturbed.
Lincoln argued that ultimately slavery must become extinct.
" After a while," said Judge Dickey, " we went upstairs to
bed. There were two beds in our room, and I remember that
Lincoln sat up in his night shirt on the edge of the bed
arguing the point with me. At last, we went to sleep. Early
in the morning I woke up and there was Lincoln half sitting
up in bed. ' Dickey,' he said, ' I tell you this nation
cannot exist half slave and half free. ' Oh, Lincoln,' said
I, ' go to sleep.' "

As the months went on this idea took deeper root, and
in August, 1855, we find it expressed in a letter to George
Robertson of Kentucky: " Our political problem now is,
' Can we as a nation continue together permanently—forever—half slave and half free?' The problem is too mighty
for me—may God, in his mercy, superintend the solution."

Not only was he beginning to see that the Union could
not exist " divided against itself," he was beginning to see
that in order to fight effectively against the repeal of the
Missouri Compromise and the admission of Kansas as a
slave State, he might be obliged to abandon the Whigs. All
his life he had been a loyal Henry Clay Whig, ardent in his
devotion to the party, sincerely attached to its principles.
His friends were of that party, and never had a man's party
friends been more willing than his to aid his ambition. But
the Whigs were afraid of the Anti-Nebraska agitation. Was
he being forced from his party? He hardly knew. " I
think I am a Whig," he wrote his friend Speed, who had
inquired where he stood, " but others say there are no

Whigs and that I am an Abolitionist." This was in August, 1855. The events of the next few months showed him that he must stand by the body of men of all parties—Whig, Democratic, Abolition, Free Soil—who opposed the repeal of the Missouri Compromise, and were slowly uniting into the new Republican party to fight it.

The first decisive step to organize these elements in Illinois was an editorial convention held on February 22, 1856, at Decatur. One of the editors interested, Paul Selby, relates the history of the convention in an unpublished manuscript on the " Formation of the Republican Party in Illinois," from which the following account is quoted:

" This movement, first suggested by ' The Morgan Journal ' at Jacksonville, having received the approval of a considerable number of the Anti-Nebraska papers of the State, resulted in the issue of the following call:

" ' *Editorial Convention.*—All editors in Illinois opposed to the Nebraska bill are requested to meet in Convention at Decatur, Illinois, on the 22d of February next, for the purpose of making arrangements for organizing the Anti-Nebraska forces in this State for the coming contest. All editors favoring the movement will please forward a copy of their paper containing their approval to the office of the Illinois ' State Chronicle,' Decatur.

" Twenty-five papers indorsed the call, but on the day of the meeting only about half that number of editors put in an appearance. One reason for the small number was the fact that, on the night before a heavy snow-storm had fallen throughout the State, obstructing the passage of trains on the two railroads centering at Decatur. The meeting was held in the parlor of the ' Cassell House '—afterwards the ' Oglesby House,' now called the ' St. Nicholas Hotel.' Those present and participating in the opening proceedings, as shown by the official report, were: E. C. Dougherty, 'Register,' Rockford; Charles Faxon, ' Post.' Princeton; A. N. Ford, ' Gazette,' Lacon; Thomas J. Pickett, ' Republican,' Peoria; Virgil Y. Ralston, ' Whig,' Quincy; Charles

(19)

H. Ray, 'Tribune,' Chicago; George Schneider, 'Staats
Zeitung,' Chicago; Paul Selby, 'Journal,' Jacksonville; B.
F. Shaw, 'Telegraph,' Dixon; W. J. Usrey, 'Chronicle,'
Decatur, and O. P. Wharton, 'Advertiser,' Rock Island. In
the organization Paul Selby was made Chairman and W. J.
Usrey, Secretary, while Messrs. Ralston, Ray, Wharton,
Dougherty, Prickett and Schneider constituted a Committee
on Resolutions. The platform adopted as 'a basis of common and concerted action' among the members of the
new organization, embraced a declaration of principles that
would be regarded in this day as most conservative Republicanism, recognizing 'The legal rights of the slave States
to hold and enjoy their property in slaves under their State
laws;' reaffirming the principles of the Declaration of Independence, with its correlative doctrine that 'Freedom is
national and slavery sectional;' declaring assumption of the
right to extend slavery on the plea that it is essential to the
security of the institution 'an invasion of our rights' which
'must be resisted;' demanding the restoration of the Missouri Compromise and 'the restriction of slavery to its
present authorized limits;' advocating the maintenance of
'the naturalization laws as they are' and favoring 'the
widest tolerance in matters of religion and faith' (a rebuke
to Know-Nothingism); pledging resistance to assaults upon
the common school system, and closing with a demand for
reformation in the administration of the State Government
as 'second only in importance to the question of slavery
itself.' Mr. Lincoln was present in Decatur during the day,
and, although he did not take part in the public deliberations
of the convention, he was in close conference with the Committee on Resolutions, and the impress of his hand is seen in
the character of the platform adopted. Messrs. Ray and
Schneider, of the Chicago press, were also influential fac-
tors in shaping the declaration of principles with which the
new party in Illinois started on its long career of almost un-
interrupted success.

"The day's proceedings ended with a complimentary banquet given to the editors at the same hotel by the citizens
of Decatur. Speeches were made in response to toasts by
Mr. Lincoln, R. J. Oglesby (afterwards Major-General of

Volunteers and three times Governor of Illinois—then a young lawyer of Decatur), Ray of the Chicago ' Tribune,' Ralston of the Quincy 'Whig' and others among the editors. In the course of his speech, referring to a movement which some of the editors present had inaugurated to make him the Anti-Nebraska candidate for Governor at the ensuing election, Mr. Lincoln spoke (in substance) as follows: ' I wish to say why I should not be a candidate. If I should be chosen, the Democrats would say it was nothing more than an attempt to resurrect the dead body of the old Whig party. I would secure the vote of that party and no more, and our defeat will follow as a matter of course. But I can suggest a name that will secure not only the old Whig vote, but enough Anti-Nebraska Democrats to give us the victory. That man is Colonel William H. Bissell.'

" Here Mr. Lincoln again displayed his characteristic unselfishness and sagacity. That he would, at that time, have regarded an election to the Governorship of the great State of Illinois as an honor not worth contending for, will scarcely be presumed. He was seeking more important results, however, in the interest of freedom and good government—the ending of the political chaos that had prevailed for the past two years and the consolidation of the forces opposed to slavery extension in a compact political organization. Bissell had been an officer in the Mexican War with a good record; had afterwards, as a member of Congress from the Belleville District, opposed the Kansas-Nebraska bill, and had refused to be brow-beaten by Jefferson Davis into the retraction of statements he had made on the floor of Congress. As will appear later, he was nominated and Lincoln's judgment vindicated by his election and the unification of the elements which afterwards composed the Republican party.

" One of the last acts of the editorial convention was the appointment of a State Central Committee, consisting of one member for each Congressional District and two for the State at large. Some of the names were suggested by Mr. Lincoln, while the others received his approval. . . . A supplementary resolution recommended the holding of a State Convention at Bloomington, on the 29th of May following, and requested the committee just appointed to issue the necessary call. . . . . . . . . . . . . .

" It is a coincidence of some interest that, on the day the Illinois editors were in session at Decatur a convention of representatives from different States, with a similar object in view for the country at large, was in session at Pittsburg, Pa. The latter was presided over by the venerable Francis P. Blair, of Maryland, while among its most prominent members appear such names as those of Governor E. D. Morgan of New York, Horace Greeley, Preston King, David Wilmot, Oliver P. Morton, Joshua R. Giddings, Zachariah Chandler and many others of national reputation. A National Committee there appointed called the first National Convention of the Republican party, held at Philadelphia on the 17th of June."

In the interval between the Decatur meeting and the Bloomington Convention called for May 29, the excitement in the county over Kansas grew almost to a frenzy. The new State was in the hands of a pro-slavery mob, her Governor a prisoner, her capital in ruins, her voters intimidated. The newspapers were full of accounts of the attack on Sumner in the United States Senate by Brooks. One of the very men who had been expected to be a leader in the Bloomington Convention, Paul Selby, was lying at home prostrated by a cowardly blow from a political opponent. Little wonder then that when the Convention met its members were resolved to take radical action. The convention was opened with John M. Palmer, afterwards United States Senator, in its chair, and in a very short time it had adopted a platform, appointed delegates to the National Convention, nominated a State ticket, completed, in short, all the work of organizing the Republican Party in Illinois. After this work of organizing and nominating was finished, there was a call for speeches. The convention felt the need of some powerful amalgamating force which would weld its discordant elements. In spite of the best intentions of the members, their most manful efforts, they knew in their hearts that they were still political enemies, that the Whig was still a Whig, the Democrat a Democrat, the Abolitionist an Abolitionist. Man after man was called to the platform and spoke without producing any marked effect, when suddenly there was a call raised of a name not on the program—" Lincoln "—" Lincoln "—" give us Lincoln! " The crowd took it up and made the hall ring until a tall figure rose in the back of the audience and slowly strode down the aisle. As he turned to his audience there came gradually a great change upon his face. " There was an expression of intense emotion," Judge Scott, of Bloomington, once told the author. " It was the emotion of a great soul. Even in stature he seemed greater. He seemed to realize it was a crisis in his life."

Lincoln, in fact, had come to the parting of the ways in his political life, to the moment when he must publicly break with his party. For two years he had tried to fight slavery extension under the name of a Whig. He had found it could not be done, and now in spite of the efforts of his conservative friends who had vainly tried to keep him away from the Bloomington Convention, he was facing that convention, was openly acknowledging that henceforth he worked with the Republican Party.

Lincoln's extraordinary human insight and sympathy told him as he looked at his audience that what this body of splendid, earnest, but groping men needed was to feel that they had undertaken a cause of such transcendent value that beside it all previous alliances, ambitions and duties were as nothing. If he could make them see the triviality of their differences as compared with the tremendous principle of the new party, he was certain they would go forth Republicans in spirit as well as in name.

He began his speech, then, deeply moved, and with a profound sense of the importance of the moment. At first he spoke slowly and haltingly, but gradually he grew in force and intensity until his hearers arose from their chairs and with pale faces and quivering lips pressed unconsciously towards him. Starting from the back of the broad platform on which he stood, his hands on his hips, he slowly advanced towards the front, his eyes blazing, his face white with passion, his voice resonant with the force of his conviction. As he advanced he seemed to his audience fairly to grow, and when at the end of a period he stood at the front line of the stage, hands still on the hips, head back, raised on his tip toes, he seemed like a giant inspired. " At that moment he was the handsomest man I ever saw," Judge Scott declared.

So powerful was his effect on his audience that men and women wept as they cheered and children there that night still remember the scene, though at the time they understood nothing of its meaning. As he went on there came upon the convention the very emotion he sought to arouse. " Every one in that before incongruous assembly came to feel as one man, to think as one man and to purpose and resolve as one man," says one of his auditors. He had made every man of them pure Republican. He did something more. The indignation which the outrages in Kansas and throughout the country had aroused was uncontrolled. Men talked passionately of war. It was at this meeting that Lincoln, after firing his hearers by an expression which became a watchword of the campaign, " We won't go out of the Union and you shan't," poured oil on the wrath of the Illinois opponents of the Nebraska bill by advising " ballots, not bullets."

Nothing illustrates better the extraordinary power of Lincoln's speech at Bloomington than the way he stirred up the newspaper reporters. It was before the stenographer had become acclimated in Illinois, though long-hand reports were regularly taken. Of course, all the leading papers of the State leaning towards the new party, had reporters at the convention. Among these was Mr. Joseph Medill.

" It was my journalistic duty," says Mr. Medill, " though a delegate to the convention, to make a ' long-hand ' report of the speeches delivered for the Chicago ' Tribune.' I did make a few paragraphs of what Lincoln said in the first eight or ten minutes, but I became so absorbed in his magnetic oratory that I forgot myself and ceased to take notes; and joined with the convention in cheering and stamping and clapping to the end of his speech.

" I well remember that after Lincoln sat down and calm had succeeded the tempest, I waked out of a sort of hypnotic trance, and then thought of my report for the ' Tribune.' There was nothing written but an abbreviated introduction.

" It was some sort of satisfaction to find that I had not been ' scooped,' as all the newspaper men present had been equally carried away by the excitement caused by the wonderful oration and had made no report or sketch of the speech."

A number of Lincoln's friends, young lawyers, most of them, were accustomed to taking notes of speeches, and as usual sharpened their pencils as he began. " I attempted for about fifteen minutes," says Mr. Herndon, Lincoln's law partner, " as was usual with me then to take notes, but at the end of that time I threw pen and paper away and lived only in the inspiration of the hour." The result of this excitement was that when the convention was over there was no reporter present who had anything for his newspaper. They all went home and wrote burning editorials about the speech and its great principle, but as to reproducing it they could not. Men came to talk of it all over Illinois. They realized that it had been a purifying fire for the party, but as to what it contained no one could say. Gradually it became known as Lincoln's "lost speech." From the very mystery of it its reputation grew greater as time went on.

But though the convention so nearly to a man lost its head, there was at least one auditor who had enough control to pursue his usual habit of making notes of the speeches he heard. This was a young lawyer on the same circuit as Lincoln, Mr. H. C. Whitney. For some three weeks before the convention Lincoln and Whitney had been attending court at Danville. They had discussed the political situation in the State carefully, and to Whitney Lincoln had stated his convictions and determinations. In a way Whitney had absorbed Lincoln's speech beforehand, as indeed any one must have done who was with Lincoln when he was preparing an address, it being his habit to discuss points and to repeat them aloud indifferent to who heard him. Whitney had gone to the convention intending to make notes, knowing, as he did, that Lincoln had not written out what he was going to say. Fortunately he had a cool enough head to keep to his purpose. He made his notes, and on returning to Judge Davis's home in Bloomington, where he, with Lincoln and one or two others, were staying, he enlarged them while the others discussed the speech. These notes Whitney kept for many years, always intending to write them out, but never attending to it until the author, in 1896, learned that he had them and urged him to expand them. This Mr. Whitney did, and the speech was first published in "McClure's Magazine" for September, 1896. Mr. Whitney does not claim that he has made a full report. He does claim that the argument is correct and that in many cases the expressions are exact. A few quotations will show any one familiar with Lincoln's speeches that Mr. Whitney has caught much of their style, for instance, the following:

*     *     *     *     *     *     *     *     *     *

" We come—we are here assembled together—to protest
as well as we can against a great wrong, and to take measures, as well as we now can, to make that wrong right; to
place the nation, as far as it may be possible now, as it was
before the repeal of the Missouri Compromise; and the plain
way to do this is to restore the Compromise, and to demand
and determine that *Kansas shall be free!* While we affirm,
and reaffirm, if necessary, our devotions to the principles of
the Declaration of Independence, let our practical work here
be limited to the above. We know that there is not a perfect
agreement of sentiment here on the public questions which
might be rightfully considered in this convention, and that
the indignation which we all must feel cannot be helped;
but all of us must give up something for the good of the
cause. There is one desire which is uppermost in the mind,
one wish common to us all—to which no dissent will be
made; and I counsel you earnestly to bury all resentment,
to sink all personal feeling, make all things work to a common purpose in which we are united and agreed about, and
which all present will agree is absolutely ncessary—which
*must* be done by any rightful mode if there be such : *Slavery
must be kept out of Kansas!* The test—the pinch—is right
there. If we lose Kansas to freedom, an example will be
set which will prove fatal to freedom in the end. We, therefore, in the language of the *Bible,* must ' lay the axe to the
root of the tree.' Temporizing will not do longer; now
is the time for decision—for firm, persistent, resolute action.

*     *     *     *     *     *     *     *

"We have made a good beginning here to-day. As our
Methodist friends would say, ' I feel it is good to be here.'
While extremists may find some fault with the moderation
of our platform, they should remember that ' the battle is not
always to the strong, nor the race to the swift.' In grave
emergencies, moderation is generally safer than radicalism;
and as this struggle is likely to be long and earnest, we must
not, by our action, repel any who are in sympathy with us
in the main, but rather win all that we can to our standard.

We must not belittle nor overlook the facts of our condition —that we are new and comparatively weak, while our enemies are entrenched and relatively strong. They have the administration and the political power; and, right or wrong, at present they have the numbers. Our friends who urge an appeal to arms with so much force and eloquence, should recollect that the government is arrayed against us, and that the numbers are now arrayed against us as well; or, to state it nearer to the truth, they are not yet expressly and affirmatively for us; and we should repel friends rather than gain them by anything savoring of revolutionary methods. As it now stands, we must appeal to the sober sense and patriotism of the people. We will make converts day by day; we will grow strong by calmness and moderation; we will grow strong by the violence and injustice of our adversaries. And, unless truth be a mockery and justice a hollow lie, we will be in the majority after a while, and then the revolution which we will accomplish will be none the less radical from being the result of pacific measures. The battle of freedom is to be fought out on principle. Slavery is a violation of the eternal right. We have temporized with it from the necessities of our condition, but *as sure as God reigns and school children read,* THAT BLACK FOUL LIE CAN NEVER BE CONSECRATED INTO GOD'S HALLOWED TRUTH!

.    .    .    .    .    .    .    .

"I will not say that we may not sooner or later be compelled to meet force by force; but the time has not yet come, and if we are true to ourselves, may never come. Do not mistake that the ballot is stronger than the bullet. Therefore, let the legions of slavery use bullets; but let us wait patiently till November, and fire ballots at them in return; and by that peaceful policy, I believe we shall ultimately win.

.    .    .    .    .    .    .    .

"Did you ever, my friends, seriously reflect upon the speed with which we are tending downwards? Within the memory of men now present the leading statesmen of Virginia could make genuine, red-hot abolitionist speeche in old Virginia; and, as I have said, now even in 'free Kansas' it is a crime to declare that it is 'free Kansas.' The very sentiments that I and others have just uttered, would entitle us, and each of us, to the ignominy and seclusion of a dungeon; and yet I suppose that, like Paul, we were 'free born.' But if this thing is allowed to continue, it will be but one step further to impress the same rule in Illinois.

"The conclusion of all is, that we must restore the Missouri Compromise. We must highly resolve that *Kansas must be free!* We must reinstate the birthday promise of the Republic; we must reaffirm the Declaration of Independence; we must make good in essence as well as in form Madison's avowal that 'the word *slave* ought not to appear in the Constitution;' and we must even go further, and decree that only local law, and not that time-honored instrument, shall shelter a slave-holder. We must make this a land of liberty in fact, as it is in name. But in seeking to attain these results—so indispensable if the liberty which is our pride and boast shall endure—we will be loyal to the Constitution and to the 'flag of our Union,' and no matter what our grievance—even though Kansas shall come in as a slave State; and no matter what theirs—even if we shall restore the Compromise—WE WILL SAY TO THE SOUTHERN DISUNIONISTS, WE WON'T GO OUT OF THE UNION, AND YOU SHAN'T!!!

# CHAPTER XVIII

## THE LINCOLN-DOUGLAS DEBATES

" THE greatest speech ever made in Illinois, and it puts
Lincoln on the track for the Presidency," was the comment
made by enthusiastic Republicans on Lincoln's speech before the Bloomington Convention. Conscious that it was
he who had put the breath of life into their organization,
the party instinctively turned to him as its leader. The
effect of this local recognition was at once perceptible in
the national organization. Less than three weeks after the
delivery of the Bloomington speech, the national convention of the Republican party met in Philadelphia June
17, to nominate candidates for the presidency and vice-
presidency. Lincoln's name was the second proposed for
the latter office, and on the first ballot he received one hundred and ten votes. The news reached him at Urbana, Ill.,
where he was attending court, one of his companions reading from a daily paper just received from Chicago, the
result of the ballot. The simple name Lincoln was given,
without the name of the man's State. Lincoln said indifferently that he did not suppose it could be himself; and
added that there was " another great man " of the name,
a man from Massachusetts. The next day, however, he
knew that it was himself to whom the convention had given
so strong an endorsement. He knew also that the ticket
chosen was Frémont and Dayton.

The campaign of the following summer and fall was one
of intense activity for Lincoln. In Illinois and the neighboring States he made over fifty speeches, only fragments

320

of which have been preserved. One of the first important ones was delivered on July 4, 1856, at a great mass meeting at Princeton, the home of the Lovejoys and the Bryants. The people were still irritated by the outrages in Kansas and by the attack on Sumner in the Senate, and the temptation to deliver a stirring and indignant oration must have been strong. Lincoln's speech was, however, a fine example of political wisdom, an historical argument admirably calculated to convince his auditors that they were right in their opposition to slavery extension, but so controlled and sane that it would stir no impulsive radical to violence. There probably was not uttered in the United States on that critical 4th of July, 1856, when the very foundation of the government was in dispute and the day itself seemed a mockery, a cooler, more logical speech than this by the man who, a month before, had driven a convention so nearly mad that the very reporters had forgotten to make notes. And the temper of this Princeton speech Lincoln kept throughout the campaign.

In spite of the valiant struggle of the Republicans, Buchanan was elected; but Lincoln was in no way discouraged. The Republicans had polled 1,341,264 votes in the country. In Illinois, they had given Frémont nearly 100,-000 votes, and they had elected their candidate for governor, General Bissell. Lincoln turned from arguments to encouragement and good counsel.

" All of us," he said at a Republican banquet in Chicago, a few weeks after the election, " who did not vote for Mr. Buchanan, taken together, are a majority of four hundred thousand. But in the late contest we were divided between Frémont and Fillmore. Can we not come together for the future? Let every one who really believes and is resolved that free society is not and shall not be a failure, and who can conscientiously declare that in the last contest he has done only what he thought best—let every such one have charity to believe that every other one can say as much. Thus let bygones be bygones; let past differences as nothing be; and with steady eye on the real issue let us reinaugurate the good old 'central idea' of the republic. We can do it. The human heart is with us; God is with us. We shall again be able, not to declare that 'all States as States are equal,' nor yet that 'all citizens as citizens are equal,' but to renew the broader, better declaration, including both these and much more, that 'all men are created equal.'"

The spring of 1857 gave Lincoln a new line of argument. Buchanan was scarcely in the Presidential chair before the Supreme Court, in the decision of the Dred Scott case, declared that a negro could not sue in the United States courts and that Congress could not prohibit slavery in the Territories. This decision was such an evident advance of the slave power that there was a violent uproar in the North. Douglas went at once to Illinois to calm his constituents. "What," he cried, "oppose the Supreme Court! Is it not sacred? To resist it is anarchy."

Lincoln met him fairly on the issue in a speech at Springfield in June, 1857.

"We believe as much as Judge Douglas (perhaps more) in obedience to and respect for the judicial department of government. . . . But we think the Dred Scott decision is erroneous. We know the court that made it has often overruled its own decisions, and we shall do what we can to have it overrule this. We offer no resistance to it. . . . If this important decision had been made by the unanimous concurrence of the judges, and without any apparent partisan bias, and in accordance with legal public expectation and with the steady practice of the departments throughout our history, and had been in no part based on assumed historical facts which are not really true; or if, wanting in some of these, it had been before

the court more than once, and had there been affirmed and
reaffirmed through a course of years, it then might be, perhaps would be, factious, nay, even revolutionary, not to
acquiesce in it as a precedent.  But when, as is true, we
find it wanting in all these claims to the public confidence, it
is not resistance, it is not factious, it is not even disrespect-
ful, to treat it as not having yet quite established a settled
doctrine for the country."

Let Douglas cry " awful," " anarchy," " revolution," as
much as he would, Lincoln's arguments against the Dred
Scott decision appealed to common sense and won him
commendation all over the country.  Even the radical leaders of the party in the East—Seward, Sumner, Theodore
Parker—began to notice him, to read his speeches, to consider his arguments.

With every month of 1857 Lincoln grew stronger, and
his election in Illinois as United States senatorial candidate
in 1858 against Douglas would have been insured if Douglas
had not suddenly broken with Buchanan and his party in
a way which won him the hearty sympathy and respect of
a large part of the Republicans of the North.  By a flagrantly unfair vote the pro-slavery leaders of Kansas had
secured the adoption of the Lecompton Constitution allowing slavery in the State.  President Buchanan urged Congress to admit Kansas with her bogus Constitution.  Douglas, who would not sanction so base an injustice, opposed
the measure, voting with the Republicans steadily against
the admission.  The Buchananists, outraged at what they
called " Douglas's apostasy," broke with him.  Then it
was that a part of the Republican party, notably Horace
Greeley at the head of the New York " Tribune," struck
by the boldness and nobility of Douglas's opposition, began
to hope to win him over from the Democrats to the Republicans.  Their first step was to counsel the leaders of their

party in Illinois to put up no candidate against Douglas for the United States senatorship in 1858.

Lincoln saw this change on the part of the Republican leaders with dismay. "Greeley is not doing me right," he said. ". . . I am a true Republican, and have been tried already in the hottest part of the anti-slavery fight; and yet I find him taking up Douglas, a veritable dodger,—once a tool of the South, now its enemy,—and pushing him to the front." He grew so restless over the returning popularity of Douglas among the Republicans that Herndon, his law-partner, determined to go East to find out the real feeling of the Eastern leaders towards Lincoln. Herndon had, for a long time, been in correspondence with the leading abolitionists and had no difficulty in getting interviews. The returns he brought back from his canvass were not altogether reassuring. Seward, Sumner, Phillips, Garrison, Beecher, Theodore Parker, all spoke favorably of Lincoln, and Seward sent him word that the Republicans would never take up so slippery a quantity as Douglas had proved himself. But Greeley—the all-important Greeley—was lukewarm. "The Republican standard is too high," he told Herndon. "We want something practical. . . . Douglas is a brave man. Forget the past and sustain the righteous." "Good God, *righteous,* eh!" groaned Herndon in his letter to Lincoln.

But though the encouragement which came to Lincoln from the East in the spring of 1858 was meagre, that which came from Illinois was abundant. There the Republicans supported him in whole-hearted devotion. In June, the State convention, meeting in Springfield to nominate its candidate for Senator, declared that Abraham Lincoln was its *first and only choice* as the successor of Stephen A. Douglas. The press was jubilant. "Unanimity is a weak word," wrote the editor of the Bloomington "Pantagraph," "to express the universal and intense feeling of the convention. *Lincoln!* LINCOLN!! LINCOLN!!! was the cry everywhere, whenever the senatorship was alluded to.   Delegates from Chicago and from Cairo, from the Wabash and the Illinois, from the north, the center, and the south, were alike fierce with enthusiasm, whenever that loved name was breathed.   Enemies at home and misjudging friends abroad, who have looked for dissension among us on the question of the senatorship, will please take notice that our nomination is a *unanimous* one; and that, in the event of a Republican majority in the next Legislature, no other name than Lincoln's will be mentioned, or thought of, by a solitary Republican legislator.   One little incident in the convention was a pleasing illustration of the universality of the Lincoln sentiment.   Cook county had brought a banner into the assemblage inscribed, ' Cook County for Abraham Lincoln.'   During a pause in the proceedings, a delegate from another county rose and proposed, with the consent of the Cook county delegation, ' to *amend the banner* by substituting for " Cook County " the word which I hold in my hand,' at the same time unrolling a scroll, and revealing the word ' Illinois ' in huge capitals.   The Cook delegation promptly *accepted the amendment,* and amidst a perfect hurricane of hurrahs, the banner was duly altered to express the sentiment of the whole Republican party of the State, thus: ' Illinois for Abraham Lincoln.' "

On the evening of the day of his nomination, Lincoln addressed his constituents.   The first paragraph of his speech gave the key to the campaign he proposed.   "A house divided against itself cannot stand.   I believe this government cannot endure permanently half slave and half free.   I do not expect the house to fall—but I do expect it will cease to be divided.   It will become all one thing or all the other."

Then followed the famous charge of conspiracy against

the slavery advocates, the charge that Pierce, Buchanan, Chief Justice Taney, and Douglas had been making a concerted effort to legalize the institution of slavery " in all the States, old as well as new, North as well as South." He marshalled one after another of the measures that the proslavery leaders had secured in the past four years, and clinched the argument by one of his inimitable illustrations:

" When we see a lot of framed timbers, different portions of which we know have been gotten out at different times and places and by different workmen,—Stephen, Franklin, Roger and James,* for instance,—and we see these timbers joined together, and see they exactly make the frame of a house or a mill, all the tenons and mortises exactly fitting, and all the lengths and proportions of the different pieces exactly adapted to their respective places, and not a piece too many or too few, not omitting even scaffolding—or, if a single piece be lacking, we see the place in the frame exactly fitted and prepared yet to bring such a piece in—in such a case we find it impossible not to believe that Stephen and Franklin and Roger and James all understood one another from the beginning, and all worked upon a common plan or draft, drawn up before the first blow was struck."

The speech was severely criticised by Lincoln's friends. It was too radical. It was sectional. He heard the complaints unmoved. " If I had to draw a pen across my record," he said, one day, " and erase my whole life from sight, and I had one poor gift or choice left as to what I should save from the wreck, I should choose that speech and leave it to the world unerased."

The speech was, in fact, one of great political adroitness. It forced Douglas to do exactly what he did not want to do in Illinois: explain his own record during the past four years; explain the true meaning of the Kansas-Nebraska

---

* *Stephen* A. Douglas, *Franklin* Pierce, *Roger* Taney, *James* Buchanan.

bill; discuss the Dred Scott decision; say whether or not he thought slavery so good a thing that the country could afford to extend it instead of confining it where it would be in course of gradual extinction. Douglas wanted the Republicans of Illinois to follow Greeley's advice: "Forgive the past." He wanted to make the most among them of his really noble revolt against the attempt of his party to fasten an unjust constitution on Kansas. Lincoln would not allow him to bask for an instant in the sun of that revolt. He crowded him step by step through his party's record, and compelled him to face what he called the "profound central truth" of the Republican party, "slavery is wrong and ought to be dealt with as wrong."

But it was at once evident that Douglas did not mean to meet the issue squarely. He called the doctrine of Lincoln's "house-divided-against-itself" speech "sectionalism;" his charge of conspiracy "false;" his talk of the wrong of slavery extension "abolitionism." This went on for a month. Then Lincoln resolved to force Douglas to meet his arguments, and challenged him to a series of joint debates. Douglas was not pleased. His reply to the challenge was irritable, even slightly insolent. To those of his friends who talked with him privately of the contest, he said: "I do not feel, between you and me, that I want to go into this debate. The whole country knows me, and has me measured. Lincoln, as regards myself, is comparatively unknown, and if he gets the best of this debate,—and I want to say he is the ablest man the Republicans have got,—I shall lose everything and Lincoln will gain everything. Should I win, I shall gain but little. I do not want to go into a debate with Abe." Publicly, however, he carried off the prospect confidently, even jauntily. "Mr. Lincoln," he said patronizingly, "is a kind, amiable, intelligent gentleman." In the mean time his constituents boasted loudly of the fine spectacle they were

going to give the State—" the Little Giant chawing up Old
Abe!"

Many of Lincoln's friends looked forward to the encounter
with foreboding.   Often, in spite of their best intentions,
they showed anxiety.   " Shortly before the first debate came
off at Ottawa," says Judge H. W. Beckwith of Danville, Ill.
" I passed the Chenery House, then the principal hotel in
Springfield.   The lobby was crowded with partisan leaders
from various sections of the State, and Mr. Lincoln, from
his greater height, was seen above the surging mass that
clung about him like a swarm of bees to their ruler.   He
looked careworn, but he met the crowd patiently and kindly,
shaking hands, answering questions, and receiving assurances of support.   The day was warm, and at the first
chance he broke away and came out for a little fresh air,
wiping the sweat from his face.

"As he passed the door he saw me, and, taking my hand,
inquired for the health and views of his ' friends over in
Vermilion county.'   He was assured they were wide awake,
and further told that they looked forward to the debate
between him and Senator Douglas with deep concern.   From
the shadow that went quickly over his face, the pained look
that came to give quickly way to a blaze of eyes and quiver
of lips, I felt that Mr. Lincoln had gone beneath my mere
words and caught my inner and current fears as to the result.
And then, in a forgiving, jocular way peculiar to him, he
said, ' Sit down; I have a moment to spare and will tell you
a story.'   Having been on his feet for some time, he sat on
the end of the stone step leading into the hotel door, while I
stood closely fronting him.

" 'You have,' he continued, ' seen two men about to fight?'

" ' Yes, many times.'

" ' Well, one of them brags about what he means to do.
He jumps high in the air cracking his heels together, smites

his fists, and wastes his breath trying to scare somebody. You see the other fellow, he says not a word,'—here Mr. Lincoln's voice and manner changed to great earnestness, and repeating—' you see the other man says not a word. His arms are at his side, his fists are closely doubled up, his head is drawn to the shoulder, and his teeth are set firm together. He is saving his wind for the fight, and as sure as it comes off he will win it, or die a-trying.'

" He made no other comment, but arose, bade me good-by, and left me to apply the illustration."

It was inevitable that Douglas's friends should be sanguine, Lincoln's doubtful. The contrast between the two candidates was almost pathetic. Senator Douglas was the most brilliant figure in the political life of the day. Winning in personality, fearless as an advocate, magnetic in eloquence, shrewd in political manœuvring, he had every quality to captivate the public. His resources had never failed him. From his entrance into Illinois politics in 1834, he had been the recipient of every political honor his party had to bestow. For the past eleven years he had been a member of the United States Senate, where he had influenced all the important legislation of the day and met in debate every strong speaker of North and South. In 1852, and again in 1856, he had been a strongly supported, though unsuccessful, candidate for the Democratic presidential nomination. In 1858 he was put at or near the head of every list of possible presidential candidates made up for 1860.

How barren Lincoln's public career in comparison! Three terms in the lower house of the State Assembly, one term in Congress, then a failure which drove him from public life. Now he returns as a bolter from his party, a leader in a new organization which the conservatives are denouncing as " visionary," " impractical," " revolutionary."

No one recognized more clearly than Lincoln the difference between himself and his opponent. " With me," he said, sadly, in comparing the careers of himself and Douglas, " the race of ambition has been a failure—a flat failure. With him it has been one of splendid success." He warned his party at the outset that, with himself as a standard-bearer, the battle must be fought on principle alone, without any of the external aids which Douglas's brilliant career gave. " Senator Douglas is of world-wide renown," he said; " All the anxious politicians of his party, or who have been of his party for years past, have been looking upon him as certainly, at no distant day, to be the President of the United States. They have seen in his round, jolly, fruitful face, post-offices, land-offices, marshalships, and cabinet appointments, chargéships and foreign missions, bursting and sprouting out in wonderful exuberance, ready to be laid hold of by their greedy hands. And as they have been gazing upon this attractive picture so long, they cannot, in the little distraction that has taken place in the party, bring themselves to give up the charming hope; but with greedier anxiety they rush about him, sustain him, and give him marches, triumphal entries, and receptions beyond what even in the days of his highest prosperity they could have brought about in his favor. On the contrary, nobody has ever expected me to be President. In my poor, lean, lank face, nobody has ever seen that any cabbages were sprouting out. These are disadvantages, all taken together, that the Republicans labor under. We have to fight this battle upon principle, and upon principle alone."

If one will take a map of Illinois and locate the points of the Lincoln and Douglas debates held between August 21 and October 15, 1858, he will see that the whole State was traversed in the contest. The first took place at Ottawa, about seventy-five miles southwest of Chicago, on August 21; the second at Freeport, near the Wisconsin boundary, on August

27. The third was in the extreme southern part of the
State, at Jonesboro, on September 15. Three days later the
contestants met one hundred and fifty miles northeast of
Jonesboro, at Charleston. The fifth, sixth, and seventh debates were held in the western part of the State; at Galesburg, October 7; Quincy, October 13; and Alton, October 15.

Constant exposure and fatigue were unavoidable in meeting these engagements. Both contestants spoke almost every
day through the intervals between the joint debates; and as
railroad communication in Illinois in 1858 was still very in-
complete, they were often obliged to resort to horse, carriage, or steamer to reach the desired points. Judge Douglas
succeeded, however, in making this difficult journey something of a triumphal procession. He was accompanied
throughout the campaign by his wife—a beautiful and brilliant woman—and by a number of distinguished Democrats.
On the Illinois Central Railroad he had always a special car,
sometimes a special train. Frequently he swept by Lincoln,
side-tracked in an accommodation or freight train. "The
gentleman in that car evidently smelt no royalty in our carriage," laughed Lincoln one day, as he watched from the
caboose of a laid-up freight train the decorated special of
Douglas flying by.

It was only when Lincoln left the railroad and crossed the
prairie, to speak at some isolated town, that he went in state.
The attentions he received were often very trying to him.
He detested what he called "fizzlegigs and fireworks," and
would squirm in disgust when his friends gave him a genuine
prairie ovation. Usually, when he was going to a point
distant from the railway, a "distinguished citizen" met him
at the station nearest the place with a carriage. When they
were come within two or three miles of the town, a long procession with banners and band would appear winding across

the prairie to meet the speaker. A speech of greeting was made, and then the ladies of the entertainment committee would present Lincoln with flowers, sometimes even winding a garland about his head and lank figure. His embarrassment at these attentions was thoroughly appreciated by his friends. At the Ottawa debate the enthusiasm of his supporters was so great that they insisted on carrying him from the platform to the house where he was to be entertained. Powerless to escape from the clutches of his admirers, he could only cry, " Don't, boys; let me down; come now, don't." But the " boys " persisted, and they tell to-day proudly of their exploit and of the cordial hand-shake Lincoln, all embarrassed as he was, gave each of them when at last he was free.

On arrival at the towns where the joint debates were held, Douglas was always met by a brass band and a salute of thirty-two guns (the Union was composed of thirty-two States in 1858), and was escorted to the hotel in the finest equipage to be had. Lincoln's supporters took delight in showing their contempt of Douglas's elegance by affecting a Republican simplicity, often carrying their candidate through the streets on a high and unadorned hay-rack drawn by farm horses. The scenes in the towns on the occasion of the debates were perhaps never equalled at any other of the hustings of this country. No distance seemed too great for the people to go; no vehicle too slow or fatiguing. At Charleston there was a great delegation of men, women, and children present which had come in a long procession from Indiana by farm wagons, afoot, on horseback, and in carriages. The crowds at three or four of the debates were for that day immense. There were estimated to be from eight thousand to fourteen thousand people at Quincy, some six thousand at Alton, from ten thousand to fifteen thousand at Charleston, some twenty thousand at Ottawa. Many of those at Ottawa came the night before. " It was a matter of but a short time," says Mr. George Beatty of Ottawa, "until the few hotels, the livery stables, and private houses were crowded, and there were no accommodations left. Then the campaigners spread out about the town, and camped in whatever spot was most convenient. They went along the bluff and on the bottom-lands, and that night the camp-fires, spread up and down the valley for a mile, made it look as if an army was gathered about us."

When the crowd was massed at the place of the debate, the scene was one of the greatest hubbub and confusion. On the corners of the squares, and scattered around the outskirts of the crowd, were fakirs of every description, selling pain-killers and ague cures, watermelons and lemonade; jugglers and beggars plied their trades, and the brass bands of all the four corners within twenty-five miles tooted and pounded at "Hail Columbia, Happy Land," or "Columbia, the Gem of the Ocean."

Conspicuous in the processions at all the points was what Lincoln called the "Basket of Flowers," thirty-two young girls in a resplendent car, representing the Union. At Charleston, a thirty-third young woman rode behind the car, representing Kansas. She carried a banner inscribed: "I will be free;" a motto which brought out from nearly all the newspaper reporters the comment that she was too fair to be long free.

The mottoes at the different meetings epitomized the popular conception of the issues and the candidates. Among the Lincoln sentiments were:

Illinois born under the Ordinance of '87.

Free Territories and Free Men,
   Free Pulpits and Free Preachers,
Free Press and a Free Pen,
   Free Schools and Free Teachers.

" Westward the star of empire takes its way;
   The girls link on to Lincoln, their mothers were for Clay."

Abe the Giant-Killer.

Edgar County for the Tall Sucker.

A striking feature of the crowds was the number of women they included. The intelligent and lively interest they took in the debates caused much comment. No doubt Mrs. Douglas's presence had something to do with this. They were particularly active in receiving the speakers, and at Quincy, Lincoln, on being presented with what the local press described as a " beautiful and elegant bouquet," took pains to express his gratification at the part women everywhere took in the contest.

While this helter-skelter outpouring of prairiedom had the appearance of being little more than a great jollification, a lawless country fair, in reality it was with the majority of the people a profoundly serious matter. With every discussion it became more vital. Indeed, in the first debate, which was opened and closed by Douglas,* the relation of the two speakers became dramatic. It was here that Douglas, hoping to fasten on Lincoln the stigma of " abolitionist," charged him with having undertaken to abolitionize the old Whig party, and having been in 1854 a subscriber to a radical platform proclaimed at Springfield. This platform Douglas read. Lincoln, when he replied, could only say he was never at the convention—knew nothing of the resolutions; but the impression prevailed that he was cornered. The next issue of the Chicago " Press and Tribune " dispelled it. That paper had employed to report the debates the first short-

---

* By the terms agreed upon by Douglas and Lincoln for regulating the debates Douglas opened at Ottawa, Jonesboro, Galesburg, and Alton with an hour's speech; was followed by Lincoln with a speech of one and a half hours, and closed with a half-hour speech. At the three remaining points, Freeport, Charleston, and Quincy, Lincoln opened and closed.

hand reporter in Chicago, Mr. Robert L. Hitt—now a Member of Congress and the Chairman of the Committee on Foreign Affairs. Mr. Hitt, when Douglas began to read the resolutions, took an opportunity to rest, supposing he could get the original from the speaker. He took down only the first line of each resolution. He missed Douglas after the debate, but on reaching Chicago, where he wrote out his report, he sent an assistant to the files to find the platform adopted at the Springfield Convention. It was brought, but when Mr. Hitt began to transcribe it he saw at once that it was widely different from the one Douglas had read. There was great excitement in the office, and the staff, ardently Republican, went to work to discover where the resolutions had come from. It was found that they originated at a meeting of radical abolitionists with whom Lincoln had never been associated.

The " Press and Tribune " announced the " forgery," as it was called in a caustic editorial, " The Little Dodger Cornered and Caught." Within a week even the remote school-districts of Illinois were discussing Douglas's action, and many of the most important papers of the nation had made it a subject of editorial comment.

Almost without exception Douglas was condemned. No amount of explanation on his part helped him. " The particularity of Douglas's charge," said the Louisville " Journal," " precludes the idea that he was simply and innocently mistaken." Lovers of fair play were disgusted, and those of Douglas's own party who would have applauded a trick too clever to be discovered could not forgive him for one which had been found out. Greeley came out bitterly against him, and before long wrote to Lincoln and Herndon that Douglas was " like the man's boy who (he said) didn't weigh so much as he expected and he always knew he wouldn't."

Douglas's error became a sharp-edged sword in Lincoln's

hand. Without directly referring to it, he called his hearers'
attention to the forgery every time he quoted a document
by his elaborate explanation that he believed, unless there
was some mistake on the part of those with whom the matter
originated and which he had been unable to detect, that this
was correct. Once when Douglas brought forward a document, Lincoln blandly remarked that he could scarcely be
blamed for doubting its genuineness since the introduction
of the Springfield resolutions at Ottawa.

It was in the second debate, at Freeport, that Lincoln made
the boldest stroke of the contest. Soon after the Ottawa
debate, in discussing his plan for the next encounter, with a
number of his political friends,—Washburne, Cook, Judd,
and others,—he told them he proposed to ask Douglas four
questions, which he read. One and all cried halt at the second question. Under no condition, they said, must he put it.
If it were put, Douglas would answer it in such a way as to
win the senatorship. The morning of the debate, while on
the way to Freeport, Lincoln read the same questions to Mr.
Joseph Medill. "I do not like this second question, Mr.
Lincoln," said Mr. Medill. The two men argued to their
journey's end, but Lincoln was still unconvinced. Even
after he reached Freeport several Republican leaders came to
him pleading, "Do not ask that question." He was obdu-
rate; and he went on the platform with a higher head, a
haughtier step than his friends had noted in him before. Lincoln was going to ruin himself, the committee said despond-
ently; one would think he did not want the senatorship.

The mooted question ran in Lincoln's notes: "Can the
people of a United States territory in any lawful way, against
the wish of any citizen of the United States, exclude slavery from its limits prior to the formation of a State Constitution?" Lincoln had seen the irreconcilableness of Douglas's own measure of popular sovereignty, which declared

that the people of a territory should be left to regulate their domestic concerns in their own way subject only to the Constitution, and the decision of the Supreme Court in the Dred Scott case that slaves, being property, could not under the Constitution be excluded from a territory. He knew that if Douglas said *no* to this question, his Illinois constituents would never return him to the Senate. He believed that if he said *yes,* the people of the South would never vote for him for President of the United States. He was willing himself to lose the senatorship in order to defeat Douglas for the Presidency in 1860. " I am after larger game; the battle of 1860 is worth a hundred of this," he said confidently.

The question was put, and Douglas answered it with rare artfulness. " It matters not," he cried, " what way the Supreme Court may hereafter decide as to the abstract question whether slavery may or may not go into a territory under the Constitution; the people have the lawful means to introduce it or exclude it as they please, for the reason that slavery cannot exist a day or an hour anywhere unless it is supported by local police regulations. Those police regulations can only be established by the local legislature, and if the people are opposed to slavery, they will elect representatives to that body who will, by unfriendly legislation, effectually prevent the introduction of it into their midst. If, on the contrary, they are for it, their legislation will favor its extension."

His Democratic constituents went wild over the clever way in which Douglas had escaped Lincoln's trap. He now practically had his election. The Republicans shook their heads. Lincoln only was serene. He alone knew what he had done. The Freeport debate had no sooner reached the pro-slavery press than a storm of protest went up. Douglas had betrayed the South. He had repudiated the Supreme Court decision. He had declared that slavery could be kept out of the territories by other legislation than a State Constitution. " The Freeport doctrine,"or " the theory of unfriendly legislation," as it became known, spread month by month, and slowly but surely made Douglas an impossible candidate in the South. The force of the question was not realized in full by Lincoln's friends until the Democratic party met in Charleston, S. C., in 1860, and the Southern delegates refused to support Douglas because of the answer he gave to Lincoln's question in the Freeport debate of 1858.

" Do you recollect the argument we had on the way up to Freeport two years ago over the question I was going to ask Judge Douglas?" Lincoln asked Mr. Joseph Medill, when the latter went to Springfield a few days after the election of 1860.

" Yes," said Medill, " I recollect it very well."

" Don't you think I was right now? "

" We were both right. The question hurt Douglas for the Presidency, but it lost you the senatorship."

" Yes, and I have won the place he was playing for."

From the beginning of the campaign Lincoln supplemented the strength of his arguments by inexhaustible good-humor. Douglas, physically worn, harassed by the trend which Lincoln had given the discussions, irritated that his adroitness and eloquence could not so cover the fundamental truth of the Republican position but that it would up again, often grew angry, even abusive. Lincoln answered him with most effective raillery. At Havana, where he spoke the day after Douglas, he said:

" I am informed that my distinguished friend yesterday became a little excited—nervous, perhaps—and he said something about *fighting,* as though referring to a pugilistic encounter between him and myself. Did anybody in this audience hear him use such language? [Cries of " Yes."]

I am informed further, that somebody in *his* audience, rather more excited and nervous than himself, took off his coat, and offered to take the job off Judge Douglas's hands, and fight Lincoln himself. Did anybody here witness that warlike proceeding? [Laughter and cries of "Yes."] Well, I merely desire to say that I shall fight neither Judge Douglas nor his second. I shall not do this for two reasons, which I will now explain. In the first place, a fight would prove *nothing* which is in issue in this contest. It might establish that Judge Douglas is a more muscular man than myself, or it might demonstrate that I am a more muscular man than Judge Douglas. But this question is not referred to in the Cincinnati platform, nor in either of the Springfield platforms. Neither result would prove him right nor me wrong; and so of the gentleman who volunteered to do this fighting for him. If my fighting Judge Douglas would not prove anything, it would certainly prove nothing for me to fight his bottle-holder.

"My second reason for not having a personal encounter with the judge is, that I don't believe he wants it himself. He and I are about the best friends in the world, and when we get together he would no more think of fighting me than of fighting his wife. Therefore, ladies and gentlemen, when the judge talked about fighting, he was not giving vent to any ill feeling of his own, but merely trying to excite—well, *enthusiasm* against me on the part of his audience. And as I find he was tolerably successful, we will call it quits."

More difficult for Lincoln to take good-naturedly than threats and hard names was the irrelevant matters which Douglas dragged into the debates to turn attention from the vital arguments. Thus Douglas insisted repeatedly on taunting Lincoln because his zealous friends had carried him off the platform at Ottawa. "Lincoln was so frightened by the questions put to him," said Douglas, "that he could not walk." He tried to arouse the prejudice of the audience by absurd charges of abolitionism. Lincoln wanted to give negroes social equality; he wanted a negro wife; he was willing to allow Fred Douglass to make speeches for him. Again he took up a good deal of Lincoln's time by forcing him to answer to a charge of refusing to vote supplies for the soldiers in the Mexican War. Lincoln denied and explained, until at last, at Charleston, he turned suddenly to Douglas's supporters, dragging one of the strongest of them—the Hon. O. B. Ficklin, with whom he had been in Congress in 1848—to the platform.

" I do not mean to do anything with Mr. Ficklin," he said, " except to present his face and tell you that he personally knows it to be a lie." And Mr. Ficklin had to acknowledge that Lincoln was right.

" Judge Douglas," said Lincoln in speaking of this policy, " is playing cuttlefish—a small species of fish that has no mode of defending himself when pursued except by throwing out a black fluid which makes the water so dark the enemy cannot see it, and thus it escapes."

The question at stake was too serious in Lincoln's judgment, for platform jugglery. Every moment of his time which Douglas forced him to spend answering irrelevant charges he gave begrudgingly. He struggled constantly to keep his speeches on the line of solid argument. Slowly but surely those who followed the debates began to understand this. It was Douglas who drew the great masses to the debates in the first place; it was because of him that the public men and the newspapers of the East, as well as of the West, watched the discussions. But as the days went on it was not Douglas who made the impression.

During the hours of the speeches the two men seemed well mated. " I can recall only one fact of the debates," says Mrs. William Crotty of Seneca, Illinois, " that I felt so sorry for Lincoln while Douglas was speaking, and then to my surprise I felt *so* sorry for Douglas when Lincoln replied." The disinterested to whom it was an intellectual game, felt the power

and charm of both men.    Partisans had each reason enough
to cheer.    It was afterwards, as the debates were talked over
by auditors as they lingered at the country store or were
grouped on the fence in the evening, or when they were read
in the generous reports which the newspapers of Illinois and
even of other States gave, that the thoroughness of Lincoln's
argument was understood.    Even the first debate at Ottawa
had a surprising effect.    " I tell you," says Mr. George Beatty
of Ottawa, " that debate set people thinking on these important questions in a way they hadn't dreamed of.    I heard any
number of men say : ' This thing is an awfully serious question, and I have about concluded Lincoln has got it right.'
My father, a thoughtful, God-fearing man, said to me, as
we went home to supper, ' George, you are young, and don't
see what this thing means, as I do.    Douglas's speeches of
" squatter sovereignty " please you younger men, but I tell
you that with us older men it's a great question that faces us.
We've either got to keep slavery back or it's going to spread
all over the country.    That's the real question that's behind
all this.    Lincoln is right.'    And that was the feeling that
prevailed, I think, among the majority, after the debate was
over.    People went home talking about the danger of slavery getting a hold in the North.    This territory had been
Democratic;  La Salle County, the morning of the day of the
debate, was Democratic; but when the next day came around,
hundreds of Democrats had been made Republicans, owing
to the light in which Lincoln had brought forward the fact
that slavery threatened."

It was among Lincoln's own friends, however, that his
speeches produced the deepest impression.    They had believed him to be strong, but probably there was no one of
them who had not felt dubious about his ability to meet
Douglas.    Many even feared a fiasco.    Gradually it began
to be clear to them that Lincoln was the stronger.    Could it

be that Lincoln really was a great man? The young Republican journalists of the " Press and Tribune "—Scripps, Hitt, Medill—began to ask themselves the question. One evening as they talked over Lincoln's arguments a letter was received. It came from a prominent Eastern statesman. " Who is this man that is replying to Douglas in your State? " he asked. " Do you realize that no greater speeches have been made on public questions in the history of our country; that his knowledge of the subject is profound, his logic unanswerable, his style inimitable? " Similar letters kept coming from various parts of the country. Before the campaign was over Lincoln's friends were exultant. Their favorite was a great man, " a full-grown man," as one of them wrote in his paper.

The country at large watched Lincoln with astonishment. When the debates began there were Republicans in Illinois of wider national reputation. Judge Lyman Trumbull, then Senator, was better known. He was an able debater, and a speech which he made in August against Douglas's record called from the New York " Evening Post " the remark: " This is the heaviest blow struck at Senator Douglas since he took the field in Illinois; it is unanswerable, and we suspect that it will be fatal." Trumbull's speech the " Post " afterwards published in pamphlet form. Besides Trumbull, Owen Lovejoy, Oglesby, and Palmer were all speaking. That Lincoln should not only have so far outstripped men of his own party, but should have out-argued Douglas, was the cause of comment everywhere. " No man of this generation," said the " Evening Post " editorially, at the close of the debate, " has grown more rapidly before the country than Lincoln in this canvass." As a matter of fact, Lincoln had attracted the attention of all the thinking men of the country. " The first thing that really awakened my interest in him," says Henry Ward Beecher. " was his speech parallel

with Douglas in Illinois, and indeed it was that manifesta-
tion of ability that secured his nomination to the presidency."

But able as were Lincoln's arguments, deep as was the impression he had made, he was not elected to the senatorship.
Douglas won fairly enough; though it is well to note that if
the Republicans did not elect a senator they gained a substantial number of votes over those polled in 1856.

Lincoln accepted the result with a serenity inexplicable
to his supporters. To him the contest was but one battle in
a "durable" struggle. Little matter who won now, if in
the end the right triumphed. From the first he had looked
at the final result—not at the senatorship. "I do not claim,
gentlemen, to be unselfish," he said at Chicago in July. "I
do not pretend that I would not like to go to the United States
Senate; I make no such hypocritical pretense; but I do say
to you that in this mighty issue, it is nothing to you, nothing
to the mass of the people of the nation, whether or not Judge
Douglas or myself shall ever be heard of after this night; it
may be a trifle to either of us, but in connection with this
mighty question, upon which hang the destinies of the nation perhaps, it is absolutely nothing."

The intense heat and fury of the debates, the defeat in
November, did not alter a jot this high view. "I am glad I
made the late race," he wrote Dr. A. G. Henry. "It gave
me a hearing on the great and durable question of the age
which I would have had in no other way; and though I now
sink out of view and shall be forgotten, I believe I have made
some marks which will tell for the cause of civil liberty long
after I am gone."

At that date perhaps no one appreciated the value of what
Lincoln had done as well as he did himself. He was absolutely sure he was right and that in the end people would
see it. Though he might not rise, he knew his cause would.

" Douglas had the ingenuity to be supported in the late contest both as the best means to break down and to uphold the slave interest," he wrote. " No ingenuity can keep these antagonistic elements in harmony long. Another explosion will soon occur." His whole attention was given to conserving what the Republicans had gained,—" We have some one hundred and twenty thousand clear Republican votes. That pile is worth keeping together; " to consoling his friends,—" You are feeling badly," he wrote to N. B. Judd, Chairman of the Republican Committee, " and this too shall pass away, never fear; " to rallying for another effort,— " The cause of civil liberty must not be surrendered at the end of one or even one hundred defeats."

If Lincoln had at times a fear that his defeat would cause him to be set aside, it soon was dispelled. The interest awakened in him was genuine, and it spread with the wider reading and discussion of his arguments. He was besieged by letters from all parts of the Union, congratulations, encouragements, criticisms. Invitations for lectures poured in upon him, and he became the first choice of his entire party for political speeches.

The greater number of these invitations he declined. He had given so much time to politics since 1854 that his law practice had been neglected and he was feeling poor; but there were certain of the calls which could not be resisted. Douglas spoke several times for the Democrats of Ohio in the 1859 campaign for governor and Lincoln naturally was asked to reply. He made but two speeches, one at Columbus on September 16 and the other at Cincinnati on September 17, but he had great audiences on both occasions. The Columbus speech was devoted almost entirely to answering an essay by Douglas which had been published in the September number of " Harper's Magazine," and which began by asserting that—" Under our complex system of gov-

ernment it is the first duty of American statesmen to mark
distinctly the dividing-line between Federal and Local authority." It was an elaborate argument for " popular sovereignty " and attracted national attention. Indeed, at the
moment it was the talk of the county. Lincoln literally tore
it to bits.

" What is Judge Douglas's popular sovereignty? " he
asked. " It is, as a principle, no other than that if one
man chooses to make a slave of another man, neither that
other man nor anybody else has a right to object. Applied
in government, as he seeks to apply it, it is this: If, in a
new territory into which a few people are beginning to
enter for the purpose of making their homes, they choose
to either exclude slavery from their limits or to establish it
there, however one or the other may affect the persons to
be enslaved, or the infinitely greater number of persons who
are afterward to inhabit that Territory, or the other members of the families of communities, of which they are but
an incipient member, or the general head of the family of
States as parent of all—however their action may affect one
or the other of these, there is no power or right to interfere.
That is Douglas's popular sovereignty applied."

It was in this address that Lincoln uttered the oft-quoted
paragraphs:

" I suppose the institution of slavery really looks small
to him. He is so put up by nature that a lash upon his back
would hurt him, but a lash upon anybody else's back does
not hurt him. That is the build of the man, and consequently he looks upon the matter of slavery in this unim-
portant light.

" Judge Douglas ought to remember, when he is endeavoring to force this policy upon the American people, that
while he is put up in that way, a good many are not. He
ought to remember that there was once in this country a
man by the name of Thomas Jefferson, supposed to be a
Democrat—a man whose principles and policy are not very

prevalent amongst Democrats to-day, it is true; but that
man did not take exactly this view of the insignificance of
the element of slavery which our friend Judge Douglas
does. In contemplation of this thing, we all know he was led
to exclaim, ' I tremble for my country when I remember that
God is just!' We know how he looked upon it when he
thus expressed himself. There was danger to this country,
danger of the avenging justice of God, in that little unim-
portant popular-sovereignty question of Judge Douglas. He
supposed there was a question of God's eternal justice
wrapped up in the enslaving of any race of men, or any
man, and that those who did so braved the arm of Jehovah—
that when a nation thus dared the Almighty, every friend of
that nation had cause to dread his wrath. Choose ye between Jefferson and Douglas as to what is the true view
of this element among us."

One interesting point about the Columbus address is that
in it appears the germ of the Cooper Institute speech delivered five months later in New York City.

Lincoln made so deep an impression in Ohio by his
speeches that the State Republican Committee asked permission to publish them together with the Lincoln-Douglas
Debates as campaign documents in the presidential election
of the next year.

In December he yielded to the persuasion of his Kansas
political friends and delivered five lectures in that State,
only fragments of which have been preserved.

Unquestionably the most effective piece of work he did
that winter was the address at Cooper Institute, New York,
on February 27. He had received an invitation in the fall
of 1859 to lecture at Plymouth Church, Brooklyn. To his
friends it was evident that he was greatly pleased by the
compliment, but that he feared that he was not equal to
an Eastern audience. After some hesitation he accepted,
provided they would take a political speech if he could find

time to get up no other. When he reached New York he found that he was to speak there instead of Brooklyn, and that he was certain to have a distinguished audience. Fearful lest he was not as well prepared as he ought to be, conscious, too, no doubt, that he had a great opportunity before him, he spent nearly all of the two days and a half before his lecture in revising his matter and in familiarizing himself with it. In order that he might be sure that he was heard he arranged with his friend, Mason Brayman, who had come on to New York with him, to sit in the back of the hall and in case he did not speak loud enough to raise his high hat on a cane.

Mr. Lincoln's audience was a notable one even for New York. It included William Cullen Bryant, who introduced him, Horace Greeley, David Dudley Field and many more well known men of the day. It is doubtful if there were any persons present, even his best friends, who expected that Lincoln would do more than interest his hearers by his sound arguments. Many have confessed since that they feared his queer manner and quaint speeches would amuse people so much that they would fail to catch the weight of his logic. But to the surprise of everybody Lincoln impressed his audience from the start by his dignity and his seriousness. " His manner was, to a New York audience, a very strange one, but it was captivating," wrote an auditor. " He held the vast meeting spellbound, and as one by one his oddly expressed but trenchant and convincing arguments confirmed the soundness of his political conclusions, the house broke out in wild and prolonged enthusiasm. I think I never saw an audience more thoroughly carried away by an orator."

The Cooper Union speech was founded on a sentence from one of Douglas's Ohio speeches :—" Our fathers when they framed the government under which we live understood

this question just as well, and even better, than we do now."
Douglas claimed that the " fathers " held that the Constitution forbade the Federal government controlling slavery in
the Territories. Lincoln with infinite care had investigated
the opinions and votes of each of the " fathers "—whom
he took to be the thirty-nine men who signed the Constitution—and showed conclusively that a majority of them
" certainly understood that no proper division of local from
Federal authority nor any part of the Constitution forbade
the Federal government to control slavery in the Federal
Territories." Not only did he show this of the thirty-nine
framers of the original Constitution, but he defied anybody
to show that one of the seventy-six members of the Congress which framed the amendments to the Constitution ever
held any such view.

" Let all," he said, " who believe that ' our fathers who
framed the government under which we live understood this
question just as well, and even better, than we do now,' speak
as they spoke, and act as they acted upon it. This is all Republicans ask—all Republicans desire—in relation to slavery. As those fathers marked it, so let it be again marked,
as an evil not to be extended, but to be tolerated and pro-
tected only because of and so far as its actual presence among
us makes that toleration and protection a necessity. Let all
the guaranties those fathers gave it be not grudgingly, but
fully and fairly, maintained. For this Republicans contend,
and with this, so far as I know or believe, they will be content."

One after another he took up and replied to the charges
the South was making against the North at the moment :—
Sectionalism, radicalism, giving undue prominence to the
slave question, stirring up insurrection among slaves, refusing to allow constitutional rights, and to each he had an un-
impassioned answer impregnable with facts.

The discourse was ended with what Lincoln felt to be a precise statement of the opinion of the question on both sides, and of the duty of the Republican party under the circumstances. This portion of his address is one of the finest early examples of that simple and convincing style in which most of his later public documents were written.

" If slavery is right," he said, " all words, acts, laws, and constitutions against it are themselves wrong, and should be silenced and swept away. If it is right, we cannot justly object to its nationality—its universality; if it is wrong, they cannot justly insist upon its extension—its enlargement. All they ask we could readily grant, if we thought slavery right; all we ask they could as readily grant, if they thought it wrong. Their thinking it right and our thinking it wrong is the precise fact upon which depends the whole controversy. Thinking it right, as they do, they are not to blame for desiring its full recognition as being right; but thinking it wrong, as we do, can we yield to them? Can we cast our votes with their view, and against our own? In view of our moral, social, and political responsibilities, can we do this?

" Wrong, as we think slavery is, we can yet afford to let it alone where it is, because that much is due to the necessity arising from its actual presence in the nation; but can we, while our votes will prevent it, allow it to spread into the national Territories, and to overrun us here in these free States? If our sense of duty forbids this, then let us stand by our duty fearlessly and effectively. Let us be diverted by none of those sophistical contrivances wherewith we are so industriously plied and belabored—contrivances such as groping for some middle ground between the right and the wrong: vain as the search for a man who should be neither a living man nor a dead man; such as a policy of ' don't care ' on a question about which all true men do care; such as Union appeals beseeching true Union men to yield to Disunionists, reversing the divine rule, and calling, not the sinners, but the righteous to repentance; such as invocations to Washington, imploring men to unsay what Washington said and undo what Washington did.

" Neither let us be slandered from our duty by false accusations against us, nor frightened from it by menaces of destruction to the government, nor of dungeons to ourselves. Let us have faith that right makes might, and in that faith let us to the end dare to do our duty as we understand it."

From New York Lincoln went to New Hampshire to visit his son Robert, then at Phillips Exeter Academy. His coming was known only a short time before he arrived and hurried arrangements were made for him to speak at Concord, Manchester, Exeter and Dover. At Concord the address was made in the afternoon on only a few hours' notice, nevertheless, he had a great audience, so eager were men at the time to hear anybody who had serious arguments on the slavery question. Something of the impression Lincoln made in New Hampshire may be gathered from the following article, " Mr. Lincoln in New Hampshire," which appeared in the Boston " Atlas and Bee " for March 5:

The Concord " Statesman " says that notwithstanding the rain of Thursday, rendering travelling very inconvenient, the largest hall in that city was crowded to hear Mr. Lincoln. The editor says it was one of the most powerful, logical and compacted speeches to which it was ever our fortune to listen; an argument against the system of slavery, and in defence of the position of the Republican party, from the deductions of which no reasonable man could possibly escape. He fortified every position assumed, by proofs which it is impossible to gainsay; and while his speech was at intervals enlivened by remarks which elicited applause at the expense of the Democratic party, there was, nevertheless, not a single word which tended to impair the dignity of the speaker, or weaken the force of the great truths he uttered.

The " Statesman " adds that the address " was perfect, and was closed by a peroration which brought his audience to their feet. We are not extravagant in the remark, that a political speech of greater power has rarely if ever been uttered in the Capital of New Hampshire. At its conclusio nine roof-raising cheers were given; three for the speaker, three for the Republicans of Illinois, and three for the Republicans of New Hampshire."

On the same evening Mr. Lincoln spoke at Manchester, to an immense gathering in Smyth's Hall. The "Mirror," a neutral paper, gives the following enthusiastic notice of his speech: " The audience was a flattering one to the reputation of the speaker. It was composed of persons of all sorts of political notions, earnest to hear one whose fame was so great, and we think most of them went away thinking better of him than they anticipated they should. He spoke an hour and a half with great fairness, great apparent candor, and with wonderful interest. He did not abuse the South, the Administration, or the Democrats, or indulge in any personalities, with the solitary exception of a few hits at Douglas's notions. He is far from prepossessing in personal appearance, and his voice is disagreeable, and yet he wins your attention and good will from the start.

" He indulges in no flowers of rhetoric, no eloquent passages; he is not a wit, a humorist or a clown; yet, so great a vein of pleasantry and good nature pervades what he says, gilding over a deep current of practical argument, he keeps his hearers in a smiling good mood with their mouths open ready to swallow all he says. His sense of the ludicrous is very keen, and an exhibition of that is the clincher of all his arguments; not the ludicrous acts of persons, but ludicrous ideas. Hence he is never offensive, and steals away willingly into his train of belief, persons who are opposed to him. For the first half hour his opponents would agree with every word he uttered, and from that point he began to lead them off, little by little, cunningly, till it seemed as if he had got them all into his fold. He displays more shrewdness, more knowledge of the masses of mankind than any public speaker we have heard since long Jim Wilson left for California."

From New Hampshire Lincoln went to Connecticut, where on March 5 he spoke at Hartford, on March 6 at New Haven, on March 8 at Woonsocket, on March 9 at Norwich. There are no reports of the New Hampshire speeches, but two of the Connecticut speeches were published in part and one in full. Their effect was very similar, according to the newspapers of the day, to that in New Hampshire, described by the "Atlas and Bee."

By his debates with Douglas and the speeches in Ohio, Kansas, New York and New England, Lincoln had become a national figure in the minds of all the political leaders of the country, and of the thinking men of the North. Never in the history of the United States had a man become prominent in a more logical and intelligent way. At the beginning of the struggle against the repeal of the Missouri Compromise in 1854, Abraham Lincoln was scarcely known outside of his own State. Even most of the men whom he had met in his brief term in Congress had forgotten him. Yet in four years he had become one of the central figures of his party; and now, by worsting the greatest orator and politician of his time, he had drawn the eyes of the nation to him.

It had been a long road he had travelled to make himself a national figure. Twenty-eight years before he had deliberately entered politics. He had been beaten, but had persisted; he had succeeded and failed; he had abandoned the struggle and returned to his profession. His outraged sense of justice had driven him back, and for six years he had travelled up and down Illinois trying to prove to men that slavery extension was wrong. It was by no one speech, by no one argument that he had wrought. Every day his ceaseless study and pondering gave him new matter, and every speech he made was fresh. He could not repeat an old speech, he said, because the subject enlarged and widened so in his mind as he went on that it was "easier to make a new one than an old one." He had never yielded in his campaign to tricks of oratory—never played on emotions. He had been so strong in his convictions of the right of his case that his speeches had been arguments pure and simple. Their elegance was that of a demonstration in Euclid. They persuaded because they proved. He had never for a moment counted personal ambition before the cause. To insure an ardent opponent of the Kansas-Nebraska bill in the United States Senate, he had at one time given up his chance for the senatorship. To show the fallacy of Douglas's argument, he had asked a question which his party pleaded with him to pass by, assuring him that it would lose him the election. In every step of these six years he had been disinterested, calm, unyielding, and courageous. He knew he was right, and could afford to wait. " The result is not doubtful," he told his friends. " We shall not fail—if we stand firm. We shall not fail. Wise counsels may accelerate or mistakes delay it; but, sooner or later, the victory is sure to come."

The country, amazed at the rare moral and intellectual character of Lincoln, began to ask questions about him, and then his history came out; a pioneer home, little schooling, few books, hard labor at all the many trades of the frontiersman, a profession mastered o' nights by the light of a friendly cooper's fire, an early entry into politics and law— and then twenty-five years of incessant poverty and struggle.

The homely story gave a touch of mystery to the figure which loomed so large. Men felt a sudden reverence for a mind and heart developed to these noble proportions in so unfriendly a habitat. They turned instinctively to one so familiar with strife for help in solving the desperate problem with which the nation had grappled. And thus it was that, at fifty years of age, Lincoln became a national figure.

# CHAPTER XIX

THE possibility of Abraham Lincoln becoming the presidential candidate of the Republican party in 1860 was probably first discussed by a few of his friends in 1856. The dramatic speech which in May of that year gave him the leadership of his party in Illinois, and the unexpected and flattering attention he received a few weeks later at the Republican national convention suggested the idea; but there is no evidence that anything more was excited than a little speculation. The impression Lincoln made two years later in the Lincoln and Douglas debates kindled a different feeling. It convinced a number of astute Illinois politicians that judicious effort would make Lincoln strong enough to justify the presentation of his name as a candidate in 1860 on the ground of pure availability.

One of the first men to conceive this idea was Jesse W. Fell, a local politician of Bloomington, Illinois. During the Lincoln and Douglas debates Fell was travelling in the Middle and Eastern States. He was surprised to find that Lincoln's speeches attracted general attention, that many papers copied liberally from them, and that on all sides men plied him with questions about the career and personality of the new man. Before Fell left the East he had made up his mind that Lincoln must be pushed by his own State as its presidential candidate. One evening, soon after returning home, he met Lincoln in Bloomington, where the latter was attending court, and drew him into a deserted law-office for a confidential talk.

"I have been East, Lincoln," said he, "as far as Boston, and up into New Hampshire, travelling in all the New England States, save Maine; in New York, New Jersey, Pennsylvania, Ohio, Michigan, and Indiana; and everywhere I hear you talked about. Very frequently I have been asked, 'Who is this man Lincoln, of your State, now canvassing in opposition to Senator Douglas?' Being, as you know, an ardent Republican and your friend, I usually told them we had in Illinois *two* giants instead of one; that Douglas was the *little* one, as they all knew, but that you were the *big* one, which they didn't all know.

"But, seriously, Lincoln, Judge Douglas being so widely known, you are getting a national reputation *through him,* and the truth is, I have a decided impression that if your popular history and efforts on the slavery question can be sufficiently brought before the people, you can be made a formidable, if not a successful, candidate for the presidency."

"What's the use of talking of me for the presidency," was Lincoln's reply, "whilst we have such men as Seward, Chase, and others, who are so much better known to the people, and whose names are so intimately associated with the principles of the Republican party? Everybody knows them; nobody scarcely outside of Illinois knows me. Besides, is it not, as a matter of justice, due to such men, who have carried this movement forward to its present status, in spite of fearful opposition, personal abuse, and hard names? I really think so."

Fell continued his persuasions, and finally requested Lincoln to furnish him a sketch of his life which could be put out in the East. The suggestion grated on Lincoln's sensibilities. He had no chance. Why force himself? "Fell," he said, rising and wrapping his old gray shawl around his tall figure, "I admit that I am ambitious and would like to be President. I am not insensible to the compliment you pay me and the interest you manifest in the matter; *but there is no such good luck in store for me as the presidency of these United States.* Besides, there is nothing in my early history that would interest you or anybody else; and, as Judge Davis says, '*it won't pay.*' Good night." And he disappeared into the darkness.

Lincoln's defeat in November, 1858, in the contest for the United States senatorship, in no way discouraged his friends. A few days after the November election, when it was known that Douglas had been reëlected senator, the Chicago "Democrat," then edited by "Long John" Wentworth, printed an editorial, nearly a column in length, headed "Abraham Lincoln." His work in the campaign then just closed was reviewed and commended in the highest terms.

"His speeches," the "Democrat" declared, "will be recognized for a long time to come as the standard authorities upon those topics which overshadow all others in the political world of our day; and our children will read them and appreciate the great truths which they so forcibly inculcate, with even a higher appreciation of their worth than their fathers possessed while listening to them.

"We, for our part," said the "Democrat" further, "consider that it would be but a partial appreciation of his services to our noble cause that our next State Republican Convention should nominate him for governor as unanimously and enthusiastically as it did for senator. With such a leader and with our just cause, we would sweep the State from end to end, with a triumph so complete and perfect that there would be scarce enough of the scattered and demoralized forces of the enemy left to tell the story of its defeat. And this State should also present his name to the National Republican Convention, first for President and next for Vice-President. We should then say to the United States at large that in our opinion the Great Man of Illinois is Abraham Lincoln, and none other than Abraham Lincoln."

All through the year 1859 a few men in Illinois worked quietly but persistently to awaken a demand throughout the State for Lincoln's nomination. The greater number of these were lawyers on Lincoln's circuit, his life-long friends, men like Judge Davis, Leonard Swett, and Judge Logan, who not only believed in him, but loved him, and whose efforts were doubly effective because of their affection. In addition to these were a few shrewd politicians who saw in Lincoln the "available" man the situation demanded; and a group represented by John M. Palmer, who, remembering Lincoln's magnanimity in throwing his influence to Trumbull in 1854, in order to send a sound Anti-Nebraska man to the United States Senate, wanted, as Senator Palmer himself put it, to "pay Lincoln back." Then there were a few young men who had been won by Lincoln in the debates with Douglas, and who threw youthful enthusiasm and conviction into their support. The first time his name was suggested as a candidate in the newspapers, indeed, was because the young editor of the Central Illinois "Gazette," Mr. W. O. Stoddard, had caught a glimpse of Lincoln's inner might and concluding in a sudden burst of boyish exultation that Lincoln was "the greatest man he had ever seen or heard of," had rushed off and written an editorial nominating him for the presidency; this editorial was published on May 4, 1859.

The work which these men did at this time cannot be traced with any definiteness. It consisted mainly in "talking up" their candidate. They were greatly aided by the newspapers. The press, indeed, followed a concerted plan that had been carefully laid out by the Republican State Committee in the office of the Chicago "Tribune." To give an appearance of spontaneity to the newspaper canvass it was arranged that the country papers should first take up Lincoln's name. Joseph Medill, editor of the "Tribune," and secretary of the committee, says that a Rock Island paper opened the campaign.

Lincoln soon felt the force of this effort in his behalf. Letters came to him from unexpected quarters, offering aid. Everywhere he went on the circuit, men sought him to discuss the situation. In the face of an undoubted movement for him he quailed. The interest was local; could it ever be more? Above all, had he the qualifications for President of the United States? He asked himself these questions as he pondered a reply to an editor who had suggested announcing his name, and he wrote; "I must in all candor say I do not think myself fit for the presidency."

This was in April, 1859. In the July following he still declared himself unfit. Even in the following November he had little hope of nomination. "For my single self," he wrote to a correspondent who had suggested the putting of his name on the ticket, "I have enlisted for the permanent success of the Republican cause, and for this object I shall labor faithfully in the ranks, unless, as I think not probable, the judgment of the party shall assign me a different position."

The last weeks of 1859 and the first of 1860 convinced Lincoln, however, that, fit or not, he was in the field. Fell, who as corresponding secretary of the Republican State Central Committee had been travelling constantly in the interests of the organization, brought him such proof that his candidacy was generally approved of, that in December, 1859, he consented to write the "little sketch" of his life now known as Lincoln's "autobiography."

He wrote it with a little inward shrinking, a half shame that it was so meagre. "There is not much of it," he apologized in sending the document, "for the reason, I suppose, that there is not much of me. If anything be made out of it, I wish it to be modest, and not to go beyond the material."

By the opening of 1860 Lincoln had concluded that, though he might not be a very promising candidate, at all events he was now in so deep that he must have the approval of his own State, and he began to work in earnest for that. "I am not in a position where it would hurt much for me to not be nominated on the national ticket," he wrote to Norman B. Judd, "but I am where it would hurt some for me to not get the Illinois delegates. . . . Can you help me a little in your end of the vineyard?"

The plans of the Lincoln men were well matured. About the first of December, 1859, Medill had gone to Washington, ostensibly as a "Tribune" correspondent, but really to promote Lincoln's nomination. "Before writing any Lincoln letters for the "Tribune,'" says Mr. Medill in his "Reminiscences," "I began preaching Lincoln among the Congressmen. I urged him chiefly upon the ground of availability in the close and doubtful States, with what seemed like reasonable success."

February 16, 1860, the "Tribune" came out editorially for Lincoln, and Medill followed a few days later with a ringing letter from Washington, naming Lincoln as a candidate on whom both conservative and radical sentiment could unite, and declaring that he now heard Lincoln's name mentioned for President in Washington "ten times as often as it was one month ago." About the time when Medill was writing thus, Norman B. Judd, as member of the Republican National Committee, was executing a manœuvre the importance of which no one realized but the Illinois politicians. This was securing the convention for Chicago.

As the spring passed and the counties of Illinois held their conventions, Lincoln found that, save in the North, where Seward was strong, he was unanimously recommended as the candidate at Chicago. When the State Convention met at Decatur, May 9 and 10, he received an ovation of so

picturesque and unique a character that it colored all the rest
of the campaign. The delegates were in session when Lincoln came in as a spectator and was invited to a seat on the
platform. Soon after, Richard Oglesby, one of Lincoln's
ardent supporters, asked that an old Democrat of Macon
County be allowed to offer a contribution to the convention.
The offer was accepted, and a curious banner was borne up
the hall. The standard was made of two weather-worn
fence-rails, decorated with flags and streamers, and bearing
the inscription:

## ABRAHAM LINCOLN

### THE RAIL CANDIDATE

### FOR PRESIDENT IN 1860

Two rails from a lot of 3,000 made in 1830
by Thos. Hanks and Abe Lincoln — whose
father was the first pioneer of Macon County.

A storm of applause greeted the banner, followed by cries
of " Lincoln! Lincoln!" Rising, Lincoln said pointing to
the banner, " I suppose I am expected to reply to that. I cannot say whether I made those rails or not, but I am quite
sure I have made a great many just as good." The speech
was warmly applauded, and one delegate, an influential German and an ardent Seward man, George Schneider, after wit-
nessing the demonstration, turned to his neighbor and said,
" Seward has lost the Illinois delegation." He was right;
for when, later, John M. Palmer brought forth a resolution
that " Abraham Lincoln is the choice of the Republican party
of Illinois for the presidency, and the delegates from this
State are instructed to use all honorable means to secure his
nomination by the Chicago Convention, and to vote as a
unit for him," it was enthusiastically adopted.

While the politicians of Illinois were thus preparing for
the campaign, the Republicans of the East hardly realized

that Lincoln was or could be made a possibility. In the first four months of 1860 his name was almost unmentioned as a presidential candidate in the public prints of the East. In a list of twenty-one " prominent candidates for the presidency in 1860," prepared by D. W. Bartlett and published in New York towards the end of 1859, Lincoln's name is not mentioned; nor does it appear in a list of thirty-four of " our living representative men," prepared for presidential purposes by John Savage, and published in Philadelphia in 1860. The most important notice at this period of which we know was a casual mention in an editorial in the New York " Evening Post," February 15. The " Post " considered it time for the Republicans to speak out about the nominee at the coming convention, and remarked: " With such men as Seward and Chase, Banks and *Lincoln,* and others in plenty, let us have two Republican representative men to vote for." This was ten days before the Cooper Union speech and the New England tour, which undoubtedly did much to recommend Lincoln as a logical and statesmanlike thinker and debater, though there is no evidence that it created him a presidential following in the East, save, perhaps, in New Hampshire. Indeed it was scarcely to be expected that prudent and conservative men would conclude that, because he could make a good speech, he would make a good President. They knew him to be comparatively untrained in public life and comparatively untried in large affairs. They naturally preferred a man who had a record for executive statesmanship.

Up to the opening of the convention in May there was, in fact, no specially prominent mention of Lincoln by the Eastern press. Greeley, intent on undermining Seward, though as yet nobody perceived him to be so, printed in the New York weekly " Tribune"—the paper which went to the country at large—correspondence favoring the nomination of

Bates and Read, McLean and Bell, Cameron, Frémont, Dayton, Chase, Wade; but not Lincoln. The New York " Herald " of May 1, in discussing editorially the nominee of the " Black Republicans," recognized " four living, two dead, aspirants." The " living " were Seward, Banks, Chase, and Cameron; the " dead," Bates and McLean. May 10 " The Independent," in an editorial on " The Nomination at Chicago," said : " Give us a man known to be true upon the only question that enters into the canvass—a Seward, a Chase, a Wade, a Sumner, a Fessenden, a Banks." But it did not mention Lincoln. His most conspicuous Eastern recognition before the convention was in " Harper's Weekly " of May 12, his face being included in a double page of portraits of " eleven prominent candidates for the Republican presidential nomination at Chicago." Brief biographical sketches appeared in the same number—the last and the shortest of them being of Lincoln.

It was on May 16 that the Republican Convention of 1860 formally opened at Chicago, but for days before the city was in a tumult of expectation and preparation. The audacity of inviting a national convention to meet there, in the condition in which Chicago chanced to be at that time, was purely Chicagoan. No other city would have risked it. In ten years Chicago had nearly quadrupled its population, and it was believed that the feat would be repeated in the coming decade. In the first flush of youthful energy and ambition the town had undertaken the colossal task of raising itself bodily out of the grassy marsh, where it had been originally placed, to a level of twelve feet above Lake Michigan, and of putting underneath a good, solid foundation. When the invitation to the convention was extended, half the buildings in Chicago were on stilts; some of the streets had been raised to the new grade, others still lay in the mud;

half the sidewalks were poised high on piles, and half were still down on a level with the lake. A city with a conventional sense of decorum would not have cared to be seen in this demoralized condition, but Chicago perhaps conceived that it would but prove her courage and confidence to show the country what she was doing; and so she had the convention come.

But it was not the convention alone which came. Besides the delegates, the professional politicians, the newspaper men, and the friends of the several candidates, there came a motley crowd of men hired to march and to cheer for particular candidates,—a kind of out-of-door *claque* which did not wait for a point to be made in favor of its man, but went off in rounds of applause at the mere mention of his name. New York brought the greatest number of these professional applauders, the leader of them being a notorious prize-fighter and street politician,—" a sort of white black-bird," says Bromley,—one Tom Hyer. With the New York delegation, which numbered all told fully two thousand Seward men, came Dodworth's Band, one of the celebrated musical organizations of that day.

While New York sent the largest number, Pennsylvania was not far behind, there being about one thousand five hundred persons present from that State. From New England, long as was the distance, there were many trains of excursionists. The New England delegation took Gilmore's Band with it, and from Boston to Chicago stirred up every community in which it stopped, with music and speeches. Several days before the convention opened fully one-half of the members of the United States House of Representatives were in the city. To still further increase the throng were hundreds of merely curious spectators whom the flattering inducements of the fifteen railroads centring in Chicago at that time had tempted to take a trip. There were fully forty thousand strangers in the city during the sitting of the convention.

The streets for a week were the forum of this multitude. Processions for Seward, for Cameron, for Chase, for Lincoln, marched and counter-marched, brave with banners and transparencies, and noisy with country bands and hissing rockets. Every street corner became a rostrum, where impromptu harangues for any of a dozen candidates might be happened upon. In this hurly-burly two figures were particularly prominent: Tom Hyer, who managed the open-air Seward demonstration, and Horace Greeley, who was conducting independently his campaign against Seward. Greeley, in his fervor, talked incessantly. It was only necessary for some one to say in a rough but friendly way, " There's old Greeley," and all within hearing distance grouped about him. Not infrequently the two or three to whom he began speaking increased until that which had started as a conversation ended as a speech.

In this half-spontaneous, half-organized demonstration of the streets, Lincoln's followers were conspicuous. State pride made Chicago feel that she must stand by her own. Lincoln banners floated across every street, and buildings and omnibuses were decorated with Lincoln emblems. When the Illinois delegation saw that New York and Pennsylvania had brought in so many outsiders to create enthusiasm for their respective candidates, they began to call in supporters from the neighboring localities. Leonard Swett says that they succeeded in getting together fully ten thousand men from Illinois and Indiana, ready to march, shout, or fight for Lincoln, as the case required.

Not only was the city full of people days before the convention began, but the delegations had organized and actual work was in progress. Every device conceivable by an ingenious opposition was resorted to in order to weaken Seward, the most formidable of the candidates. The night before the opening of the convention a great mass meeting was held in the Wigwam. The Seward men had arranged to have only advocates of their own candidate speak. But the clever opposition detected the game, and William D. Kelley of Pennsylvania, who was for Lincoln or for Wade, got the floor and held it until nearly midnight, doggedly talking against time until an audience of twelve thousand had dwindled to less than one thousand.

One of the first of the delegations to begin activities was that of Illinois. The Tremont House had been chosen as its headquarters, and here were gathered almost all the influential friends Lincoln had in the State. They came determined to win if human effort could compass it, and men never put more intense and persistent energy into a cause. Judge Davis was naturally the head of the body; but Judge Logan, Leonard Swett, John M. Palmer, Richard Oglesby, N. B. Judd, Jesse W. Fell, and a score more were with him. " We worked like nailers," Governor Oglesby often declared in after years.

The effort for Lincoln had to begin in the Illinois delegation itself. In spite of the rail episode at Decatur, the State convention was by no means unanimous for Lincoln. " Our delegation was instructed for him," wrote Leonard Swett to Josiah Drummond,* " but of the twenty-two votes in it, by incautiously selecting the men, there were *eight* who would have gladly gone for Seward. The reason of this is in this fact: the northern counties of this State are more overwhelmingly Republican than any other portion of the continent. I could pick twenty-five contiguous counties giving larger Republican majorities than any other adjacent

---

* This letter, written by Mr. Swett on May 27, 1860, to Josiah Drummond of Maine, is one of the best documents on the convention. It was published in the New York " Sun " of July 26, 1891, and is printed in O. H. Oldroyd's " Lincoln's Campaign."

counties in any State. The result is, many people there are for Seward, and such men had crept upon the delegation. They intended in good faith to go for Lincoln, but talked despondingly, and really wanted and expected finally to vote as I have indicated. We had also in the North and about Chicago a class of men who always want to turn up on the winning side, and who would do no work, although their feelings were really for us, for fear it would be the losing element and would place them out of favor with the incoming power. These men were dead weights. The centre and South, with many individual exceptions to the classes I have named, were warmly for Lincoln, whether he won or lost.

"The lawyers of our circuit went there determined to leave no stone unturned; and really they, aided by some of our State officers and a half dozen men from various portions of the State, were the only tireless, sleepless, unwavering, and ever vigilant friends he had."

The situation which the Illinois delegation faced, briefly put, was this: the Republican party had in 1860 but one prominent candidate, William H. Seward. By virtue of his great talents, his superior cultivation, and his splendid services in anti-slavery agitation, he was the choice of the majority of the Republican party. It was certain that at the opening of the convention he would have nearly enough votes to nominate him. But still there was a considerable and resolute opposition. The grounds of this were several, but the most substantial and convincing was that Illinois, Indiana, Pennsylvania, and New Jersey all declared that they could not elect Seward if he was nominated. Andrew G. Curtin of Pennsylvania, and Henry S. Lane of Indiana, candidates for governor in their respective States, were both his active opponents, not from dislike of him, but because they were convinced that they would themselves be defeated if he headed the Republican ticket. It was clear to the entire party that Pennsylvania and Indiana were essential to Republican success; and since many States with which Seward was the first choice held success in November as more important than Seward, they were willing to give their support to an " available " man. But the difficulty was to unite this opposition. Nearly every State which considered Seward an unsafe candidate had a " favorite son " whom it was pushing as " available." Pennsylvania wanted Cameron; New Jersey, Dayton; Ohio, Chase, McLean, or Wade; Massachusetts, Banks; Vermont, Collamer. Greeley, who alone was as influential as a State delegation, urged Bates of Missouri.

Illinois's task was to unite this opposition on Lincoln. She began her work with a next-door neighbor. " The first State approached," says Mr. Swett, " was Indiana. She was about equally divided between Bates and McLean.* Saturday, Sunday, and Monday were spent upon her, when finally she came to us, unitedly, with twenty-six votes, and from that time acted efficiently with us."

With Indiana to aid her, Illinois now succeeded in drawing a few scattering votes, in making an impression on New Hampshire and Virginia, and in persuading Vermont to think of Lincoln as a second choice. Matters began to look decidedly cheerful. May 14 (Monday) the New York " Herald's " last despatch declared that the contest had narrowed down to Seward, Lincoln, and Wade. The Boston " Herald's " despatch of the same day reported; " Abe Lincoln is booming up to-night as a compromise candidate, and his friends are in high spirits." And this was the situation when the convention finally opened on Wednesday, May 16.

The assembly-room in which the convention met was situ-

---

* Mr. Joseph Medill once told the writer that half the Indiana delegation had been won for Lincoln on the ground of availability before the convention met.

ated conveniently at the corner of Market and Lake Streets. It had been built especially for the occasion by the Chicago Republican Club, and in the fashion of the West in that day was called by the indigenous name of Wigwam. It was a low, characterless structure, fully one hundred and eighty feet long by one hundred feet wide. The roof rose in the segment of a circle, so that one side was higher than the other; and across this side and the two ends were deep galleries. Facing the ungalleried side was a platform reserved for the delegates—a great floor one hundred and forty feet long and thirty-five feet deep, raised some four feet from the ground level, with committee-rooms at each end. This vast structure of pine boards had been rescued from ugliness through the energetic efforts of the committee, assisted by the Republican women of the city, who, scarcely less interested than their husbands and brothers, strove in every way to contribute to the success of the convention. They wreathed the pillars and the galleries with

masses of green; hung banners and flags; brought in busts of American notables; ordered great allegorical paintings of Justice, Liberty, and the like, to suspend on the walls; borrowed the whole series of Healy portraits of American statesmen—in short, made the Wigwam at least gay and festive in aspect. Foreign interest added something to the furnishings; the chair placed on the plat-

CHAIR OCCUPIED BY THE CHAIRMAN OF THE REPUBLICAN NATIONAL CONVENTION OF 1860.

It was the first chair made in the State of Michigan.—Reproduced from "Harper's Weekly" of May 19, 1860, by permission of Messrs. Harper and Brothers.

form for the use of the chairman of the convention was donated by Michigan, as the first chair made in that State. It was an arm-chair of the most primitive description, the seat dug out of an immense log and mounted on large rockers. Another chair, one made for the occasion, attracted a great deal of attention. It was constructed of thirty-four kinds of wood, each piece from a different State or Territory, Kansas being appropriately represented by the "weeping willow" a symbol of her grief at being still excluded from the sisterhood of States. The gavel used by the chairman was more interesting even than his chair, having been made from a fragment of Commodore Perry's brave *Lawrence*.

Into the Wigwam, on the morning of the 16th of May, there crowded fully ten thousand persons. To the spectator in the gallery the scene was vividly picturesque and animated. Around him were packed hundreds of women, gay in the high-peaked, flower-filled bonnets and the bright shawls and plaids of the day. Below, on the platform and floor, were many of the notable men of the United States—William M. Evarts, Thomas Corwin, Carl Schurz, David Wilmot, Thaddeus Stevens, Joshua Giddings, George William Curtis, Francis P. Blair and his two sons, Andrew H. Reeder, George Ashmun, Gideon Welles, Preston King, Cassius M. Clay, Gratz Brown, George S. Boutwell, Thurlow Weed. In the multitude the newspaper representatives outnumbered the delegates. Fully nine hundred editors and reporters were present, a body scarcely less interesting than the convention itself. Horace Greeley, Samuel Bowles, Murat Halstead, Isaac H. Bromley, Joseph Medill, Horace White, Joseph Hawley, Henry Villard, A. K. McClure, names so familiar to-day, all represented various journals at Chicago in 1860, and in some cases were active workers in the caucuses. It was evident at once that the members of the convention—some five hundred out of the attendant ten thousand —were not more interested in its proceedings than the spectators, whose approval and disapproval, quickly and emphatically expressed, swayed, and to a degree controlled, the delegates. Wednesday and Thursday mornings were passed in the usual opening work of a convention. While officers were formally elected and a platform adopted, the real interest centred in the caucuses, which were held almost uninterruptedly. Illinois was in a frenzy of anxiety. " No men ever worked as our boys did," wrote Mr. Swett; " I did not, the whole week, sleep two hours a night." They ran from delegation to delegation, haranguing, pleading, promising. But do their best they could not concentrate the opposition. " Our great struggle," says Senator Palmer, " was to prevent Lincoln's nomination for the vice-presidency. The Seward men were perfectly willing that he should go on the tail of the ticket. In fact, they seemed determined that he should be given the vice-presidential nomination. We were not troubled so much by the antagonism of the Seward men as by the overtures they were constantly making to us. They literally overwhelmed us with kindness. Judge David Davis came to me in the Tremont House, greatly agitated at the way things were going. He said: ' Palmer, you must go with me at once to see the New Jersey delegation.' I asked what I could do. ' Well,' said he, ' there is a grave and venerable judge over there who is insisting that Lincoln shall be nominated for Vice-President and Seward for President. We must convince the judge of his mistake.' We went; I was introduced to the gentleman, and we talked about the matter for some time. He praised Seward, but he was especially effusive in expressing his admiration for Lincoln. He thought that Seward was clearly entitled to first place and that Lincoln's eminent merits entitled him to second place. I listened for some time, and then said: 'Sir, you may nominate Mr. Lincoln for Vice-President if you please. But I want you to understand that there are 40,000 Democrats in Illinois who will support this ticket if you give them an opportunity. We are not Whigs, and we never expect to be Whigs. We will never consent to support two old Whigs on this ticket. We are willing to vote for Mr. Lincoln with a Democrat on the ticket, but we will not consent to vote for two Whigs.' I have seldom seen a more indignant man. Turning to Judge Davis he said: 'Judge Davis, is it possible that party spirit so prevails in Illinois that Judge Palmer properly represents public opinion?' 'Oh,' said Davis, affecting some distress at what I had said, 'oh, Judge, you can't account for the conduct of these old Locofocos.' 'Will they do as Palmer says?' 'Certainly. There are 40,000 of them, and, as Palmer says, not one of them will vote for two Whigs.' We left the New Jersey member in a towering rage. When we were back at the Tremont House I said: 'Davis, you are an infernal rascal to sit there and hear that man berate me as he did. You really seemed to encourage him.' Judge Davis said nothing, but chuckled as if he had greatly enjoyed the joke. This incident is illustrative of the kind of work we had to do. We were compelled to resort to this argument—that the old Democrats then ready to affiliate with the Republican party would not tolerate two Whigs on the ticket—in order to break up the movement to nominate Lincoln for Vice-President. The Seward men recognized in Lincoln their most formidable rival, and that was why they wished to get him out of the way by giving him second place on the ticket."

The uncertainty on Thursday was harrowing, and if the ballot had been taken on the afternoon of that day, as was at first intended, Seward probably would have been nominated. Illinois, Indiana, and Pennsylvania all felt this, and shrewdly

managed to secure from the convention a reluctant adjourn-
ment until Friday morning. In spite of the time this manœuvre gave, however, Seward's nomination seemed sure;
so Greeley telegraphed the "Tribune" at midnight on Thursday. At the same hour the correspondent of the " Herald "
(New York) telegraphed: " The friends of Seward are
firm, and claim ninety votes for him on the first ballot. Opposition to Seward not fixed on any man. Lincoln is the
strongest, and may have altogether forty votes. The various
delegations are still caucusing."

It was after these messages were sent that Illinois and Indiana summoned all their energies for a final desperate effort
to unite the uncertain delegates on Lincoln, and that Pennsylvania went through the last violent throes of coming to a
decision. The night was one of dramatic episodes of
which none, perhaps, was more nearly tragic than the spectacle of Seward's followers, confident of success, celebrating
in advance the nomination of their favorite, while scores of
determined men laid the plans ultimately effective, for his
overthrow. All night the work was kept up. " Hundreds
of Pennsylvanians, Indianians, and Illinoisans," says Murat
Halstead, " never closed their eyes. I saw Henry S. Lane
at one o'clock, pale and haggard, with cane under his arm,
walking as if for a wager from one caucus-room to another
at the Tremont House. In connection with them he had been
operating to bring the Vermonters and Virginians to the
point of deserting Seward."

In the Pennsylvania delegation, which on Wednesday had
agreed on McLean as its second choice and Lincoln as its third,
a hot struggle was waged to secure the vote of the delegation
*as a unit* for Cameron until a majority of the delegates directed otherwise. Judge S. Newton Pettis, who proposed
this resolution, worked all night to secure votes for it at the
caucus to be held early in the morning. The Illinois men

ran from delegate to caucus, from editor to outsider. No man who knew Lincoln and believed in him, indeed, was allowed to rest, but was dragged away to this or that delegate to persuade him that the " rail candidate," as Lincoln had already begun to be called, was fit for the place. Colonel Hoyt, then a resident of Chicago, spent half the night telling Thaddeus Stevens of Pennsylvania what he knew of Lincoln. While all this was going on, a committee of twelve men from Pennsylvania, New York, Ohio, Indiana, Illinois, and Iowa were consulting in the upper story of the Tremont House. Before their session was over they had agreed that in case Lincoln's votes reached a specified number on the following day, the votes of the States represented in that meeting, so far as these twelve men could effect the result, should be given to him.

The night was over at last, and at ten o'clock the convention reassembled. The great Wigwam was packed with a throng hardly less excited than the members of the actual convention, while without, for blocks away, a crowd double that within pushed and strained, every nerve alert to catch the movements of the convention.

The nominations began at once, the Hon. William M. Evarts presenting the name of William H. Seward. The New Yorkers had prepared a tremendous *claque,* which now broke forth—" a deafening shout which," says Leonard Swett, " I confess, appalled us a little." But New York in preparing her *claque* had only given an idea to Illinois. The Illinois committee, to offset it, had made secret but complete preparations for what was called a " spontaneous demonstration." From lake front to prairie the committee had collected every stentorian voice known, and early Friday morning, while Seward's men were marching exultantly about the streets, the owners of these voices had been packed into the Wigwam, where their special endowment would be most effective. The women present had been requested to wave their handkerchiefs at every mention of Lincoln's name, and hundreds of flags had been distributed to be used in the same way. A series of signals had been arranged to communicate to the thousands without the moment when a roar from them might influence the convention within. When N. B. Judd nominated Lincoln this machinery began to work. It did well; but a moment later, in greeting the seconding of Seward's nomination, New York out-bellowed Illinois. "Caleb B. Smith of Indiana then seconded the nomination of Lincoln," says Mr. Swett, "and the West came to his rescue. No mortal ever before saw such a scene. The idea of us Hoosiers and Suckers being outscreamed would have been as bad to them as the loss of their man. Five thousand people at once leaped to their seats, women not wanting in the number, and the wild yell made soft vesper breathings of all that had preceded. No language can describe it. A thousand steam whistles, ten acres of hotel gongs, a tribe of Comanches, headed by a choice van-guard from pandemonium, might have mingled in the scene unnoticed."

As the roar died out a voice cried, "Abe Lincoln has it by the sound now; let us ballot!" and Judge Logan, beside himself with screeching and excitement, called out: "Mr. President, in order or out of order, I propose this convention and audience give three cheers for the man who is evidently their nominee."

The balloting followed without delay. The Illinois men believed they had one hundred votes to start with; on counting they found they had 102. More hopeful still, no other opposition candidate approached them. Pennsyl-vania's man, according to the printed reports of that day, had but fifty and one-half votes; Greeley's man, forty-eight; Chase, forty-nine; while McLean, Pennsylvania's second

choice, had but twelve. If Seward was to be beaten, it must
be now; and it was for Pennsylvania to say. The delegation hurried to a committee-room, where Judge Pettis, dis-
regarding the action of the caucus by which McLean had
been adopted as the delegation's second choice, moved that,
on the second ballot, Pennsylvania's vote be cast solidly for
Lincoln. The motion was carried. Returning to the hall
the delegation found the second ballot under way. In a
moment the name of Pennsylvania was called. The whole
Wigwam heard the answer: "Pennsylvania casts her fifty-
two votes for Abraham Lincoln." The meaning was clear.
The break to Lincoln had begun. New York sat as if
stupefied, while all over the hall cheer followed cheer.

It seemed but a moment before the second ballot was
ended, and it was known that Lincoln's vote had risen from
102 to 181. The tension as the third ballot was taken was
almost unbearable. A hundred pencils kept score while the
delegations were called, and it soon became apparent that
Lincoln was outstripping Seward. The last vote was hardly
given before the whisper went around, "Two hundred and
thirty-one and one-half for Lincoln; two and one-half more
will give him the nomination." An instant of silence followed, in which the convention grappled with the idea, and
tried to pull itself together to act. The chairman of the
Ohio delegation was the first to get his breath. "Mr. President," he cried, springing on his chair and stretching out
his arm to secure recognition, "I rise to change four votes
from Mr. Chase to Mr. Lincoln."

It took a moment to realize the truth. New York saw it,
and the white faces of her noble delegation were bowed in
despair. Greeley saw it, and a guileless smile spread over
his features as he watched Thurlow Weed press his hand
hard against his wet eyelids. Illinois saw it, and tears
poured from the eyes of more than one of the overwrought,

devoted men as they grasped one another's hands and vainly struggled against the sobs which kept back their shouts. The crowd saw it, and broke out in a mad hurrah. " The scene which followed," wrote one spectator, " baffles all human description. After an instant's silence, as deep as death, which seemed to be required to enable the assembly to take in the full force of the announcement, the wildest and mightiest yell (for it can be called by no other name) burst forth from ten thousand voices which we ever heard from mortal throats. This strange and tremendous demonstration, accompanied with leaping up and down, tossing hats, handkerchiefs, and canes recklessly into the air, with the waving of flags, and with every other conceivable mode of exultant and unbridled joy, continued steadily and without pause for perhaps ten minutes.

" It then began to rise and fall in slow and billowing bursts, and for perhaps the next five minutes these stupendous waves of uncontrollable excitement, now rising into the deepest and fiercest shouts, and then sinking like the ground swell of the ocean into hoarse and lessening murmurs, rolled through the multitude. Every now and then it would seem as though the physical power of the assembly was exhausted and that quiet would be restored, when all at once a new hurricane would break out, more prolonged and terrific than anything before. If sheer exhaustion had not prevented, we don't know but the applause would have continued to this hour."

Without, the scene was repeated. At the first instant of realization in the Wigwam a man on the platform had shouted to a man stationed on the roof, " Hallelujah; Abe Lincoln is nominated!" A cannon boomed the news to the multitude below, and twenty thousand throats took up the cry. The city heard it, and one hundred guns on the Tremont House, innumerable whistles on the river and lake front, on locomotives and factories, and the bells in all the steeples, broke forth. For twenty-four hours the clamor never ceased. It spread to the prairies, and before morning they were afire with pride and excitement.

And while all this went on, where was Lincoln? Too much of a candidate, as he had told Swett, to go to Chicago, yet hardly enough of one to stay away, he had ended by remaining in Springfield, where he spent the week in restless waiting and discussion. He drifted about the public square, went often to the telegraph office, looked out for every returning visitor from Chicago, played occasional games of ball, made fruitless efforts to read, went home at unusual hours. He felt in his bones that he had a fighting chance, so he told a friend, but the chance was not so strong that he could indulge in much exultation. By Friday morning he was tired and depressed, but still eager for news. One of his friends, the Hon. James C. Conkling, returned early in the day from Chicago, and Lincoln soon went around to his law office. " Upon entering," says Mr. Conkling, " Lincoln threw himself upon the office lounge, and remarked rather wearily, ' Well, I guess I'll go back to practising law.' As he lay there on the lounge, I gave him such information as I had been able to obtain. I told him the tendency was to drop Seward; that the outlook for him was very encouraging. He listened attentively, and thanked me, saying I had given him a clearer idea of the situation than he had been able to get from any other source. He was not very sanguine of the result. He did not express the opinion that he would be nominated."

But he could not be quiet, and soon left Mr. Conkling, to join the throng around the telegraph office, where the reports from the convention were coming in. The nominations were being reported, his own among the others. Then news

came that the balloting had begun.   He could not endure to
wait for the result.   He remembered a commission his wife
had given him that morning, and started across the square to
execute it.   His errand was done, and he was standing in the
door of the shop, talking, when a shout went up from the
group at the telegraph office.   The next instant an excited
boy came rushing pell-mell down the stairs of the office, and,
plunging through the crowd, ran across the square, shouting,
" Mr. Lincoln, Mr. Lincoln, you are nominated ! "   The cry
was repeated on all sides.   The people came flocking about
him, half laughing, half crying, shaking his hand when they
could get it, and one another's when they could not.   For a
few minutes, carried away by excitement, Lincoln seemed
simply one of the proud and exultant crowd.   Then remembering what it all meant, he said, " My friends, I am glad to
receive your congratulations, and as there is a little woman
down on Eighth street who will be glad to hear the news, you
must excuse me until I inform her."   He slipped away,
telegram in hand, his coat-tails flying out behind, and strode
towards home, only to find when he reached there that his
friends were before him, and that the " little woman " already knew that the honor which for twenty years and more
she had believed and stoutly declared her husband deserved,
and which a great multitude of men had sworn to do their
best to obtain for him, at last had come.

# CHAPTER XX

## THE CAMPAIGN OF 1860.

THIRTY-SIX hours after Lincoln received the news of his nomination, an evening train from Chicago brought to Springfield a company of distinguished-looking strangers. As they stepped from their coach cannon were fired, rockets set off, bands played, and enthusiastic cheering went up from a crowd of waiting people. A long and noisy procession accompanied them to their hotel and later to a modest two-storied house in an unfashionable part of the town. The gentlemen whom the citizens of Springfield received with such demonstration formed the committee, sent by the Republican National Convention to notify Abraham Lincoln that he had been nominated as its candidate for the presidency of the United States.

The delegation had in its number some of the most distinguished workers of the Republican party of that day:—Mr. George Ashmun, Samuel Bowles, and Governor Boutwell of Massachusetts, William M. Evarts of New York, Judge Kelley of Pennsylvania, David K. Carter of Ohio, Francis P. Blair of Missouri, the Hon. Gideon Welles of Connecticut, Amos Tuck of New Hampshire, Carl Schurz of Wisconsin. Only a few of these gentlemen had ever seen Mr. Lincoln and to many of them his nomination had been a bitter disappointment.

As the committee filed into Mr. Lincoln's simple home there was a sore misgiving in more than one heart, and as Mr. Ashmun, their chairman, presented to him the letter notifying him of his nomination they eyed their candidate with

359

critical keenness. They noted his great height; his huge hands and feet; his peculiar lankness of limb. His shoulders drooped as he stood, giving his form a look of irresolution. His smooth shaven face seemed of bronze as he listened to their message and amazed them by its ruggedness. The cheeks were sunken, the cheek bones high, the nose large, the mouth unsymmetrical, the under lip protruding a little. Irregular seams and lines cut and creased the skin in every direction. The eyes downcast as he listened were sunken and somber. Shaded by its mass of dark hair, the face gave an impression of a sad impenetrable man.

Mr. Ashmun finished his speech and Mr. Lincoln lifting his bent head began to reply. The men who watched him thrilled with surprise at the change which passed over him. His drooping form became erect and firm. The eyes beamed with fire and intelligence. Strong, dignified and self-possessed, he seemed transformed by the simple act of self-expression.

His remarks were brief, merely a word of thanks for the honor done him, a hint that he felt the responsibility of his position, a promise to respond formally in writing and the expression of a desire to take each one of the committee by hand, but his voice was calm and clear, his bearing frank and sure. His auditors saw in a flash that here was a man who was master of himself. For the first time they understood that he whom they had supposed to be little more than a loquacious and clever State politician, had force, insight, conscience, that their misgivings were vain. " Why, sir, they told me he was a rough diamond," said Governor Boutwell to one of Lincoln's townsmen, " nothing could have been in better taste than that speech." And a delegate who had voted against Lincoln in the convention, turning to Carl Schurz, said, " Sir, we might have done a more daring thing, but we certainly could not have done a better thing," and it was with that feeling that the delegation, two hours later, left Mr. Lincoln's home, and it was that report they carried to their constituents.

But one more formality now remained to complete the ceremony of Abraham Lincoln's nomination to the presidency,—his letter of acceptance. This was soon written. The candidates of the opposing parties all sent out letters of acceptance in 1860 which were almost political platforms in themselves. Lincoln decided to make his merely an acceptance with an expression of his intention to stand by the party's declaration of principles. He held himself rigidly to this decision, his first address to the Republican party being scarcely one hundred and fifty words in length. Though so short, it was prepared with painstaking attention. He even carried it when it was finished to a Springfield friend, Dr. Newton Bateman, the State Superintendent of Education, for correction.

"Mr. Schoolmaster," he said, "here is my letter of acceptance, I am not very strong on grammar and I wish you to see if it is all right. I wouldn't like to have any mistakes in it."

The doctor took the MS. and after reading it, said:

"There is only one change I should suggest, Mr. Lincoln, you have written 'It shall be my care *to not* violate or disregard it in any part,' you should have written 'not to violate.' Never split an infinitive, is the rule."

Mr. Lincoln took the manuscript, regarding it a moment with a puzzled air, "So you think I better put those two little fellows end to end, do you?" he said as he made the change.

His nomination an accomplished fact, the all-important question for Mr. Lincoln was "can I be elected." Six months before when he had asked himself "Can I be nominated?" he had been forced to reply "Not probable." Even

the very morning of the nomination he had said despond-
ently to a friend, " I guess I'll go back to practising law,"
but now when he asked himself " Can I be elected? " the answer he gave was far from uncertain.  With the tables of
the popular vote since 1856 before him he reckoned his
chances.  Twenty-four States out of the thirty-three which
then formed the Union had taken part in the Chicago Convention.  These twenty-four States held 234 of the 303 electoral
votes to be cast.  On how many of them could he depend?
In 1856 the first time the party had appeared in a presidential contest it had secured for Frémont eleven States,* 114
electoral votes.  On these Lincoln felt he still could count.
But that was not enough, nor was it all the Republicans
claimed.  The growth of the party had been steady and
vigorous since 1856.  The whole country saw that if the
Chicago Convention chose a presidential candidate accepta-
ble to New Jersey, Pennsylvania, Indiana and Illinois, those
States would certainly go Republican.  Lincoln added their
votes to the 114 of the certain States.  It gave him 169—a
respectable majority of the 303 which the electoral college
would cast.

The tables were in his favor; but that was not all in the
situation which encouraged him.  Lincoln saw that, as his
nomination in Chicago had been largely the result of dis-
agreement among the Republicans, so there was a possibility
of his election being the result of quarrels among the Democrats.  The National Democratic Convention had met in
Charleston, South Carolina, on April 23.  From the opening, the sessions were stormy.  One vital difference divided
the body.  The South was determined that a platform should
be adopted stating unequivocally that slaves could be car-

---

* The states which went for Frémont in 1856 were Connecticut, Iowa
Maine, Massachusetts, Michigan, New Hampshire. New York, Ohio
Rhode Island, Vermont, Wisconsin.

ried into the Territories and that neither Congressional nor Territorial legislation could interfere with them. The Democracy of the North was determined to adopt a platform in which Douglas's doctrine of popular sovereignty was the central plank. The time had been when the South had been thoroughly satisfied with the Douglas theory; that it was not so now was due largely to Lincoln. He had discovered that Douglas in presenting his attractive dogma that the people of the States should be left to regulate their domestic concerns in their own way, subject only to the Constitution, gave one interpretation in the South, another in the North. Knowing that Illinois would never consent to the doctrine as the South understood it, nor the South to the Northern notion, Lincoln forced Douglas in 1858 in a debate at Freeport, Illinois, to explain his meaning. Illinois was satisfied with the explanation, but the South saw the deceit. From the day of the Freeport Debate Douglas's power in the South declined. When the Charleston Convention met the Southern Democrats were fully determined to defeat the man who had so nearly persuaded them to a doctrine which he interpreted according to the prejudices of the section in which he spoke. When a Douglas platform was adopted by the convention they withdrew. The upshot of this secession was that the two factions called fresh conventions to meet in Baltimore in June. There the Northern Democracy nominated as its candidates Douglas and Johnson. A few days later the Southern Democrats named Breckinridge and Lane.

Thus when Lincoln was nominated his opponents were divided. The opposition to him was still further weakened by the appearance of a sporadic party the Constitutional Union which in a vague and general platform shirked the very precise and vital question at issue and declared finely for " the Constitution of the country, the Union of the States, and the enforcement of the laws." This party nominated Bell and Everett, known as the "Kangaroo Ticket" because "the hind part was the stronger."

The tables were in his favor. If his own party stood by him, he felt sure of his election. There was every sign that it would. "So far as I can learn," he wrote his friend Washburne a few days after the convention, " the nominations start well everywhere; and, if they get no back-set, it would seem as if they were going through."

The " start " of the nominations had in fact been very good. Nothing more jubilant could have been conceived than the reception given Lincoln's name in the Northwest. " There won't be a tar barrel left in Illinois to-night," said Douglas, in Washington, to his senatorial friends, who asked him when the news of the nomination reached them, " Who is this man Lincoln, anyhow ? " Douglas was right. Not only the tar barrels but half the fences of the State went up in the fire of rejoicing.

The demonstrations in the Middle States and in the East were hardly less exultant. There was a striking difference in them, however. In the Northwest it was the candidate, in the rest of the country the platform and the probability of its success, which inspired the popular outbursts. And this was inevitable, so little was Lincoln known outside of his own part of the country. The orators at the ratification meetings of the East found it necessary to look up his history to tell their audiences who he was. The newspapers printed biographical sketches, and very meagre ones they were; for up to this time almost no details of his life had been published. These facts filled many a serious-minded Republican with dismay. To them there seemed but one explanation for the choice of Lincoln over the heads of so many more experienced and distinguished men—it had been a political trick born of the sentiment " Anything to beat Seward." " I remember," says a Republican of 1860, "that when I first read the news on a bulletin board as I came down street in Philadelphia that I experienced a moment of intense physical pain, it was as though some one had dealt me a heavy blow over the head, then my strength failed me. I believed our cause was doomed."

The opposition press found in Lincoln's obscurity abundant editorial material. He was a "third-rate country lawyer, poorer even than poor Pierce," said the New York "Herald." Of course, he would be a "nullity" if he were elected. How could a man be otherwise who had never done anything but deliver a few lectures and get himself beaten by Douglas in the campaign of '58. They hooted at his "coarse and clumsy jokes," declared that he "could not speak good grammar," and that all he was really distinguished for was rail-splitting, running a "broad-horn," and bearing the sobriquet of "honest old Abe." The snobbishness of the country came out in full. He was not a gentleman; that is, he did not know how to wear clothes, perhaps sat at times in shirt sleeves, tilted back his chair. He could quote neither Latin nor Greek, had never travelled, had no pedigree.

The Republican press took up the gauntlet. To the charge that he would be a "nullity" the "Tribune" replied "A man who by his own genius and force of character has raised himself from being a penniless and uneducated flat boatman on the Wabash River to the position Mr. Lincoln now occupies is not likely to be a nullity anywhere." And Bryant answered all the sneering by a noble editorial in which he claimed Mr. Lincoln to be "A Real Representative Man."

Nevertheless the eagerness with which the Republican press hastened to show that Lincoln was not the coarse backwoodsman the Democrats painted him showed how much they winced under the charges. Reporters were sent West to describe his home, his family, and his habits, in order to prove that he did not live in "low Hoosier style." They told with great satisfaction that he wore daily a broadcloth suit "almost elegant," they described his modest home as a "mansion" and "an elegant two-story dwelling" and they never failed to note that Mrs. Lincoln spoke French fluently and that he had a son in Harvard College. When they could with reasonable certainty connect him with the Lincolns of Hingham, Mass., they heralded his "good blood" with pride and marshalled the Lincolns who had distinguished themselves in the history of the country.

Among the common people the jeers that Lincoln was but a rail-splitter was a spur to enthusiasm. Too many of the solid men of the North had swung an axe, too many of them had passed from log hut to mansion, not to blaze with sympathetic indignation when the party was taunted with nominating a backwoodsman. The rail became their emblem and their rallying cry, and the story of the rail fence Lincoln had built a feature of every campaign speech and every country store discussion. In a week after his nomination two rails declared to have been split by Lincoln were on exhibition in New York, and certain zealous Pennsylvanians had sent to Macon, Ill., asking to buy the whole fence and have it shipped East. It was the rail which decorated campaign medals, inspired campaign songs, appeared in campaign cartoons. There was something more than a desire to "stand by the candidate" in the enthusiasm. At bottom it was a popular vindication of the American way of making a man.

More important to Lincoln than any popular enthusiasm was the ratification given his nomination by the rival candidates. What would they do? The whole party held its breath until Seward was heard from. No man could have taken a crushing defeat more nobly. He was at his home in Auburn, New York, on May 18, the day of the nomination, and when the news of Lincoln's success was brought him, his informer told him that there was not a Republican to be found in town who had the heart left to write an editorial for the "Daily Advertiser" approving the nomination. Seward smilingly took his pen and wrote the following paragraph, which appeared that evening:—

"No truer exposition of the Republican creed could be given, than the platform adopted by the convention contains. No truer or firmer defenders of the Republican faith could have been found in the Union, than the distinguished and esteemed citizens on whom the honors of the nomination have fallen. Their election, we trust by a decisive majority, will restore the Government of the U. S. to its Constitutional and ancient course. Let the watch-word of the Republican party be 'Union and Liberty,' and onward to victory."

A few days later Seward went to Washington where a number of disappointed and rebellious Republicans called upon him to offer their condolence. "Mr. Seward," they said, "we cannot accept this situation. We want you to bolt the nomination and run on an independent ticket."

Mr. Seward smiled: "Gentlemen," he said, "your zeal outruns your discretion. There are many of you giving this advice now, say perhaps three hundred. Two weeks hence there would be one hundred and fifty and the next week fifty. After that only William H. Seward. No, gentlemen, the Republican party was not made for William H. Seward, but Mr. Seward, if he is worth anything for the Republican party, and I believe I have still work to do, I must therefore decline to accept your advice. I have had some experience of this kind. I ran once as a candidate for the nomination to the governorship of New York; I was defeated; my friends wanted me to bolt and run independently, but I declined. My opponent who had received the nomination, was defeated in the election. I would have been defeated.

Another year I did receive the nomination and I was elected, but if I had consented in the first place to bolt the regular nominee I would never have received the nomination regularly a second time and so would never have been Governor of New York."*

Seward wrote Lincoln very soon congratulating him and promising support. So did the other leading rivals. The letters were grateful to Lincoln. " Holding myself the humblest of all those whose names were before the convention," he wrote Chase, " I feel in special need of the assistance of all; and I am glad—very glad—of the indication that you stand ready."

With these congratulations and promises of support from his rivals came others from men not less known. Joshua Giddings wrote Lincoln an admirable letter on May 19:

" Dear Lincoln: You're nominated. You will be elected. After your election, thousands will crowd around you, claiming rewards for services rendered. I, too, have my claims upon you. I have not worked for your nomination, nor for that of any other man. I have labored for the establishment of principles; and when men came to me asking my opinion of you, I only told them, ' Lincoln is an honest man.' All I ask of you in return for my services is, *make my statement good through your administration.* Yours, GIDDINGS."

Lincoln soon saw that not only the strong men of his party were supporting him, but that they were working harmoniously in an excellent organization. The Republicans all agreed with the " Tribune " that " the election of Mr. Lincoln though it could not be accomplished without work, was eminently a thing that could be done," and they set themselves vigorously to do it. As the party was composed largely of young men who felt that the cause was worthy of their best

* The Hon. H. L. Dawes in interview corrected by him and published with his permission.

efforts, great zest and ingenuity were thrown into the campaigning. Arrangements were immediately made for a systematic stumping of the whole country. The speakers engaged were of a very high order, among them being Sumner, Seward, Chase, Cassius M. Clay, Greeley, Stevens. Many of the speeches were of more than usual dramatic interest. Such was Sumner's great speech at Cooper Institute, July 11, on "The Origin, Necessity and Permanence of the Republican Party." It was the first speech Sumner had made in public since the attack on him in the Senate in 1856, and attracted immense attention. Seward made a five weeks' trip through the West, often speaking several times a day. No one worked harder than Carl Schurz. "I began speaking shortly after the convention," Mr. Schurz once told the author, "and continued until the day of the election, making from one to three speeches, with the exception of about ten days in September when I was so fatigued that I had to stop for a little while. I spoke in both English and German, under the auspices of the National Committee and not only in the larger towns, but frequently also in country districts." No speaker of the campaign touched the people more deeply. "Young, ardent, aspiring," said the New York "Evening Post," in speaking of Mr. Schurz, "the romances connected with his life and escape from his fatherland, his scholarly attainments, and, above all, his devotion to the principles which cast him an exile on our shores, have all combined to render him dear to the hearts of his countrymen and to place him in the foremost rank of their leaders."

Beside this educational work on the stump was that by pamphlets. After the campaign lives of Lincoln and Hamlin, of which there were many,* the "campaign tracts" is-

---

* On May 19, the day after the nominations were made, five different lives of Lincoln were announced by the New York "Evening Post." The first to appear was the Wigwam Edition, which was ready at the

sued by the " Tribune " were the most widely circulated documents.  There were several of these, the most popular being
Carl Schurz's speech on the Doom of Slavery, and Seward's
on the Irrepressible Conflict.  There was at the same time,
of course, an immense amount done in the press, and much
of it by the ablest literary men the United States has produced, thus Lowell wrote essays for the "Atlantic," Whittier
verses for the " Tribune " and the " Atlantic," Bryant, Greeley, Raymond, Bowles editorials for their journals.

The Republican campaign of 1860 had one distinguishing
feature,—the Wide Awakes, bands of torch-bearers who in
a simple uniform of glazed cap and cape, and carrying colored lanterns or blazing coal-oil torches, paraded the streets
of almost every town of the North throughout the summer
and fall, arousing everywhere the wildest enthusiasm.  Their
origin was purely accidental.  In February, Cassius M. Clay
spoke in Hartford, Connecticut.  A few ardent young Republicans accompanied him as a kind of body guard, and to
save their garments from the dripping of the torches a few
of them wore improvised capes of black glazed cambric.  The
uniform attracted so much attention that a campaign club
formed in Hartford soon after adopted it.  This club called
itself the Wide-Awakes.  Other clubs took up the idea, and
soon there were Wide-Awakes drilling regularly from one
end of the North to the other.

A great many fantastic movements were invented by them,
a favorite one being a peculiar zig-zag march—an imita-

---

beginning of June.  The best were those by W. D. Howells and David
W. Bartlett.

The Illinois "State Journal" of June 5, 1860, quoted a paragraph from
the Cincinnati "Commercial" to the effect that " it is stated that there
have already been fifty-two applications to Mr. Lincoln to write his
biography."

The "Journal" of June 15, 1860, said that none of the numerous biog-
raphies announced by publishers as "authorized" or the "only authorized" has been in fact authorized by Mr. Lincoln.  "He is ignorant of
their contents and is not responsible for anything they contain."

tion of the party emblem—the rail-fence. Numbers of the clubs adopted the rules and drills of the Chicago Zouaves—one of the most popular military organizations of the day. In the summer of 1860 Colonel Ellsworth, the commanding officer of the Zouaves, brought them East. The Wide-Awake movement was greatly stimulated by this tour of the Zouaves.

Almost all of the clubs had their peculiar badges, Lincoln splitting rails or engineering a flat-boat being a favorite decoration for them. There were many medals worn as well. Many of these combined business and politics adroitly, the obverse advising you to " vote for the rail-splitter," the reverse to buy somebody's soap, or tea, or wagons.

Many of the clubs owned Lincoln rails which were given the place of honor on all public occasion and the " Originals," as the Hartford Wide-Awakes were called, possessed the identical maul with which Lincoln had split the rails for the famous fence. It had been secured in Illinois together with such weighty credentials that nobody could dispute its claim, and was the pride of the club. It still is to be seen in Hartford occupying a conspicuous place in the collection of the Connecticut Historical Society.

Campaign songs set to familiar airs were heard on every hand. Many of these never had more than a local vogue, but others were sung generally. One of the most ringing was E. C. Stedman's " Honest Abe of the West," sung to the air of " The Star Spangled Banner ":

"Then on to the holy Republican strife!
  And again, for a future as fair as the morning,
For the sake of that freedom more precious than life,
  Ring out the grand anthem of Liberty's warning!
Lift the banner on high, while from mountain and plain,
  The cheers of the people are sounded again;
Hurrah! for our cause—of all causes the best!
Hurrah! for Old Abe, Honest Abe of the West!"

One of the campaign songs which will never be forgotten
was Whittier's " The Quakers Are Out :—"

> " Give the flags to the winds!
> Set the hills all aflame!
> Make way for the man with
> The Patriarch's name!
> Away with misgivings—away
> With all doubt,
> For Lincoln goes in when the
> Quakers are out!"

In many of the States great rallies were held at central
points, at which scores of Wide-Awake clubs and a dozen
popular speakers were present. The most enthusiastic of all
these was held in Mr. Lincoln's own home, Springfield, on
August 8. Fully 75,000 people gathered for the celebration,
by far the greater number coming across the prairies on
horseback or in wagons. A procession eight miles long filed
by Mr. Lincoln's door.

Mr. E. B. Washburne, who was with Mr. Lincoln in
Springfield that day, says of this mass meeting:

" It was one of the most enormous and impressive gatherings I had ever witnessed. Mr. Lincoln, surrounded by
some intimate friends, sat on the balcony of his humble
home. It took hours for all the delegations to file before
him, and there was no token of enthusiasm wanting. He
was deeply touched by the manifestations of personal and
political friendships, and returned all his salutations in that
off-hand and kindly manner which belonged to him. I know
of no demonstration of a similar character that can compare with it except the review by Napoleon of his army for
the invasion of Russia, about the same season of the year in
1812."

From May until November this work for the ticket went
on steadily and ardently. Mr. Lincoln during all this time
remained quietly in Springfield. The conspicuous position
in which he was placed made almost no difference in his sim-

ple life. He was the same genial, accessible, modest man as ever, his habits as unpretentious, his friendliness as great. The chief outward change in his daily round was merely one of quarters. It seemed to his friends that neither his home nor his dingy law office was an appropriate place in which to receive his visitors and they arranged that a room in the State House which stood on the village green in the centre of the town, be put at his disposal. He came down to this office every morning about eight o'clock, always stopping on his way in his old cordial fashion to ask the news or exchange a story when he met an acquaintance. Frequently he went to the post-office himself before going to his office and came out his arms loaded with letters and papers.

He had no regular hours for visitors; there was no ceremony for admittance to his presence. People came when they would. Usually they found the door open; if it was not, it was Mr. Lincoln's own voice which answered, " come in," to their knock. These visitors were a strange medley of the curious, the interested and the friendly. Many came simply to see him, to say they had shaken hands with him; numbers to try to find out what his policy would be if elected; others to wish him success. All day long they filed in and out leaving him some days no time for his correspondence, which every day grew larger. He seemed never to be in a hurry, never to lose patience, however high his table was piled with mail, however closely his room was crowded with visitors. He even found time to give frequent sittings to the artists sent from various parts of the country to paint his portrait. Among those who came in the summer after the nomination were Berry, of Boston; Hicks, of New York; Conant, of St. Louis; Wright, of Mobile; Brown, and Atwood, of Philadelphia; Jones, of Cincinnati. Mr. Lincoln took the kindliest interest in these men, and later when President did more than one of them a friendly turn; thus in

March, 1865 he wrote to Seward in regard to Jones and Piatt, that he had " some wish " that they might have " some of those moderate sized consulates which facilitate artists a little in their profession." They in their turn never forgot him. Sitting over their easels by the hour in the corner of his office assigned them they got many glimpses into the man's great heart, and nowhere do we get pleasanter pictures of Mr. Lincoln in this period than from their journals.

To those who observed Mr. Lincoln closely as he received his visitors one thing was apparent: he always remained master of the interview. While his visitors told him a great deal, they learned nothing from him which he did not wish to give. The following observations, published in the Illinois "State Journal" in November, 1860, illustrate very well what happened almost every day in his office:

" While talking to two or three gentlemen and standing up, a very hard looking customer rolled in and tumbled into the only vacant chair and the one lately occupied by Mr. Lincoln. Mr. Lincoln's keen eye took in the fact, but gave no evidence of the notice. Turning around at last he spoke to the odd specimen, holding out his hand at such a distance that our friend had to vacate the chair if he accepted the proffered shake. Mr. Lincoln quietly resumed his chair. It was a small matter, yet one giving proof more positively than a larger event of that peculiar way the man has of mingling with a mixed crowd.

" He converses fluently on all subjects, illustrates everything by a merry anecdote, of which article he has an abundant supply. I said on all subjects. He does not talk politics. He passes from that gracefully the moment it is introduced. Hundreds seek him every week to get his opinion on this or that subject. He has a jolly way of disposing of that matter by saying, ' Ah! you haven't read my speeches. Let me make you a present of my speeches.' And the earnest inquirer finds himself the happy possessor of some old documents."

Among his daily visitors there were usually men of eminence from North and South. He received them all with perfect simplicity and always even on his busiest days, found a moment to turn away from them to greet old friends who had known him when he kept grocery in New Salem or acted as deputy-surveyor of Sangamon County. One day as he talked to a company of distinguished strangers an old lady in a big sun-bonnet, heavy boots and short skirts walked into the office. She carried a package wrapped in brown paper and tied with a white string. As soon as Mr. Lincoln saw her he left the group, went to meet her and, shaking her hand cordially, inquired for her " folks." After a moment the old lady opened her package and taking out a pair of coarse wool socks she handed them to him. " I wanted to give you somethin', Mr. Linkin," she said, " to take to Washington, and that's all I hed. I spun that yarn and knit them socks myself." Thanking her warmly, Mr. Lincoln took the socks and holding them up by the toes, one in each hand, he turned to the astonished celebrities and said in a voice full of kindly amusement, " The lady got my latitude and longitude about right, didn't she, gentlemen? "

The old lady was not the only one, however, who gave Mr. Lincoln " something to carry to Washington." From the time of his nomination gifts poured in on him. Many of these came in the form of wearing apparel. Mr. George Lincoln, of Brooklyn, who in January carried a handsome silk hat to the President-elect, the gift of a New York hatter, says that in receiving the hat, Mr. Lincoln laughed heartily over the gifts of clothing and remarked to Mrs. Lincoln:

" Well, wife, if nothing else comes out of this scrape, we are going to have some new clothes, are we not? "

To those who observed Mr. Lincoln superficially in this period, it might have seemed that he was doing nothing of any value to himself or to his party. Certainly he was taking no active part in the campaign. He was making no speeches —writing no letters—giving no interviews. This policy of silence he had adopted at the outset. The very night of his nomination his townspeople in serenading him had called for a speech. Standing in the doorway of his house he said to them that he did not suppose the honor of such a visit was intended particularly for himself as a private citizen, but rather as the representative of a great party; that as to his position on the political questions of the day he could only refer them to his previous speeches, and he added:—" Fellow citizens and friends: The time comes upon every public man, when it is best for him to keep his lips closed. That time has come upon me." When in August the monster mass meeting was held in Springfield every effort was made to persuade Mr. Lincoln to speak. All he would consent to do was to appear and in a few words excuse himself. Up to the time he left for Washington to be inaugurated, he kept his resolve.

Nor would he write letters explaining his position, or defending himself. So many letters were received asking his political opinion that he found it necessary soon after his nomination to prepare the following form of reply to be sent out by his secretary:

" Dear Sir: Your letter to Mr. Lincoln of ——, and by which you seek to obtain his opinions on certain political points, has been received by him. He has received others of a similar character, but he also has a greater number of the exactly opposite character. The latter class beseech him to write nothing whatever upon any point of political doctrine. They say his positions were well known when he was nominated, and that he must not now embarrass the canvass by undertaking to shift or modify them. He regrets that he cannot oblige all, but you perceive it is impossible for him to do so.           Yours, etc.,
          " JNO. G. NICOLAY."

To one gentleman who asked him to write something disclaiming all intention to interfere with slaves or slavery in the States, he replied, " I have already done this many many times; and it is in print and open to all who will read. Those who will not read or heed what I have already publicly said would not read or heed a repetition of it. If they hear not Moses and the prophets, neither will they be persuaded though one rose from the dead."

And to another correspondent who suggested that he set forth his conservative views, he wrote :—

***" I will not forbear from doing so merely on punctilio and pluck. If I do finally abstain, it will be because of apprehension that it would do harm. For the good men of the South—and I regard the majority of them as such—I have no objection to repeat seventy and seven times. But I have bad men to deal with, both North and South; men who are eager for something new upon which to base new misrepresentations; men who would like to frighten me, or at least to fix upon me the character of timidity and cowardice. They would seize upon almost any letter I could write as being an ' awful coming down.' I intend keeping my eye upon these gentlemen, and to not unnecessarily put any weapons in their hands."

Nor would he defend himself against the " campaign stories " which appeared in numbers. One of which his enemies made much was that he had received two hundred dollars for the Cooper Union speech in February, 1860. They claimed that as it was a political speech it was contrary to political etiquette to accept pay. Lincoln explained the affair in a letter to a gentleman who had been disturbed by it and added :—

" I have made this explanation to you as a friend, but I wish no explanation made to our enemies. What they want is a squabble and a fuss, and that they can have if we explain; and they cannot have it if we don't."

Another foolish tale which caused Lincoln's partisans unrest was that when he was a member of Congress he had charged several pairs of *boots* to his stationery account and that they had been paid for out of public funds. One of Lincoln's friends took the trouble to examine the stationery account for the Thirtieth Congress and to publish a certified denial of the story.

Lincoln's silence and inactivity were merely external. As a matter of fact no one was busier than he. No one was following more intently and thoughtfully the gradual development of the situation and the daily fluctuation of opinion. By correspondence, from the press, through his visitors many of whom came to Springfield at his request, he kept himself informed of how the campaign was going from Maine to California. Whenever he feared a break in the ranks he put in a word of warning or of advice. He warned Thurlow Weed that Douglas was "managing the Bell element with great adroitness." He cautioned Hannibal Hamlin against a break the latter feared in Maine, "Such a result as you seem to predict in Maine"—he wrote, "would, I fear, put us on the down-hill track, lose us the State elections in Pennsylvania and Indiana, and probably ruin us on the main turn in November." While he gave the strictest attention to the progress of the elections all over the country, he managed to keep above local issues and to hold himself aloof from the personal contests and rivalries within the party.

In fact Lincoln kept in perfect touch with the progress of his party from May to November and was able to say at any time with accuracy just what his chances were in each State. He seems at no time to have had any serious fear that he would be defeated.

There was a tragic side to this very certainty of election which Lincoln felt deeply. In the Convention which had nominated him, nine States of the Union had not been rep-

**resented.** If he should be elected these States would have had no voice in his choice. He knew that he was pledged to a platform whose principles these States stigmatized as "deception and fraud," and that if elected he must deny what they claimed as rights. He knew that in at least one State, Alabama, the legislature two months before his nomination had pledged itself by an almost unanimous vote in case of his election to call a convention to consider what should be done for "the protection of their rights, interests and honor." He knew that numbers of influential Southern men were repeating daily with Wm. L. Yancey, "I want the cotton states precipitated in a revolution," or declaring with Mr. Crawford of Georgia, "We will never submit to the inauguration of a Black Republican President."

From May to November he watched anxiously for every sign that the South was preparing to make good the threats with which its orators were inflaming their audiences, which a hostile press reiterated day by day, which teemed in his mail, and which brought scores of timorous men to Springfield to advise and warn him. How serious was it all? He did his utmost to discover; even writing in October to Major David Hunter to find out how much truth there was in the report of disaffection in a Western fort: "I have a letter from a writer unknown to me," he said, "saying the officers of the army at Fort Kearney have determined, in case of Republican success, at the approaching presidential election, to take themselves, and the arms at that point, South, for the purpose of resistance to the government. While I think there are many chances to one that this is a humbug, it occurs to me that any real movement of this sort in the army would leak out and become known to you. In such case, if it would not be unprofessional, or dishonorable (of which you are to be judge), I shall be much obliged if you will apprise me of it."

In spite of all that Lincoln knew of the temper of the South, in spite of his close study of events there through the summer of 1860, he did not believe secession probable. " The people of the South have too much good sense and good temper to attempt the ruin of the government rather than see it administered as it was administered by the men who made it. At least so I hope and believe," he wrote a correspondent in August. And in September he said to a visitor, " There are no real disunionists in the country."

There were reasons for this confidence. In every State of the South there was a Union party working to meet the crisis which Lincoln's election was sure to produce; many of the members sent him cheering letters. In acknowledging such a letter in August, Lincoln wrote: " It contains one of the many assurances I receive from the South, that in no probable event will there be any very formidable effort to break up the Union."

Then, too, Lincoln had heard this threat of secession for so long that he had grown slightly indifferent to it. He remembered that in the Frémont campaign it had been employed with even more violence than now. Again in 1858 the clamor of disunion had risen. He believed that now much of the noise about disunion was merely political, raised by the friends of Breckenridge, Douglas, or Bell, to drive voters from him. The leading men of the party sustained Lincoln in this belief. Seward and Schurz both confidently assured Republicans in their speeches that they might vote for Lincoln without fear, and Bryant, in the " Evening Post," laughed at the " conservative distresses " of those who supposed that Lincoln's election would cause secession and war; reminding them that when Jefferson was a candidate it was said his election would " let loose the flood-gates of French Jacobinism " and that Henry Clay had declared that " nothing short of universal commercial ruin " would follow Jack-

son's election.  Lincoln was sustained not only by the assurances of the Union party of the South and by the buoyant
hopefulness of the Republicans of the North, he had a powerful moral support in his own conviction that no matter what
effort the South made to secede the North could and would
prevent it.  He was and had been for years perfectly clear
on this subject.  In the Frémont campaign he had said in
reply to the threat of disunion, " No matter what our grievance—even though Kansas shall come in as a slave State;
and no matter what theirs—even if we shall restore the compromise—we will say to the Southern disunionists we won't
go out of the Union and you *shan't*."

It was then with the belief that he was going to be elected
and that while his election would produce a serious uproar in
the South, that no successful resistance would follow, that
Lincoln approached election day.  He had grown materially
in the estimation of the country in the interval between May
and November.  Many of the leading men of his party who
had deplored his nomination had come to believe him a wise,
strong man.  Those who sought personal interviews with
him, and they were many, went home feeling like Thurlow
Weed who, heart-sick over Seward's defeat and full of
distrust, not to say contempt, of Lincoln's ability, visited
him soon after the nomination at the earnest request of David
Davis and Leonard Swett.  " I found Mr. Lincoln," wrote
Weed afterward, " sagacious and practical.  He displayed
throughout the conversation so much good sense, such intu-
itive knowledge of human nature, and such familiarity with
the virtues and infirmities of politicians, that I became impressed very favorably with his fitness for the duties which
he was not unlikely to be called upon to discharge.  This
conversation lasted some five hours, and when the train arrived in which we were to depart, I rose all the better prepared to ' go to work with a will ' in favor of Mr. Lincoln's

election, as the interview had inspired me with confidence in his capacity and integrity." . . .

In the very South where a fury of prejudice had burst and where, as was to be expected, Lincoln was popularly regarded as an odious and tyrannical monster, much as later the North regarded Jefferson Davis, there were signs that he was at least considered honest in his views.

"It may seem strange to you," wrote a Kentuckian, who was quoted by the New York "Evening Post," August 17, 1860, "but it is nevertheless true that the South looks for the election of Lincoln by the people and would prefer him to Douglas. Our most ultra Southern men seem to respect him and to have confidence in his honesty, fairness and conservatism. They concede that he stands on a moderate platform, that his antecedents are excellent, and that he is not likely to invade the rights of any one; but they can't go for him because he holds opinions relative to the rights of slavery in the Territories directly opposite to the Southern view, still he is an open and candid opponent, and therefore commands Southern respect."

"Some of the most interesting interviews which Mr. Lincoln has had," wrote some one to the Baltimore "Patriot," "have been with extreme Southern gentlemen, who came full of prejudice against him, and who left satisfied with his loyalty to all the constitutional rights of the South. I could tell you of some most interesting cases, but it is enough to know that the general sentiment of all Southern men who have conversed with him is the same as that publicly expressed by Mr. Goggin, of Virginia; Mr. Perry, of South Carolina; Mr. McRae, of North Carolina, and many others, who have not hesitated to avow their intention of accepting Mr. Lincoln's election and holding him to the constitutional discharge of the presidential office. . . ."

The most significant element in the estimate of Lincoln which the country formed between May and November was the respect and affection which was awakened among the common people.   There sprang up all over the country among plain people a feeling for him not unlike that which had long existed in Illinois.  The general distribution made of his speeches had something to do with this.   There was published in 1860 in Columbus, Ohio, an edition of the Lincoln and Douglas debates of 1858, which was used freely as a campaign document.  Lincoln himself gave away scores of these books to his friends and to persons who came to him begging for an expression of his views.  To-day copies bearing his autograph are to be seen, treasured volumes in the libraries of many public men.  The Cooper Union speech was published by the Young Men's Republican Club of New York and circulated widely.  To the hard-working farmer, mechanic, store-keeper, who thought slowly but surely, and whose sole political ambition was to cast an honest vote, these speeches were like a personal face-to-face talk.  The argument was so clear, the illustration so persuasive, the statement so colloquial and natural, that they could not get away from them.  " Lincoln's right," was the general verdict among masses of people who, hesitating between Republicanism and Popular Sovereignty, read the speeches as a help to a decision.

While Lincoln's speeches awakened respect for and confidence in his ability, the story of his life stirred something deeper in men.  Here was a man who had become a leader of the nation by the labor of his hands, the honesty of his intellect, the uprightness of his heart.  Plain people were touched by the hardships of this life so like their own, inspired by the thought that a man who had struggled as they had done, who had remained poor, who had lived simply, could be eligible to the highest place in the nation.  They had believed that it could be done.  Here was a proof of it. They told the story to their boys.  This, they said, is what American institutions make possible; not glitter or wealth, trickery or demagogy is necessary, only honesty, hard thinking, a fixed purpose. Affection and sympathy for Lincoln grew with respect. It was the beginning of that peculiar sympathetic relation between him and the common people which was to become one of the controlling influences in the great drama of the Civil War.

Election day in 1860 fell on the 6th. Springfield, although a town of strong Democratic sympathy, realized the importance of the occasion, and by daylight was booming away with cannon; before noon numbers of bands which came, the citizens hardly knew from where, were playing on the corners of every street. Mr. Lincoln, as was his custom, came down to his room at the State House by eight o'clock, where he went over his big mail as coolly as if it were not election day and he a candidate for the presidency of the United States. He had not been there long before his friends began to flock in in such numbers that it was proposed that the doors be closed and he be allowed to remain by himself, but he said he had never done such a thing in his life as to close the door on his friends and that he did not intend to begin now, and so the day wore away in the entertainment of visitors.

It had not been Mr. Lincoln's intention to vote, the obstacle which he found in the way being that his own name headed the Republican ticket and that he did not want to vote for himself. One of his friends suggested that his name might be cut off and he vote for the rest of the ticket. He fell in with this suggestion, and late in the afternoon, when the crowd around the polls, which were just across the street from his office, had subsided somewhat, he went over to cast his ballot. He was recognized immediately and his friends were soon about him, cheering wildly and contending good-naturedly for an opportunity to shake his hand. Even the Democrats, with their hands full of documents which they were distributing, joined in this enthusiastic demonstration and cheered at the top of their voices for their beloved townsman.

No returns were expected before seven o'clock, and it was a little later than that when Mr. Lincoln returned from his supper to the State House. The first despatches that came were from different parts of Illinois, the very first being from Decatur, where a Republican gain was announced. Soon after, Alton, which was expected to go for Douglas, sent in a majority of twelve for Lincoln. There was a tremendous sensation in the company, and Mr. Lincoln asked that the despatch be sent out to the "boys," meaning the crowd which had gathered in and about the State House. After an hour or more news began to come from Missouri. " Now," said Mr. Lincoln, " they should get a few licks back at us." But to everybody's surprise, there was more good news from Missouri than had been expected. Towards midnight news began to come from Pennsylvania: " Allegheny County, 10,-000 majority for Lincoln;" " Philadelphia, 15,000 plurality, 5,000 majority over all;" then a telegram from Simon Cameron, " Pennsylvania 70,000 for you. New York safe. Glory enough." This was the first news from New York, and since ten o'clock the company had been waiting impatiently for it. A fusion ticket, it was feared, might go through there, and if it did the disaster to the Republicans would be serious.

While waiting anxiously for something definite from New York, a delegation of Springfield ladies came in to invite Mr. Lincoln and his friends to a hall near by, where they had prepared refreshments for all the Republican politicians of the town. The party had not been there long before there came a telegram announcing that New York city had gone Republican. Such a cheering was probably never heard in Springfield before. The hall full of people, beside themselves with joy, began a romping promenade around the

(25)

tables, singing at the top of their voices the popular campaign song, "Oh ain't you glad you joined the Republicans?" Here at intervals further telegrams came from New York, all announcing large majorities. The scene became one of the wildest excitement, and Mr. Lincoln and his friends soon withdrew to a little telegraph office on the square, where they could receive reports more quietly. Up to this time the only anxiety Mr. Lincoln had shown about the election was in the returns from his State and town. He didn't "feel quite easy," as he said, "about Springfield." Towards morning, however, the announcement came that he had a majority in his own precinct. Then it was that he showed the first emotion, a jubilant chuckle, and soon after he remarked cheerfully to his friends, that he "guess'd he'd go home now," which he did. But Springfield was not content to go home. Cannon banged until daylight, and on every street corner and in every alley could be heard groups of men shouting at the top of their voices, "Oh, ain't you glad you joined the Republicans?"

Twenty-four hours later and the full result of that Tuesday's work was known. Out of 303 electoral votes, Lincoln had received 180. Of the popular vote he had received 1,866,452—nearly a half million over Douglas, a million over Breckenridge, a million and a quarter over Bell. It was a victory, but there were facts about the victory which startled the thoughtful. If Lincoln had more votes than any one opposing candidate, they together had nearly 1,000,000 over him. Fifteen States of the Union gave him no electoral votes, and in ten States he had not received a single popular vote.

# CHAPTER XXI

## MR. LINCOLN AS PRESIDENT-ELECT

ALTHOUGH the election of November 6 made Lincoln the President-elect of the United States, for four months, he could exercise no direct influence on the affairs of the country. If the South tried to make good her threat to secede in case he was elected, he could do nothing to restrain her. The South did try, and at once. With the very election returns the telegraph brought Lincoln news of disruption. Day by day this news continued, and always more alarming. On November 10, the United States senators from South Carolina resigned. Six weeks later, that State passed an ordinance of secession and began to organize an independent government. By the end of December, the only remnant of United States authority in South Carolina was the small garrison commanded by Major Anderson which occupied Fort Sumter, in Charleston harbor. The remaining forts and batteries of that harbor, the lighthouse tender, the arsenal, the post-office, the custom-house, in short, everything in the State over which the Stars and Stripes had floated, was under the Palmetto Flag.

In his quiet office in Springfield, Mr. Lincoln read, in January, reports of the proceedings of conventions in Mississippi, Florida, Alabama, Georgia, and Louisiana, by all of which States, in that month, ordinances of secession were adopted. In February, he saw representatives of these same States unite in a general convention at Montgomery, Alabama, and the newspapers told him how promptly and intelligently they went to work to found a new nation, the Southern Confederacy, to provide it with a constitution, and to give it officers.

Mr. Lincoln observed that each State, as she went out of the Union, prepared to defend her course if necessary. On November 18, Georgia appropriated $1,000,000 to arm the State, and in January she seized Forts Pulaski and Jackson and the United States arsenal. Louisiana appropriated all the federal property in her borders, even to the mint and custom-house and the money they contained. Georgia, Florida, Alabama, and Mississippi were not behind in their seizures, and when the new government was formed at Montgomery, it promptly took up the question of defending its life.

Mr. Lincoln was not only obliged to sit inactive and watch this steady dissolution of the Union, but he was obliged to see what was still harder—that the administration which he was to succeed was doing nothing to check the destructionists. Indeed, all through this period proof accumulated that members of Mr. Buchanan's cabinet had been systematically working for many months to disarm the North and equip the South. The quantity of arms sent quietly from Northern arsenals was so great that the citizens of the towns from which they went became alarmed. Thus the Springfield "Republican" of January 2, 1861, noted that the citizens of that town were growing excited over "the procession of government licenses which, during the last spring and summer, and also quite recently, have been engaged in transporting from the United States Armory to the United States freight station, an immense quantity of boxes of muskets marked for Southern distribution." "We find," the paper continues, "that in 1860 there were removed for safe-keeping in other arsenals 135,430 government arms. This has nothing to do with the distribution occasionally made for

State militia." And when, in December, the citizens of Pittsburg, Pennsylvania, found that 123 cannon had been ordered South from the arsenal there, they made such energetic protests that President Buchanan was obliged to countermand the order of his Secretary of War.

The rapid disintegration which followed the election of Mr. Lincoln filled the North with dismay. There was a general demand for some compromise which would reassure the South and stop secession. It was the place of the Republicans, the conservatives argued, to make this compromise. A furious clamor broke over Mr. Lincoln's head. His election had caused the trouble; now what would he do to quell it? How much of the Republican platform would he give up? Among the newspapers which pleaded with the President-elect to do something to reassure the South the most able was the New York " Herald." Lincoln was a " sectional President," declared the " Herald," who, out of 4,700,000 votes cast, had received but 1,850,000, and whom the South had had no part in electing.

If Mr. Lincoln intends to carry on the government according to the principles laid down in the Chicago platform and the documents issued under the authority of the Republican " national " committee, the inevitable tendency of his administration will be to encourage servile insurrections and to make the Southern States still more uncomfortable within the Union than they could by any possibility be without it. . . . If the new President recognizes the fact that he is not bound by the Chicago platform—the people having repudiated it; . . . if he comes out and tells the people that he will govern the country according to the views of the majority, and not to serve the purposes of the minority, all may yet be well. . . . Mr. Lincoln must throw his pledges to the winds, let his party go to perdition in its own way, and devote himself to the service of the whole country. It is Mr. Lincoln's bounden duty to come out now and declare his views.

It was not only the opposition press which urged Lincoln to offer some kind of compromise; many frightened Republican newspapers added their influence. The appeals of thousands of letters and of scores of visitors were added to the arguments of the press. Lincoln, however, refused to express his views anew. " I know the justness of my intentions," he told an interviewer in November, " and the utter groundlessness of the pretended fears of the men who are filling the country with their clamor. If I go into the presidency, they will find me as I am on record, nothing less, nothing more. My declarations have been made to the world without reservation. They have been often repeated, and now self-respect demands of me and of the party which has elected me that, when threatened, I should be silent."

Business was brought almost to a standstill throughout the North by the prospect of disunion. " It is an awful time for merchants," wrote a correspondent to Charles Sumner, " worse than in 1857. And if there is not some speedy relief, more than half of the best concerns in the country will be ruined." Numbers of prominent men urged the President-elect to say something conciliatory for the sake of trade. His replies published in Nicolay and Hay's " Abraham Lincoln " are marked by spirit and decision. To one man of wealth he wrote on November 10:

I am not insensible to any commercial or financial depression that may exist, but nothing is to be gained by fawning around the " respectable scoundrels " who got it up. Let them go to work and repair the mischief of their own making, and then perhaps they will be less greedy to do the like again.

And to Henry J. Raymond, the editor of the New York " Times," he gave, on November 28, in answer to a request for his views, what he called a " demonstration " of the correctness of his judgment that he should say nothing for the public:

On the 20th instant, Senator Trumbull made a short speech, which I suppose you have both seen and approved. Has a single newspaper, heretofore against us, urged that speech upon its readers with a purpose to quiet public anxiety? Not one, so far as I know. On the contrary, the Boston " Courier " and its class hold me responsible for that speech, and endeavor to inflame the North with the belief that it foreshadows an abandonment of Republican ground by the incoming administration while the Washington " Constitution " and its class hold the same speech up to the South as an open declaration of war against them. This is just as I expected, and just what would happen with any declaration I could make. These political fiends are not half sick enough yet. Party malice, and not public good, possesses them entirely. " They seek a sign, and no sign shall be given them." At least such is my present feeling and purpose.

While refusing positively to express himself for the general public at this time, Lincoln wrote and talked freely to the Republican leaders, almost all of whom were busy with one or another scheme for quieting the distracted nation. On the opening of Congress, a committee of thirty-three had been appointed by the House to consider " the present perilous condition of the country," and the Republican members wished to know what Mr. Lincoln would yield. The Hon. William Kellogg, the Illinois member of the committee, wrote to him. His reply, dated December 11, is unmistakable:

Entertain no proposition for a compromise in regard to the extension of slavery. The instant you do, they have us under again: all our labor is lost, and sooner or later must be done over. Douglas is sure to be again trying to bring in his " popular sovereignty." Have none of it. The tug has to come, and better now than later. You know I think the fugitive slave clause of the Constitution ought to be enforced—to put it in its mildest form, ought not to be resisted.

While the committee of thirty-three was seeking grounds for a settlement in the House, a committee of thirteen was busy in the Senate in the same search. On the latter committee was William H. Seward, and he too sent to Mr. Lincoln for a suggestion. In reply, the President-elect sent Mr. Seward, by Thurlow Weed, a memorandum which was supposed to have been lost until a few months ago when it was discovered by Mr. Frederick Bancroft in course of his researches for a Life of Seward. Two points are covered in this memorandum. The first that the fugitive slave law should be enforced, the second that the Federal Union must be preserved. In a letter to the Hon. E. B. Washburne, written on December 13th, Lincoln again stated his views on slavery extension:

Prevent, as far as possible, any of our friends from demoralizing themselves and our cause by entertaining propositions for compromise of any sort on " slavery extension." There is no possible compromise upon it but which puts us under again and leaves all our work to do over again. Whether it be a Missouri line or Eli Thayer's popular sovereignty, it is all the same. Let either be done, and immediately filibustering and extending slavery recommences. On that point hold firm, as with a chain of steel.

These counsels were given while secession was still in its infancy. The alarming developments which followed did not cause Lincoln to waver. On January 11, he wrote to the Hon. J. T. Hale a letter published by Nicolay and Hay, in which he said:

What is our present condition? We have just carried an election on principles fairly stated to the people. Now we are told in advance the government shall be broken up unless we surrender to those we have beaten, before we take the offices. In this they are either attempting to play upon us or they are in dead earnest. Either way, if we surrender, it is the end of us and of the government. They will repeat the experiment upon us *ad libitum.* A year will not pass till we shall have to take Cuba as a condition upon which they will stay in the Union. They now have the Constitution under which we have lived over seventy years, and acts of Congress of their own framing, with no prospect of their being changed; and they can never have a more shallow pretext for breaking up the government, or extorting a compromise, than now. There is, in my judgment, but one compromise which would really settle the slavery question, and that would be a prohibition against acquiring any more territory.

It was not the North and the Republicans alone that appealed to Mr. Lincoln; the Unionists of the South urged him for an explanation which they might present to the people as proof that there was nothing to fear from his election. Lincoln had no faith that any expression of his would be heeded; yet he did, confidentially, express himself frankly to many Southerners who came to him in Springfield, and there are two letters of his published by Nicolay and Hay which show how completely he grasped the essential difference between the North and the South, and with what justice and kindness he put the case to those who disagreed with him. The first of these letters was written to John A. Gilmer, a member of Congress from North Carolina, who desired earnestly to preserve the Union, but not unless the opinions of the South were considered. Mr. Gilmer had written to Mr. Lincoln, asking his position on certain questions. Lincoln replied:

Carefully read pages 18, 19, 74, 75, 88, 89, and 267 of the volume of joint debates between Senator Douglas and myself, with the Republican platform adopted at Chicago, and all your questions will be substantially answered. I have no thought of recommending the abolition of slavery in the District of Columbia, nor the slave-trade among the slave States, even on the conditions indicated; and if I were to make such recommendation, it is quite clear Congress would not follow it.

As to employing slaves in arsenals and dock-yards, it is a thing I never thought of in my life, to my recollection, till I saw your letter; and I may say of it precisely as I have said of the two points above.

As to the use of patronage in the slave States, where there are few or no Republicans, I do not expect to inquire for the politics of the appointee, or whether he does or not own slaves. I intend, in that matter, to accommodate the people in the several localities, if they themselves will allow me to accommodate them. In one word, I never have been, am not now, and probably never shall be in a mood of harassing the people either North or South.

On the territorial question I am inflexible, as you see my position in the book. On that there is a difference between you and us; and it is the only substantial difference. You think slavery is right and ought to be extended; we think it is wrong and ought to be restricted. For this neither has any just occasion to be angry with the other.

As to the State laws mentioned in your sixth question, I really know very little of them. I never have read one. If any of them are in conflict with the fugitive-slave clause, or any other part of the Constitution, I certainly shall be glad of their repeal; but I could hardly be justified, as a citizen of Illinois, or as President of the United States, to recommend the repeal of a statute of Vermont or South Carolina.

A week later, Mr. Lincoln wrote to A. H. Stephens, of Georgia, in reply to a note in which Stephens had said: " The country is certainly in great peril, and no man ever had heavier or greater responsibilities resting upon him than you have in the present momentous crisis."

I fully appreciate the present peril the country is in, and the weight of responsibility on me. Do the people of the

South really entertain fears that a Republican administration would, directly or indirectly, interfere with the slaves, or with them about the slaves? If they do, I wish to assure you, as once a friend, and still, I hope, not an enemy, that there is no cause for such fears. The South would be in no more danger in this respect than it was in the days of Washington. I suppose, however, this does not meet the case. You think slavery is right and ought to be extended, while we think it is wrong and ought to be restricted. That, I suppose, is the rub. It certainly is the only substantial difference between us.

The uproar which raged about Mr. Lincoln soon became quite as loud over " coercion " as over " compromise." Each passing week made conciliation more difficult, saw new elements of disunion realized. What was to be done with the seceding States? What was to be done about the forts and arsenals, custom-houses and post-offices, they were seizing? If Mr. Lincoln would not compromise, was he going to let the States and the federal property go, or was he going to compel them to return with it? Did he propose to coerce the South? Though the President-elect refused to give any expression of opinion on the subject to the country, it was not because he was not perfectly clear in his own mind. Secession he considered impossible. " My opinion is," he wrote Thurlow Weed on December 17, " that no State can in any way lawfully get out of the Union without the consent of the others; and that it is the duty of the President and other government functionaries to run the machine as it is."

When Horace Greeley began a series of editorials in the " Tribune " contending that if seven or eight States sent agents to Washington saying, " We want to get out of the Union," he should feel constrained by his devotion to Human Liberty to say " Let them go," Lincoln said nothing publicly, though in Springfield it was believed that he considered the policy " dangerous and illogical." He certainly was only

amused at Fernando Wood's scheme to take New York City
out of the Union and make it a free city—another Hamburg.
" I reckon," he said to a New Yorker in February, in discussing the subject, " that it will be some time before the
front door sets up house-keeping on its own account."

As to the forts and other federal property seized by the
outgoing States, he seems to have felt from the first that they
were to be retaken. In this matter he sought guidance from
Andrew Jackson. Less than a week after his election, a correspondent of the " Evening Post " found him engaged in
reading the history of the nullifiers of 1832 and 1833 and of
the summary way in which " Old Hickory " dealt with them.
In December, he wrote to his friend E. B. Washburne, who
had just reported to him an interview with General Scott,
the general in command of the army, on the dangers of the
situation :

Please present my respects to the General, and tell him,
confidentially, that I shall be obliged to him to be as well
prepared as he can to either hold or retake the forts, as the
case may require, at and after the inauguration.

And the very next day, he wrote to Major David Hunter :

The most we can do now is to watch events, and be as
well prepared as possible for any turn things may take. If
the forts fall, my judgment is that they are to be retaken.

From the foregoing letters it will be seen that Mr. Lincoln
had stripped his opinions on the questions of the day of all
verbiage and non-essentials and reduced them to the following simple propositions.

(1) Slavery is wrong, and must not be extended.
(2) Entertain no proposition for a compromise in regard
to the extension of slavery.
(3) No State can in any way lawfully get out of the
Union, without the consent of the others. It is the duty of

the President and other government functionaries to run the
machine as it is.

(4) If the forts fall, my judgment is that they are to be
retaken.

To these simple statements he stuck throughout this period of confusion and distress, refusing to allow them to be
obscured by words and passion, and making them his guide
in the work of preparation for his inauguration.

Three things especially occupied him in this preparation:
(1) Making the acquaintance of the men with whom he was
to be associated in the administration. (2) His cabinet.
(3) His inaugural address.

The first letter Lincoln wrote after his election was to
Hannibal Hamlin, the Vice-President-elect, asking for an
interview. The two gentlemen met at the Tremont House,
Chicago, on November 23. Mr. Hamlin once gave to a
friend, Mr. C. J. Prescott, of New York, an account of this
meeting, which Mr. Prescott has written out for this work:

Mr. Hamlin was for many years a member of the Board
of Trustees of Waterville College now Colby University,
Waterville, Maine. On one of the annual Commencement
occasions, I found him one afternoon seated on the piazza
of the Elmwood, for the moment alone and unoccupied.
Taking a chair by his side, I said: " Mr. Hamlin, when did
you first meet Mr. Lincoln? " " Well," said he, " I very
plainly recall the circumstances of our first meeting. It was
in Chicago. Some time before the inauguration, I received
a letter from Mr. Lincoln, asking me to see him before I
went to Washington. So I went to Chicago, where I was to
meet Mr. Lincoln. Sending my card to Mr. Lincoln's room,
I received word to ' come right up.' I found the door open,
and Mr. Lincoln approaching with extended hand. With a
hearty welcome, he said, ' I think I have never met you before, Mr. Hamlin, but this is not the first time I have seen
you. I have just been recalling the time when, in '48, I went
to the Senate to hear you speak. Your subject was not new,

but the ideas were sound. You were talking about slavery, and I now take occasion to thank you for so well expressing what were my own sentiments at that time.'

" ' Well, Mr. President,' said I, ' this is certainly quite a remarkable coincidence. I myself have just been recalling the first time I ever saw you. It must have been about the same time to which you allude. I was passing through the House, and was attracted by some remarks on the subject of slavery from one of the new members. They told me it was Lincoln, of Illinois. I heard you through, and I very well remember how heartily I endorsed every point you made. And, Mr. President, I have no doubt we are still in perfect accord on the main question.' "

The result of the Chicago interview was a cordial understanding between the two men which lasted throughout their administration. This was to be expected, for they were not unlike in character and experience. The same kind of democratic feeling inspired their relations with others. Both " marched with the boys." Both were eminently companionable. Hamlin liked a good story as well as Lincoln, and told almost as many. He had, too, the same quaint way of putting things. Like Lincoln, Hamlin had been born poor, and had had a hand-to-hand struggle to get up in the world. He had worked on a farm, chopped logs, taught school, studied law at night; in short, turned his hand cheerfully and eagerly to anything that would help him to realize his ambitions. Like Lincoln, he had gone early into politics, and, like Lincoln again, he had revolted from his party in 1856 to join the Republicans.

A great many men were summoned to Springfield by Lincoln, in order that he might learn their views more perfectly. Among those who came, either by his direct or indirect invitation, were Edward Bates, Thurlow Weed, David Wilmot, A. K. McClure, George W. Julian, E. D. Baker, William Sweeney, Horace Greeley, and Carl

Schurz. With many of them Lincoln did not hesitate to talk over his cabinet. Thurlow Weed says that when he visited the President-elect in December, the latter introduced the subject of the cabinet, saying that " he supposed I had had some experience in cabinet-making, that he had a job on hand, and as he had never learned that trade, he was disposed to avail himself of the suggestions of friends." " The making of a cabinet," he continued, " now that he had it to do, was by no means as easy as he had supposed; that he had, even before the result of the election was known, assuming the probability of success, fixed upon the two leading members of his cabinet; but that, in looking about for suitable men to fill the other departments, he had been much embarrassed, partly from his want of acquaintance with the prominent men of the day, and partly, he believed, because that, while the population had greatly increased, really great men were scarcer than they used to be."

The two members of his cabinet on whom Lincoln fixed so early were Seward and Chase. He wrote Seward on December 8, asking permission to nominate him as Secretary of State, and saying:

It has been my purpose, from the day of the nomination at Chicago, to assign you, by your leave, this place in the administration. I have delayed so long to communicate that purpose in deference to what appeared to me a proper caution in the case. Nothing has been developed to change my view in the premises; and I now offer you the place, in the hope that you will accept it, and with the belief that your position in the public eye, your integrity, ability, learning, and great experience, all combine to render it an appointment pre-eminently fit to be made.

Seward took three weeks to consider, and finally, on December 28, wrote that, " after due reflection and much self-distrust," he had concluded it was his duty to accept.

Lincoln did not approach Chase on the subject of the cabinet until some three weeks after he had written Seward.
Then, on December 31, he wrote him this brief note:

In these troublous times I would much like a conference
with you.   Please visit me here at once.

Chase reached Springfield on the evening of January 3,
and Lincoln, in his informal way, went to the hotel to see
him.   Chase afterward described the interview in a letter to
a friend:

He said he had felt bound to offer the position of Secretary
of State to Mr. Seward as the generally recognized leader
of the Republican party, intending, if he declined it, to offer
it to me.   He did not wish that Mr. Seward should decline
it, and was glad that he had accepted, and now desired to
have me take the place of Secretary of the Treasury.

Chase did not promise to accept, only to think it over, and
so the situation stood until the appointment was actually
made in March.

It was Pennsylvania and the South that gave Lincoln the
greatest trouble.  " Pennsylvania,"he told Weed, " any more
than New York or Ohio, cannot be overlooked.   Her strong
Republican vote, not less than her numerical importance, en-
titles her to a representative in the cabinet."   After a careful
" balancing of matters," as he called it, he concluded to appoint Simon Cameron as the Pennsylvania cabinet member,
and on December 31 he gave Cameron, who had been for
three days in Springfield discussing the situation, the following letter:

HON. SIMON CAMERON.

*My dear Sir:* I think fit to notify you now that, by your
permission, I shall at the proper time nominate you to the
United States Senate for confirmation as Secretary of the

Treasury, or as Secretary of War—which of the two I have not yet definitely decided.    Please answer at your earliest convenience.    Your obedient servant,

A. LINCOLN.

Cameron had scarcely reached home with his letter before those opposed to him in Pennsylvania had frightened Lincoln into believing that the lack of trust in Cameron's political honesty which existed throughout the country would destroy faith in the new cabinet.    Lincoln immediately wrote Cameron that things had developed which made it impossible to take him into the cabinet.    Later he assured Cameron that the withdrawal did not spring from any change of view as to the ability or faithfulness with which he would discharge the duties of the place, and he promised not to make a cabinet appointment for Pennsylvania without consulting him and giving all the weight he consistently could to his views and wishes.    There the matter remained until March.

Among conciliatory Republicans there was a strong desire that Lincoln find a member of his cabinet in the South. It was believed that such an act would be taken as proof that the new President intended to consider the claims of the South.    Lincoln did not believe the idea practical, and he showed the difficulties in the way very shrewdly by causing to be inserted, on December 12, in the " Illinois Journal," a paper popularly called his " organ," the following short editorial:

We hear such frequent allusions to a supposed purpose on the part of Mr. Lincoln to call into his cabinet two or three Southern gentlemen from the parties opposed to him politically, that we are prompted to ask a few questions.

First. Is it known that any such gentlemen of character would accept a place in the cabinet?

Second. If yea, on what terms does he surrender to Mr. Lincoln, or Mr. Lincoln to him, on the political differences between them; or do they enter upon the administration in open opposition to each other?

The demand continued, however. Weed told Lincoln in December that, in his opinion, at least two of the members of the cabinet should be from the South. Lincoln was doubtful if they could be trusted. " There are men in Maryland, Virginia, North Carolina, and Tennessee," replied Weed, " for whose loyalty under any circumstances, and in any event, I would vouch."

" Well," said Lincoln, " let me have the names of your white blackbirds." Weed gave him four names. Mr. Seward, a little later, suggested several, and Mr. Greeley likewise sent him a list of five Southerners whom he declared it would be safe to take into the official family. Of all those named, Lincoln preferred John A. Gilmer, of North Carolina, and he invited him to come to Springfield for an interview. As late as January 12, he wrote to Seward:

I still hope Mr. Gilmer will, on a fair understanding with us, consent to take a place in the cabinet. . . . I fear, if we could get, we could not safely take more than one such man— that is, not more than one who opposed us in the election, the danger being to lose the confidence of our own friends.

Mr. Gilmer did not accept Mr. Lincoln's invitation to Springfield, however, and nothing ever came of the overture made him. The nearest approach Lincoln made to selecting a cabinet member from the South was in the appointment of Edward Bates, of Missouri. He was one of the men whom Lincoln had decided upon as soon as he knew of his election, and he was the first after Seward to be notified. A representative from Indiana was desirable, and Caleb Smith was put on the slate provisionally. It was necessary, too, that New England have a place in the cabinet. Mr. Lincoln had three candidates, of all of whom he thought well—Tuck, of

New Hampshire; Banks, of Massachusetts; Gideon Welles, of Connecticut; but he made no decision until after he reached Washington.

About the middle of January, 1861, Lincoln began to prepare his inaugural address.  A more desperate situation than existed at that moment it would be hard to imagine. Thus far every peace measure had failed, and the endless discussions of press and senate chamber were daily increasing the anger and the bewilderment of the people.   Four States had left the Union, and the South was rapidly accepting the idea of separate nationality.   The North was desperate and helpless.  All the bitterness and confusion centred about Lincoln.  A hundred things told him how serious was the situation; the averted faces of his townsmen of Southern sympathies, the warnings of good men who sought him from North, and South, letters threatening him with death, sketches of gibbets and stilettos in every mail.

But in spite of all these distracting circumstances, when he thought it time to write the inaugural address, he calmly locked himself up in an upper room over a store, across the street from the State House, where he had his office, and there, with no books but a copy of the " Constitution," Henry Clay's " Speech of 1850," Jackson's " Proclamation against Nullification," and Webster's " Reply to Hayne," he prepared the document.   Wishing to have several copies of it, he went to the general manager of the Illinois " State Journal," Major Wm. H. Bailhache, now of San Diego, California, to arrange for them.   Major Bailhache has prepared for this work a statement of the incident :

" In relation to the printing of the draft of his first inaugural address, my recollection is very clear that his manner was as free from formality and affectation as it would have been had he been ordering the printing of a legal document.   He merely asked me, one day early in January, 1861, if I could

print his address in a certain style without its contents becoming known, and upon being assured that I could do so, he
remarked that he would give me the manuscript in a few
days.  Not long after this, he placed the momentous paper in
my hands.  I had the work done at once, under my personal
supervision, in a private room in the "Journal" building,
by a trusted employé, sworn to secrecy.  When it was
finished, I returned the manuscript to Mr. Lincoln, together
with the twenty printed copies ordered, one of which he
himself gave to me, and it has been retained in my possession
ever since.  I may remark in passing, that the manuscript
was all in his own handwriting and was almost entirely free
from alterations or interlineations.  He did not ask to see a
proof, reposing entire confidence in my careful supervision.
Neither the original draft nor the printed sheets were ever
out of my immediate custody for an instant during the time
occupied in the printing, and I doubt whether any of the
score or more of "typos" employed in the "Journal" office
had even the slightest suspicion that this important state
paper was then being put in type under the same roof with
them.  Be this as it may, the secret was well kept, although
the newspapers employed every conceivable means to obtain
a hint of its tenor, and the whole country was in a state of
feverish anxiety to learn what the policy of the new President was to be."

Although Lincoln met the appalling events which preceded
his inauguration with an outward calm, which led many
people to say that he did not realize the seriousness of the
situation, he was keenly alive to the dangers of the country
and to the difficulty of his own position.  So full of threats
and alarms had his life become by the time of his election
that the mysticism of his nature was awakened, and he was
the victim of an hallucination which he afterwards described
to different friends, among them Noah Brooks, who tells the
story in Lincoln's own words:

It was just after my election in 1860, when the news had
been coming in thick and fast all day and there had been a

great " hurrah boys," so that I was well tired out and went home to rest, throwing myself down on a lounge in my chamber.   Opposite where I lay was a bureau with a swinging glass upon it (and here he got up and placed furniture to illustrate the position), and looking in that glass, I saw myself reflected nearly at full length; but my face, I noticed, had *two* separate and distinct images, the tip of the nose of one being about three inches from the tip of the other.   I was a little bothered, perhaps startled, and got up and looked in the glass, but the illusion vanished.   On lying down again, I saw it a second time, plainer, if possible, than before; and then I noticed that one of the faces was a little paler—say, five shades—than the other.   I got up, and the thing melted away, and I went off, and in the excitement of the hour forgot all about it—nearly, but not quite, for the thing would once in a while come up, and give me a little pang, as if something uncomfortable had happened.   When I went home again that night, I told my wife about it, and a few days afterward I made the experiment again, when (with a laugh), sure enough! the thing came again; but I never succeeded in bringing the ghost back after that, though I once tried very industriously to show it to my wife, who was somewhat worried about it.   She thought it was a " sign " that I was to be elected to a second term of office, and that the paleness of one of the faces was an omen that I should not see life through the last term.

Of far deeper significance than this touch of superstition is a look into the man's heart which Judge Gillespie, a lifelong friend of Lincoln, left, and which his daughter, Mrs. Josephine Gillespie Prickett, of Edwardsville, Illinois, has kindly put at my service.   Early in January, Judge Gillespie was in Springfield, and spent the night at Mr. Lincoln's home.   It was late before the President-elect was free, and then the two men seated themselves by the fire for a talk.

" I attempted," says Judge Gillespie, " to draw him into conversation relating to the past, hoping to divert him from the thoughts which were evidently distracting him.  ' Yes,

yes, I remember,' he would say to my references to old scenes and associations; but the old-time zest was not only lacking, but in its place was a gloom and despondency entirely foreign to Lincoln's character as I had learned to know it. I attributed much of this to his changed surroundings. He sat with his head lying upon his arms, which were folded over the back of his chair, as I had often seen him sit on our travels after an exciting day in court. Suddenly he roused himself. 'Gillespie,' said he, 'I would willingly take out of my life a period in years equal to the two months which intervene between now and my inauguration to take the oath of office now.' 'Why?' I asked. 'Because every hour adds to the difficulties I am called upon to meet, and the present administration does nothing to check the tendency toward dissolution. I, who have been called to meet this awful responsibility, am compelled to remain here, doing nothing to avert it or lessen its force when it comes to me.'

"I said that the condition of which he spoke was such as had never risen before, and that it might lead to the amendment of such an obvious defect in the federal Constitution. 'It is not of myself I complain,' he said, with more bitterness than I ever heard him speak, before or after. 'But every day adds to the difficulty of the situation, and makes the outlook more gloomy. Secession is being fostered rather than repressed, and if the doctrine meets with a general acceptance in the border States, it will be a great blow to the government.'

"Our talk then turned upon the possibility of avoiding a war. 'It is only possible,' said Mr. Lincoln, 'upon the consent of this government to the erection of a foreign slave government out of the present slave States. I see the duty devolving upon me. I have read, upon my knees, the story of Gethsemane, where the Son of God prayed in vain that the cup of bitterness might pass from him. I am in the garden of Gethsemane now, and my cup of bitterness is full and overflowing.'

"I then told him that as Christ's prayer was not answered and his crucifixion had redeemed the great part of the world from paganism to Christianity, so the sacrifice demanded of him might be a great beneficence. Little did I then think how prophetic were my words to be, or what a great sacrifice he was called to make.

"I trust and believe that that night, before I let him go, I shed some rays of sunlight into that troubled heart. Ere long he came to talk of scenes and incidents in which he had taken part, and to laugh over my reminders of some of our professional experiences. When I retired, it was the master of the house and chosen ruler of the country who saw me to my room. 'Joe,' he said, as he was about to leave me, 'I suppose you will never forget that trial down in Montgomery County, where the lawyer associated with you gave away the whole case in his opening speech. I saw you signaling to him, but you couldn't stop him. Now, that's just the way with me and Buchanan. He is giving away the case, and I have nothing to say, and can't stop him. Good-night.'"

But the time for going to Washington was drawing near. There had been considerable discussion about when he had better go. So many threats had been made and so many rumors were in the air, that the party leaders had begun to feel, as early as December, that the President-elect might never get to Washington alive. Even Seward, optimist as he was, felt that precautions had better be taken, and he wrote Lincoln, from Washington, on December 28:

There is a feverish excitement here which awakens all kinds of apprehensions of popular disturbance and disorders, connected with your assumption of the government.

I do not entertain these apprehensions myself. But it is worth consideration, in our peculiar circumstances, that accidents themselves may aggravate opinion here. Habit has accustomed the public to anticipate the arrival of the President-elect in this city about the middle of February; and evil-minded persons would expect to organize the demonstrations for that time. I beg leave to suggest whether it would not be well for you, keeping your own counsel, to be prepared to drop into the city a week or ten days earlier. The effect would be, probably, reassuring and soothing.

Mr. Lincoln replied:

I have been considering your suggestions as to my reaching Washington somewhat earlier than is usual.   It seems to
me the inauguration is not the most dangerous point for us.
Our adversaries have us now clearly at disadvantage.   On
the second Wednesday of February, when the votes should
be officially counted, if the two Houses refuse to meet at
all, or meet without a quorum of each, where shall we be?   I
do not think that this counting is constitutionally essential
to the election; but how are we to proceed in absence of it?

In view of this, I think it best for me not to attempt
appearing in Washington till the result of that ceremony is
known.

The peace of the capital was, however, in good hands.
General Scott, the general in command of the army, had,
even before the election, seen the trouble coming, and had
pleaded with the administration to dispose of the United
States forces in such a way as to protect threatened property.
Early in January, he succeeded in securing a guard for
Washington.   The fear that the electoral vote would never
be counted partially subsided then, and Lincoln announced
that he would leave Springfield on February 11.

The fortnight before his departure he gave to settling up
his private business and saying good-by to his old friends.
His stepmother was still living near Charleston, in Coles
County, and thither he went to spend a day with her and to
visit his father's grave.   The comfort and happiness of his
stepmother had been one of his cares from the time he began
to be self-supporting, and in this farewell visit he assured
himself that her future was provided for.   Mrs. Lincoln, who
was now a very old woman and might naturally doubt
whether she would live to see her son again, was not concerned about herself at this time.   The threats which pursued
Lincoln had reached her, and in bidding him good-by, she
sobbed out her belief that she would never see him again;

that his life would be taken.   This same fear was expressed
by many of Lincoln's early friends who came to Springfield
to say good-by to him.

In the multitude of partings which took place in these last
days none was more characteristic than that with his law
partner, Herndon.   The day before his departure, Mr. Lincoln went to the office to settle some unfinished business.

"After those things were all disposed of," writes Mr.
Herndon, " he crossed to the opposite side of the room and
threw himself down on the old office sofa, which, after many
years of service, had been moved against the wall for support.
He lay for some moments, his face towards the ceiling, without either of us speaking.   Presently he inquired, ' Billy '—
he always called me by that name— ' how long have we been
together?'   'Over sixteen years,' I answered.   'We've
never had a cross word during all that time, have we?' . . .
He gathered a bundle of papers and books he wished to take
with him, and started to go; but before leaving he made the
strange request that the sign-board which swung on its rusty
hinges at the foot of the stairway should remain.   ' Let it
hang there undisturbed,' he said, with a significant lowering
of the voice.   ' Give our clients to understand that the election of a president makes no change in the firm of Lincoln &
Herndon.   If I live, I am coming back some time, and then
we'll go right on practising law as if nothing had happened.'
He lingered for a moment, as if to take a last look at the old
quarters, and then passed through the door into the narrow
hallway."

Herndon says that he never saw Lincoln more cheerful
than on that day, and Judge Gillespie, who visited him a few
days earlier, found him in excellent spirits.   " I told him that
I believed it would do him good to get down to Washington."   " I know it will," he replied.   " I only wish I could
have got there to lock the door before the horse was stolen.
But when I get to the spot, I can find the tracks."

Mr. Lincoln and his party were to leave Springfield by a special train at eight o'clock on Monday morning, February 11. And at precisely five minutes before eight o'clock, he was summoned from the dingy waiting-room of the station. Slowly working his way through the crowd of friends and townspeople that had gathered to bid him good-by, he mounted the platform of the car, and turning, stood looking down into the multitude of sad, friendly upturned faces. For a moment a strong emotion shook him; then, removing his hat and lifting his hand to command silence, he spoke:

My friends, no one, not in my situation, can appreciate my feeling of sadness at this parting. To this place, and the kindness of these people, I owe everything. Here I have lived a quarter of a century, and have passed from a young to an old man. Here my children have been born and one is buried. I now leave, not knowing when or whether ever I may return, with a task before me greater than that which rested upon Washington. Without the assistance of that Divine Being who ever attended him, I cannot succeed. With that assistance, I cannot fail. Trusting in Him who can go with me, and remain with you, and be everywhere for good, let us confidently hope that all will yet be well. To His care commending you, as I hope in your prayers you will commend me, I bid you an affectionate farewell. *

A sob went through the listening crowd as Mr. Lincoln's broken voice asked their prayers, and a choked exclamation, "We will do it! We will do it!" rose as he ceased to speak. Upon all who listened to him that morning his words produced a deep impression. "I was only a lad of fourteen," says Mr. Lincoln Dubois, of Springfield, "but to this day I can recall almost the exact language of that speech." "We have known Mr. Lincoln for many years," wrote the editor of the "State Journal." "We have heard him speak upon a

---

* The version of the farewell speech here used is that given by Nicolay and Hay in their "Complete Works of Abraham Lincoln."

hundred different occasions; but we never saw him so profoundly affected, nor did he ever utter an address which
seemed to us so full of simple and touching eloquence, so
exactly adapted to the occasion, so worthy of the man and the
hour.   Although it was raining fast when he began to speak,
every hat was lifted and every head bent forward to catch
the last words of the departing chief.   When he said, with
the earnestness of a sudden inspiration of feeling, that *with
God's help he should not fail,* there was an uncontrollable
burst of applause."

The speech was of course telegraphed over the country,
and though politicians sneered at it, the people were touched.
He had appealed to one of their deepest convictions, the belief
in a Providence whose help was given to those who sought
it in prayer.   The new President, they said to one another,
was not only a man who had struggled with life like common
people; he was a man who believed, as they did, in God, and
was not ashamed to ask the prayers of good men.

The journey eastward through Illinois, which now began,
was full of incident.   No better description of it was ever
given than that of Thomas Ross, a brakeman on the presidential train.

" The enthusiasm all along the line was intense.   As we
whirled through the country villages, we caught a cheer from
the people and a glimpse of waving handkerchiefs and of hats
tossed high into the air.   Wherever we stopped there was
a great rush to shake hands with Mr. Lincoln, though of
course only a few could reach him.   The crowds looked as if
they included the whole population.   There were women and
children, there were young men, and there were old men
with gray beards.   It was soul-stirring to see these white-
whiskered old fellows, many of whom had known Lincoln
in his humbler days, join in the cheering, and hear them
shout after him, ' Good-by, Abe.   Stick to the Constitution,
and we will stick to you.'   It was my good fortune to stand

beside Lincoln at each place at which he spoke—at Decatur, Tolono, and Danville. At the State line the train stopped for dinner. There was such a crowd that Lincoln could scarcely reach the dining-room. ' Gentlemen,' said he, as he surveyed the crowd, ' if you will make me a little path, so that I can get through and get something to eat, I will make you a speech when I get back.'

" I never knew where all the people came from. They were not only in the towns and villages, but many were along the track in the country, just to get a glimpse of the President's train. I remember that, after passing Bement, we crossed a trestle, and I was greatly interested to see a man standing there with a shot-gun. As the train passed he presented arms. I have often thought he was there, a volunteer, to watch the trestle and to see that the President's train got over it in safety. As I have said, the people everywhere were wild. Everybody wanted to shake hands with Lincoln, and he would have to say : ' My friends, I would like to shake hands with all of you, but I can't do it.' At Danville I well remember seeing him thrust his long arm over several heads to shake hands with George Lawrence. Walter Whitney, the conductor, who went on to Indianapolis, told me when he got back that, after Lincoln got into a carriage, men got hold of the hubs and carried the vehicle for a whole block. At the State line, I left the train, and returned to Springfield, having passed the biggest day in my whole life."

It was nearly five o'clock in the afternoon before the party reached Indianapolis, where they were to spend the night. An elaborate reception had been prepared, and here Mr. Lincoln made his first speech. It was not long, but it contained a paragraph of vital importance. The discussion over the right of the government to coerce the South was at its height. Lincoln had never publicly expresssed himself on this point. In the Indianapolis speech he said :

The words " coercion " and " invasion " are much used in these days, and often with some temper and hot blood. Let us make sure, if we can, that we do not misunderstand the meaning of those who use them. Let us get exact definitions of these words, not from dictionaries, but from the men themselves, who certainly deprecate the things they would represent by the use of words. What, then, is " coercion " ? What is " invasion " ? Would the marching of an army into South Carolina without the consent of her people, and with hostile intent toward them, be " invasion " ? I certainly think it would; and it would be " coercion " also if the South Carolinians were forced to submit. But if the United States should merely hold and retake its own forts and other property, and collect the duties on foreign importations, or even withhold the mails from places where they were habitually violated, would any or all of these things be " invasion " or " coercion " ? Do our professed lovers of the Union, but who spitefully resolve that they will resist coercion and invasion, understand that such things as these on the part of the United States would be coercion or invasion of a State? If so, their idea of means to preserve the object of their great affection would seem to be exceedingly thin and airy. If sick, the little pills of the homeopathist would be much too large for them to swallow. In their view, the Union as a family relation would seem to be no regular marriage, but rather a sort of " free-love " arrangement, to be maintained only on " passional attraction."

The speech was warmly applauded by the Republican press. It was the sign they had been seeking from Mr. Lincoln. But to the advocates of compromise it was a bitter message. " The bells of St. Germain l'Auxerrois have at length tolled forth the signal for massacre and bloodshed by the incoming administration," said the New York "Herald."

A long public reception in the evening, a breakfast the next morning with the Governor of the State, another reception at the hotel, and then, at ten o'clock on the morning of the 12th, Mr. Lincoln's party left Indianapolis for Cincinnati. Several of the friends who had come from Springfield left Mr. Lincoln at Indianapolis, but others joined him, and the train was as full of life and interest as it had been the day before. There was, too, the same succession of decorated, cheering towns; the same eager desire to see and hear the President at every station. At Cincinnati, where the second night was spent and where a magnificent reception was given him, Lincoln made two brief addresses. In that to the Mayor and citizens he was particularly happy:

"I have spoken but once before this in Cincinnati," he said. "That was a year previous to the late presidential election. On that occasion, in a playful manner, but with sincere words, I addressed much of what I said to the Kentuckians. I gave my opinion that we as Republicans would ultimately beat them as Democrats, but that they could postpone that result longer by nominating Senator Douglas for the presidency than they could in any other way. They did not, in any true sense of the word, nominate Mr. Douglas, and the result has come certainly as soon as ever I expected. I also told them how I expected they would be treated after they should have been beaten; and I now wish to recall their attention to what I then said upon that subject. I then said, ' When we do as we say—beat you—you perhaps want to know what we will do with you. I will tell you, so far as I am authorized to speak for the opposition, what we mean to do with you. We mean to treat you, as near as we possibly can, as Washington, Jefferson, and Madison treated you. We mean to leave you alone, and in no way interfere with your institutions; to abide by all and every compromise of the Constitution; and, in a word, coming back to the original proposition, to treat you, so far as degenerate men—if we have degenerated—may, according to the examples of those noble fathers, Washington, Jefferson, and Madison. We mean to remember that you are as good as we; that there is no difference between us other than the difference of circumstances. We mean to recognize and bear in mind always that you have as good hearts in your bosoms as other people, or as we claim to have, and treat you accordingly.'

"Fellow-citizens of Kentucky!—friends!—brethren! may I call you in my new position? I see no occasion, and feel no inclination, to retract a word of this.    If it shall not be made good, be assured the fault shall not be mine."

These conciliatory remarks were received with great enthusiasm, the crowd rushing at him as soon as he had finished, patting him on the back, and almost wrenching his arms off in their efforts at showing their approval.

On Wednesday morning, Mr. Lincoln left Cincinnati for Columbus.    Although few stops were made, he was kept busy receiving the committees and politicians who boarded the train here and there, and who were indefatigable in their efforts to draw from him some expression of his views.    Mr. Lincoln felt that to answer their questions would be the gravest indiscretion, and he resorted to stories and jests in his efforts not to commit himself or offend his visitors.    The reports of his " levity," as more than one felt this practice to be, were telegraphed over the country and bitterly commented upon by a large part of the press.    So far, however, as the stories Mr. Lincoln told on his journey have come to us, they contain quite as much political wisdom as a sober dissertation could have contained.    Thus there was a great deal of discussion *en route* about the possibility of reconciling the Northern and Southern Democrats.    Mr. Lincoln was appealed to.    " Well," he said, " I once knew a good sound churchman called Brown, who was on a committee to erect a bridge over a very dangerous and rapid river.    Several engineers had failed, and at last Brown said he had a friend Jones, who, he believed, could build the bridge.    Jones was accordingly summoned.    ' Can you build this bridge?' asked the committee.    ' Yes,' replied Jones; ' I could build a bridge to the infernal regions if necessary.'    The committee was horrified; but after Jones had retired, Brown said thoughtfully, ' I know Jones so well, and he is so honest a man and so good a builder, that if he says he can build a

**bridge** to Hades, why, I believe it; but I have my doubts about the abutments on the infernal side.' So," said Lincoln, " when politicians say they can harmonize the Northern and Southern wings of the Democracy, why, I believe them, but I have my doubts about the abutments on the Southern side."

At Columbus, the brilliant receptions of Indianapolis and Cincinnati were repeated, and here Mr. Lincoln addressed briefly the State Legislature. One clause of his remarks proved to be most unfortunate:

Allusion has been made to the interest felt in relation to the policy of the new administration. In this I have received from some a degree of credit for having kept silence, and from others some depreciation. I still think that I was right. . . .

In the varying and repeatedly shifting scenes of the present, and without a precedent which could enable me to judge by the past, it has seemed fitting that, before speaking upon the difficulties of the country, I should have gained a view of the whole field, being at liberty to modify and change the course of policy as future events may make a change necessary.

I have not maintained silence from any want of real anxiety. It is a good thing that there is no more than anxiety, for there is nothing going wrong. It is a consoling circumstance that when we look out there is nothing that really hurts anybody. We entertain different views upon political questions, but nobody is suffering anything. This is a most consoling circumstance, and from it we may conclude that all we want is time, patience, and a reliance on that God who has never forsaken this people.

A hostile press took the phrases " there is nothing going wrong "—" there is nothing that really hurts anybody "— " nobody is suffering anything," and used them apart from the context, to prove that the President-elect did not grasp

the situation.  At Newark, New Jersey, a week later, just before the presidential party passed through, a poster appeared
in the town quoting these sentences and calling on the unem-
ployed to meet at the station when Mr. Lincoln's train arrived and show the President that "they emphatically dif-
fered from these sentiments." Nothing came of this attempt
to create a disturbance.

On Thursday morning, February 14, the presidential
party was again *en route*, this time bound for Pittsburg.
Lincoln must have made this journey with a lighter heart
than that of the day before, for the danger that the counting of the electoral vote would be interfered with, was now
over.  The night before at Columbus, he had received a telegram which read: " The votes have been peaceably counted.
You are elected." The ceremony had passed off without incident.

At Pittsburg, where the night of the 14th was spent, the
President spoke to an immense crowd, and as the issue in
Pennsylvania had been so largely protection, it was to that
doctrine that he gave his chief attention.  Nothing could
have pleased the Iron City better.  The people were so wild
with enthusiasm that it took the combined efforts of the police and militia to get the presidential party on the train and
out of town.

From the hour that Lincoln's coercion remarks at Indianapolis reached the country, he had received telegraphic congratulations and remonstrances at almost every stop of the
train.  The remarks at Columbus produced a similar result,
and he seems to have concluded at this point to make his future speeches more general.  At Cleveland, Buffalo, Albany,
and New York there was nothing in what he said that his
enemies could fasten on.  His journey from Pittsburg eastward was in no way different from what it had been previously.  There were the same crowds of people at every

station, the same booming of cannon, gifts of flowers, recep
tions at hotels, breakfasts, dinners, and luncheons with local
magnates.  All along the route in the East, as in the West,
the people were out; everywhere there were flags and banners and mottoes.  The party in the train continued to
change as it had done, committees and "leading citizens"
replacing each other in rapid succession.  None of these
accessions aroused more interest among the other members
of the party than Horace Greeley, who appeared unexpect-
edly at Girard, Ohio, bag and blankets in hand, and after
a ride of twenty miles with Mr. Lincoln, departed.

At Buffalo, where Mr. Lincoln spoke on Saturday, the
16th, a bit of variety was infused into the celebration by the
fulfilment of an election wager.  The loser was to saw a cord
of wood in front of the American House and present it to
the poorest negro to be found.  He accordingly appeared
with a wagon-load of cord-wood just before Mr. Lincoln
began his speech from the hotel balcony, and during the address sawed vigorously.

The journey through New York State, with the elaborate
ceremonies at Albany and New York City, occupied three
days, and it was not until the evening of February 21 that
Lincoln reached Philadelphia.  The day had been a hard one.
He had left New York early, had replied to greetings at Jersey City and again at Newark, had addressed both branches
of the New Jersey Legislature at Trenton and gone through
a formal dinner there, and now, though it was dark and cold,
he was obliged to ride in state through the streets of Philadelphia to his hotel, where hundreds of visitors soon were
surging in to shake his hand.  The hotel was still crowded
with guests when he was summoned to the room of one of
his party, Mr. Norman Judd.  There he was introduced to
Mr. Allan Pinkerton, who, as Mr. Judd explained, was a
Chicago detective and had a story to lay before him.

"Pinkerton informed me," said Mr. Lincoln afterwards, in relating the affair to Benson J. Lossing, "that a plan had been laid for my assassination, the exact time when I expected to go through Baltimore being publicly known. He was well informed as to the plan, but did not know that the conspirators would have pluck enough to execute it. He urged me to go right through with him to Washington that night. I did not like that. I had made engagements to visit Harrisburg, and go from there to Baltimore, and I resolved to do so. I could not believe that there was a plot to murder me. I made arrangements, however, with Mr. Judd for my return to Philadelphia the next night, if I should be convinced that there was danger in going through Baltimore. I told him that if I should meet at Harrisburg, as I had at other places, a delegation to go with me to the next place (then Baltimore), I should feel safe, and go on."

Mr. Lincoln left Mr. Pinkerton, and started to his room. On the way he met Ward Lamon, also a member of his party, who introduced Frederick Seward, the son of the Senator. Mr. Seward, who relates this story in his life of his father, told Mr. Lincoln that he had a letter for him from his father. The letter informed Mr. Lincoln that General Scott and Colonel Stone, the latter the officer commanding the District of Columbia militia, had just received information which seemed to them convincing, that a plot existed in Baltimore to murder him on his way through that city. Mr. Seward besought the President to change his plan and go forward secretly.

Mr. Lincoln read the note through twice slowly and thoughtfully; then looked up, and said to Mr. Seward, "Do you know anything about the way this information was obtained?"

No, Mr. Seward knew nothing.

"Did you hear any names mentioned? Did you, for instance, ever hear anything said about such a name as Pinkerton?"

No, Mr. Seward had heard no names mentioned save those of General Scott and Colonel Stone.

" I may as well tell why I ask," said Mr. Lincoln. " There were stories and rumors some time ago, before I left home, about people who were intending to do me a mischief. I never attached much importance to them—never wanted to believe any such thing. So I never would do anything about them in the way of taking precautions and the like. Some of my friends, though, thought differently—Judd and others —and, without my knowledge, they employed a detective to look into the matter. It seems he has occasionally reported what he found; and only to-day, since we arrived at this house, he brought this story, or something similar to it, about an attempt on my life in the confusion and hurly-burly of the reception at Baltimore."

" Surely, Mr. Lincoln," said Mr. Seward, " that is a strong corroboration of the news I bring you."

He smiled, and shook his head. " That is exactly why I was asking you about names. If different persons, not know-ing of each other's work, have been pursuing separate clews that led to the same result, why, then, it shows there must be something in it. But if this is only the same story, fil-tered through two channels, and reaching me in two ways, then that don't make it any stronger. Don't you see? "

After a little further discussion of the subject, Mr. Lin-coln rose and said:  " Well, we haven't got to decide it to-night, anyway, and I see it is getting late. You need not think I will not consider it well. I shall think it over care-fully, and try to decide it right; and I will let you know in the morning."

The next day was Washington's birthday. The hauling down of the Stars and Stripes in the South and the substi-tuting of State flags had stirred the North deeply. The day the first Palmetto Flag was raised in South Carolina, a new reverence for the national emblem was born in the North. The flag began to appear at every window, in every buttonhole. On January 29 Kansas was admitted into the Union, without slavery, thus adding a new star to the thirty-three then in the field; and for raising the new flag thus made necessary, Washington's birthday became almost a universal choice. In Philadelphia, it was arranged that the new flag for Independence Hall be raised by Mr. Lincoln. The ceremony took place at seven o'clock in the morning. Mr. Lincoln's brief speech was one of the best received of all he made on the journey:

I am filled with deep emotion at finding myself standing in this place, where were collected together the wisdom, the patriotism, the devotion to principle from which sprang the institutions under which we live. You have kindly suggested to me that in my hands is the task of restoring peace to our distracted country. I can say in return, sir, that all the political sentiments I entertain have been drawn, so far as I have been able to draw them, from the sentiments which originated in and were given to the world from this hall. I have never had a feeling, politically, that did not spring from the sentiments embodied in the Declaration of Independence. I have often pondered over the dangers which were incurred by the men who assembled here and framed and adopted that Declaration. I have pondered over the toils that were endured by the officers and soldiers of the army who achieved that independence. I have often inquired of myself what great principle or idea it was that kept this Confederacy so long together. It was not the mere matter of separation of the colonies from the motherland, but that sentiment in the Declaration of Independence which gave liberty not alone to the people of this country, but hope to all the world, for all future time. It was that which gave promise that in due time the weights would be lifted from the shoulders of all men, and that all should have an equal chance. This is the sentiment embodied in the Declaration of Independence. Now, my friends, can this country be saved on that basis?

If it can, I will consider myself one of the happiest men in the world if I can help to save it. If it cannot be saved upon that principle, it will be truly awful. But if this country cannot be saved without giving up that principle, I was about to say I would rather be assassinated on this spot than surrender it. Now, in my view of the present aspect of affairs, there is no need of bloodshed and war. There is no necessity for it. I am not in favor of such a course, and I may say in advance that there will be no bloodshed unless it is forced upon the government. The government will not use force, unless force is used against it.

My friends, this is wholly an unprepared speech. I did not expect to be called on to say a word when I came here. I supposed I was merely to do something toward raising a flag. I may, therefore, have said something indiscreet. [Cries of "No, no."] But I have said nothing but what I am willing to live by, and, if it be the pleasure of Almighty God, to die by.

It was after returning from the flag-raising at Philadelphia that Lincoln told his friends that he had decided to go on to Washington at whatever time they thought best after his only remaining engagement was filled; viz., to meet and address the Pennsylvania Legislature at Harrisburg that afternoon. The engagement was carried out, and late in the afternoon he was free. It had been arranged that he leave Harrisburg secretly at six o'clock in the evening with Colonel Lamon, the rest of his party to know nothing of his departure. But Mr. Lincoln did not like to go without at least informing his companions, and asked that they be called. " I reckon they'll laugh at us, Judd," he said, " but you had better get them together." Several of the party, when told of the project, opposed it violently, arguing that it would expose Mr. Lincoln to ridicule and to the charge of cowardice. He, however, answered that unless there was something besides ridicule to fear, he was disposed to carry out Mr. Judd's plan.

At six o'clock he left his hotel by a back door, bareheaded, a soft hat in his pocket, and entering a carriage, was driven to the station, where a car and engine, unlighted save for a headlight, awaited him.  A few minutes after eleven o'clock, he was in Philadelphia, where the night train for Washington was being held by order of the president of the road for an "important package."  This package was delivered to the conductor as soon as it was known that Mr. Lincoln was on the train.  At six o'clock the next morning, after an undisturbed night, he was in Washington, where Mr. Washburne and Mr. Seward met him, and, with devout thanksgiving, conducted him to Willard's Hotel, there to remain until after the inauguration.

There were still nine days before the inauguration, and nine busier days Mr. Lincoln had not spent since his election.  He was obliged to make visits to President Buchanan, Congress and the Supreme Court, and under Mr. Seward's guidance, this was done at once.  He received, too, great numbers of visitors, including many delegations and committees.  The Hon. James Harlan, of Iowa, at that time United States Senator, called on Mr. Lincoln on February 23, the day of his arrival.  "He was overwhelmed with callers," says Mr. Harlan.  "The room in which he stood, the corridors and halls and stairs leading to it, were crowded full of people, each one, apparently, intent on obtaining an opportunity to say a few words to him *privately*."

It was in these few days before his inauguration that the great fight over the future Cabinet was made.  As we have seen, Lincoln had made his selections, subject to events, before he left Springfield.  When he reached Washington he sought counsel on his proposed appointments from great numbers of the leading men of the country.  If they did not come to him, he went to them.  Thus ex-Senator Harlan, in an unpublished manuscript "Recollections of Abraham Lin-

coln," tells how the President-elect sounded him on the Cabinet. "A page came to me at my desk in the Senate Chamber," writes Mr. Harlan, "and said, 'The President-elect is
in the President's room and wishes to see you.' I confess
that I felt a little flurried by this announcement. I had not
been accustomed to being called in by Presidents of the
United States; hence, to gain a little time for self-composure,
I said to the little page, 'How do you know that the President-elect wishes to see me?' 'Oh,' said he, 'his messenger came to the door of the Senate Chamber, and sent me to
tell you.' 'All right,' said I. 'You may tell the President's
messenger that I will call immediately,' which, of course, I
did without the least delay.

"I was received by the President in person, who, after the
ordinary greetings, offered me a seat, and seated himself
near me. No one else was in the room. He commenced the
conversation, saying in a half-playful, half-serious tone and
manner, 'I sent for you to tell me whom to appoint as members of my Cabinet.' I responded, saying, 'Mr. President,
as that duty, under the Constitution, devolves, in the first
instance, on the President, I have not given to the subject a
serious thought; I have no names to suggest, and expect to
be satisfied with your selections.' He then said he had about
concluded to nominate William H. Seward, of New York, as
Secretary of State; Edward Bates, of Missouri, for Attorney-General; Caleb B. Smith, of Indiana, for Secretary of
the Interior; Gideon Welles, of Connecticut, for Secretary of
the Navy; Montgomery Blair, of Maryland, for Postmaster-
General; and that he thought he ought to appoint Simon
Cameron, of Pennsylvania, and Salmon P. Chase, of Ohio,
for the remaining two places, but was in doubt which one to
offer Mr. Cameron and would like to have me express my
opinion frankly on the point.

"'Well,' said I. 'Mr. President, if that is the only question involved, I have not the slightest doubt that Mr. Chase ought to be made Secretary of the Treasury,' and then I proceeded to mention, without hesitation or reserve, my reasons for this opinion.  He thanked me cordially for my frankness. I took my leave.  This interview lasted probably about ten or fifteen minutes."

Not all of those with whom Mr. Lincoln talked about his Cabinet professed, like Senator Harlan, to be satisfied with his selections.  Radical Republicans, mistrusting Seward's spirit of compromise, besought him to take Chase and drop Seward altogether.  Conservatives, on the contrary, fearing Chase's implacable " no compromise " spirit, urged Lincoln to omit him from the Cabinet.  Seward finally, on March 2, probably thinking to force Lincoln's hand, withdrew his consent to take an appointment.  He said later that he feared a " compound Cabinet " and did not wish to " hazard " himself in the experiment.  This action brought no immediate reply from Mr. Lincoln.  He simply left Seward's name where he had placed it at the head of the slate.  The struggle over Cameron's appointment, which had been going on for more than two months, now culminated in a desperate encounter.  The appointment of Blair was hotly contested. Caleb Smith's seat was disputed by Schuyler Colfax.  In short, it was a day-and-night battle of the factions of the Republican party, which raged around Lincoln from the hour he appeared in Washington until the hour of his inauguration.

In spite of all the arguments and threats from excited and earnest men, to which he listened candidly and patiently; Lincoln found himself, on the eve of his inauguration, with the Cabinet which he had selected four months before unchanged.  This fact, had it been known, might have modified somewhat the opinion expressed generally at the time, that the new President would never be anything but the tool of

Chase or Seward, or of whoever proved to be the strong man of his Cabinet—that is, if he was ever inaugurated. Of this last many had doubts, and even, at the last hour, were betting in the hotel corridors and streets of Washington that Abraham Lincoln would never be President of the United States.